20 STUPID THINGS WOMEN & COUPLES DO TO MESS UP THEIR LIVES

Dr. Laura Schlessinger

HarperCollins*Publishers*

Ten Stupid Things Women Do to Mess Up Their Lives

Dr. Laura C. Schlessinger

HARPER

NEW YORK • LONDON • TORONTO • SYDNEY

Ten Stupid Things Women Do to Mess Up Their Lives was originally published in 1994 by Villard Books, a division of Random House Inc. It is reprinted here by permission of Villard Books. First published in paperback in 1995 by Harper Paperbacks, an imprint of HarperCollins Publishers Inc. *Ten Stupid Things Couples Do to Mess up Their Relationships* was originally published in 2001 by HarperCollins Publishers Inc.

Library of Congress Cataloging-in-Publication Data is available.

ISBN: 978-0-06-191170-5

09 10 11 12 13   /RRD   10 9 8 7 6 5 4 3 2 1

To my husband, Lew Bishop,
and my son, Deryk, who
never stopped telling me
I was the "little engine that could."

With all my love.

PREFACE

It ever has been since time began,
*   And ever will be, till time lose breath,*
That love is a mood—no more—to man,
*   And love to a woman is life or death.*

Ella Wheeler Wilcox
1850–1919

My hope is that this book will help both men and women put love and work in more harmonious balance; hence, learn to live together with more joy and meaning.

ACKNOWLEDGMENTS

I don't have any "little people" to thank. I have been fortunate to have had support, pushes, pulls, and nudges by many people of immense talent, heart, and friendship. I have regrets that I may not have always demonstrated the appreciation they deserved. I hope in these words, and in my life's actions, I show them all the respect, love, and gratitude they earned.

Dr. Bernard Abbott, once chairman of the Department of Biological Sciences at USC, gave me my first big break. After sending me a pleasant "Sorry, we don't have any permanent, full-time positions available," he responded with great humor to my follow-up call, "Okay, but might you have some not-so-permanent, part-time position?" That preceeded five wonderful years as an assistant professor teaching biology, physiology, and human sexuality.

It was the last course that helped me discover my interest in psychotherapy.

Thanks, then, to Dr. Carlfred Broderick, director of the USC Human Relations Center. What makes him remarkable and memorable to me is that he didn't "impose" ideas; he excavated my mind and heart to have me see and accept and nurture what might be special in me. He was the beginning of my self-confidence.

Marcia Lasswell, current president of the American Association of Marriage and Family Therapists, was my mentor, teacher, supervisor, and role model. She is the most incredible combination of womanly charm, beauty, decisive wit, and intellect. Her energy is boundless, and her commitment and accomplishments in the field of marriage and family are legendary.

Dr. Jim Hedstrom, chairman of the graduate program in psychology at Pepperdine, gave me the opportunity to teach, therefore to truly learn my craft. He is a man of heart and integrity and gentle understanding.

Running parallel with my academic and professional growth was my introduction to its practical application: radio and, inevitably, this book. This interface belongs to Bill Ballance, the pioneer and "father" of personal-style talk radio. He literally "discovered me on the phone" and put me on his daily L.A. radio program once a week. No matter how many times I wanted to quit out of fear and self-doubt, he kept me going.

Time-out came when I decided to withdraw from the fray to produce and nurture the next miracle in my life, my son, Deryk. When Deryk was three I got back on the microphone on KWNK, walking distance from my house, thanks to the warmest, mushiest guy, sometimes disguised as a curmudgeon, Manny Cabranes.

From that jump start back into my professional life, I landed on KFI AM 640 thanks to George Oliva, then program director. I started on Sundays, then weekends, then six nights a week till 1:00 A.M., until the current program director, David G. Hall, switched me to middays . . . just to prove I wasn't a vampire and could be out in sunlight! I owe them both. David is my boss and friend—only he would know how to balance those so well.

Larry Metzler is my radio board operator and dear friend. He helped me keep my book and thoughts organized by producing "dubs" of significant calls for me to review. While I'm doing my show, his input during commercial breaks and news keeps up my spirits and, therefore, improves my performance. "Couldn't have done this without ya, Larry!" He's also been there when I've had a hurt in my heart.

The rest of my on-air team includes Susanne Whatley, news anchor, and Mark Denis, traffic reports. We've become a great team and great friends.

My therapy colleagues for closing in on two decades, Dr. Rhoda Marcovitch and Dr. Judith Friedman, have been there as creative critics and, more important, friends. I finally feel I have friends for life. There are so many times I could not have gotten through without them.

My husband, Lew Bishop, requires special attention here. Sometimes I think he's just crazy, because I can't fathom the magnitude of his uninterrupted love, loyalty, faith, friendship, and unrelenting efforts in behalf of my career. And Deryk thinks he's just the "best daddy" going.

Suzanne Wickham from Random House just called me one day and said, "You have a book in you. Write it!" I'd been scared to write a book—something about the exposure to criticism and judgment, I think. However, her positiveness and enthusiasm got me through the worst of it. Now I can't wait to start on the next!

Carolyn Fireside, my editor, is a special human being as well as an incredible professional. Before she got started with her red pencil, she listened to hours of tapes and read volumes of my writings to get to know me, my style, my voice, my message. She edited this book honoring all of those, making all the suggestions and improvements that made this a finished product about which I have great pride. Thank you, Carolyn.

Writing this acknowledgment section has been like counting my blessings. I am blessed. I am grateful.

—L. C. Schlessinger, 1993

CONTENTS

This book is going to be difficult for you to read—and maybe even hurtful to you—and you may get angry.

There are ten million exceptions to everything I say. Nonetheless, EVERYTHING I SAY IS TRUE!

INTRODUCTION

This is not a self-help book, but it will help women help themselves. Sound like double-talk? Kindly read on!

Here's another apparent contradiction. The inspiration for *Ten Stupid Things Women Do to Mess Up Their Lives* comes from two male sources: the first engineer on my KFI AM 640 Los Angeles call-in radio program, and my father.

First, the engineer. After working with me for more than six months, three hours a night, five days a week, Dan Mandis was hearing approximately twenty-five women per show agonize over "some dumb guy." "You know, Laura," he told me in an unguarded moment. "If you listen to your show long enough, you begin to think women are stupid!"

In my psychotherapeutic, compassionate, nonjudgmental opinion, that comment amounted to heresy. Yet after a while, I began to wonder if there was some truth to it. Yes, we are motivated by unrealistic drives and primal needs related to yearnings for a paradise-never-visited in childhood. And yes, practicalities sometimes make our choices and directions seem almost too complex to fathom, much less handle. That's part and parcel of the human condition. But I had to admit that women knowingly do stupid things—like using complaining, whining, anger, depression, anxiety, food, and chemicals to avoid taking active steps to improve their lot. They "cop out." They get "chicken." *They act stupid.*

An example: One of my callers, who was "having trouble" losing weight, claimed that she had looked in every available self-help book for a scenario she could really relate to. She called because she was frustrated she hadn't found it yet.

Oh, great! In other words, until she finds herself in a book (which I bet will never happen), she has a perfect excuse for doing nothing—and that "nothing" includes confronting the fact that she is basically lazy. Her goal in life may be to look like a model, which could be foolish and unrealistic in itself, but she's totally unwilling to put in any effort whatsoever to achieve it.

Granted, there are no psychiatric diagnostic categories for laziness, immaturity, cowardice, selfishness, and downright stupidity. Even if there were, it wouldn't matter because no one bothers to consider them anymore. Know why? In the Age of the Victim, nothing is anybody's fault! All the personality and behavioral traits I just listed have been swept clean away as women, aided and abetted by a torrent of apologetic self-help books, insist on rationalizing their self-destructive behavior by identifying themselves as "sick." Codependent, addicted, loved too much, scarred by a dysfunctional past, whatever—we've provided ourselves with a virtual boutique of new "identities" designed to enable us to marinate in our weaknesses.

Listen to Dr. Laura! For improvement to happen, these weaknesses need airing and exercising. Until you take them on, you are a victim. And you don't have to be a female rocket scientist to figure out who the perpetrator is! Dan the engineer—a man—could tell you in a second. It's you! That's what he meant when he said women seemed stupid. The ultimate stupidity is withholding from yourself the respect you deserve.

Bottom line: If you want a higher self-esteem, there's only one, admittedly old-fashioned, way to get it: Earn it!

On to the second motivation for this book: my father, who once remarked at dinner that men couldn't get away with anything rotten, political or personal, unless women let them. He listed every conceivable transgression—petty robbery, abuse, war, governmental corruption, you name it. According to his argument, the ultimate power of women over men was their sexual acceptance and/or approval.

My father loved to bait me, especially at the dinner table, so I must have made his day when I immediately became outraged at the very notion that men would shunt off responsibility for their actions. As with Dan's comment, though, I continued to ponder the possibility that there might be some truth to my father's theory. A woman, I reasoned, is not responsible for a man's choices. She is, however, responsible for her own—which too often entail tolerating some obnoxious male behaviors in order to avoid, for example, loneliness, self-assertiveness, and self-sufficiency.

If, from the first meeting with an ill-mannered lout, a woman expressed her disdain clearly and confidently, the guy would either shape up or expect to get shipped out. If, instead, she focuses on her dependency and desperate need for male acceptance while forgetting about his dependency and craving for approval and then continues to be sexually receptive, she'll be giving him a strong signal that she condones his behavior. So I have to concede my father had a point. Unfortunately, now that he's passed on, this intellectual arm-wrestle is history.

By the way, I'm aware that women psychologists are generally mistrusted by men as male-bashers. If any of you

guys are sneaking a peek at this book, you can relax. If anything, I'm woman-bashing! And get ready, women, because I'm taking off the gloves and telling you the naked
truth. You can take it. You need to hear it.

Here goes. Men are not keeping you miserable. You
are! If you are unhappy with your man, straighten yourself
out and pick better! Put all this low self-esteem stuff in perspective. Life is hard. Only those willing to sustain themselves through self-doubt and difficult periods of pain, loss,
even dread, will achieve enhanced self-respect. It's that
simple.

If you don't want to put in the effort, accept that
you've made a decision not to grow. If changing is simply
too much trouble, just forget it—and at least give yourself
some peace. If you're bent on excusing your inner weakness and passivity by spending decades "recovering," go
right ahead. It's your life. If you're more interested in helping yourself than in so-called self-help, which means eternally searching for a miracle cure via the latest guru's new
cop-out title-of-the-month, this is the book for you!

Women, rebel! Don't fall for yet another slick explanation of the pathetic yet understandable motivation for
your weak-kneed behavior. My book was written to encourage you to show yourself what you're made of. And
when you do, I guarantee you, you'll be impressed!

Ten Stupid Things Women Do to Mess Up Their Lives
is not about steps, syndromes, or programs. It's not about
"recovery." It's not a "miracle cure" for your problems
that promises gain without pain.

This book is intended to open your eyes, startle you
into awareness, and smarten you up.

But it will not do the trick for all women.

Some of you will resent it, even reject it, because
"looking in the mirror" does not always reflect a "pretty
picture" and because confronting your own stupidity can

really hurt. You may even know I'm right but still not be consciously ready to take an objective look at yourself.

So feel free to hurl the fruit of my labors across the room or call it nasty names or just ignore it. Just, please, for your own good, keep it around!

Because someday, when things get bad enough and the pain and feelings of helplessness get too acute to bear, you'll go to it. And it will be there for you as you make your most important decision ever: to fight your way out of misery and go take on your life!

TEN STUPID THINGS WOMEN DO TO MESS UP THEIR LIVES

1 **Stupid Attachment**

IS A WOMAN JUST A WO- WO- WO- ON A MAN?

I remember precisely when I knew I had to write this book. It was a few years ago when my husband, Lew, and I were leaving a screening of Robin Williams's *Dead Poets Society*. The movie, you may recall, concerns the students and faculty of an exclusive boys' school and is set in the fifties. So? What's the big deal? Not exactly the subject to inspire strong emotions in a nineties woman, yet I found myself deeply upset—and equally puzzled because my feelings did seem so way out of proportion to the specific dramatic events of the film.

As I struggled to understand my "overreaction," I found myself focusing on my anger at the mother of the main student in the film, a sensitive sort, whose father refuses to allow him to follow his dream of a career in the theater! The boy is to be a doctor, the father froths, and that's that!

While the father declaims, the mother just sits in a corner suffering in silence. She watches the complete demoralization of her son, yet does nothing. Before she dutifully follows her husband to his bed, she gently hugs the boy, pats him solemnly on the back, and then walks away sadly.

The young man uses his father's gun to kill himself.

I went absolutely crazy with pain.

That a mother could stand by and allow the selfish insensitivity of her husband to destroy her own child absolutely horrified me.

By the time my husband and I reached the parking lot, I had worked myself up into a rage at the character's weakness, her cowardice, her subservience. In fact, I held her more responsible for the boy's death than the father!

The father was all caught up in his competitive macho behavior of using his son as his ego extension. After all, could being a doctor be considered such a bad thing to wish on someone?

But the mother knew her son's heart. She knew he had poetry in his heart, which did not need a stethoscope over it.

She just would not stand up to her controlling husband.

A middle-aged woman who was parked next to us heard me railing and anguishing over the mother's spineless culpability and took it upon herself to calm me down. "Well," she said firmly, "that's just how women were in those . . . my . . . days!" Her tone actually seemed quite sympathetic toward the servile woman of forty years ago; and that made me even angrier and sadder.

BOYS YEARN FOR COURAGE AND NO "CHAPTER 11" . . . WHILE GIRLS YEARN FOR CURLS AND NO CELLULITE

As my husband and I drove home, my mood became even more melancholy as I continued to ruminate. I surprised even myself with this next observation: "You know, Lew, *Dead Poets Society* could not have been written about a girls school—whether it was set in the fifties or now! It is a movie about ideals and aspirations, about personal discovery by courageous actions, not just by attending 'Adult Children of Some Kind of Imperfect Parent' organization.

"Let me ask you something. If the movie was set in a girls prep school, would anybody 'buy' it? Would it make sense? Would it make the point the author was trying to make?"

My husband thought for a moment, then told me, "No, I guess not."

ARE YOU JUST A WO- WO- WO- ON A MAN?

His agreement about the obviousness of this sad truth made me feel tearful, profoundly sad, frustrated, angry, and ashamed both at women and for women—women as personified by my comforter in the parking lot. Women possibly like your mother or aunt, your teacher or female friends, maybe even like yourself, who use an entire arsenal of excuses to avoid facing the fact that they define themselves and their role in the world exclusively through men—and it almost "don't" matter what "kinda" man! (More about that later . . . much, much, much more.)

DON'T DISCOUNT THE POSITIVE ASPECTS
OF MALE BEHAVIOR

In the nearly fifteen years I have worked with men and women in private practice and on radio, I am constantly amazed by how myopic women are about life and themselves, and how much they complain about men! I wonder if the absence of complaining about men would eliminate the talk show industry. Most of what you hear on these talk shows is whining about how men are unwilling to commit to women after minutes or millennia of dating.

Women seem to like more to whine about problems than to solve them. Men, more typically, want to solve problems rather than talk on and on about them. Men are being maligned because they are not behaving like women: Talk, talk, talk, whine, whimper, analyze, reanalyze, etc. Ugh.

To use a familiar saying, "Why can't a woman be more like a man" is sometimes not such a bad idea. Women are so driven by the desire to exist through men that they miss the positive examples male behavior can offer them as a model.

Contrary to much of the feminist cant, there are many things we can learn from men's perspective about life and personal identity. To refuse to learn anything that could prove beneficial to yourself is a working definition of stupid. I sincerely believe that if women studied male lessons in concepts of assertion, courage, destiny, purpose, honor, dreams, endeavor, perseverance, goal orientation, etc., they would have a more fulfilling life, pick better men with whom to be intimate, and have better relationships with them.

"I AM BARBIE, SEE MY HAIR GROW!"

Of course, there are already special, spectacular women out there who were born and/or imbued with a strong sense of personal destiny—you may even be one of them. Generally, aspirations and lofty intentions don't dovetail with women's concept of femininity, because the determination to make your life extraordinary is not a typical part of female thinking. To be completely honest, there is no realization of dreams and purpose for either women or men without difficulty, opposition, disappointment, and failure. When the French say, *"La vie est dure,"* life is hard, it pertains to everyone who's ever lived, not just womankind. In order to grow, you've got to face the fact that painless change happens only in fairy tales.

So stop blaming men or society or anything else for your personal disappointments. Decide to become more meaningful to yourself and to others. Then you can go take on the day every day of your life.

THE "HIGH" PRICE OF "LOW" FEMALE SELF-ESTEEM

The price for not making a move toward personal specialness has always been and continues to be too great. Since women do not typically define self-esteem and purpose in terms of personal accomplishment, the ways they have gone about getting some sense of identity, value, and meaning in their lives have been primarily through relationships. That has been disappointing and destructive. In the 1830s Lord Byron wrote, "For men, love is a thing apart, for women it is their whole existence."

Unfortunately, it is still all too true today.

"WE HAVEN'T COME A LONG ENOUGH WAY, BABY!"

Whitney Houston was quoted in the *Los Angeles Times* (11/22/92—that's 1992, not 1892) as having said, "Women are supposed to have husbands. We are validated by that, and we validate ourselves that way."

Even today, on the eve of the twenty-first century,

there are young women for whom the very possibility that there is life separate from attachment to some guy comes as a revelation. Read these amazing words a *Los Angeles Times* article (11/2/93) called "New Rules for Teen Love": ". . . she never had thought it possible for a girl to spend a Saturday night without a date—and still be happy: 'I grew up thinking that if you're not with [some guy], you're nothing. Then, last Saturday I went with Michelle to the movies. I couldn't believe it was fun to go out with girls.' "

A twinkle of hope? Well, perhaps, but . . .

A thirty-one-year-old woman who has had affairs with athletes in two sports said this to *Time* magazine (11/25/91): "For women, many of whom don't have meaningful work, the only way to identify themselves is to say whom they have slept with. A woman who sleeps around is called a whore. But a woman who has slept with Magic Johnson is a woman who has slept with Magic Johnson. It's almost as if it gives her legitimacy."

So here it is—nothing new—identity through attachment to a man perceived as super-special. And God help you if that perception changes, because once the star falls from grace, so does the woman's sense of worth. She simply ceases to exist. It's no wonder that so many women get furious with their men for having even reasonable human frailties and don't "stand by their man" during the harder times.

MATHEMATICS 1: MARRIAGE DOES NOT EQUAL SELF-WORTH

"And now, from Santa Clarita, Susan, you're on KFI," the conversation began. And Susan, twenty-nine, came on the line by telling me she'd been married for five and a half months but still felt an overwhelming sense of insignificance. Her husband, the marital state itself—well, things just hadn't turned out the way she'd imagined.

"Nothing in my life," she said mournfully, "affirms my worth to myself."

Think of it like this: If you bring your own goals and dreams and self-awareness to a marriage, the other person can be a tremendous source of comfort and support when your career or one of your friendships is going through a rough patch. That's true for anything that causes your ego to suffer a blow—and you can and should do the same for your partner.

If you bring to the relationship nothing but your neediness, the balance is all off. You become your husband's baby, his perpetual "damsel in distress." Though a damsel may be macho-assuaging for a while, it is not long before she becomes a constant emotional drain and a total "taker."

In such a lopsided situation, you're bound to feel lonely, because feelings of self-worth do not come from the mere existence or presence of someone in your life. Counting on that, in fact, just makes the pain of your sense of personal nothingness even worse.

WANT SELF-ESTEEM? GET IT
THE OLD-FASHIONED WAY . . . EARN IT!

On this very important subject of self-esteem, social psychologist Carol Tavris makes a valid point when she writes that self-esteem is now a mere shadow of its former self. "Once," she claims, "it referred to a fundamental sense of self-worth; today that meaning has narrowed into merely feeling good about oneself. Self-esteem used to rest on the daily acts of effort, care and accomplishment that are the bedrock of character; now it rests on air, on being instead of doing."

So when women stuck in Susan's depressed, low-self-esteem quagmire ask: "How can I increase my self-esteem? Can you recommend a book? A seminar? A workshop? A group?" here's my answer: Self-esteem is earned! When you dare to dream, dare to follow that dream, dare to suffer through the pain, sacrifice, self-doubts, and friction from the world—when you show such courage and tenacity—you will genuinely impress yourself. And most important, you will treat yourself accordingly and not settle for less from others—at least, not for long.

Self-esteem is always forged from your efforts. I still cannot believe the self-defeating moves women make to avoid those efforts.

A LOUSY RELATIONSHIP IS NEVER BETTER
THAN NO RELATIONSHIP AT ALL

Vanessa, a twenty-seven-year-old caller, was furious that her physically and verbally abusive boyfriend had broken off with her to go back to his ex-girlfriend, whom he had also abused.

What astonished me was that Vanessa wasn't calling in anger about his abuse. She called because she was angry that he decided to leave!

I said to her, with some irony, "If you took all that crap, at least he should be giving it only to you!" She came back with "I know," and giggled!

Vanessa continued, "I gave so much away. And my self-acceptance was based on his acceptance of me. I just don't understand why he's done what he's done."

Here she had taken all this abuse, hoping this would

ensure his undying love and attachment, and it didn't work. What a blow!

When I suggested that Vanessa tell me about her goals, to name only one, she couldn't. When I talked to her about hard work and sacrifice as a means of building something special, she dismissed the whole idea by claiming she guessed she was just lazy.

I asked her if all this *sturm und drang* of the relationship with this crazy guy was "exciting." She giggled again, and admitted that it was. "The fighting, the making up, the wondering, the pain. It is pretty exciting in a way. Certainly takes up my life."

This is what you call a life?

DON'T EXPECT A MAN TO SHARE YOUR "ALL-FOR-LOVE" ATTITUDE

I sincerely hope I helped Vanessa see a little light by chipping away at her denial. I sincerely hope I helped you see a little more clearly, too. It just seems such a tragic waste to see young women suffering needlessly by having no independent goals, to observe them acting so stupidly. I can't tell you how many twenty-something women I've talked to over the years who are furious with the young men in their lives who don't want to get married just yet because they're working practically full-time getting their education and/or building their careers. If you're one of these women, take his hint—or follow his example! Because, as I've said, men do have traits we'd be smart to adapt.

THE GOOD LIFE REQUIRES GUTS

Let me describe a fantastic cartoon—by a male, Jules Feiffer. A man meets a guru in the road. The man asks the guru, "Which way is success?" The berobed, bearded sage speaks not but points to a place off in the distance. The man, thrilled by the prospect of quick and easy success, rushes off in the appropriate direction. Suddenly, there comes a loud "SPLAT." Eventually, the man limps back, tattered and stunned, assuming he must have misinterpreted the message. He repeats his question to the guru, who again points silently in the same direction. The man obediently walks off once more. This time the splat is deafening, and when the man crawls back, he is bloody, broken, tattered, and irate. "I asked you which way is success," he screams at the guru. "I followed the direction you indicated. And all I got was splatted! No more of this pointing! Talk!" Only then does the guru speak, and what he says is this: "Success *is* that way. Just a little *past* splat."

Accomplishment, leading to self-esteem, is not just about doing something. . . . It is about the courage to persist through pain and failure and self-doubt; to go past splat.

I've lost count of all the callers who give sad testimony to the extraordinary and wholly inappropriate "romantic" situations in which women find themselves because they have never found the courage to go past splat, to focus on self-effort as the avenue to self-esteem and positive identity.

I can just feel that ultra-feminists reading this want to knock me upside my head right about now with some complaint that woman just haven't been able to do important things because men haven't let them. While I'm not going to deny the realities of the male power structure, I do want to reprimand you sternly about passing the buck. I recently spoke to a group of educated, accomplished women who belong to a group called American Association of University Women. The approach of the meeting had to do with what stood in the way of women accomplishing more.

The irony was deafening. Here I am, surrounded by hundreds of successful women of all ages and races who managed to do it. Why aren't we studying them?

Obviously, it can be done. If, if, if, you're not lazy or cowardly.

THERE OUGHT TO BE A LAW AGAINST ROMANTIC ENTRAPMENT

Tragically, when a woman doesn't dare to dream or endeavor to a purpose, a sense of meaning generally comes from excessive emphasis on a relationship with a man and/or producing babies—sometimes even using the latter to ensure the former. Perhaps the most shocking (and unhappy) proponent of this approach was Jennifer, age twenty-two, from Glendale.

Jennifer tearfully reported that she'd "been with" her fiancé for two years, although they weren't living together. Now she was pregnant, but when she told the daddy, he was furious and wanted her to have an abortion. She was distraught that the relationship had turned upside down, that her man was terribly disturbed about the baby and felt betrayed . . .

Basically, though, her call was about her being angry with him!

DR. LAURA: Were you guys using contraception?

JENNIFER: Well, I was taking the Pill, but I went off it when I decided to—

DR. LAURA: —decided to get pregnant intentionally?

JENNIFER: Um . . . yes. . . . He wanted to go to school and get a better job before we got married and I didn't want to wait four or five years.

DR. LAURA: I can't believe this, Jennifer. Do you realize you did a terrible thing?

JENNIFER: Well, yeah . . . but . . .

DR. LAURA: Forget the "but"! When you unilaterally decide to trick someone—even when you think it's out of love—they're well within their right not to trust you and not to feel the same way about you.

JENNIFER: But how can I be happy with myself, about the baby?

DR. LAURA: That's a tough one. This pregnancy was never about becoming a mother or being a family. It was about coercing and manipulating somebody into changing his life before he was committed to the change. And the reason you did it is because you don't have a life outside of what you thought being married would give you. I know I'm telling you things you don't want to hear. But I doubt I'm telling you things you don't already know.

If you realize you're not ready to be a mom and he's unwilling to be a dad, you might want to think of adoption as an option, so that this child will be raised by a loving couple who truly want it, are ready for it, and can take care of it.

JENNIFER: I just don't know what I need to do to make things better . . .

DR. LAURA: Now, he may not want to marry you, but he is the father of a child, whether it was his plan or not. You forced him to be a dad when he didn't feel ready. I don't know how all of this is going to turn out between you. But you need to pick yourself up in a spurt of maturity and take full responsibility for what you've done and realize how frightened you are in anticipating a grown-up life that you would go to this end.

That is not what being a wife is about, or mother, or grown-up. You're pregnant right now, so you have big decisions to make, and being angry with him for not "falling into place" is not the kind of thinking you need to do.

His angry reaction is reasonable and you need to tell him so.

JENNIFER: I need to tell him I betrayed, tricked him?

DR. LAURA: You can't be truthful with him and yet you want to marry him? Listen, the hallmark of a marriage, of any intimate relationship, is truth, especially about your weaknesses and vulnerabilities. You know what I think? I think this guy would be crazy to marry you right now. If you want his attitude to change, first tell him you're terribly sorry. Then commit to being honest—with him and with yourself. Admit to the truth of your fears, and take them where they belong, to a counselor. You've got to stop acting out and deal directly with your dread of not having an identity. These fears are things we can talk through, survive, and grow from. And remember, Jennifer, you have no real future with your fiancé at all—unless you start with the truth!

YOU CAN'T SHARE WHAT YOU DON'T HAVE, AND THAT GOES DOUBLY FOR RESPONSIBILITY

When she rang off, Jennifer sounded a lot more centered and resolved than she had at the beginning of our encounter. But you may be thinking I was too hard on her, that her anger with her boyfriend wasn't entirely unjustified; after all, he was engaging in a sexual relationship with her, and he knew that sexuality brings risk along with the pleasure. The birth-control pill does have a 2 percent failure rate, which means that of one hundred women using the birth-control pill for one year, two will become pregnant. This is the actual *vs.* theoretical failure rate, which is smaller because it doesn't include human error.

In fact, if the fiancé had called, angrily condemning his girlfriend for having gotten pregnant while on the Pill and interrupting his personal life's plans (and I have gotten many such calls from men), I would have told him that regardless of whether his girlfriend got pregnant because the Pill failed or she failed to take the Pill, he is responsible for his own sperm! His plans now need to include fatherhood. When adults are sexually active, they assume responsibility for the risks and consequences.

I intentionally didn't mention this shared responsibility to Jennifer because I wanted to emphasize what her responsibilities were. I wanted to stress to her, and to listeners identifying with her personal fears of life and autonomy, that any and all decisions and actions intended to manipulate men into enforced caretaking are unconscionable, cowardly, selfish, and destructive. End of story.

You'll read more about this terrible ploy in a later chapter, but it's still only one of the stupid ways in which women mess up their lives.

OBSESSIONS AND MARTYRDOM (UNPAID SOCIAL WORK) ARE WOEFULLY INEFFECTIVE HEDGES AGAINST FEMALE AUTONOMY

Are you obsessed with your weight, your thighs, your breasts, the thinness of your hair? If they were only different, you'd be loved?

Sylvia did have a real physical problem: male-pattern baldness in women. She was quite self-conscious about this rare medical problem and was working with a physician to get it under control.

Understandably, she felt uncomfortable about her looks, but the degree of her concern was obsessive: the reading, buying, trying, worrying, remedies, etc.

I asked her when she seemed to focus in on her hair problem the most.

Sylvia admitted, "I've been trying to go to school for the last five years and I've been having problems with that. I work and go to school and it's hard. And it's a difficult course—court reporting. And it's hard to concentrate sometimes; it just doesn't come easy to me."

I explained that when things are tough, stressful, scary, it's sometimes a lot easier to find other things to worry about rather than do your work. There is no surprise there. Every college student knows that feeling and the games of procrastination and distraction.

"When you're stressed," I told her, "you obsess." I also suggested that she fight through the discomfort of having to work hard, of feeling different. I offered that she needed to be more positive in her attitude and have more fun in her life.

Obsessing about imperfections makes for low self-evaluation, obviously. And just like water seeks its own level, equal self-evaluations match up in men and women, too. It just doesn't seem to be obvious.

There are legions of women who stay with men who are drug or alcohol abusers, and/or who are immature and irresponsible, and/or who betray trust emotionally, sexually, and financially, and/or who aren't loyal or supportive—who basically are not one of the good guys who are out there.

Generally, you discover these realities early on in the relationship—and that realization is the seductive hook that reels you in instead of signaling you to run for cover.

By continuing the relationship, you—out of cowardice and self-denial—short-circuit your progress toward "purpose" by martyring yourself on the altar of someone else's pain or need. Therein lies the appeal—the probability that the guy will "stay with you" because of his dependency on your caretaking. Between his dependency and your "mission," you have an identity and a sense of security, however skewed, which eventually leads you to be nonsexually screwed.

WHEN YOU DEVOTE YOUR LIFE TO "FINDING YOURSELF," YOU PROBABLY WON'T

Yet another style of struggling with purpose and identity is to bury your head in the sand, run away, and just keep putting off commitment to some purpose in any form! That was the case with Sibella, a thirty-year-old who called from Santa Monica.

Sibella was trying to decide whether to move to Germany, where she would be living with a boyfriend and taking a philosophical/spiritual seminar, or to stay in California and start a career. The only catch was that she hadn't a clue about what kind of career to start. She admitted to me that she felt she hadn't really ever achieved anything, despite the fact that all her life she'd been told she had tremendous potential . . .

DR. LAURA: Pretty scary, huh? To finally have to test that potential?

SIBELLA: Yeah, and it's funny . . . I am not—at least I think I'm not—afraid of failure.

DR. LAURA: Oh man, then you are the only person on the face of the earth who isn't. That's a fib, Sibella, but nice try. And I'll tell you, one of the things women types do when they get in this kind of predicament is to go live with a boyfriend while he does "his thing," which they ultimately come to resent as a competitor for attention. You're just postponing, postponing, postponing.

SIBELLA: Yes. And it's because . . . well . . . I've done a lot of soul-searching, but I feel I still don't know the real purpose of life.

DR. LAURA: You make purpose each day. I see the purpose of life when I look into my boy's sweet face. I feel the purpose of my life when I get on the phones here at KFI and have a conversation with someone, and feel it might have helped either the caller or some listener.

Perhaps the purpose of life is forged moment by moment. If you're going to wait till you find something "bigger than that" before you do anything, then you're doing a sixties kind of "I can't do anything till I find myself." And, my love, the nothingness you are giving, doing, and creating is yourself.

SIBELLA: Yes, exactly!

DR. LAURA: That is an avoidance of life. Life is not a coordinated complete picture of any kind for anyone. It is creating something for every day as best you can.

SIBELLA: And yet most people go through life with a goal in mind or something specific in their heart.

DR. LAURA: I think most people go through life trying to figure out how to survive each day. A goal? Build a Taj Mahal. A goal? Give someone else hope. A goal? Learn something new, exciting, and then wonder about a new and special use for it.

SIBELLA: And so basically you just think it's a matter of getting over the fear? I'm just procrastinating?

DR. LAURA: That's a pretty big "just"! Sibella, you've got to commit to something. I'm not telling you it has to be your life's dream or that it'll get you a Nobel Prize. But it will earn you more ownership of yourself. Commit to something—that is the essence of soul-searching. You're not soul-searching now, you're ruminating over fears of negative judgment and failure, disguised as search for "the ultimate wisdom."
Stop it. Do something.

SIBELLA: And give up the possibility of everything else I might have found or done?

DR. LAURA: Honey, anything you do leaves out everything else at that one moment. But it's also called having a moment of some depth in your life, where you do have some meaning. While I am here with you I am not riding my bicycle—I had to give up the possibility of that journey to have a new one with you—touching another human being. I'll settle for that.

SIBELLA: Yes, me too, thank you.

I hope I helped Sibella understand that if identity is going to come only from doing that right special something, then the something becomes the everything. When identity comes from the doing, the something becomes secondary. Baking bread is as glorious as planting flowers, as doing a cardiac bypass, as teaching a child to read.

The moral of this story is to not get stuck in looking for the right thing to do, the outstanding thing that will make you special. It is the process of doing, of committing yourself to something that makes the difference in your enjoyment of life and your satisfaction with self.

The same thinking applies to the fear of settling for one man when the next one might be better. This is not the thinking of a person ready, willing, and able to be caring and committed. It's the thinking of a woman who hopes to find the miracle cure that will make her feel like a valid person, like a real woman. For many contemporary females, that hoped-for miracle continues too often to be an ill-timed, ill-selected, ill-planned marriage and motherhood.

THE FEMALE ESCAPE ROUTE: THE QUICKEST MEANS TO PAINT YOURSELF INTO A CORNER

Although I'm always aware of being a woman, the most womanly I have ever felt was when I was pregnant. Imagine, having life within your body; being able to make, sustain, nurture new life. How special and incredible!

Well, even beautiful, special things such as marriage and motherhood have their proper time and place and purpose. The problem is, many women simply want to hide there.

Just the other day, a patient, a young woman in her early thirties with three children, ages fourteen to three and a half, talked about her early family life, during which she and her sister were never expected, never encouraged, to think of their lives in terms of personal dreams. She used a phrase remarkable for its poignancy: "So, I took the female escape route and got married and made babies right out of high school."

At thirty-something, she is finally ready to "take on the world," constrained by a family she made too soon, and for the wrong reasons.

Some women get a bit luckier. They've got guys who don't want to be burdened with women who are in creative hiding.

Thirty-one-year-old Carol, who called from Holly-wood, was a study in misery. She'd followed her boyfriend from Boston to L.A., where he was trying hard to make it in the music industry. After two months here, she had no job, no car, no friends, no family, no money. She hated it. Carol admitted freely she'd relocated with no commitment from the young man, who didn't even want to think about marriage and a family until he was established in his profession. She felt desperate by the failure of her pressuring to get him to give her access to the female escape route.

When I suggested to Carol that her boyfriend was right and that she ought to adopt his way of thinking, her tears, pain, and fear kept her from hearing me at first.

The breakthrough came when I asked her what her "dreams" were. First, she denied ever having any. Then she tearfully added, "Getting married and having children."

When I asked her what she was going to do with herself until then, she quietly said, "Nothing, I guess . . . nothing."

She said she had never had any dreams or goals. I

doubt that was true, but I do believe she's just totally scared.

My advice to Carol was to move back to Boston and get an education. As it was, I told her that she was but a comma in the sentence of her boyfriend's life, while for her, he was the entire text! That brand of emotional imbalance is almost always a format for disaster.

WHEN YOU'RE READY TO CHANGE, YOU'LL HEED THE CALL

Some six months after this call, while taping a television appearance, I was approached by a young man who worked on the set. "You're Dr. Laura!" He beamed, shaking my hand enthusiastically. "My girlfriend from Boston called you about six months ago."

I remembered the girlfriend instantly! It was Carol.

"You know," he continued, "you told her what I'd been telling her. Only, she listened to you! I was so relieved."

He candidly admitted that although he really cared about Carol, she had become a burden. "I was trying to work toward my things and all she wanted me to do was to take care of her!"

"I know you'll be happy to hear," he continued, "that she did move back home to go to school. I want to thank you for both of us. Whew! And hurray!"

MARRIAGE AND MOTHERHOOD ARE FOR ADULTS ONLY

It's true that the good guys out there do want a total woman—not one who greets them at the front door wrapped in cellophane (on a daily basis, anyway), but a centered, self-aware human being who wants to, rather than needs to, be with him as a companion, lover, friend, co-parent.

As a former male patient complained, men don't easily have the privilege of running from the fear of failure—they have to do something (well, I guess they can become bums or "kept men"), while women can fall back into biology: make babies.

If I had tried to make my son my sole purpose in life, I'd probably have psychologically destroyed him with my overwhelming demand that he either fulfill my dreams or display such excellence that my craving for reflected identity would be satisfied. This same is true of my marriage, which is a joy and comfort, not an obsession or manifestation of neurotic neediness.

NOT SUPERWOMAN—JUST A SUPER WOMAN

It is your job as a woman, as a person, to become as fully realized as you can by having dreams, forging a purpose, building an identity, having courage, and making commitments to things outside yourself. In so doing, you take a more active role in the quality of your own life so that other people—friends, spouses, children—share in your growth rather than become responsible for it. You'll feel super. And you'll feel really womanly—as opposed to babyish or girlish—perhaps for the first time.

AND WHEN IT WORKS, IT'S WONDERFUL

I am heartened to know that many of you have gotten the message. This follow-up letter from a caller is an example I'm particularly proud of:

> Dr. Laura,
>   One and a half years ago you helped me see what I knew already, and I broke off a bad relationship with a man. I also went to see a therapist, who helped me make better choices. I'm now dating a kind, giving, good man (for over a year) and we have a true relationship—complete with the gives and takes and compromises that are necessary for a strong friendship and a good base for a future. Thank you so much!
>   I'm also building my career and making decisions for my future, not basing them on "what he is doing." Yours, Kitty.

It's letters like these that make me constantly realize not only how much I love what I do but that many, many women are ready to change. They just need a jump start to do it!

PERSONAL COURAGE GIVES YOU THE FREEDOM TO CHOOSE

Now, to sum up: When you choose to include ideals such as courage and personal achievement as part of your feminine identity, I'll stop hearing: "I know he lies (cheats, steals, whatever)—but I'm thirty-nine. What if I never find another guy?"

OR, "I know he's abusive to me and the kids. But I'm too afraid to be alone."

OR, "I know I should let go of him (or some compulsive behavior); it's just that I get too uncomfortable. I don't like that feeling. So I just give up."

OR many of the other traps women fall into because of their lack of recognition and exercise of their true grit. The chapters to come will deal with them.

So read and learn—and get ready to be challenged.

2 Stupid Courtship

"I FINALLY FOUND SOMEONE I COULD ATTACH TO" AND OTHER STUPID IDEAS ABOUT DATING

Problems that callers present on my radio program can sadden me, frustrate me, even upset me. But after some fifteen years of on- and off-air counseling experience, they rarely surprise me.

I was not initially surprised by this particular Saturday-night call . . . then . . .

HE'S A COMPLETE TURKEY, BUT WHY HASN'T HE CALLED?

Christine came across as a strong, positive, assertive young woman, who described her "first date from hell" as if we were two best girlfriends in a jocular, "you won't believe what happened next" mood.

She told me she'd gone to a party with a female friend but had begun talking with one particular fellow, who eventually suggested they go somewhere to talk. She agreed, left her friend to find her own way home (this behavior really deserves its own chapter!), and accompanied her new companion to an all-night coffee shop.

Her description of the rest of the evening played like

sound bites from a comedy special about the worst kind of blind or first date. The man smoked without asking her permission or even inquiring whether it bothered her. His smoking *did* bother her, and she told him so. Without consulting her or checking to see if she was hungry, he proceded to order only coffee for them both. Not only did he talk about himself the entire time, he also performed a series of tacky magic tricks, which made Christine wish the earth would swallow her up, then discoursed on the profound significance of astrology as a personal life philosophy. He never asked her one interested question about herself.

As Christine talked about the evening, she and I continued to joke about her date's narcissism and boorishness. At this point, I assumed she had called to give evidence on how difficult it was to find a good man or, perhaps, to discuss how to unload such a rude and self-centered individual without seeming too rude or critical, since women tend to be overly concerned with appearing nice.

I was wrong. So wrong.

For when I asked her why she had called, her tone changed dramatically from that of a positive good ol' girl to a deflated, disappointed li'l girl.

"I wonder," she confessed, "if I shouldn't have mentioned anything about his cigarette smoking. He hasn't called me since that night. He did ask me for my number, but he hasn't called. I know where he works. Maybe I should call him?"

Was she kidding?

I don't think so!

DATING SHOULD BE ABOUT SELECTING,
NOT BEING SELECTED

Like Christine, far too many women behave more like beggars than choosers in the dating game. For them, dating is a process of hoping-to-be-selected rather than an opportunity to select. For example:

Twenty-four-year-old Annette from L.A. called to complain about her tendency to choose "the wrong type" of man—which, at present, is a younger fellow of twenty-one. "Isn't that awful?" she asks, and when I inquire what's so awful about it, she replies that it is completely "inappropriate." "It's not just because of my age," she explains. "It's my social situation. I have a seven-year-old son, which makes me seem even older in comparison than I am chronologically." I concede that's a good point and then we get down to business.

GO WITH THE FLOW, AND YOU COULD GET
CAUGHT IN THE UNDERTOW

What I tell Annette applies to many of you. We all tend to be motivated much too much by the tremendous relief that comes with realizing someone (read anyone) is interested in us—because we're lonely or feeling amorous and would like to act it out. So we go with the flow without, indeed, making any choice at all. Do you see the crucial difference there? Acquiescing to an availability is in no way making a choice.

I point out this fundamental distinction to Annette, stressing that what she needs to do is spend time thinking about what she really wants and needs at this particular time in her life. If, as it appears to me, she is inclined to be a family person and devote her energy to her son instead of to her social life, she has to be prepared to sustain herself through those low times we all go through when we feel alone.

SWEATING OUT THE ROUGH TIMES

How do we get through rough times? By believing in ourselves enough and occupying ourselves enough, developing ourselves enough, so that we can tolerate the discomfort between now and our next triumph. As I've said, there really is no gain without pain—emotionally as well as aerobically. Why not ride the loneliness through and come out a stronger person as the result of it? Why not fill our minds and our hearts and stop using a relationship with a man as a substitute for that core fulfillment?

DOWN WITH FAIRY TALES!

None of us, thank heaven, is Cinderella—who happens to be the greatest example ever of a woman waiting for some man to come along and fix it for her. It's sad that we women grow up believing in these fairy tales and then are crushed when they turn out not to pertain to real life. In the actual world, we must concern ourselves with our personal growth. Then we'll be able to stand the wait until we encounter a man who is both special and, in Annette's term, "appropriate."

AVOIDING THE LOSER TRACK

And what are the telltale feelings that let you know you're on the loser track with an "inappropriate" man? They are relief that you're no longer alone, leading to gratitude that he's selected you and panic when he's out of your sight. These are difficult feelings to admit to because they make very conscious and concrete our fears of life, adulthood, responsibility, and autonomy. However, such fears are normal and natural. Everybody has experienced them to some degree throughout her life. But remember, the quality, satisfaction, and meaning you get out of your life depends upon how you face those fears. Using an unsatisfactory relationship to camouflage them is a sure way to diminish self-worth.

This thinking was summarized by the therapy patient of mine who coined the term "female escape route," which, as I've said, is a socially acceptable means of avoiding becoming an individual—through attachment.

YOU CAN RUN AWAY FROM YOURSELF, BUT YOU CAN'T HIDE

When she called me, twenty-two-year-old Kristin was a study in panic, hysterical that she'd made an irreversible mistake with her boyfriend of four years. Her problem had begun when the guy, whom she described as "my best friend," announced he was taking an "all-boys" trip during spring break, leaving her, or so it seemed to her, in the lurch.

Consequently, when Kristin and her boyfriend were having dinner at the house of his best friend, along with the other young men with whom he'd be vacationing, she had one drink too many and, in her words, "made a fool of myself." What she'd basically said in no uncertain terms was that if her man couldn't include her in everything he did, she wanted to end the relationship. "And it's kinda true," she told me. "But in the meantime, look what I've done, I'm totally embarrassed and my boyfriend was crying. I just created a big episode and now I don't know how to get out of it."

ATTACHMENT ISN'T INTIMACY

I first suggested that Kristin calm down, then explained that everybody loses it at one time or another. The important thing is to understand why we lost it. And it seemed to me that Kristin's explosion was indicative that she was taking the female escape route by insisting that she become an attachment to her man. Expecting a boyfriend to provide you with your life is unrealistic and actually unfair, because it's simply not his job. Men are here to share our lives, not to be our lives. It's not a question of having too many expectations; it's really about having too few expectations for yourself.

OVERCOMING FEAR THE REAL-WORLD WAY

What I recommended to Kristin, what I recommend to all women, was to do something, such as taking a class or doing community work, which would provide a sense that her life has a purpose outside herself. By so doing, you discover you're not so scared about life because you're excited about establishing your special place in it. Isn't that preferable to being so dependent that the very idea of solitude strikes fear in your heart?

I suggested to Kristin that a good way to begin becoming her own person was to call her boyfriend, tell him that she'd been concerned enough about the incident to elicit my advice and now was working to have a deeper understanding of her own autonomy, then to simply apologize and tell him, sincerely, to have a good time when he was away.

Kristin was lucky that she'd had to confront the issue of dependence on males at twenty-two instead of forty-seven. In fact, she was on the border of doing something very special at a time when she had so many productive years ahead of her to explore her feelings, desires, and the place she really wanted to carve out for herself in the world.

FEAR OF THE UNKNOWN IS HOW GREAT THINGS START

Imagine people going west in covered wagons. They were scared. They had no idea what they'd find. Imagine the first astronauts of the moon landing. Those pioneers may have been heroes, but I guarantee they had their share of fear of the unknown. It just didn't prevent them from acting. All change, as I've said, is scary, but it's the only route to progress. It might help to think of your fears as stage fright, as you prepare to give an Oscar-winning performance as yourself!

EXPECTING THE IMPOSSIBLE—A NO-WIN GAME

If you're inclined to discount my point of view as full of assumptions, as a personal agenda or bias, I understand. After all, it's unsettling to consider the possibility that most female thrusting toward men and relationships is not because women are making sensible choices. Rather, it's a case of women being driven to attach to men for identity, affirmation, approval, purpose, safety, and security—values that can really only come from within ourselves. When the inevitable disappointment happens, such women complain bitterly that their men have failed them because they don't sustain them just the way they want.

DON'T YOU DARE PICK UP THAT PHONE!

My conversation with Stephanie, twenty, made this truth abundantly clear. She immediately expressed her fear of being alone, which she defined as not being in a relationship. I asked her exactly what she feared would happen if she didn't have a guy.

STEPHANIE: I don't know . . . but this has been going on for years with me; I always seem to overlap my relationships. . . . It's almost like I don't know myself, really. And I think that, like, maybe my identity is through these guys.

DR. LAURA: So you're like some Twilight Zone toy. If someone's holding you, you're animated. If they put you down and leave the room, you become an inanimate object. No wonder you race to make sure you've always got a guy around as sort of a battery—they literally give you life.

STEPHANIE: Yes. And security.

DR. LAURA: Oh yeah? What security? You've gone from guy to guy—how secure is that? That's called an "illusion," honey.

STEPHANIE: But I don't want to be like that . . . I want to . . . take care of *me* for a while.

DR. LAURA: "Take care of me," I like that—that's well put.

STEPHANIE: I say it, but doing it . . . It seems that when I end a relationship . . .

DR. LAURA: You get right back on the "guy-patrol alert"?

STEPHANIE: I try to stop myself . . .

DR. LAURA: The same way it's hard to say no to a piece of cheesecake, right? . . . So how *are* you going to say no? When the agony of simply being with yourself, utterly devoid of a sense of importance or joy, makes you want to snort, shoot up, or ingest a guy—because that's what it's like, a drug, right?

STEPHANIE: Yes. It takes everything in me to keep from picking up the phone and calling a boyfriend.

DR. LAURA: And that's the very moment you have to keep from doing it. You know where self-esteem ultimately comes from? Surviving that painful moment and not picking up the phone. Not by seducing some new guy—but by suffering through the pain. And, Stephanie, you *do* have the personal courage it takes—you've just been too afraid to test it!

FIVE RIGHT THINGS TO DO WHEN YOU'RE
DRIVEN TO DO A WRONG ONE

What Stephanie needed was a game plan to combat those "dark nights of the soul." She needed to tell herself, "When I get scared, whether it's expressed as boredom, loneliness, feeling lost, or as if I have no meaning in my life and no direction, at that moment, I'll pull out my list of five good things to do, out of which I'll choose one or more." These things will enable women to get past that horrendous moment of self-doubting fear—and avoid "eating the cheesecake."

Those five things could include calling a friend who knows and understands you and your situation, someone who can give you "first refusal." The list may include taking a bath or a walk, writing in a journal, exercising, meditating, having a cup of hot tea—anything that puts some time and energy between the "impulse to act" and the actual choice to action. Usually, if some centering behavior intercedes, the pain can be survived and you are on to new planes of your own growing existence.

MAKING A MAN THE JUDGE AND JURY OF YOUR SELF-WORTH

Men are not only seen and used by many women as a place to hide from the difficulties and discomforts of becoming an autonomous human being, as we've seen thus far. They are often burdened with the task of being the source of affirmation and approval for the woman's young, uncertain, developing, or even somewhat damaged self-esteem.

If she can make him stay, she's okay. If he leaves, she's not okay. To attribute such godlike powers to someone you just happen to meet in the unpredictable "crapshoot" of life is, in a word, stupid. And remember, that kind of stupidity has nothing to do with I.Q. because it's a universal truth that some of the smartest women do the stupidest things.

WHAT IF I DO SOMETHING WRONG AND RUIN IT?

Emily, a twenty-year-old college student majoring in childhood education, professed to be very happy in her ten-month relationship with a twenty-seven-year-old. And yet when she called me, she was crying. When I asked her the problem, she blurted out that she was constantly terrified that she was going to do something wrong and ruin it.

I asked her if she was equally afraid that he might do something wrong and ruin it and she emphatically replied no, but, under my prodding, she soon admitted that he could get a job out of state and leave. She told me plaintively, "He could say that I am not worth it, too young or something, or not mature enough to handle it." I agreed that some of that might be true but suggested that what she was really afraid of was slipping up and showing him what she really is.

THE SMART PART

Before long, Emily was confessing to her fears of not being smart enough to achieve her goal of being a kindergarten and preschool teacher. She claimed to be both dedicated and perseverant; it was the smart part that set off her worry attacks. "People don't have confidence in me," she insisted, and when I demanded a specific example, she immediately responded, "My family."

DR. LAURA: Who in your family doesn't have confidence in you?

EMILY: My mother.

DR. LAURA: How do you know that? What does she say?

EMILY (CRYING HARDER): . . . Ohhh, I never talked to anybody like this before . . . um . . . she tells me that, you know, when I started school, that "You're not going to finish it" . . .

DR. LAURA: Go ahead, what else did she say?

EMILY (CRYING): That I'm like all my other sisters—that I'm stupid, undependable, irresponsible—but I'm not! Nothing I can say or do . . . Excuse me, I have to calm down.

DR. LAURA: I believe you're not those things—now, why do you think she would say those things if you're not?

EMILY: She can be very abusive, verbally.

DR. LAURA: Has she accomplished anything in her life?

EMILY: No.

DR. LAURA: Oh, now, how do you think that might relate to her tearing down everybody else?

EMILY: Because she feels jealousy for me. There's times she's told me, like when I go somewhere with my friends, "Why should I let you go when I never got to do that when I was your age?" And I go, "Mother, this is a different time . . ."

DR. LAURA: It's just irrelevant. You first have to know that your mother needs a lot of help.

EMILY: Yeah, she does.

DR. LAURA: Now, you may know that, but you are separating what you know intellectually from how you feel—and you feel too often like your mom is right—after all, she is your mom—while in reality you're just a young person with the normal inherent insecurities.

KNOWING IS NOT ALWAYS BELIEVING

At this point, I explained to Emily the nature of the deeper issue: She knew in her mind that her mom was jealous, a bit twisted, and even cruel; but too often she felt that her mom was right. After all, she *was* her mother, so by definition was supposed to know best. And everybody has perfectly normal periods of self-doubt. If you put these factors together, you have a desperately hurt and frightened young lady, whose core fear was that her boyfriend would have the same reaction to her as her mother did. Riddled with such insecurity and dependency, she runs the risk of becoming a pain to her man—unless she begins to work out her emotional conflicts in therapy.

MAKING MEN INTO BAND-AID SOLUTIONS

Everybody's got emotional baggage and idiosyncrasies—that's just real life. For women to expect men to be the bandage for their hurt is to surrender the opportunity to be co-equal and confident in a relationship. Women have work to do before they're ready to make a healthy choice and then to function in a relationship as a healthy partner.

I sometimes feel it should be a felony to marry before thirty. Why? Because women would then be "forced" to take the time to become self-knowledgeable and self-reliant. Then dating would not seem like such a life-and-death necessity. Decisions and choices made out of desperation generally lose you more ground than they can ever gain for you.

CHOOSE OR LOSE

You don't have to be a radical feminist to believe women should make choices. I just don't believe enough of it is happening. One of my aims in writing this book, which I can't stress too often, is that women are hooking onto men by default—with "I love him" becoming the great liberator from personal growth and self-responsibility. In addition, it's not really fair to the man himself, whom you're settling for.

DON'T GET CAUGHT IN THE "VICTIM TRAP"

Probably the single most familiar theme uttered and written by and about women in the popular media is "victimization," replete with graphic stories of dysfunctional this and alcoholic that, so that women are supported to experience interminable "recovery" from terrible pasts. I admit to having a problem with this approach.

Each human being has a story, and the traumas and betrayals are real. Each individual responds to these realities in his or her own unique way. We are not simple formulas of cause and effect. The quality of our lives ultimately depends upon the courage we extend to deal with hurt and risk in a creative way: That is the road to ever growing self-esteem.

And those challenges are available at every age.

CAN "WEDDING JITTERS" BE A WARNING TO GET OUT?

Stacy, my twenty-one-year-old caller, and her thirty-one-year-old live-out boyfriend became engaged five months after they met. Until the engagement began, things had been wonderful, but afterward, Stacy started noticing certain behavior in her Prince Charming. He had become increasingly jealous, controlling, and possessive. At this point, Stacy had had it but was still uncertain if she was doing the right thing by leaving him.

I told Stacy she was doing the right thing unless she wanted to have a life with someone who is perpetually jealous, controlling, and possessive. Then I brought up my theory of the first eighteen months of a relationship's life.

LET'S DECLARE A WAITING PERIOD FOR MARRIAGE

I wholeheartedly believe you should date for about a year and a half before even contemplating engagement. It takes that long to get a clear picture of the other person. Stacy had gotten engaged too soon, before she got that clarification. When you become engaged too quickly, when you've got the ring and announced to the world that you're getting married and then you begin seeing things about your fiancé that are totally unacceptable, it's profoundly embarrassing to do what you know you need to do, which is to get out— at any cost.

FACING REALITY: THE KEY TO GROWTH

Stacy quickly admitted she hadn't really wanted to get engaged in the first place but that the man had insisted on it. Here she was, a nineteen-year-old living in a free country who, because she didn't yet have the strength of her own convictions, bowed to the greater will of an insecure bully who most probably chose a much younger woman so he could order around someone weaker.

YOU'VE GOT TO LEARN TO TRUST YOURSELF

I advised Stacy that the chances of her fiancé changing were slight to nonexistent, as she must by now have surmised, and that what she should do, what she really wanted to do, was gather her courage, take the ring off her finger, give it back to him, and say, "This is too controlling. I have a life I want to develop first. I cannot cater to your fears and your insecurities."

What was clear to me, and what I hope became clear to Stacy, is that she knew what she wanted to do before she called me. In her words, she just "needed to hear it from somebody else." Honestly, what she needed most of all was to learn to trust herself, to hear it from her own mind and accept that it's the right move and go on and live it. That's part and parcel of being a grown-up.

A MAN'S-EYE VIEW OF THE DATING GAME

Now, women, let's take a moment out and explore dating from the guy's point of view. Do you think men are so emotionally dense that they can't sense the difference between your really wanting them and desperately needing attachment? Well, they can! And some of these men, like Stacy's boyfriend, use it to bolster their own insecurity. Too often that sort of situation can become abusive as the controlling aspects of the relationship increase—perhaps in response to the woman's evolving maturity and independence as manifested by her desire to split up.

MEN CAN FEEL LIKE OBJECTS, TOO

Let's not forget that many men are sensitive to our attachment desperation and don't feel wanted for themselves but instead are aware they're being used.

Tony, twenty-nine, had been dating a certain woman for almost a year. He was in therapy in order to deal with his own intimacy problems but was growing increasingly dismayed by the behavior of his girlfriend. She would always look at him with goo-goo eyes and extol the perfection of the relationship even though he was not reciprocating on anything even remotely close to her level. Despite her extraordinary devotion, she never seemed interested in what he was really feeling or thinking. Maybe, he suggested, she didn't want to confront a truth that might interfere with her fantasy.

TONY: I don't understand. I go, "How could you want to be with someone who is not giving you back what you're giving?" And she basically said at the end of the conversation, "Look, I'm tired of being the suffering female . . ."

DR. LAURA: Good, I'm glad she is.

TONY: So she said that and that was fine. But she's still calling me and suffering and saying she doesn't understand why she is in so much pain, she didn't do anything to earn it, and so on. Like last night she just moved into a new apartment and it was raining, you know that's kind of creepy stuff, so she called me . . . real late . . . terrified . . .

DR. LAURA: Clearly, she's trying to make you feel responsible for her and suck you back in. And you don't even describe her as wanting an intimate relationship with you. You describe her as wanting a RELATIONSHIP—in capital letters. But she can't have it by telling you it's perfect or that she's scared in her apartment, because it's not you she is really learning anything about—thoughts, feelings, needs—it's just you as a generic man, date, or boyfriend. Am I right?

TONY: A thousand percent.

THERE AIN'T NOTHING LIKE THE REAL THING

No one will deny the enormous ego gratification involved in having someone attracted to you. There is pleasure in having a good time with somebody. There is comfort in having somebody share many of your perspectives. Affirmation, approval, and attachment are beneficial and wonderful aspects of relationships. The excitement of all those feelings coming together is exhilarating. And they are some of the many benefits of relating to other human beings.

If you are desperate for affirmation, approval, and attachment, if you're grateful to be chosen, so you're not too choosy, if you are settling instead of being selective, then you are probably making stupid dating choices. Think about it: Would the kind of man you really want want a gal who behaves like you? No.

. . .

On January 7, 1993, Suzanne, thirty, called me, all confused about whether or not she should continue to date her thirty-two-year-old boyfriend of three months. It seems that when his mother comes to town she stays at his house. Well, it's more than that. She sleeps with him in his bed.

"He says that they don't 'do' anything," she whimpered. "So I asked him why his mom doesn't just sleep in another bed in his house. He answered me back by saying I'm too conservative.

"Is this okay? I just don't know if I should date him anymore. Am I overreacting?"

Need I say more?

3 Stupid Devotion

"BUT I LOVE HIM" AND MORE STUPID ROMANTIC STUFF

You cannot imagine how frustrating it is to hear over and over "I love him" as the justification for a bad choice in a man. These women can't face the fact that they're immobilized in an obviously self-defeating situation, gratefully tolerating attitudes and behaviors no man would give quarter to for five seconds. Their definition of love is—with a lot of confirmation from popular culture—way off the mark and has become synonymous with attachment.

WHOEVER SAID SURRENDER IS ROMANTIC
HAD A MAJOR PROBLEM

Let's look briefly at current popular role models for women in love as personified by contemporary fairy tales, which all our children know by heart.

Ariel, the Little Mermaid, aspires to "greater things" and ends up with a stupid prince, who "loved whoever had that 'voice,'" no matter how wonderful Ariel was. For this, she gives up her world, her family, her fins.

Belle, in *Beauty and the Beast,* aspires to "greater

things" and ends up with a rotten (oh, maybe he'll change . . .) prince who at first worked on being nice to her only to break a curse. Okay, okay, so he came around—but would Prince Handsome have hung around that long for a witch? I hardly think so. For this she gave up her plans and dreams of journeying into the world.

I would have been happier had she been a part of his successful spiritual transformation, patted him on the head, and gave him her forwarding address at the university.

In *Aladdin,* the princess also gives up her dreams of venturing into the world, independently, when her beggar-turned-prince takes her off on a magic carpet. He's going to show her the world—of course, that he's never seen it himself is irrelevant.

If you're thinking these "fairy tales" do not apply to real life, think again! Remember, billions of girls and boys who see these films are going to grow up believing this romantic nonsense and dreaming dreams that could later turn into nightmares.

DREAMS CAN BE DANGEROUS

Since we're on the subject of dreams, I want to point out the crucial difference between really caring for someone in particular and caring desperately for the dream. By caring more for the dream, by being dependent upon making an attachment, women make compromises that can destroy them. Consider Lisa's story:

COME GET ME, CONVINCE ME, SHOW ME YOU LOVE ME!

Lisa described herself as "kind of in a predicament right now," which turned out to be the understatement of the week. She had been dating a man for a year and a half (my recommended minimum waiting period for marriage), and he had recently proposed to her. Having taken the time to get clarification, she told him no because of his many problems, which included drug use and abusive behavior.

Although she claimed her boyfriend was trying to curb his temper and hadn't pushed her around for three months, Lisa was still concerned because that last abuse had taken place when she had tried to break off the relationship.

DR. LAURA: Lisa, what the heck are you doing there?

LISA: I don't know. I really have been trying to get out . . . but I can't get rid of him. I'll refuse to take his phone calls or answer the door—anything—and he'll still come over or he'll bust through the door. . . .

DR. LAURA: Then you call the police.

LISA: I haven't had the heart . . .

DR. LAURA: The heart! Lisa, what he is doing is against the law. Breaking and entering and stalking are crimes!

LISA: But sometimes he can be—

DR. LAURA: Sometimes, nothing! Lisa. I'm going to sound very harsh for a moment. You cannot afford to be a wimpy, overcompassionate, frightened female, because you'll be putting yourself in real physical danger. You need to take the appropriate steps to protect yourself and let him know you are not playing a dramatic love game of "come get me—convince me—make me know you love me—when I say no." Can you do that?

LISA: Yesss . . .

DR. LAURA: You must convince him you're really serious when you say, "Go away." Even if he's nice from time to time. Even if he gets down on his knees and swears he'll try to change. I just don't think an abusive, intrusive drug addict is a good father for your children-to-be. Do you think so?

LISA: No . . . but is it natural to still feel like I love him?

DR. LAURA: Perhaps you're feeling for your dream, for those moments when it's pleasant. Unfortunately, a relationship is not about moment-to-moment. It's about totality. What you have to do is stand back and not look at any one moment. You have to say, "Overall, this is a really bad choice," and get the heck out!

LISA: Okay, thank you.

NO MORE MS. NICE GAL!

Although Lisa can clearly see this man is a major problem, she continues to have feelings for him. So what's really at issue? That's extremely complicated, but here's at least a partial explanation.

We all know the phrase "a face only a mother could

love." Therein lies a clue to solving the mystery. I can't tell you precisely what combination of nature and nurture is at work here, but women do seem able (and all too willing) to search really hard for redeeming qualities in their men. With such a mind-set, they are ripe to be overly tolerant of grossly negative qualities in exchange for what may be only moments of happiness or peace.

THE DETESTABLE DOUBLE STANDARD

I'm reminded of the Ann Landers column in which a woman was complaining about how difficult it was for a "quality lady over thirty-five" to find a "nice guy": "I find it fascinating," she wrote, "that women are willing to overlook balding heads, beer bellies and plaid shirts with polka-dot ties, but a man will take me aside and whisper, 'She's okay but she has thighs in two different time zones.' "

And think of all those beer commercials in which the guys are schleppy but their dream women have to be at least in the running for the cover of the *Sports Illustrated* swimsuit issue. Are we, as "normal" women, expected not only to be satisfied with such jerks but deeply gratified when they deign to favor us with their attention?

SELECT, DON'T SETTLE

Unfortunately, women's willingness to overlook troubling traits doesn't stop at schleppiness. It includes, for instance, drug and alcohol problems, abusiveness, immaturity, irresponsibility—and more.

Much too much more.

And all in order to settle for fantasy versions of love, commitment, security, attachment, identity, and purpose.

Why are you settling? Why are you not more selective? Why are you not more critical?

Why are you calling it love?

Because you haven't come to believe in yourself!

And when you don't believe in yourself, you find yourself believing in things considerably more foolish than the Tooth Fairy.

WHY DO WOMEN PUT UP WITH BAD-NEWS BOORS?

Suzanne had been seeing her boyfriend for six months when he broke the news that he was moving back with his ex-wife—for three months, for financial reasons. To add insult to injury, she subsequently discovered he was still married to the woman, although they'd been separated for seven years, and had a seven-year-old son by her.

After meeting the wife, Suzanne realized the "divorce" was only the tip of an iceberg of dishonesty: The entire time he'd been romancing her, even suggesting they marry, the man had been sleeping with his wife. As far as the other woman knew, there were no financial reasons and no three-month time limit on his living with her; they were simply getting back together. When Suzanne confronted the louse, he not only denied everything, but he made her feel as if *she* were the one with the problem. Then came this shocking statement:

"BUT I . . . I STILL JUST . . . REALLY LOVE HIM."

When I suggested to Suzanne that she was probably dealing with a sociopath—a master at manipulating women who were made vulnerable by self-doubt into assuming guilt—she didn't disagree. When she told me he had been in AA for over a year, she listened with interest as I countered, "So what, Suzanne. I don't care what he's been in or for how long. The most adequate measure of the man is what he does when he's not in meetings." When she confessed she knew he'd cheated on his wife with at least five other women and I groused, she told me, "I've heard it from everybody, but I needed to hear it from a professional, I guess."

DR. LAURA: Suzanne, this is a bad person, a liar and manipulator. Why aren't you angry and horrified and disgusted enough to make this decision on your own?

SUZANNE: I guess because of my upbringing. A lot of manipulation—but never really lying . . . yeah . . . lying too.

DR. LAURA: So all this is "normal" to you. You're going to have to struggle against that "normal" so that your new normal is a healthier one. Because he is going to wine, dine, and send you flowers and try to get you back. But people like that don't change. Ask his wife how much he's changed over two decades. Ask yourself how much your family's changed.

SUZANNE: Right, you're right. . . . But is there anything I can do so I don't go back to him? Because—I'm in AA, so I have a support group, but I'm still really scared . . .

DR. LAURA: You have to use your courage. There's no magic here. AA isn't going to give you the courage. And I'm not going to give you the courage. Nothing and nobody has your power to do what you need to do.

SUZANNE (QUIETLY): Yeah.

DR. LAURA: It's up to you, kiddo. You want to have something beautiful and meaningful in your life; you have to hold out for it and in your own mind become the receptacle for it.

SUZANNE (LONG PAUSE WITH SIGHS): I still can't believe I thought he was a good person.

DR. LAURA: You wanted to believe it because he said things you so wanted to hear. He made you feel ways you so badly wanted to feel that you didn't care who he was, really. I can almost still hear it in your voice now. You want too much not to care who he is even now. It's just his wife—right? She's a bitch—we get rid of her and everything will be swell?

SUZANNE: Yeah, I mean, no . . . I really like her!

DR. LAURA: Good, then go out with her instead!

LINDA: Really! Thank you so much.

DENIAL GETS YOU NOTHING

If you kiss a toad, you don't get a prince—you get slime in your mouth and bad memories. You do everything but accept reality: You deny, ignore, rationalize, justify, and ultimately go back to that most pathetic defensive position: "But I love him."

What's that supposed to mean, anyway? "I love him," therefore your rational sensibilities are suspended? Now, that's stupid!

THE "BUT I LOVE HIM" FOLLIES

When my caller Jody pleaded, "But I love him . . . ," I suggested that her idea of love—from what she'd described to me—had gotten her into trouble so many times before and was getting her into trouble again. My advice was emphatically not to use those feelings she calls love to make a relationship decision. Since they inevitably led her to the wrong decision, she would do better to tough it out now and spare herself the endless anguish she might otherwise be setting herself up for.

THE LOVE STUFF ISN'T A DIVINE DIRECTIVE

Women like Jody must learn that hormones and heart are not necessarily our best leaders. This love stuff is not an omen or divine directive—so stop wallowing in it! If you find your rational sense being overridden by mushy feelings . . . know that you are probably on the wrong track!

Stop with the "Oh, I know he's ——— (fill in the blank with *abusive, mean, cold, uncommunicative, negative, bullying, violent, addicted, controlling, workaholic, jealous,* etc.), but I love him." The "I love him" does not erase what came before!

MY ACID TEST FOR GENUINE LOVE

I feel certain that what many women call love, under so many obviously ugly, hurtful, and sometimes downright dangerous situations, is more about passion and promise and fantasies and desperate dependencies and fears about taking on alternatives.

Real love is a long marination of qualities having to do with respect, admiration, appreciation, character, affection, cooperation, honor, and sacrifice. I ask all these "But I love him" women the same question: "If you were a parent, would you introduce this kind of guy—or even this guy—to your daughter?"

Funny how the answer is always an emphatic No!

WHY CAN'T YOU PUT YOURSELF FIRST?

My comeback is then, "Why would you not be as caring about yourself, as rational about yourself, as you'd be about a daughter?"

Why? Why? Why?

What goes through your mind?

- "If he doesn't want me, I'm no good."
- "I'll never find anyone else to tolerate me."
- "I don't want to be alone."
- "It's better than nothing."
- "It's better than I've had."
- "I'm twenty-nine (thirty-nine, forty-nine, fifty-nine —it's always with a "-nine") and it's getting late for me."
- "I don't really think I could find anybody better."
- "Sometimes he's not so bad."
- "I don't know where I'm going in my life anyway."
- "I'm too uncomfortable with my own problems to face them. Trying to help him makes me feel better."
- "Caring for him makes me feel more meaningful."
- "I'm too scared to face unknowns, inside myself or in the world."
- "It's not so bad."
- "It's hard to find people to have fun with."

LOW SELF-ESTEEM IS NO EXCUSE FOR INACTION

All the above sound like self-esteem problems, don't they?

They are, but the entire low-self-esteem issue is particularly complex, since negative self-worth can also serve as a weapon that women wield against themselves. So many times I'll be asking a woman about her often unfortunate choices and impotent participation in her own life's direction, and the reason she'll give me is "Oh well, I guess it's because I have low self-esteem."

Now, while there is no doubt in my mind that the price tag you put on yourself will determine in large part the value of the people and the situations you'll pick and tolerate, I'm more and more concerned about low self-esteem becoming an excuse for inaction in your own behalf in this sense: You don't feel special, or worthy or competent—therefore, you don't dare take risks.

PAST HURTS DON'T EXCUSE PRESENT COWARDICE

So what do you do when you're feeling consistently down about yourself? You probably search for the childhood hurts that landed you in this pickle, then join an "Adult Child of Whatever" group to give validation to your helplessness. The information you glean and the support you get from self-help books and groups and/or from therapy should help you fight through those reflexive, emotionally induced self-defeating behaviors and choices and to take risks, not linger in negativity.

For it is in the taking of risks, especially in the face of emotional motivations to the contrary, that you grow in autonomy and personal power.

Remember, self-esteem is not simply a product of the

existence or lack of verbal, emotional, or physical abuse. There are many, many people walking around with positive self-images and expansive worldviews in spite of their terrible upbringings. So the equation between past trauma and low self-esteem can't be one-to-one. I'm not denying the negative impact of early family crises, disruption, or destructiveness. History is not destiny. You have free will to overcome, grow, change: Invent yourself.

WHICH COMES FIRST, COURAGE OR POSITIVE SELF-ESTEEM?

The concept of courage is one I hear discussed almost only when watching *Rescue 911*, but courage is crucial to building, or repairing, a self-image or identity.

Here's my point: Life, with its risks and challenges, is scary. Just as we often turn to instant gratification instead of a more mature postponement of pleasure for some future gain, we often turn too quickly to mechanisms of instant avoidance to deflect risk of failure or hurt.

So, which comes first? Low self-esteem or the absence of an independent, creative effort in life? As with the time-honored "chicken or egg" riddle, which comes first is irrelevant. A lack of self-esteem and a lack of courageous, independent, creative effort on your own behalf will reinforce each other—forever. I suspect this dual failure of the will becomes a self-perpetuating bad habit.

SELF-WORTH: THE GIFT YOU HAVE TO EARN

If you wait for good self-esteem to set in before you take on life, we'll probably share rocking chairs together as we talk over what might have been.

Your actions often have to come before the feelings, maybe even despite them. As I said before, courage is not the lack of fear, it is fear plus action. You must begin thinking of self-esteem and rational behavior as a continuous loop, each perpetually feeding the other.

THERAPY IS HEALTHY, DESPERATE ATTACHMENT IS NOT

You are ultimately the architect of your life. Some raw materials might have been left out—or damaged along the way—but you are still the architect of your own life.

So when you examine the blueprints of your relationship, do you—honestly—see a sturdy building or a house of cards? The ultimate quality of your existence will depend upon your exercising the courage to make rational decisions about your relationships early on. That means you'll have to cope with real and irrational feelings of self-doubt and meaninglessness directly, through therapy, for example, rather than indirectly, through desperate attachment.

Otherwise, what you'll call loving feelings are really desperate cries for significance. The loss of that so-called love becomes more than a personal loss—it becomes a person loss: you! And that is the pain thirty-six-year-old Linda was suffering.

HOW TO SURVIVE THE LOSS OF AN ATTACHMENT

Linda was involved with another woman, a twenty-four-year-old, who had informed her that she didn't love Linda and wanted to see other people. But Linda was finding herself unable to let go. I pointed out to her that the issue really was not one of letting go of her lover but of not being able to hold on to herself! There is, after all, a big difference between being hurt and disappointed that someone has rejected you—since we have all been rejected—and making the leap to "I'm worthless and unlovable," which was the tack Linda was taking.

CONNECTING VS. ATTACHING

As the conversation proceded and Linda admitted she had a tendency to make all her intimate relationships the center of her universe, I observed that such behavior is typically female. Men don't feel they have to be attached to a woman in order to exist. They feel they have to be doing something: racing a car faster, inventing something, climbing a mountain, running a company—doing something in the world. That's how they find an identity. Women tend not to do that enough. Linda certainly didn't.

DON'T EXPECT MOTIVATION TO FALL FROM THE SKY

"So one of things you should be working out in therapy," I advised her, "is the evolution, in your original family perhaps, of your discouragement in being independent and autonomous. Second, you'll have to get off your *tush* and have the courage to create something in this world that you can look at and be proud of. And don't expect motivation to fall from the sky. At this point, the motivation will probably have to come from rational thinking. And the rational thought is: If I don't do this, I will always feel this pain."

Dependent women acquire the self-esteem they lack through their attachments to other people. It's a foolhardy means of building self-esteem. Claiming as love the attachment to anyone who barely shows a hint of approval is a desperate state of being. You worry that any minute change in that person's demeanor or behavior might mean his or her lack of interest—and the loss of you. It makes life a fragile experience.

It is just this kind of state of mind that leads women to look for potential in all the wrong places, and to have the following laments:

LEONORA: I'm kinda hurt and disappointed. I met a guy at work and I've been dating him one month and it's clear that he drinks a lot. What do you think is his potential?

DR. LAURA: Potential for what? Drunk-driving arrests?

DEBBY: I met a man three months ago—we've had a few dates. I found out he's been involved in a shooting. Should I stay?

DR. LAURA: Only after watching *Bonnie and Clyde* for wardrobe suggestions.

LINDA: Well, he has a tendency to lie—actually, he lies a lot. But he is good at other things, if you get what I'm saying. So, what do you think?

DR. LAURA: What "hooks you in"? Does his potency increase in proportion to his lies? Will you really be satisfied with a highly sexed Pinocchio?

DENISE: I'm twenty-eight and I've been dating him for five years. We're engaged for two months. I don't know why, but I still don't trust him. He is irresponsible with money and has been with other women. But he says he loves me. Should I trust him?

DR. LAURA: Why, yes! You should trust that he'll probably be consistently untrustworthy. Which is great if you're not into surprises.

SELLING YOURSELF TO THE LOWEST BIDDER

Can you believe it? These are typical questions! It's not as though the woman has known the man for years and he's recently had a life crisis to which he's responding poorly. These ugly situations generally show themselves in their true light quite early in a relationship. Instead of saying to yourself, "Uh-oh, this is a definite no-no," you act out of a compulsion to grab what's available and make it work no matter what. You too often sell yourself to the available (and usually the lowest) bidder.

GRASPING FOR HOPE MEANS RISKING DESPAIR

A listener letter that can truly be described as heartbreaking illustrates this point perfectly. In it, the writer described her "relationship" with an instructor at an institution that doesn't allow fraternization with students. If the relationship were discovered, the man would be immediately dismissed. "I wonder why he would risk so much to be with me if for only a friendship," the letter continued.

It is most romantic to interpret his "fraternization" as some sort of sacrifice because of his deep feelings for the woman. Unfortunately, what seems more likely is that the teacher is both unethical and self-serving. But that jolt of reality wouldn't fulfill the writer's fantasy, hope, and need. Especially in light of her next disclosure: "I should add that the place where he works has provided me with a great deal of pleasure and friendship since the suicide of my son and subsequent death of my husband."

THE HIGH RISK OF CARING FOR THE DREAM

I can't even imagine the depth of pain, loss, perhaps guilt, fear, and need this woman is experiencing. Her grasping for the hope becomes more understandable. And more perilous. Because too often we only know what we want or need to know.

There is a world of difference between really caring for someone and caring for the dream—of frantically needing the dream as an emotional Band-Aid. If you care for the dream, you don't end up really healing or growing. You just end up hurting from a different source. If ignoring, denial, and rationalization don't work to make this relationship fit—why, become a chameleon. Make yourself fit—at all costs:

THE "VOLUNTEER" HOSTAGE CRISIS

Becky, thirty-six, is with a man who drinks, is verbally abusive, physically violent, owns guns, and now has job problems. How is that for a formula for disaster? "But," she says, "as long as I make things okay—take care of things the way he likes—then it's okay." It is? I don't think so. I think Becky is a volunteer hostage—making the best of what could literally become a life-and-death situation.

IT'S A TERRIBLE FOLLY, TRYING TO FIT

More than just trying to make things okay by appeasing the demons (those guys you just looooooove), so many of you turn yourselves inside out to make your man happy. If he's happy, then you're happy and all is well in the world. Because if he's happy, he'll be nice to you and love you and keep you happily ever after. Right? Wrong! Here's an outstanding example:

RETURNING TO THE SCENE OF THE CRIME

Twenty-year-old Valerie had been going with a young man about her age for more than two years. The relationship was troubled, and Valerie decided to fix it by changing herself to fit his ideals and trying to do everything he wanted of her. Unfortunately, the tactics hadn't worked. Her man was still discontented. At this point, she had had it, but every time she tried to end the affair, she was so overwhelmed with loneliness that she inevitably went back.

When I asked her why she kept "returning to the scene of the crime," she pleaded ignorance, then told me, "I guess it's because I miss him." Miss him? The source of perpetual negative judgment and rejection—plus some sex and handholding? For this she continued to give up pieces of herself?

I suggested that she was losing too many pieces of herself for so little positive return from this insecure, immature, controlling young man.

WHEN YOU'RE REENACTING OLD PAIN

I was particularly curious as to why Valerie was giving a youth with little more experience than she the power to define her. Under further scrutiny, the reason became clear. Valerie was the product of a broken home. She had a reservoir of unresolved emotions about the disappearance of her dad when she was only six. Now she was acting them out by being utterly submissive for fear that she, like her mother, would "do something wrong" and chase the man away, thereby losing "Daddy" again.

By the time our conversation concluded, Valerie seemed ready to unload the boyfriend, since they both needed time to grow, to face the fact that she was reenacting past pain, frustration, hurt, and loss and to begin to accept her own lovability and start exploring her own desires and dreams.

ROMANTIC INSTANT REPLAY

Valerie's predicament exemplifies behavior I encounter frequently: using the new love as a replacement part for an old loss—usually of a parent. It's not, therefore, the new guy who is the real target of your lovin' feelings. It is what he symbolizes, what he gives you a second chance to resolve. That's why his eventual loss becomes so devastating: It is an instant replay of a primal hurt!

WHY WOMEN AVOID NEW CHALLENGES—WITH ALL THEIR MIGHT

There are two powerful motivations for making it work with the most available guy—attempting to heal past hurts and avoiding risks. Sadly, neither works for long—even if a romance takes off and you're swept away by passion. When reality steps in, you go back to reading EMPTY and start trying to figure out why you're still not happy. Nine times out of ten, you come up with the following solution: Some change has to be made in him! Then everything will be okay.

RESISTANCE TO RISK-TAKING AND LOW SELF-ESTEEM— THE DEADLY DUO

Diane, forty-two, has a boyfriend whom she describes as self-centered. "He is always putting me down and discounting me," she complains. "We have fights about this all the time. I keep trying to get him to understand and to change."

I ask Diane what the benefits are to struggling to make him change. She answers, "Number one, I don't have to change.

"Number two, I don't lose what I like in the companionship and security aspects.

"Number three, it would be uncomfortable making a transition to being alone or with anyone else.

"And number four, I guess, I would take it personally—his negative perceptions of me must be right."

Wow! How is that for self-knowledge and honesty! We're back to those same old bugaboos: resistance to risk-taking and low self-esteem—hereafter to be known as "the deadly duo."

THE FATAL "BUT . . ."

Want another sure indicator that you're on the wrong track? It's when, after you admit to knowing what you're doing is probably stupid, you add anything reminiscent of the word *but*. Oh, I know, but, maybe, what if . . . ! Honey, you can't afford to live in the land of "what if." Because you—and I and everyone else—are living in the land of what is. Take up residence, please, and look at the buts as what they are, last-ditch attempts to struggle against the inevitable next step: personal growth.

HOW DO I TEACH HIM TO RESPECT ME?

Don't think you're going to trip me up on the compassion or pity issue! Elizabeth writes, "I can't take the insults anymore! They're hurtful and I never know why he gets mad till it's too late. Help! How do I teach him to respect me?" And I respond, "By doing what any truly self-respecting person would do under those circumstances: Leave. That will provide the most profound lesson he can learn from you!"

ARE YOU A ROMANTIC MARTYR?

Barbara complains, "My boyfriend and I have been dating for over a year. So far, there has been no intimacy and almost no touching. He doesn't like to be touched, or so he says. It's easy to understand why, with his background. His father was very abusive to him, his mother, five sisters, including beatings and sexual abuse . . ." And I answer, "This is a fella I would suggest you refer to a good therapist and forget. If you feel inexorably drawn in such 'what if' directions, we need to talk about your anxieties about intimacy—because the bottom line is that when you are with a guy who can't/won't do it, you're not doing it. And just maybe, that's they way you like it—safe from confronting your inner demons by martyring yourself to his."

GIVING IS NO GUARANTEE OF GETTING ANYTHING BACK

Remember that when your identity depends on becoming indispensable, you'll collect a lot of takers, but the chances are you will not often find that caretaking returned. You get something by communicating need, by being open to the gift but not, not ever, by settling.

CHANGING HIM FOR YOUR OWN GOOD

When women attempt to attain value and definition by attachment to men, a strange thing happens: They become vigilant to any imperfections in him—because if he's not perfect, then, by association, neither are they. That's when you try to fix him for your own good. Of course, this will be registered by him as behavior that is castrating, bitchy, unloving, and unaccepting. So it rarely results in any change coming from him, because he isn't the one motivated for the changes—you are. Unfortunately, you aren't exercising the option of change in the person who really needs it: you.

JUST HOW MUCH POINTLESS PAIN CAN YOU TAKE?

It's amazing how much nonproductive anguish and suffering (abuse, mismatch, disdain, disinterest) women will endure in order to avoid the productive forms of anguish and suffering (inner knowledge, independence, and challenging life for a personal dream). I stress again: No genuine, fulfilling love is possible without self-love preceding it.

THE AGE-OLD HEART VS. HEAD DEBATE

To sum up, please don't mix up feelings comprised of familiarity, investment, sex, promises, hopes, and fantasies with love. If those are the feelings tugging at your heart strings, forget it!

I'm asked all the time about whether decisions in relationships should be made from the head or the heart. You can guess my answer—the head, always. Because the heart is notorious for having a more blurry picture of reality.

And you know, when it comes to a long-term, committed relationship: Love is not enough. There are issues of honor, respect, mutuality, sacrifice, acceptance, supportiveness, similarity of life values and morality, to name only a few. They, too, don't come without struggling and striving, but, oh, are they worth it!

P.S.: IS THIS WOMAN FOR REAL?

Believe it or not, dear reader, this is a genuine news story, which the Associated Press released on March 9, 1993:

> A woman whose husband is accused of poisoning her and killing two others with cyanide-tainted cold capsules says

she considers their relationship normal even though she once dialed 911 seeking help during a fight.

Joseph Meling is charged with six counts of product tampering, two counts of perjury, and three counts of insurance fraud. He is accused of putting a cyanide capsule into a Sudafed package in February 1991 to kill his wife for $700,000 in life insurance. He also is accused of tampering with five Sudafed packages in stores to make it appear a random killer was at work.

Kathleen Daneker, 40, of Tacoma and Stan McWhorter, 44, of Lacey died of cyanide poisoning from Sudafed purchased around Tacoma and Olympia. Three other cyanide-filled capsules were found in Sudafed packages during a recall of the product.

Mrs. Meling nearly died but eventually recovered. She filed divorce papers soon after the cyanide incident, but later went back to her husband and is testifying in his defense.

Mrs. Meling said she felt the conflict in her marriage was normal. At times in tears, Mrs. Meling said she still loves Meling, and believes he is innocent.

Go figure!

4 Stupid Passion

"OHHH, AHHH, WE'RE BREATHING HARD. . . . IT MUST MEAN LOVE"

I remember a series of commercials some years ago in which Orson Welles intoned: "We will sell no wine before its time." Would that more women would display the same attitude toward sex!

And please don't accuse me of being a throwback to the double-standard days without considering the increasing numbers of unwanted pregnancies, abortions, venereal diseases, and broken hearts since the sexual revolution told us: "Hey, baby, you have the same right to fun 'n' games as men do."

I agree we've come a long way, dahlin', but we're still not where we want to be—because women continue to overromanticize sex.

IS ONE NIGHT OF HEAVEN WORTH THE AFTERMATH FROM HELL?

This from Ellen, who called in during my stint filling in for Sally Jessy Raphael on her ABC Radio Network show: "I'm a secretary who's been in love with my boss for a year. I never actually said anything about it to him. He never acted any way but businesslike with me.

"A month ago he asked me out to dinner on a Friday night. Then we went to his house to have some wine and talk, and I ended up staying the weekend. It was great. The sex was fantastic—it was all so romantic—just like a dream come true. We didn't talk about what would happen now at the office, or anything, before I went home on Sunday night. Okay. It's been over three weeks now and he treats me exactly like he did before that weekend! He hasn't said a word. My feelings are very hurt and I don't know what to do. I feel very uncomfortable."

HOPE EQUALS RESIGNATION

Find me a woman who can't relate to that caller's hurt and embarrassment—leading back to the old-fashioned now-comic question "But will he respect me in the morning?" That's yet another of our fatal buts. Still, the issue isn't really his respect. The issue is how we women can fantasize that something is so without bothering to question or discuss it. We hold our breath and hope it all turns out okay. Listen: In the words of Nobel Prize winner Albert Camus, "Hope equals resignation, and to live is not to resign yourself."

When I asked Ellen her thoughts on being sexual with her boss without a prior discussion about the relationship, she replied, "I thought that if he had sex with me, it meant that he feels like I do."

So there it is: relationship by hopeful fantasy.

THE VIRGIN-TILL-DEATH ACT

Let me repeat, this is not an issue of his respect—the old double standard. And I am not saying women should do a virgin-till-death act to make a man see them as pure, good, or a prize to be won. That would produce the desired effect only with a man who has an inferiority complex. However, a man who is heavily indoctrinated in a fundamentalist mentality would require a mate in kind—perhaps a better plan than the sexual chaos we have now.

BEWARE THE DON JUANS OF THIS WORLD!

Let's face it, it's perfectly possible to have a complete discussion with a man who seems to be on the same wavelength only to find out he is a liar, that he is someone playing a game with others. It happens. It always has. It always will. Remember Don Juan (whose real problem was his mother, of course . . .)? I'm sorry to report he's alive and well and living practically everywhere. Finally, I'm much more concerned with you playing games with yourselves—expecting pleasure while you're actually setting yourselves up for pain.

I FEEL LIKE I BETRAYED MY FRIEND!

That is what my caller Tiffany did to herself, all the while trying to believe things were more substantial than was actually the case. She came on the air telling me she was "having a lot of problems dealing with a mistake I made." The "mistake" turned out to be getting sexually involved with a very close friend's husband. (She herself was unmarried.)

Now, she regretted it tremendously, wished it had never taken place. Although it had only happened once some five weeks earlier, it plagued her. When I asked Tiffany why she'd done it in the first place, she initially claimed she didn't know, and then . . .

TIFFANY: Well, he sort of approached me about it and, um, what is killing me the most is that he approached me and I responded. And I don't know exactly why . . . except . . . I thought that I needed to help him, in a way . . . because his wife . . . my friend . . . had just died two weeks before and now I . . . I feel like I betrayed her . . . like she's going, "Why did you do this to me?"

DR. LAURA: You didn't do this to her. You obviously have done something to hurt yourself. Do you like this man? Did you have warmies for him when she was alive?

TIFFANY: I don't think so. . . . Well . . . yes and no . . . yes.

DR. LAURA: So you already coveted him in your heart. And now there was the opportunity—but now you feel uncomfortable about it because he's pulled back a bit?

TIFFANY: Yeah, me also. It was sort of a mutual thing.

DR. LAURA: Okay, would you say he pulled back a little before you pulled back? Might that be what hurts and makes you feel so bad at this point?

TIFFANY: Yes.

DR. LAURA: I think you're feeling a little used. What might be helpful is to verbalize all this to him.

TIFFANY: Well, we haven't been talking to each other at all.

DR. LAURA: Even so, I still prescribe calling him and talking it out—and, even if it makes you blush, facing it directly, matter-of-factly. Say something like "I've always been fond of you, you came on to me, and I thought I could be there for you at this time of pain . . . and now it feels like I just got used." Tell him you understand it was a mutual experience. But that what you have to do right now is pull back.

TIFFANY: Oh, I don't know if I can do that . . .

DR. LAURA: Consider the alternative. Is it easier to just sit there and obsess on how you betrayed a friend? And you didn't even do that!

TIFFANY: Yeah, okay.

DR. LAURA: And, Tiffany, if he comes on to you again, don't go with the flow until you are more certain—with the passing months or maybe years—that he's dealt with his wife's death and is really available for another relationship. Okay? Now, you take care.

TIFFANY: Thank you. Thanks a lot.

INTIMACY AND SEXUALITY ARE NOT THE SAME THING

Both men and women call me to talk about their relationships. Both use the term *intimate* to imply they've had sex. So does that mean intimacy and sexuality are synonymous? Absolutely not!

Within one hour from right now you could be having

frenzied sex with a complete stranger. This is obviously not intimacy. Intimacy is not the ability to do it—fruit flies can do it. Intimacy is the ability to talk over the doing of it—and everything else, from the meaning of sex to the meaning of life.

I have often said on the air, "Don't do anything you can't talk about—with that person!"

TALK NOW, SEX LATER

So why don't you talk first and have sex later? Well, first, there is a tremendous vulnerability associated with self-expression: the pain of anticipated rejection or criticism. A caller, when questioned about why she won't ask her fella of one month if he is dating other women, replies, "I don't want to be upset by the answer."

"But," I counter, "you are already upset by the worrying and wondering if he is or not!"

"Yeah, I know," she explains, "but the upset is in my head. If I know for sure, then it's real hurt."

SHOULD I CALL HIM—OR WAIT TILL HE CALLS ME?

Here's an example of how unarticulated fantasizing works—or, rather, doesn't work:

Diana, a single parent who'd been divorced for two years, had a certain need, a human need, the need to be connected to another human being, to be cared about, to touch and to feel close. In the course of things, she'd struck up a renewed friendship with a man she'd known as a teen-ager.

The relationship initially consisted of his doing odd

jobs around the house when she needed male help—until the night her children were away, and she invited him over for dinner "to thank him." Thanking him consisted of sleeping with him. And she hadn't heard from him since—although she freely admitted she was the one who had been doing the calling all along.

SEXUALIZING INSTEAD OF ROMANTICIZING

When Diana used the term *romantic* to describe their encounter, I pointed out that to men, sex doesn't necessarily include romance—although, since we women tend to put them together in our minds, we assume our partner does too. In Diana's case, the reality was that a situation had been sexualized, not romanticized. At least, not for him.

DIANA: Right. So I don't know if I should just leave it and not call again or call him and clear the air or . . .

DR. LAURA: When you say "clear the air," what might you say? Because you need to be real clear about the message you want to give him. He may think you're getting serious now that you two have had sex—and he may not want that responsibility.

DIANA: Uh-huh. Yeah. Yeah.

DR. LAURA: So you need clarity. To be mad at him isn't fair because you didn't ever say, "Let's have a discussion about our relationship and what sex will mean for you." You guys didn't agree to anything. It just happened.

DIANA: Yeah, part of me is mad about that—but I needed, I guess, the nurturing. It's been a long, long time. And it felt good at the time, and he did say, "You'll be hearing from me" before he left, then I thought, "Oh, what did I do?" And a month has gone by and I've been patiently waiting—because I didn't want to seem like I'm chasing him. And I haven't heard anything.

DR. LAURA: Well, Diana, that is your answer.

DIANA: Yeah. But I don't know if I should . . .

DR. LAURA: When you say, "I don't know if I should . . . ," it's as though you mean, "If I make this phone call, I'll still have this nurturing support system." What you really have to adjust to is that you don't.

DIANA: It was really nice when we were just friends.

DR. LAURA: You know, Diana, I think women have to cut out the romantic fantasy and talk turkey before they get into bed. Because if we don't clarify what it is we're doing before we do it, we can't complain about being misunderstood or used.

DIANA: But, right now, what do you think I should do? Never call him, or just wait for him to call me?

DR. LAURA: You might call to talk or leave a message on his machine saying, "I don't want to lose what was a friendship by over-romanticizing what was a very nice but clearly a sexual evening. I'd still like you to come over from time to time, without any commitment and responsibility." And I would hope he would respect that amount of chutzpah. But, Diana, don't make that call unless that is exactly what you mean. Otherwise, you are just manipulating.

DIANA: Yeah, okay. That sounds good to me. Thanks so much.

SEEING ONLY WHAT YOU WANT TO SEE

That Diana's friend did odd jobs for her and ate her meals gave her hope. That he never called or showed initiative in any more personal way she ignored. Sex, she figured incorrectly, would make it be okay. As in Diana's case, sex too often happens too soon because it is used to satisfy loneliness or starvation for approval.

THE SEXUAL VICIOUS CIRCLE

Maria, nineteen, called to say, "I'm having sex with this guy who has said plainly that he doesn't love me and that he doesn't want to marry me. I don't know why, but I don't stop seeing him and having sex with him. He's older. I guess I keep thinking that he must love me if he has sex with me. But then, I know it's not true."

Maria told me she never felt love from her parents and that the only moments she thought she'd ever experienced as love were those sexual moments. It was just too much to give up. And so, the vicious circle: not feeling loved or lovable—having sex to feel love—realizing later that it was sex and not love—not feeling loved or lovable, etc. The catastrophe here is that the current reality of her behavior perpetually reinforces an assumed notion of herself as unlovable.

STOP GROVELING FOR AFFECTION!

I stressed to Maria that children are inherently lovable. And if parents don't love, it's because they can't love—they are the ones who are broken. I also pointed out that her desperate attachment to this man was actually retarding her development toward being able to love.

"Maria," I concluded, "all of your energies are directed toward getting what you interpret as affection or approval. Be careful you don't find yourself living a life that way; never giving, never growing—just always trying to harvest empty fields."

EXPLODING THE MYTH OF SEX AS AN ANTIDOTE FOR LONELINESS

Sex never works as a hoped-for cure or anesthesia for feelings of inadequacy, emptiness, shame, loneliness, fearfulness, self-disgust, and more. Oh, that it had that much power! I have worked with so many women, educated and successful or not, who have used a man's sexual interest and approval as a means of buoying a sinking feeling of worthlessness. The problem is that it just doesn't work for longer than the moment—if that.

WAKING UP WITH A STRANGER YOU CAN'T STAND

Caroline, a private patient, was in her late thirties and recently divorced from a fellow who, according to her, was extraordinarily handsome but congenitally immature. Although attractive, extremely bright, creative, and talented, she was not as pretty as her ex. She was an artsy type while her family were all lawyers. She was tall and gangly and didn't really seem to fit in. It wasn't that her family didn't love and support her—they did. It was just that she still felt very "unattractive and weird" because of the difference she perceived between herself and them.

Caroline's prototypical relationship was getting sexually passionate immediately, then waking up the next morning feeling uninterested in—or disgusted by—the guy. Any man she stayed with for more than a night was inevitably an offbeat type with whom she felt more comfortable.

THERE ARE SUCCESS STORIES!

When the pain of this pattern just got too great, Caroline turned to therapy to work on it. I'm happy to report that as a result of treatment, she became closer to her family and more sanguine about herself. The rule we established for her was: When you meet a new guy, no sex for six weeks (for her, an eternity!). She kept to it—allowing time for a relationship of communication and some vulnerability to be established before plunging between the sheets.

In Caroline's case, the pattern of sex-too-soon served the purpose of making her feeling accepted and in control; she rejected first, saving herself from anticipated rejection.

DARE TO PUT YOUR NEGATIVE SELF-IMAGE TO THE TEST

Another patient of mine, Martha, muses aloud, "I feel that sex is the only thing I really have going for me. What would a guy be attracted to me for without that? How would I keep him?"

I suggest we put her supposition to the test. Martha goes back to school as a means of building self-esteem and does great. Now she experiments with men differently: She spends time with them to see if she's right—that is, if without sex no one will be interested in her. To her amazement, she discovers she's wrong. This reality checking takes courage, but then, so does everything else worth having in life.

SEXUAL PASSION VS. MATURE LOVE

Sexual passion is a consuming feeling. You can't think, work, sleep, or do anything without the distraction of a tidal wave of visceral emotion. Mature love puts sexual passion in a context and perspective that is less all-consuming. For some women, that reality is disappointing because they're left with themselves—unmasked again.

WHEN THE THRILL GOES

Twenty-five-year-old Monica called to say, "I've been in a relationship for almost three years now, and sexually it was very good for the first year or so. When it was good, the sex was very satisfying for both of us. I felt very sexy and very free to be myself with him and I had a really good time." Then, about a year and a half into the relationship, Monica noticed that "for some reason something was freezing" her sexually.

When I pushed her, she admitted the reason: She wasn't feeling comfortable with herself because, although she had always been conscious of her figure, she'd begun gaining weight—at the same time that her sexual drive began to diminish. Under my urging, she admitted that she thought the weight gain was the result of her no longer going to a gym. And that was provoked by her unhappiness with her job, which was—and never had been—fulfilling.

DR. LAURA: So you were never doing your dream.

MONICA: Exactly!

DR. LAURA: What is your dream?

MONICA: To work with animals. I'd like to go work for the zoo.

DR. LAURA: So why didn't you go do that?

MONICA: Well, I just think they wouldn't want me.

DR. LAURA: Who? The animals?

MONICA: No, the people who would interview me.

DR. LAURA: Well, you had to interview to get the job you have now. What about you would turn them off?

MONICA: Maybe that I'm not skilled enough.

DR. LAURA: Of course you're not! You've got to learn it. So you were unhappy with yourself and with your life and you found this boyfriend who made you feel great and you had the infatuation. And frankly, those feelings took you away from all the bad stuff. But those feelings only lasted so long and now you are back confronting Monica. This is not about sex. This is about your impotency in your own life!

MONICA: That's interesting.

DR. LAURA: So, what you may want to do is go put on some decent clothes—the army boots they wear when they march around the zoo—call up, make an appointment, and go get a job, however menial. And learn all you can and work your way up to your dream. And that's okay. It's called "experience" and it's a blessing, not a curse. Because when you work toward your dream and away from the ache, you'll stop using sex as a painkiller.

MONICA: Wow! I thought there was something wrong with me sexually.

DR. LAURA: The only thing wrong with you is that you quit on your dream! That's what's wrong with you, woman! Go for it, Monica. This is your one life. Go for it!

MONICA: That's great. Thank you for the encouragement!

BUT I CAN'T HELP MYSELF—I'M SEXUALLY ADDICTED

Monica expected sexual passion to carry her through the rest of her life. But that only works if every year you get a new guy and start out with infatuation all over again. Many people do that and then call it a disease: "I'm sexually addicted."

But I say you are not sick—all you are doing is trying to get a high instead of dealing with personal empowerment and self-control. Monica's in for a pleasant surprise: the tremendous and lasting high of going for the interview, and the second one, and saying, "Please, I'll do anything, I'll sweep up after the elephants, just give me a chance to work here."

Many women, like Monica, hope or expect that sexual

passion or love will carry them through their lives, without their going for their dreams. They're dead wrong.

THE SHOCKING ADMISSION THAT IT'S ALL UP TO YOU

Some women who have sex-too-soon in their lives figure it out:

Lisa, twenty-two, began our conversation by telling me she'd left her husband a year earlier. She'd been married at eighteen, right out of high school, because of an unplanned pregnancy. She was now the mother of a three-year-old son. At that time, she had no plans for the future outside of being an ideal wife and mother. Describing herself as "not the school type," she admitted that as a teen, she was totally "boy crazy," then surprised me by explaining that behavior with a great deal of clarity. "I just wanted a boyfriend to make me feel good about myself. I had very low self-esteem, so I always had a boyfriend . . . always . . . and this guy was 'wanted' by everyone. And I got him."

"So," I said, "this marriage didn't really have to do with love, it had more to do with filling what felt empty." She agreed, then proceeded to describe the genuine fulfillment of motherhood and added, "And I'm working on my own," something of which her ex had told her she was incapable.

THE PROFOUND SATISFACTION OF INDEPENDENCE

Lisa's ex-husband had merely echoed her own fears. He would tell her, "You'll never do anything!" Now she found herself in the enviable position of knowing they were both wrong. Even the hassle of trying to perform well at work and be there for her adored son twenty-four hours a day was a source of satisfaction because she was doing it by herself. She'd even been dating a lot, but so far had found nobody worthwhile. When she laughingly told me, "My ex isn't bad, I'm just not attracted to him anymore," I replied, "You know, you really didn't get married out of love—and he wasn't supportive of your growth—a foundation for true loving. You got married out of desperation. You were sexual even before that out of desperation—emotional desperation. That's not love. So I'm not surprised you're not attracted to him anymore."

ACKNOWLEDGING THAT A MISTAKE IS NEVER A MISTAKE

My advice to Lisa was to acknowledge the fact that her marriage had been a mistake and continue moving on with her life. As far as having a man was concerned, I suggested that her son might, for the moment, be the only male she needed. Lisa seemed to know instinctively that the only person who could provide her with a feeling of self-worth was . . . herself. In closing, I told her, "Start dreaming about twenty years from now—I'd like a call from you when you've got a dream—it doesn't necessarily have to come to pass. The dreams I've had have changed. But it's important that you dream. Because if you can dream for your future, it means you believe in yourself now."

DON'T OVERLOOK YOUR OWN GROWTH

Lisa was figuring it all out but didn't realize and appreciate her own growth. I was thrilled to be able to point it out to her. Which shows you how much we all need objective feedback and a good support system. Our inner changes happen so slowly that we sometimes don't see them—we're too into survival mode.

"SEX-TOO-SOON" CAN BECOME A LIFE SENTENCE

The consequences of engaging in sexual relationships before a woman is ready (in her head, her heart, and her life) are quite serious. And sometimes quite complex and emotionally disastrous.

Karen's voice, when I took her call, clued me in at once that she was upset—and angry. But she started blandly enough by telling me she was in a three-year live-in relationship with "a gentleman." Then she said she was twenty (uh-oh!) and—here's the kicker—that they had an eight-month-old baby together. Although she assured me that she and the father were engaged to be married, she dropped another bomb when she added, "And I just found out yesterday that he has another child, a newborn, by an ex-girlfriend." Suggesting that her guy (I couldn't bear to call him her "gentleman") liked to keep his options open, I asked if he'd actually agreed to a wedding date. Of course, he hadn't.

"So I'm dying to hear your question," I told her.

"I'm just not sure what to do," she answered.

SEXUAL INTIMACY RARELY LEADS TO INSTANT COMMITMENT

My response was to tell her that wasn't accurate. She was sure what to do—or what she would have done if she wasn't locked into a seemingly no-win situation. "If you had been going with this guy for a bit and had a job with a future and no kid," I said, "I bet you'd tell him to leave." She agreed. I pointed out he didn't sound like a good bet for a lifelong partner in any case; it was Karen's romantic notion that sexual intimacy leads to instant commitment that had blurred her judgment about him all along.

Since rushing into things she wasn't ready for had caused her present difficulties, I advised Karen not to marry anybody for several years and to stop living with her so-called fiancé. Over the cooling-off period, while they remained civil and worked at parenting their baby, Karen would see if the guy was capable of the loving monogamy she desired as well as fulfilling his complicated obligations to both his children.

"The best thing you can do," I reiterated in closing, "is to give yourself these two years before making a decision—even if you have to fight the urge to marry or dump him. That's a very small percentage of time to make a decision that will affect a significant amount of your life."

AS LONG AS YOU'RE ALIVE, YOU HAVE CHOICES

Karen's relief was so apparent I realized she hadn't even considered the possibility that she had choices. My heart goes out to young women like her, struggling through what ought to be the freest time of their lives. As with pregnant teenagers, women in general refuse to read the handwriting on the wall until they are compelled to by the sheer weight of the graffiti bringing the whole wall down. Then, in such sad ways, it's often too late.

THE YOUNGER THE WOMAN, THE GREATER THE FANTASY

Just yesterday, an angry father called my program wondering how to punish his sixteen-year-old daughter for having lost her virginity. He'd learned this from the girl's grandmother, who accidently (how do you do that?) read her diary. I told him that a week without Nintendo probably wouldn't have the impact he hoped for and that the discussion had to be more profound than that and called for greater sensitivity and understanding on his part. I don't think he heard me—but I'd like to share what I tried to explain to him with you:

Once sex, especially sex-too-soon, enters a young woman's relationship with a man, she perceives the affair to be a far more meaningful situation than it probably would be without the physical intimacy.

As a woman caller said, "I made a mistake early by becoming sexually involved before knowing more about this person. From that point on, because we were intimately connected 'in that sense,' I feel like I'm kind of stuck."

This perception is all the more magnified by young people's lack of integrated identity and life experiences, and their greater dependency needs.

IS THERE A RIGHT AGE TO BEGIN BEING SEXUAL?

During an appearance on the now defunct Ron Reagan TV show, I was badgered by Mr. Reagan to give an exact "age" at which kids should begin to have sex. My answer, obviously unsatisfactory to his TV talk-show format, was that we shouldn't engage in activities until we are mature enough to comprehend, anticipate, and accept the possible consequences of the behaviors. To give a universal age would be possible only if everyone alive matured at the same rate and, in fact, had an identical nature. That they don't is the crux of the problem.

Ovaries, testes, penises, vaginas, and uteri are in operational status long before the individuals housing them have the wisdom and maturity to be responsible for the consequences: pregnancy or venereal disease or emotional pain from this disappointment of counting on sex to be not only the "glue" in the relationship but the saving grace in a frightened life. But sex-too-soon doesn't only happen to teenagers . . .

SEX-TOO-SOON IS SELF-LOVE-TOO-LATE

Hilda, twenty-five, commenting on getting into a sexual relationship immediately, says, "I want it all at once to hide who I am." Sex-too-soon is self-love-too-late.

Carolyn, thirty-three, realizes that.

Carolyn has a three-year-old son, the product of a one-night stand with a neighborhood fellow. She says, "I knew at the time it wasn't right. I just went ahead and did it anyway."

"Why?" I ask, rather bluntly.

"Well, quite honestly," she responds, "I was lonely, overweight, not too many suitors, no sex since sixteen years old, and was feeling isolated, having just recently moved into a new house in a new neighborhood. All in all, it felt good at the time."

"And now?" I asked.

"Now, I've got a wonderful little boy, whom I love dearly, but who's got no daddy."

The emotional vacuum of Carolyn's life obviously gave birth to an impulsive act, which gave birth to a son.

ULTIMATELY, THE ISSUE IS SELF-ESTEEM

Joan, forty-two, was wondering about even calling the man in question a boyfriend, since, after only four weeks in a relationship, he'd dumped her two weeks before, claiming he wanted a looser relationship, without requirements or commitments. In other words, he was willing to have "fun and chuckles," aka sex, with her, but didn't want a relationship.

"On the one hand," she lamented, "I'm going to miss the sex. On the other hand, it's not good for my self-esteem."

So I asked her, "Which one is more important?"

"Well," she replied, "at certain times of the month . . . the sex!"

We both laughed at that! Still, Joan's is a typical female pattern: I want to feel good. I want to feel secure. I want to be loved and cherished. I want it all right now. Therefore, I'll have sex now. That will ensure me the rest. Then I can complain to my girlfriends and him about how he's hurting me.

WHAT SEX-TOO-SOON CAN DO TO YOU

Before we move on, I want to stress this: No matter what your age is, sex—a powerful experience and driving force—doesn't have the power to validate you or your relationship. It's actually the other way around. Sex-too-soon can end up making you feel even more self-denigrated, desperate—and terribly alone.

5 Stupid Cohabitation

THE ULTIMATE FEMALE SELF-DELUSION

When I began working on radio some fifteen years ago, it was rare for a caller to admit she was shacking up with a guy. There seems to have been a relaxation of values and norms. Today, living-in no longer has a stigma attached to it.

The conventional wisdom in favor of living-in before marriage is that it allows the couple to get to know each other, make a better marital choice, and lay a more solid conjugal foundation than men and women who marry cold turkey.

Could this thinking be wrong?

IS LIVING-IN THE KISS OF DEATH TO A RELATIONSHIP?

According to psychologist David G. Myers, Ph.D., author of *The Pursuit of Happiness,* seven recent studies concur that couples who cohabit with their spouses-to-be have a higher divorce rate than those who don't. Three national surveys illustrate this: A U.S. survey of 13,000 adults found that couples who lived together before marriage were one-third more likely to separate or divorce within a decade. A Canadian national survey of 5,300 women found that those who cohabited were 54 percent more likely to divorce within fifteen years. And a Swedish study of 4,300 women found cohabitation linked with an 80 percent greater risk of divorce.

WHY PLAY RUSSIAN ROULETTE WITH YOUR LIFE?

Now, you and I both know how easy it is to discount all that data! You simply say, "But my situation is different."

Well, for some of you, that's true! There are those successful transitions. It happens. But it is not the rule. So why are you willing, even eager, to play Russian roulette with your life? Why? Desperation. Fear of not having somebody—of not having a life if a man doesn't want you.

In our dialogues you always come to admit it. How about saving yourself the stress of finding it out the hard way?

Perhaps waiting and growing in maturity, independence, and security-of-self are too tough to do—especially when you are young and needy and hoping to escape an unhappy past.

I LOVE HIM, BUT I JUST DON'T TRUST HIM . . .

Jessica, a nineteen-year-old aspiring dancer, came from a troubled family in which her father had played around. Her upbringing had provided her with very little security and an exaggerated inability to trust. Despite that, she had been living with her boyfriend for four months and claimed she was in love with him, although she had trouble believing in his caring and fidelity. In her words, she was "hoping for something beautiful," i.e., marriage, as proof of his caring.

I pointed out to Jessica that she was very insecure and that part of what often makes very young women move in with a man early is their hope that by association (preferably marriage) with the fellow, they will feel better about themselves and about life. And you know something? It never, never works that way.

LIVING-IN AS A RETARDANT TO MATURITY

Jessica's primary job is to build her self-esteem and competency, so that when she chooses somebody, it isn't out of a desperate need to heal the hurts of the past. It should be out of a desire to share herself, her life's experience. And that's why, in the long run, I don't think personal maturity is benefited by these living-in arrangements—especially at Jessica's age and with her history of loss and betrayal.

WHEN HOPE CAN HURT YOU

There are exceptions to everything in life, infinite combinations and permutations to experience. For the most part, living-in is usually entered into, as Jessica did, with fantasy and hopefulness and an agenda that isn't even admitted to the self. Look at Jessica's "wanting something beautiful." There is almost inevitably the vain hope that being with a man will make something magical happen.

And Jessica's not alone in that. Everybody fantasizes at some time about bypassing the hard work of growing up and growing stronger.

But nobody can—not if they want to find some fulfillment in this life. When Jessica does the work and learns to take care of herself, she won't have to hope for something beautiful. She'll be creating it.

ONLY YOU CAN MAKE YOU HAPPY

Listen, the phrase is "happily ever after." All of us girls grew up with that promise. So when you're an unhappy young girl, what better remedy than living-in with a man? The problem is that happiness just isn't won that easily—and it's not a matter of who *you* are with but who *he* is with (i.e., you!).

You and only you have the power, the sole power, to make you happy. When you blindly leap for a man, you generally end up repeating, reliving, the pain you've been trying to flee. That's why Jessica is agonizing over not being able to trust her man no matter what her instinct tells her.

DENIAL AND LIVING-IN

Denial is a big factor in this living-in arrangement. And the styles of that denial—as you'll see in the course of this chapter—run the gamut from denial of one's own true needs and wants to denial of what he is about.

One quote from a caller named Jane highlights the latter: "I feel he does love me, but he holds back" is her explanation for the live-in boyfriend's desire to sex-swap with other couples. Sadly, she goes on to say, "I might do that for him if I knew how we stood . . ."

IF HE REALLY LOVED ME, WOULDN'T HE MARRY ME?

Moving in with a man when you don't know how he feels is to try to make him feel something toward you. That's demeaning and stupid. It is about you auditioning.

Diana knew that. She and her boyfriend had been together for over a year and had been living together for five months. Although she claimed they constantly talked about marriage, a truer version would be that the "they" was really her. Her lover responded to her entreaties by saying he wanted to marry her but he didn't know when because he didn't "feel ready."

DIANA: Should I stick around and wait? It could be five or six years . . .

DR. LAURA: Diana, are you sure you're reading him right? He may not want to marry you. We can't really interpret what he means when he says he is not ready. But we can see why you put yourself in this frustrating situation. You are living-in to audition, hoping to get the part of the bride. Am I right?

DIANA: Ummm . . . yeah.

DR. LAURA: But you haven't, which means it wasn't a good plan. Look, he is content. You're anything but. You are motivated for something to change, he is not. Contented people are not motivated to make changes. Do you agree?

DIANA: Yeah.

DR. LAURA: So you're the one who's going to have to make the changes. Get out of there! Date him. If you like him, date him!

DIANA: Well, that's what we've been talking about lately.

DR. LAURA: Sounds sensible.

DIANA: He also said he'd go into therapy with me and talk about it.

DR. LAURA: That's nice, too. But right now I'm not interested in him. I'm concerned about you. Diana, leave. Leave because living with him is making you feel bad about yourself. That's why you shouldn't be there. It is damaging to you. Promise me you'll think about what I've said.

DIANA: Absolutely. And thanks. I really needed to hear that.

DR. LAURA: Take care—and move!

LIVING-IN IS NO PROOF OF GROWTH

All through this call, I had a feeling that Diana's relationship had solid potential but needed more space and time to grow. Moving in together seems to imply that this growth process has already happened. Then, when things don't fall into place as the woman thinks they should, she gets all bent out of shape.

WHAT AM I STILL DOING HERE IF HE DOESN'T WANT ME?

Jean, thirty, a part-time student with an independent income, had been living rent-free with her boyfriend for a year and a half. Prior to that, she'd been separated from her now ex-husband and hadn't been meeting many men. When she connected with her present guy and they became close, she thought, Well, this seems to feel good. "So we became closer, and I moved in." At this point, I couldn't figure out why she'd called.

As she talked, the reality of her situation became increasingly upsetting. Although Jean had no children, the man's seventeen- and thirteen-year-olds were living with them, but the father was adamant—sometimes almost violent—about Jean keeping her distance from them.

"What does that mean?" I asked her. "You're not supposed to talk to them? Give them orders?"

"He doesn't want me to participate in their lives at all," she replied. "He always tells me, 'I just want you to take care of me. Don't worry about them.'"

I still wasn't absolutely certain why Jean had called—until she mentioned that her man "goes through spells" when he wants her to leave, then relents. When she added, "I try to convince him that we have so much going for each other," I told her, "You can't convince somebody of that. They are the measure of what they think and feel. Having that argument is a waste of time and demeaning to you."

JEAN: Yes, but I keep saying to myself, "This is the move I need to do, to leave. What am I doing here if he doesn't want me?"

DR. LAURA: Notice how you don't ask yourself if you really want to be with him. Oh, I'm sure he wants you there. I'm sure he likes the sex, and you sound like a nice lady . . .

JEAN: I try to make everybody happy.

DR. LAURA: What about you, Jean? Are you making yourself happy? Is he making you happy? . . . Can I be blunt?

JEAN: Yes, please.

DR. LAURA: This arrangement is very demeaning to you. You have no long-term commitment from him, yet he has made it clear what your position is—to service him. When he feels like it, he even seems to get some pleasure from making you feel insecure. And you know why you put up with it? Because you're too scared to be on your own. You're grateful to be owned because it relieves you of responsibility.

JEAN: Is that why I don't leave? Because I'm scared to take responsibility?

DR. LAURA: Right. You let your fear have all the power. Jean, you sold out. You see, he is taking care of you in some ways—such as financially. But you are not taking care of yourself.

JEAN: Exactly. And that has to change.

DR. LAURA: Exactly. Jean, take care—of yourself!

LIVING-IN = GIVING IN

Women, remember, self-esteem is centered in the will to overcome circumstance, not to give in to being overcome. As in Jean's case, the giving in often takes the form of living-in. The results may be twofold: a roof over the head—and a sinkhole under the heart. Women have to know of their alternatives to selling themselves. And they have to be able to use their courage and creativity in ways that make them choosers, not beggars.

DON'T EVER SETTLE FOR LESS

Women ask me quite often how to get a man to respect them, to treat them with respect. My answer is always the same: Never settle for or permit less. If he can't rise to that occasion, dump him. Conversions only come from within. But some women just don't seem to get that message. They just keep hopin' and tryin', like Yolanda.

I THOUGHT I WAS IN A MONOGAMOUS RELATIONSHIP!

Yolanda, a thirty-eight-year-old social-services technician, called to discuss the fact that her live-in boyfriend of three years had admitted to spending the weekend with another woman. She was horrified that her fantasies of a monogamous relationship were dashed now that she knew he was fooling around.

I pointed out to Yolanda that when you move in with a man without a commitment, he already knows one crucial thing: He doesn't have to do much to get you. Then he fools around, and you stay, and he learns something more: He doesn't have to do much to keep you, either. And that has to be crushing to your self-respect.

Yolanda came across as a nice person, educated, a professional, who meant something in the world. I urged her to hold out for the right man, a man who would make a commitment to her, and added that she wasn't going to find one while she was frittering away her time—out of desperation—with a man who didn't seem to respect her or to be interested in pleasing her—only himself. She was clearly furious at him and disillusioned and had the financial means to move out. I only hope she had the emotional ones as well.

MAKE NO MISTAKE, COMMITMENT *IS* A BIG DEAL

Now, you might well argue: "Big deal, a commitment. Commitments don't stop people from being abusive, unloving, unfaithful, or just plain annoying. Commitments don't even stop people from dumping each other. So—big deal."

Well, the statistics prove that commitment is a big deal; as I quoted earlier in this chapter, ". . . . compared to couples who don't cohabit with their spouses-to-be, those who do have higher divorce rates."

A SOLID FOUNDATION REQUIRES TIME, EFFORT, AND SACRIFICE

The interesting question is Why? There are probably many forces at work here, worthy of a book to itself, but I feel strongly that the main contributors are maturity, patience, and the ability to postpone gratification.

When people aren't willing to put in the time and effort to build a foundation, to build something solid and meaningful, they are usually not the ones to persist with effort and sacrifice to develop it and keep it going.

Having sex-too-soon, moving in without commitments or life plans in concert, are the behaviors of basically immature, let-me-feel-good-right-now-because-I-want-it-therefore-it-is kind of people. The immaturity has to do also with not having developed an esteem and identity that permit you to be right out there with the truth of your needs and feelings.

You're scared, so you play it "safe." And then you find out that *safe* doesn't always have the big payoff! That's what my caller Sharon found out.

WHEN YOU WANT A FAMILY AND HE DOESN'T

Sharon told me she had originally decided to move in with her boyfriend because she wanted "to get to know him better." And in fact, over the course of a couple of years, they had become close. In her words, "It's the ultimate, ideal relationship. He's wonderful to me and I believe I am to him. We are very supportive of each other, have a lot in common, and we enjoy each other's company." So why was she calling?

The problem was that Sharon had moved in without marriage in her mind (consciously, at least), and the subject hadn't been discussed. Now she found herself wanting marriage and a family, but her boyfriend didn't feel he was up to the enhanced responsibilities. And he was emphatic about it. In order not to rock the boat, Sharon seemed willing to put her own desires on the back burner, but I cautioned her that as time passed, she might get increasingly frustrated—and angry at him.

"And that isn't fair," I advised her, "because every step of the way, you made the choices. Like many women, you've been lying to yourself in the hope that the relationship will evolve. That's a calculated risk. If you're able to erase the notion of marriage and babies from your mind, that's one thing. But if you're kidding yourself in order not to lose him, that's a mistake!"

IMMEDIATE LOSSES/LONG-TERM GAINS

Imagine the choices Sharon is now facing—agonizing choices: to leave a satisfying relationship or not; to leave someone she loves and enjoys to seek another who will more match what she now dares to dream—marriage and family. The immediate losses are obvious. The long-term gain is unpredictable. Often, when a woman states her intent to jump ship, suddenly the man, not wanting to experience great loss either, decides to start paddling faster.

GOOD DECISIONS REQUIRE OBJECTIVITY

Nonetheless, as we go through life, growing, changing, maturing, this type of crossroads experience is expected, typical, and human. No surprise. That's not the element that concerns me—that's just real life. My concern is that when relationships prematurely take on elements of sexuality and living-in, it makes it more difficult to have the objectivity required to make good decisions.

YOU'RE TOO BUSY MAKING SURE HE WANTS YOU TO QUESTION WHETHER YOU WANT HIM

Women do not move in to check out the guy from closer range. Women move in to be protected, taken care of, to be wanted. And when you are in that mind-set, you can't for a moment wonder (especially not out loud) if you even want the guy—you're too busy making sure he wants you.

Controlling, petty, selfish, insecure, destructive, immature, and hurtful behaviors of the man in question become things to work around rather than qualities to examine to decide on his worthiness to you! It is harder to ask yourself the very important question "Is this how I want to live the rest of my life?" when you are already dug in!

THE MATE MAKEOVER—A STUDY IN SELF-DELUSION

Susan called me to discuss her boyfriend's immature and manipulative behavior, which she was determined to change!

DR. LAURA: You live with him?

SUSAN: Yes.

DR. LAURA: You got sexual too soon. You moved in too soon. You got engaged and you are looking square into your future—and saying "yuk." But instead of making a judgment, you are asking little-girl questions about how you can make him over.

SUSAN: Yeah, I guess so.

DR. LAURA: And that's because once you've established all that you have, it is difficult to imagine backtracking. If you were simply dating, you'd look at his hypersensitivity and immaturity, be turned off, and not date him anymore—because you'd have a whole other life to fall back on. When you commit this much to living together, it makes it extremely hard to do what you need to do. So you use a Band-Aid rather than a scalpel when major surgery is required.

DATING AS A LEASE WITH AN OPTION TO BUY

Dating—not living-in—is supposed to be about learning and discerning. Dating is supposed to be a kind of lease with option—so don't get sexual and cohabit right away and change the meaning of dating to a "lease with premature obligations" situation!

THE RETURN OF THE LIVING DREAD: "BUT I . . ."

Since our dating and love chapters we haven't invoked the old reliable "But he said," as motivation for our stupid choices. Let's do it now.

Dana, a thirty-three-year-old divorcée with two children, called to say she was considering leaving a five-year relationship. She and her kids were living with the boyfriend, who had a problem: He was not divorced. "He's been pretty much back and forth for several years," she told me, "because, I'd say, of guilt. He is very Catholic. I'm not. Maybe that's just an excuse . . . anyway, I feel like I'm coaching him all the time, 'Did you talk to the attorney? Did you talk to the therapist?' "

To make matters worse, his wife wouldn't allow his kids to visit his new household, which meant that any time the fellow spent with them, such as holidays, were awful for Dana and her daughters. "And if he is with us, he might as well not be because he's so depressed," Dana told me. "And in this past year he has done nothing legally to change things."

When I asked her why she moved in to begin with, she responded, "Because he kept telling me everything was going to change. And I . . . I just believed him." To which I countered, "That's like jumping off the end of a swimming pool, saying, 'He told me there would be water in it by the time I hit bottom!' "

YOU DON'T REALLY HAVE A MAN, ANYWAY

This is what I advised Dana: "I think that no matter what he does to straighten himself out, you and the children have got to get your own place and start leading your own lives. That would be a better climate for your kids—first of all, because I don't think the decisions you are making are good for them. I think it would be a step forward from where you are now. Especially in terms of maturity and how to handle grown-up situations of commitment and attachment.

"Dana, he is weak, and you've made it easy for him. You must know by now, it doesn't matter what he promises. Until he has fixed his life and shown some strength and integrity and maturity to handle that appropriately, you don't have much of a man anyway."

I FEEL GREAT ABOUT MOVING IN—EXCEPT
FOR THESE NAGGING DOUBTS . . .

Nicole knew I wasn't an advocate of living-in when she called, but she claimed, as many do, "We have a little bit more of a situation than that." Whatever that meant—because when I asked her directly, "Nicole, are you trying to convince yourself to move in?" she responded, "Well, I want to—but there is still a part of me that is hesitating."

DR. LAURA: Listen to that part of you. When you guys are both ready to make that commitment, make it! The indication is that living-in doesn't work if you think it's supposed to help you work on how to be together. And I've got to tell you I think it's a stupid idea. The only reason I would live with somebody is if I didn't want to get married.

NICOLE: Well, I do want to marry him. But he says it's a big step for him.

DR. LAURA: Then wait till he's ready to take that step. A commitment is a social statement and an inner promise—if he's not ready, pretending that he is by moving in won't make it so!

NICOLE: I'm trying to compromise.

DR. LAURA: I don't even believe I heard you say that! No compromise, honey. Don't you compromise yourself. If you want to get married and you feel this is the guy, date him, enjoy him, and see if in time you both feel the desire for that commitment. If he doesn't want to get married and you do and you move in to play marriage, you really have compromised—and gained nothing.

NICOLE: I think I knew all this!

DR. LAURA: Well, you certainly knew how I felt about this living-in issue before you called. So maybe you wanted some confirmation. Good for you! And don't back down when he flashes his baby browns at you. Okay?

NICOLE: Okay, thanks.

HE'S THE ONE WHO SHOULD FEEL GUILTY, NOT YOU!

So he says it is a big step for him and she is supposed to feel guilty and greedy for wanting more. Women, don't let yourselves be beguiled and manipulated by that. And don't tolerate the injunction that you are being manipulative. Grown-ups should know that they don't get the goodies legitimately unless they have earned them. Look out for the word *compromise* if it ends up meaning you give up what is precious to you so that maybe you'll get what you want later.

You will live to regret it—Jackie did!

WHY IS MY LIVE-IN LOVER SEXUALLY HARASSING ME?

Jackie calls to discuss the fact that her live-in boyfriend of three years has begun constantly fondling her breasts—at inappropriate times.

"He only does it at home," she complains, "but it still just drives me crazy. Like, when I'm washing the dishes or just walking by, instead of giving me a hug, he grabs my boobs. When I tell him it bothers me, he goes, 'Fine, I'll never touch you again.' I just don't know how to respond—we get nowhere."

Under my prodding, Jackie admits there was a time when such behavior was mutually pleasing but that something has changed in her attitude, then confesses they've been angry at each other because she wants the relationship to graduate to a level other than just living together. Consequently, she feels annoyed when he takes intimate liberties without reciprocating with what she wants—marriage.

"So," I observe, "this is not about boobs—this is about a commitment. This is about you feeling insulted that you are in the no-win position of being totally available without a reciprocal agreement from him." When she agrees, I urge her to move out. If she wishes, she can continue to see him, making it clear she wants to be married to him but that she doesn't want to start hating him—which she surely will if things continue along their present course.

And Jackie agrees to try to establish some independence for herself.

LIVING TOGETHER AND MATURITY GO HAND IN HAND

To sum up: People have problems. There are no relationships without problems. The issue is whether people have the maturity and the commitment to hang in there with each other and work out the problems. Or do they have the inner strength and courage to admit to a mistake and let go. That's what makes the difference.

A living-in arrangement does not inherently have that kind of commitment; nor is it a further step in that direction. Living-in is more a convenience and a fantasy; typically the former for men, the latter for women. As you've surely guessed by now, I'm very agin' it. Let's get pragmatic: Statistics show that living-in doesn't ensure a quality, long-lasting marriage, probably because the attitude of one of the partners is more "Let's see if this feels good to me every day," and the attitude of the other is "I'll be careful, lest he not feel good about me today." The true tragedy is when the more-available sex brings forth a child into this situation. The child usually ends up the product of a never-was but still-broken home.

LOVE IS ABOUT A LOT MORE THAN PASSION

So, couples have problems. But with maturity, caring, and commitment, they can get through them. Those are the relationships that last and grow into love. Because love isn't instant. It takes years and working through problems together and growth and nurturing each other's growth. That's what grows love, and it involves a lot more than passion. It takes commitment.

P.S.: PARDON A PERSONAL PAT ON THE BACK

On Mother's Day I received this letter from a happy mom: "After listening to you, my twenty-three-year-old daughter opted for marriage instead of their living-in arrangement." And that, as they say, made my day.

6 Stupid Expectations

**FIRST YOU COMMIT TO HIM,
THEN YOU HATE HIM!?**

This query is addressed to every woman who married "the man of her dreams," only to feel as though she's passed through the Twilight Zone into a perpetual nightmare:

Q: Why is it that the very qualities that mesmerized you about him in courtship are now seemingly more repellent than bathing in worms marinated in manure?

A: Simple. You are disappointed. Somehow, the fantasies and the hopes turned threatening.

DID YOU MISREAD THE HANDWRITING ON THE WALL?

Is your disappointment justified? Only when it's a rare case of "bait 'n' switch"—in which your Dr. Jekyll boyfriend metamorphoses into a marital Mr. Hyde.

More typically, women see the handwriting on the wall quite clearly but are later struck down due to their own ancient emotional black holes.

In other words, you picked him because of your own unmet needs and frustrated yearnings. And then you hate him because of your own unmet needs and frustrated yearnings.

How do we make sense out of that?

ARE ALL DISAPPOINTMENTS MISTAKES?

Surprise! The answer is no!

The disappointment may be a great opportunity for personal growth and emotional healing of childhood hurts—if you are ready to assume personal responsibility and endure the discomforts of change.

THE PERILS OF CLINGING TO THE PAST

As a case in point, let me share with you the story of Kenny and Maureen.

Maureen told me she was calling for an appointment out of concern for her sixteen-month-old baby, who was "acting up a lot." Since I already had the notion that the child was Maureen's ticket into therapy, I suggested she also bring her husband to the session. The young couple arrived on time, with an adorable baby in their arms. The "problem"—the infant's chronic upset, crying, nervousness—I recognized quickly as a response to the chronic upset, crying, and nervousness of her mom and dad.

Critical Attraction

Maureen came from a very poor, very unstable southern family, complete with repeatedly vanishing father. A veritable Blanche DuBois, she was childlike in her demeanor, weepy, anxious, and very unhappy. Her main complaints about Kenny concerned his—she was so furious, she couldn't say his name!—coldness, argumentativeness, criticalness, bossiness, and lack of affection.

Kenny, on the other hand, was from an ultra-stable, decidedly patriarchal family that gave little quarter or value to any accomplishment that wasn't goal-oriented. He complained about Maureen's overemotionality, flightiness, lack of competency in areas of grown-up responsibility (such as being able to balance a checkbook), and general immaturity.

With the baby on her lap getting more and more restless (subsequent sessions did not include the child), Maureen finally uttered those sad words, "I think I want a divorce."

Attaching to Repair Childhood Hurts

This couple's pain brought into focus for me the underlying, perhaps even unconscious, mechanism we have for attaching to repair early childhood hurts. And don't try to get away with "that stuff is all behind me because I'm a grown-up now." We are all composites of every moment and experience in our lives.

Of course, the meaning and magnitude of the impact of any life experience depends upon our individual interpretation—which depends on our personal vulnerabilities as well as the quality of our support systems and general healthfulness of our emotional environment. In other words, what may be a trauma to you can seem to a friend simply a sad, painful, upsetting life experience to get through in order to go forward.

Dueling Priorities

Through our discussions, it became clear that Kenny's priorities included the work ethic, being responsible, being right. Issues of emotions, spirituality, philosophy, even relationships, he considered "things in the way." He was focusing exclusively on those values that would please his father—no matter how Kenny himself felt or what he needed.

Maureen's priorities were to stay attached and ensure what she saw as security. For her, issues of will, opinion, personal goals, and competency were the "things in the way." She was focusing on avoiding the traumas that had dominated her emotional life since childhood.

What I Told Kenny

"You do not permit yourself to get in touch with your gentler, dependent, needy, emotional self. I'm pretty sure that's because your father didn't admit that this self exists in all of us. He even went so far as to punish you when you did display it. Kenny, do you realize you are mostly leading your life unaware you're still programmed to please your dad?

"Now. You married Maureen because she embodied the fulfillment, reservoir, and expression of those 'taboo' parts of yourself. Why else choose someone you see as having all the parts you disdain? In addition, her apparent weakness makes you feel secure because she so clearly needs you. Once we accept ourselves, Kenny, we don't labor to disavow parts of ourselves, do we?"

What I Told Maureen

"Your personal insecurity is a reaction to the very real and repetitive abandonment and consequent insecurity that marked your childhood. It seems to me that your fear of not having a daddy or even food to eat has made you gear up to make sure your grown-up life would not repeat that pain.

"So you married Mr. Responsible. Now you can tell time by when he comes and goes and what he does, and it's driving you up a wall. And that's because you haven't worked on your own personal growth—and for a very potent reason. Because it leads toward autonomy, while you've been striving for attachment, so that this time you could keep your dad. Well, babe, you wanted a strong fellow you could count on—and you got him."

What I Told Them Both

"Both of you got exactly what you hoped for and needed in a mate. To that extent you picked right! But the original pain out of which this choice was made hasn't been relieved. That is so tremendously disappointing and puzzling that you end up blaming each other as if the pain were new.

"The issue at this point," I concluded, "ought not be how you can divorce each other. It should be how you have divorced important parts of yourselves out of need for a parent. You are adults, and that parental loss (emotional or actual) must be accepted. In so doing, you will take on the more grown-up role of giving and taking with a healthier balance and range of behaviors. Right now both of you are playing only one tiny, perpetual role."

Mutual Support Is Key

I'm happy to report that as the result of our work together, Kenny began to allow Maureen to mother and "lover" him, while Maureen began assuming more responsibility in her own right. They supported each other's measured growth—and were mutually pleased with the results. And, hallelujah, the baby calmed down!

MALE DEPENDENCY: THE OTHER SIDE OF THE COIN

You must realize that if you are aware of your low self-esteem and dependency, the man in your life may be, too, but he's probably manifesting it differently. Maureen and Kenny are prime examples of that fact.

Dependent women get weepy and clingy, while dependent men get blustery and controlling. Still, those behaviors are really different sides of the same coin. Since people with low self-esteem tend to seek their own level when pairing up, never feel you're beneath the man you're with, because he's probably your camouflaged match—and has an equal problem!

When Maureen picked Kenny to avoid the hurts of childhood, she relinquished her need for personal growth and power. She thought she hated Kenny because he kept her down. In reality, she traded off being "one down" in exchange for not being one alone. Understandably, she hated what she had become. It is not unusual to deny, ignore, or not understand that you hate yourself—and simply hate him instead.

KNOWING BETTER—AND DOING IT ANYWAY—THIS DISAPPOINTMENT DOES MEAN MISTAKE!

How can you tell if you're getting into one of these no-win situations? It's easy, actually. From discussions I have had with women over the years, I have a distinct impression that you know . . . and do it anyway.

When she called, Lila immediately announced she was in a long-distance relationship. She lived in L.A. while her boyfriend lived in northern California, and they'd been commuting for a year. They were at the point where they had a crucial decision to make: either break up or spend more time together in order to test the solidity of their feelings for each other.

Lila freely admitted she was thirty-eight and tired of

being alone, living alone, and being lonely. She had a good professional life and friends, but she felt they weren't adequate substitutes for someone at home and a family. Ultimately, she and her man had decided to live together, which meant Lila would have to relocate. Now she was getting cold feet and starting to experience doubt about him and about the relationship—wondering if she'd been deceiving herself about the man and had chosen him purely out of loneliness.

DR. LAURA: What about him is giving you these second thoughts?

LILA: The biggest thing is he's a rather cold, remote, emotionally distant person.

DR. LAURA: And you're worried about not being lonely if you live with him? Doesn't sound like a good choice on that level, hon.

LILA: Well . . . we do have some good things in common, but I still feel like I'm doing a lot of work for the intimacy and if I don't, it just doesn't happen. But you know, I just haven't met a lot of men in my age group that I could consider marrying.

DR. LAURA: You still shouldn't be with a man by default! I grant you that everybody has their limitations, but ultimately, being cold, distant, and remote . . . I don't think that should be on the priority list!

LILA: Hmm . . . yeah . . .

DR. LAURA: Does he remind you of either one of your parents?

LILA: My father—in terms of being emotionally distant.

DR. LAURA: Lila, it's not unusual for women to pick a replica of "dear old Dad," because the ultimate in happiness would be if dear old Dad had actually changed to become truly "dear" and nurturing. So to fulfill the possibility of that dream, we try to make the facsimile change or just hope that he will.

LILA: There is something that feels like "home" about him and I'm not sure it's a good thing. But we've never really spent enough time together to call our relationship real life.

DR. LAURA: Please don't move in with him. I would support your relocating only if you get your own modest digs and suggest to him you guys could use some couples therapy.

LILA: Good idea. Thanks, Laura.

I worry about Lila giving up so much in order to give this relationship a try. Because sacrifice creates an imperative to make it work. And there goes objectivity! Remember, change requires motivation. Lila's boyfriend is in for a big surprise when she lets him know she's not happy with him "as is." Will he be motivated to change? It's a big risk.

THE DAD-AND-MOM FIX

This pattern of women searching for Dad also happens with Mom.

Kathy, forty, described her premarital relationship in a way that stimulated me to nickname it a "rubber-band courtship": Before the wedding, he was constantly shifting in and out of intimacy, and that pattern continued after they'd tied the knot.

When I asked Kathy if there was a lack of loving continuity in her upbringing, she described an abandoning dad and a mom who was usually not around, with some warmies in between. I had guessed correctly that Kathy and her husband there were both wildly tentative about commitment and closeness.

This is how it worked: Kathy's instinctive avoidance of the hurt of abandonment led her to pick a man whose off-and-on behavior threatened to replicate that very abandonment. Ironically, this gave her the opportunity to stay safe. Since he is so iffy, she can justify not getting too close, therefore she can't get decimated emotionally. At the same time, the situation offered an opportunity to make the story come out better.

When she says, "I hate him," she doesn't realize that she's hating her mom and dad. She doesn't realize that the "him" she hates is the worry that she's just not lovable.

BLINDED BY THE PAIN

It is truly surprising how blind you can be to your profound fear of hurt through closeness—so blind that you blame and hate him for the lack of closeness in your life together. That turns out to be a way of not facing and taking responsibility for your inner hurts as well as the means by which you try to protect yourself from those old traumas ever happening again.

The caller named Mary seemed just that blind. She also was thirty-eight and had never been married, but Mary was in an eight-year relationship with a man who, in her words, had "finally agreed to go ahead and get married."

DR. LAURA: *Finally* he's *agreed?*

MARY: He's said he'll get married a couple of times over the years, but he always backs out. And so I am a little apprehensive now. Also, I don't know why, but I don't enjoy our sex life.

DR. LAURA: Well, help me out a little bit . . . I'm not in your bedroom. What don't you enjoy about it?

MARY: Um, I guess I kind of hold back emotionally because I . . . I don't want my feelings hurt.

DR. LAURA: You don't want your feelings hurt and that's why you're with a guy who's a master of letting you twist in the wind? I don't think you are apprehensive that he won't marry you—I think you're apprehensive that he *will!*

MARY: Hmm, I never thought of it like that.

DR. LAURA: You know what I think, Mary? The problem is not with him—it's with you. This relationship is about how you protect yourself. Withholding your emotions, withholding marriage, is about how you protect yourself. If all this is to change, you've got to be brave and look at how you make distance, safe distance, in your life.

MARY (INDIGNANT): Well, I am not the one who makes distance between us—he is!

DR. LAURA: Darling, you chose him! You've protected yourself right into this situation! That's what you've gained from protecting yourself. And that is what therapy can help you overcome.

MARY: Thank you for being so forthright, Laura. I appreciate it.

So here you have it: You choose a man to rework the most hurtful parts of your personal history or to have it come out better or to protect yourself from getting hurt like that again. And you can't miss hating him on precisely those accounts!

UNCONSCIOUS CHOICES VS. CONSCIOUS NEEDS

Here's another example of a marital situation in which you're unaware how well you have chosen unconsciously but are confounded when that choice doesn't appear to match your conscious needs.

As she came on the air, Ellen, in her early thirties, immediately announced she wanted to discuss parental influence on adult children. What she really meant is that she wanted to talk about her husband. He was from a well-off family—with whom he'd lived until he was twenty-nine—and had a brother who had already made it on his own. Ellen's husband, on the other hand, hadn't accomplished anything to speak of, certainly not as much as Ellen herself, who held a good management position.

When the couple married, Ellen's father-in-law had committed to buying them a house. "So," she told me, "we've been looking and looking and every time we find something, his father finds something wrong with it and won't give us the money." The man belittled and frustrated his son by dangling the down payment before him and then, when he was about to accept, withdrawing it. The son, afraid to confront his father despite Ellen's urgings, took out his frustration on her by "blowing his top."

MY HUSBAND THE CHILD

Ellen was married to a little boy, not an adult, and she knew it. What she didn't know was how to get him to grow up. Unfortunately, as I told her, she chose a little boy, and it's always easier to pick better than it is to change another person. Examined in that light, Ellen's expecting her husband to behave responsibly was basically unreasonable. For the five years she had been with him, she hadn't been a partner—she'd been the parent of an adult child. And I wondered what in her own childhood had led her down this road.

It turned out that Ellen's father, a traveling salesman, pretty much hadn't been there, and her mother—who doted on Ellen's brother—had been verbally abusive and extremely punishing. Now it all began to make sense:

By choosing a totally nonambitious man, Ellen ensured his not being out there in the world—as her father had been. And by selecting someone who withers under confrontation and expresses rage only by "blowing his top," she made sure that the guy was too weak and frightened to abuse her the way her mother had.

What Ellen had done was take two childhood dilemmas, which no longer existed in reality but remained as pain in her heart, and attempted to resolve them through her choice of a mate. Not only hadn't the resolution worked, it had actually created a new adult dilemma. And that—not getting her husband to face up to his father or even steering him toward maturity—was the real problem.

You know the main problem of marrying him to protect yourself from childhood hurts? It's that you end up with a mismatch in the here and now. While your history certainly gives you challenges to contend with in creative ways, you are not now living in your history unless you make choices like Ellen made. It's like a marriage made in a time warp. You are so busy taking care of yesterday that today and tomorrow get overshadowed.

THERE ARE NO SHORTCUTS TO SELF-ESTEEM

One of the more frequent themes of "women's self-help literature" (and this book too) is self-esteem. Realistically, you can't take shortcuts to it, but that doesn't stop so many of us from trying! Oh, sometimes you get lucky, but most of the time you don't. Let's consider this particular relevant shortcut—marrying from a position of low self-esteem and expecting Sir Galahad to repair it all. And when he doesn't . . . you hate him!

THE DISNEY VERSION

Twenty-nine-year-old Susan claimed that listening to other callers made her feel insignificant, and she hoped I could help her deal with her insecurity and low self-esteem. She'd been expecting her husband to fix them, and that brought only a lot of problems.

When I asked her what form she expected the fix to take, she replied she didn't really know but that she guessed she expected him to wave a magic wand and tell her everything she wanted to hear. But he didn't. Or couldn't. Whatever the case, she was furious.

DR. LAURA: We women saw too many Disney movies when we were kids, because we give men a terrible rap: They are supposed to be and do everything and provide everything, or we get so ticked off.

SUSAN: Yes.

DR. LAURA: Do you realize you came on the program heralding your problem, saying you felt "insignificant"? How have you come to feel that way? Try to answer without mentioning other people.

SUSAN: Well, um, that's hard to do . . .

DR. LAURA: See?

SUSAN: Umm . . . I have done nothing in my life which affirms my worth to myself, I guess.

DR. LAURA: So what are you going to put in your life that will affirm your worth? Notice I didn't say "who."

SUSAN (AFTER A REFLECTIVE PAUSE): I am a good mom. I have a boy, five and a half months old, and I put a lot of time and effort into reading everything and trying to be the perfect mom—

DR. LAURA: Mistake! You need to be a "good-enough mom"—attentive, loving, and responsive. No one is the perfect mom. As long as you try to be perfect, you will continue to be insignificant in your own eyes.

SUSAN: That's a good point.

DR. LAURA: Give up perfect. I'm not perfect, why should you be? (Both laugh.) Here's your assignment: Think about what you could bring into your life that would convince you—not anyone else—that you have worth. Then call me back. Okay?

SUSAN: Okay!

Now, that's an interesting scenario: not working on your own ego and well-being; instead, projecting that responsibility onto your husband and then hating him because you still don't feel great about yourself.

WHEN HE STOPS TAKING CHARGE AND STARTS TAKING CONTROL

It's not unusual for younger women to try to facilitate the leap into adulthood through the magic of marrying an older guy.

Heather, twenty-one, has been married three years and has two children by a man who is carrying on a homosexual relationship in their home! She gave up college and her family in the Midwest to go off with this guy, who is ten years older than she and who "took charge of things" and thereby made her feel more secure and settled.

After marriage, the taking charge felt more like controlling. Because of the children, she is focused on getting rid of the other guy—assuming everything will then be "all better." Somehow, I doubt it.

THE MYTH OF MASCULINE POWER

This issue of a controlling man always comes from women afraid of life. At first they see such a man as providing a sense of security reminiscent of when Daddy took care of things—maybe even find him sexy, because he embodies masculine power. Inevitably, when you make this choice and then decide to grow up a bit and start being more powerful in your own life, you become the adolescent child rebelling against the rigid dad—and you hate him.

Briana was walking right into that.

WHY CONTROL FREAKS HAVE APPEAL

Briana's boyfriend had asked her to marry him, but she was having doubts because he was a police officer who worked weird hours and expected her to stay home whenever he was on duty. When I pressed her, she insisted she found his controlling behavior neither romantic nor a sign of respect, love, or caring but saw it as an indication of her fiancé's insecurity.

When Briana asked me whether I felt her boyfriend should be in counseling, I suggested she concentrate on her own insecurity. Honestly shocked, she insisted she wasn't the one with the problem. But, of course, she was. She had chosen a control freak as a boyfriend. In the same way that water seeks its own level, she, an insecure person, had attached to a controlling person who, by the way, was also an insecure person.

Even as we ended our conversation, Briana was insisting that "everything else is so good—it's just that he wants to control me" and assuming (hoping) that marriage would make the whole problem vanish. I could just feel Briana trying it make it all better, using typical protestations of denial such as "Everything else is fine" and "Maybe he'll just stop that after we're married." The first thought is generally, It's really nothing. The second thought, He'll just stop. The third thought, I can fix him. The last thought, What have I gotten myself into?

Too often, hope is just postponed disappointment.

THE BIRD-IN-THE-HAND MIND-SET

There's far too much bird-in-the-hand mentality involved in pairing up! Take Melanie, for instance. She had been married for nine months after having dated her husband-to-be for five years. Before marriage, he'd lived with a group of other unmarried young men who, in Melanie's words, "were always smoking dope and drinking and doing all sorts of things bachelors do." He had, she claimed, a lot of bad influences, and marriage hadn't made them vanish. Melanie took denial to the nth degree!

DR. LAURA: But he hasn't stopped, and he doesn't intend to stop, right?

MELANIE: (Silence.)

DR. LAURA: You ought not to have expected that it would.

MELANIE: I guess deep down I didn't. But I've told him how much this hurts me and how much I think it is hurting him and how, when he does this to excess, it tears my heart out.

DR. LAURA: And he doesn't care much about that.

MELANIE: No. I don't know what to do to get him to stop.

DR. LAURA: Nothing.

MELANIE: I've tried to get him to go—

DR. LAURA: You're not hearing me. I said there's nothing you can do. He's not, never was, motivated to change.

MELANIE: It's just not fair when he does it.

DR. LAURA: Frankly, I don't think it was fair to marry him and expect him to become a new person, either. . . . Melanie, the choice is yours—it has always been. Just like the choice in his behavior was always his.

INSTANT REPLAY: WHY YOU DON'T GIVE UP
ON A LOST CAUSE

Melanie's apparent bad choice might be the culmination of her search for proof of her worth or lovability. I know it sounds all backward, but if you've found a parent difficult—emotionally unavailable, self-centered, addicted, or whatever—one scenario for redress is to find someone just as difficult and try to work it out with that person as a final validation of your lovability—like a belated instant replay. That certainly would explain your obvious stupid "choice" and help understand why you cling to it so tenaciously.

And perhaps sometimes you think that even a flaky someone is better than starting all over again—or reaching higher than you imagine you could attain.

MARRYING TO BE WHOLE CAN LEAVE YOU IN PIECES

Up to now I've been pointing out how you marry him and then hate him because he hasn't magically managed to repair your childhood hurts or to make the scariness of life painlessly perfect.

But there are also many women who marry to be a whole person. And when that doesn't happen, the result is hate.

IT FEELS LIKE HATE, BUT IT'S ENVY

Marge saw herself as "melancholic, sensitive, and quiet, putting everyone else first." Then, with obvious disdain, she described her husband as a self-centered type who inevitably put himself first. When I asked her if she could re-describe him—without the insults—as a person who was directed, interested, active, and goes after his dreams, she admitted she could.

The pejorative way in which Marge characterized her husband indicates to me that she covets those qualities she sees in him but doesn't dare strive for them. I suggested she was more than a little jealous and that if she took more risks and made different efforts in her own life, he wouldn't look so bad! And that would mean that she was more satisfied in her own right.

In other words, women tend to try to achieve balance in their lives by marrying it rather than becoming it. It doesn't work, because the imbalance is in two places. It is within you as you find your fulfillment and personal completion outside yourself in the man of your choice. And it is in the relationship as both you and your man retreat to those polarized corners of being.

HIM AS THE UNACCEPTABLE YOU

Too often, probably because of old parental expectations and the need for approval, women take the unacceptable from within themselves and find someone else in whom it seems to fit. That should mean you're okay because he's not. The point being that you picked him so carefully and then you hate him.

Because the "him" you hate is really the unacceptable you! So the twist here is that you're only okay when he's not.

This "being okay only if he is not okay" is tricky. Heidi, a twenty-nine-year-old nurse, called with a seemingly reasonable complaint about her husband of seven years: obesity. He is 6 feet 1½ inches tall and weighs 300 pounds.

In the first of two conversations, she complained about the possibility that her life might become caretaking a semi-invalid. Being a nurse, she fully understands the health ramifications of gross overweight.

When I asked her more about her history, she mentioned that her folks were alcoholics and that she had repeatedly stayed home to attend to them. Taking a big leap—big risk—I suggested she consider the possibility that if her husband suddenly lost his excess weight, she might actually miss it.

She was unhappy—even appalled—at my words but agreed to think about what I'd said and call back in a week.

She did.

YES, THERE ARE NEW BEGINNINGS!

Heidi confessed that admitting to all those feelings was tremendously painful but revealing, because she'd come to realize that her husband's obesity gave her what she termed the three *C's*: a caretaking role, a controlling power, and a complaining outlet. She now knew that if her husband were thinner, she'd run the risk of losing control and might no longer be able to feel superior to him. Most important, she'd be afraid of not meeting his standards of expectations toward her!

Wow! This was without doubt some of the most intense work I'd ever heard anyone on the air or in my office do totally on her own. What an achievement! And what a wonderful beginning to personal growth—and, I bet, to getting her husband to go on a diet.

NOBODY'S PERFECT—INCLUDING YOUR MATE

Heidi needed to hate her husband to feel better in herself. Which means you don't always hate the hate. In fact, it can become a treasured possession! Nonetheless, sometimes you simply have to accept the fact that no man is going to be perfect—and that means you don't have to be perfect, either.

DON'T MARRY AN ELEPHANT IF YOU WANT SOMETHING THAT PURRS

Sometimes you hate your men even though they give you what you want—just not in the form you want it in. That kind of pickiness is a definite "cut off your nose to spite your face" attitude.

Janine has a two-year-old and is pooped much of the time. She is really bent out of shape because her husband did not show interest in lying down under the evening stars and chatting with her one evening. I asked her if he had ever been the romantic type and she said, "No, but . . ." It's the "but" that gets you in trouble. If the answer is no, then it is no! He didn't push her away; he suggested cuddling on the couch, watching TV. But it wasn't her romantic vision. She married a nice guy, more mechanical and practical—not an artsy type. And that's fine. It's when you push a man to be other than what he is that he becomes less of who he is. And then you have nothing . . . even though something was available for comfort, which you reject out of your inflexible romantic fantasy.

THROWN FOR A LOOP

Betty, fifty-four, called because she was thrown for a loop. Her live-in boyfriend of one year was doing a big favor for his very ex-wife. Betty was wondering if she had the right to feel angry or jealous or whatever. I asked her if she believed in his loyalty, fidelity, commitment, etc. She said, emphatically, "Yes."

When I asked her what kind of a man he was, she told me, "He plays Big Daddy." I suggested that she enjoyed that quality when he displayed it with her but seemed to want him to change when he was with others. In the course of our talk, Betty realized that the very characteristic she loved about her husband—his big heart—was what she was hating, because she was momentarily insecure.

In the end, they were fine!

WHEN YOU HATE *HIM*, LOOK INSIDE YOURSELF

When you marry and hate him, look inside yourself first for the source of that hate. If you don't clarify those issues, you may marry and hate, marry and hate, marry and hate—and think that all men are the problem.

THE HAPPINESS OPTION

One final P.S.:

Dear Dr. Laura:
Your comment to someone on your show regarding the character of a person being infinitely more important than their success or accomplishments (something I really

shouldn't have to have been told) has cemented in me the greatest love and appreciation for my husband.

I come from a family of outwardly successful individuals, and all our friends make much more money than we do as city employees. For a while I allowed myself to become critical and frustrated until you reminded me that what I have—a true, loving, kind, honest, fun, hardworking, and gorgeous man—mattered most of all. Thanks for that reminder. I had my share of those horrendous roller-coaster high-intensity relationships, until I made a smart intellectual choice to be happy. And it's the best.

Best regards, M.

My dear, you are more than welcome!

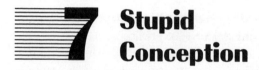

7 Stupid Conception

MAKING BABIES FOR THE WORST REASONS

"Obviously, people with life plans have more motivation to control their fertility."
—UC Davis sociology researcher Carole Joffe
(*Los Angeles Times,* January 6, 1993)

Having used "for the worst reasons" as part of the title for a chapter on conception, I'm left with the arrogant task of detailing what I presume to be the best reasons for having a baby.

Are they, for example: Love? Time of life? Supposed to? Your parents want to be grandparents? So as not to feel left out among pregnant friends? Prove you can? Have someone to love you? Force a marriage? Nothing else to do with your life? Baby as panacea for emotional malaise?

Notice something about all of these most typical motivations? They have nothing to do with the best interests of the child!

APPROPRIATE PARENTHOOD HONORS THE
CHILD'S NEEDS FIRST

So here's my notion of the single appropriate rationale for having a baby: You and another adult, committed partner (i.e., spouse) have the interest, intent, ability, and means to make the necessary sacrifices of time, attention, and resources to give that child the nurturing, security, support, love, and education he or she needs!

Procreation has little to do with your needs; it has everything to do with the child's needs.

When you look at making a baby solely from the vantage point of healing yourself, identifying yourself, solidifying yourself in a precarious relationship, or entertaining yourself in an otherwise ho-hum existence, you're terribly disappointed, and the children ultimately pay the price.

THE FIGURES SPEAK FOR THEMSELVES

As I mentioned in an earlier chapter, the Centers for Disease Control report that more than one third to one half of women questioned in a recent survey claimed that their last pregnancy was unwanted or that they became pregnant sooner than desired. The unintended pregnancy rate is substantially higher among women who are young or in the lowest income group or were never married.

I'm still unsure as to what unintended pregnancy really means. That a responsibly used contraceptive method failed? I don't think so. At least, not often. Remember those figures I quoted from the Alan Guttmacher Institute to the effect that of the nation's annual 3.5 million unplanned pregnancies, nearly one half resulted from inconsistent or incorrect use of contraceptives, the rest from using no birth control at all. So much for unintended!

HOW MANY ACCIDENTS ARE ACCIDENTAL?

Of the many, many, many phone calls I have taken from "oops, I'm pregnant" women, most finally admit, after some badgering from me, that they didn't use contraceptives "because . . ." And the "because" too often comes down to an immature perspective of "I thought it would all work out with him."

Sandy, thirty-five, is typical of this mentality. She called me, very angry with her ex-husband! She said he had been talking about their "possibly getting back together." One would hope that would mean counseling or talks about the problems in their marriage and ideas shared about self- and mutual growth, etc. No such luck.

Sandy, despite her initial anger, suddenly began behaving as if "everything were just peachy," as though they were a back-together-and-committed couple! Turns out, though, he already had a girlfriend. Nonetheless, Sandy assumed the reconciliation would all just work out and believed him when he told her he loved her—although he hadn't made a move to break up with his current flame. Sandy was just hoping he'd choose her, and to expedite matters, she got pregnant.

DR. LAURA: How did he react when you told him the news?

SANDY (INCREASINGLY UPSET): He went back to his girl-friend!

DR. LAURA: Sandy, did you have unprotected sex with him?

SANDY: Yes . . .

DR. LAURA: Did the both of you have firm, you know, committed plans to remarry?

SANDY: No . . .

DR. LAURA: How about agreeing to have a baby together? Ever happen? Had he ever independently mentioned wanting a child?

SANDY: No. But he said he loved me!

DR. LAURA: Sandy, that's beside the point. Can't you see that? I don't think your anger is appropriate. You had un-protected sex in a noncommitted relationship with a man who has no discernible interest in having children! So you had a plan, but it backfired.

SANDY: Well . . .

DR. LAURA: Sandy honey, you're in a tough spot, and you've got some very crucial decisions to make regarding this child. But whatever you do decide, remember this: Never dive into a swimming pool just because a guy tells you there might be water in it sometime. See what I mean?

SANDY: Yes, I think I do. Thank you.

HIS AND HERS RESPONSIBILITIES

Now, here's where the argument can get sticky. It is quite reasonable for you to say, "Hey, wait a minute, Laura! How about the guy and his responsibility!" That's fair. I think every man is responsible for his sperm, where they go and what they do when they get there. The law mandates financial child support; morality mandates actual inter-action.

So what!

The 1992 U.S. Census figures show that the problems of single parents today are still, for the great majority, the problems of single mothers. Since it is in women's bodies that the miracle of reproduction takes place and since child care is primarily women's responsibility, I don't think that arguing over men's responsibility actually accomplishes much in the real-world context of pregnancy.

Given that, my advice to you is: If a man refuses to take part in the contraceptive process, refuse sex, dump him!, or make sure you've got Norplant up your sleeve!

NO RIGHTS WITHOUT RESPONSIBILITY

Yeah, I know, it isn't politically correct to hit on the alleged supposed victim, the woman, especially while excusing the guy. There are countless cases where women with children are victimized. However, I've had the opportunity to talk to thousands of women who play director and producer in a plot line that results in children victimized by poverty and impersonal day care.

Tom Bethell, a media fellow at the Hoover Institute, wrote a *Los Angeles Times* essay that contains a thought I wholeheartedly endorse: "Pregnancy involves an antecedent consensual act, and to represent it (or an abortion) as unavoidable is implicitly to dismiss [these women] as lacking free will. Nothing could be more condescending than that."

As women, we can't afford to keep marching for the rights without taking on the responsibilities.

"BUT THINGS HAPPEN . . ."

Then, of course, we have the argument written in a letter by a listener, Rosalie, from El Monte, California: ". . . we are all human, and as such, we make mistakes and have moments of weakness. I agree 100% that birth control is a much better method of controlling one's body—but as they say, 'Things happen!' "

Boy oh boy, if that doesn't consign women to helpless, hopeless idiocy!

Look, forty-six years as a woman on this earth has shown me, firsthand, inequities based on sexism and cruelty based on sexism. But I've also seen it for people of color, Jews, the handicapped, the obese, you name it.

So at this point in my life, after spending the late sixties and part of the seventies angry at men, I firmly believe that women—through their own intelligent and courageous personal, one-at-a-time efforts—can ensure and/or improve the lot of their own lives.

And I am sick, sick, sick of using society or upbringing or anything else to excuse women's stupid behavior. Women must first help themselves, then aid other women, in rising above societal limitations—or there will be no progress.

Many women's groups, even NOW, contribute to the perpetuation of women's victim status by having a political agenda demanding and expecting little personal responsibility, it would seem, from individual women, which, basically, is my focus.

INDIVIDUAL EMPOWERMENT: THE WAY I SEE IT

When I—as a woman and therapist and broadcaster and mother—speak on the air about women's power over their own bodies, I always suggest that the moment of empowerment begins before conception. I have also frequently stated that I believe women, with all that power over bodies uniquely equipped to make babies, are therefore wholly responsible for birth control.

As you can imagine, I've gotten some very heated responses, one from a chapter of NOW—which accused me of, among other dastardly attitudes, absolving men and boys from the shared responsibility for contraception and placing it, unreasonably, on women's and girls' shoulders "in a society that does not sufficiently equip them to protect themselves."

Here we go again with the society-made-me-do-it excuse!

Well, now hear this: I don't think it is unreasonable to expect women to behave with integrity, courage, intelligence, and strength—regardless of the fact that your parents may have bought you Barbie dolls!

It's your body. Take care of it! And if that means not having sex with a guy who won't use a condom, then don't have sex with him!! Do not tolerate his cute or callous attempts to get you to relent.

WHAT IF I INSIST ON SAFE SEX AND HE LEAVES ME?

About two years ago I went on the *Geraldo* program to talk about "Safer Sex." The single most frequent question asked me on-camera, off-camera, in the halls, and in the ladies' room was "But, what do I do when he won't use a condom?" I answered jauntily, "Keep those knees together!" To a woman, they countered, "Yeah, but then maybe he'll leave me."

Egad! Is this how far we've come after thirty years of enlightenment? Women may be in Congress, but are they still panicked at the thought of some dude dumping them if they do the right thing for themselves, such as demand he take responsibility by using a condom? Pathetic!

Let me make sure I'm being totally clear. I agree that men should share the onerous responsibility of contraception—of course they should.

But, ladies, wake up. You are the ones who get pregnant. The buck (literally and figuratively) should stop at you!

BRAINWASHED

The arguments against my positions in my listener mail show, I think, that women are defensive because they've been brainwashed and simply accept the "awful plight of women."

Many of you experience and talk of women struggling daily with lousy situations, lousy husbands, etc. Every day I open my microphone reminding women of the power they have in their individual lives to rise above stereotypes and their own weak behaviors. I don't let them off with excuses! I exhort them to use, and to be more responsible with, all the power they have as individuals.

That is precisely why this whole book has been written. I want women to understand and accept that, typically, the mess that is their lives is of their own making. Simple as that. Not society. Themselves.

THIS BOOK IS ABOUT BRAINS AND GUTS

That, in a nutshell, is what this book is dedicated to.

It's dedicated to the type of women I read about who live in a small village in Africa. It seems that this village experiences much marital wife abuse as standard practice. Tragically, this is hardly news, throughout the world or throughout history.

What is news, however, is how the marriage-aged women in the village decided to deal with it: They simply refused to marry! Surely, in this little African village, with no radio and TV, no library filled with feminist manifestos, something special happened. It is called brains and guts!

You know the great quandary at the center of this whole issue? It's why in America, the most liberated country in the world, women are still taking so much abuse from men. It's not because you don't know what's going on—you're anything but dumb. But intelligence is only the beginning. You also have to have the courage of your beliefs, like those African tribeswomen. And I'd like to see women's groups do more to encourage an agenda of personal courage and responsibility.

I hope it won't sound too condescending to suggest that if African tribeswomen can do it, any woman in America, the most liberated country in the existing and real world, can do it!

This was highlighted in a letter I got from a female Japanese immigrant in 1992 (I reproduce it here as I received it):

I am Japanese. I grew up in post–WW II Japan during the MacArthur reign and Hirohito defeat. My culture, then and now, is completely different from this country. From listening your show, I am start understanding about freedom and independent meaning. I was so-called "door mat" my seven years marriage. I didn't have my say, I didn't have my identity, I didn't know how to be in my relationship or total in my life. My family and society are brought up for how to become nice girl, nice lady, nice wife, nice mother, and more you please them you are nice person. No talk back, just support.

I didn't know why, but I need more than that. I choose to come to this country early 1970. Because of my basic instinct, old culture value did hold marriage relationship seven years. Two years of my last marriage time little by little I start make my own identity. Of course, marriage start deteriorate.

Why? I really don't know. It just start like wakening time. My husband likes to make all decision or he has to agree everything, even small detail like pick toilet paper or choose cereal.

First two years of marriage didn't burden me. It was felt even nice to guy to involve making decision in household. I felt strong power in him, that time I liked strong man, so-called "macho man."

But slowly and gradually, I notice my feelings are changing.

I start to discuss with him that difference of my opinion. Of course, he panicked—every time we have different idea or opinion, he has to win. A lot of time I was lock in bathroom two to three hour, he likes to argue and likes to talk, I felt fear first fifteen or twenty minute, so, because he was very angry, but an hour and a half later, he totally convinced to me how he was right, and I was totally agree with him. By the way, he always say, "I can sale ice cream to Eskimo."

But more and more after two to three days, I felt

angry. Just like I bought car from use-car salesman with no satisfactory, feeling bitterness left deep inside. My brain agreed once but feeling wasn't, also locking me up in the bathroom felt very powerless too.

Now I got out that relationship, listening to your radio show, start understanding meaning of freedom and independent. Now I understand why I got out that relationship.

You are like magician. So many invisible psychological heavy tangle, you show like magician do magic. Strengthen out just two second, it is amazing to listening your logic.

Anyway I found out over little two years way from my husband. I met lot woman suffer from spouse abuse. It is mind burst, this United States of America, most a feminist of country in the world, still lot of woman taking a crap from men, psychologically and physically.

I think, we women must wake up, we are human being better know what deserve for our self as equally as man.

I am telling all my friend that if you have a chance, listen on radio at 12 to 2 P.M. 640 AM KFI radio show, because most people just only complain a situation.

I know I made lot of mistake, but at least I know now I am aware of me how I feel. It is great know about this feeling.

Just little bit a neglect, I wish I listening your show and understand your logic before I met my husband. Well! Maybe it was meant be.

By the way, couple days ago, I did go to vote myself. I felt so good, first time in my life I made decision for election and I proud myself.

HOW CAN YOU BE SO CAVALIER ABOUT
SUCH A VITAL ISSUE?

I am especially passionate about this chapter because I'm convinced that the contraceptive actions women take—or fail to take—end by affecting an innocent life: the child's.

What follows are the simple facts, as reported by journalist Paul Taylor in *The Washington Post:*

When you have children outside a committed relationship, the kids grow up in a single-parent household—which too often is synonymous with poverty. ". . . Between seventy and ninety per cent of all children born out of wedlock wind up on welfare at some point in their lives, and . . . such children are much more likely to stay on welfare for longer periods than children of divorce.

"In the 1960s," Taylor continues, "there was a global movement away from marriage as the locus of sexual relations. Since then we've seen an increasing detachment of childbearing from wedlock, and we may be entering a third stage in which marriage is no longer the locus of child-rearing. And we're not really sure why all this has happened."

THE ONUS OF SINGLE PARENTING

Well, if our single mom ain't rich, ain't on welfare, then with or without court-mandated child support from the sperm donor, she's probably working and the child is in institutionalized, impersonalized child care. According to renowned pediatrician and author T. Berry Brazelton, ". . . Children of single parents are haunted by two questions: Why would one parent desert me, and will this one go too? Unless that single parent is there to give the child a sense of how important he or she is, right from the first, they grow up with a pretty flaky self-image."

This is not exactly secret information. So what motivates women to be this noncircumspect about making babies?

From a letter from a listener: "I hope I can be an example to other women about having babies out of wedlock, for other reasons that are not acceptable. I have two kids, conceived out of me trying to keep a man."

GETTING HIM TO COMMIT THROUGH CONCEPTION IS CHILDISH

Then there was the twenty-five-year-old caller, worried about her unmarried nineteen-year-old sister. The sister has been in an off-again, on-again relationship with this guy, nineteen. Now she's pregnant. The caller wanted to know the right words to use to convince her sister to get an abortion. She was considering using logic about issues such as finances and education—absolutely the wrong approach!

What we agreed on during the call was to tell the sister outright that she thought she had found a way to finally solidify her relationship with this young man—a baby—and that it was a very risky enterprise. It's also a perfect example of the immaturity, naïveté, and stupidity all of us women need to talk about openly and honestly in order to educate one another.

BECOME YOUR OWN CONTROLLER!

It is not enough to get in a whiny group complaining about, for example, controlling husbands without taking responsibility for our lack of willingness to take the difficult and uncomfortable roll of controller in our own lives. We delegate that role to men willing to play it, then blame them when we don't like exactly how they use that control.

Don't tell me women have no choices because this is a sexist, male-dominated world. That statement would make me—and the millions of women just like me, who made the sacrifices, put out the effort, suffered the discomforts, to get educated and do it on our own, what?—some kind of freak, a member of a privileged elite, or just plain lucky. This is not the case. Not unlike those admirable examples from the ghettos of the world who put in the effort and succeed, we are more appropriate role models.

Because "Do as I say, and not as I do" does not work. You have to live it.

LET'S PUT STUPID BEHIND US

Okay, back to the subject at hand, which is my attempt at highlighting and minimizing typically stupid female behaviors, specifically as they relate to reproduction.

The sexual revolution said we could do *it* anytime we wanted because it no longer meant we were bad girls and because we were entitled to the same pleasures and sexual freedoms as men.

So far, so good. Unless you, or he, are sterilized, if you have intercourse enough times, considering the inherent and real failure rate of any contraceptive (and how lazy and irresponsible you may be with birth control), you will get pregnant. Plain and simple. Then you have to deal with abortion, adoption, single parenthood, or a shotgun wedding.

The equal sharing of contraceptive responsibility and child-care obligations between men and women is not evidenced in the hundreds of calls I have taken from scared, hurt, and crying women when they are "oops" pregnant.

I particularly remember Marie, twenty-two years old, possibly facing a second abortion, who told me tearfully that she didn't want a baby but was scared. The scared feelings actually turned out to be shame feelings, because she remembered that during the first abortion, people had been nice and there wasn't any physical pain . . . but . . . now . . .

DR. LAURA: Did you use contraception?

MARIE: Well, my boyfriend and I used condoms, but . . . we . . . we didn't use them that much.

DR. LAURA: Marie, let me ask you something. After you'd been through one abortion, why would you permit intercourse without protection?

MARIE: Okay, we—

DR. LAURA: This is not about we. It's about you!

MARIE: I guess I just got . . . um . . . caught up in the moment! I mean, he was willing to use a condom, but I didn't think I should have to tell him to. It's his—

DR. LAURA: Honey, whatever you do about this baby—and we can discuss the options—I'd suggest getting Norplant, because you are not showing sexual responsibility. You can't let the emotions of the moment overpower you! Look what lack of planning has caused already!

MARIE: Yeah, maybe you're right . . .

MISTAKING FANTASIES FOR ACTUAL POWER

If all that intercourse brought were orgasms, no children, no venereal disease, and no distortions of passion interpreted as love, this chapter would not even be necessary.

As long as there are such serious consequences, we women must act as adults and not as helpless, swept-away fairy princesses. The price is obviously too great for that.

Honestly, I think so many women, including Marie, don't use birth control because they are fantasizing about being in a perfect situation of love and commitment, and they mistake fantasizing for actual power.

USING THE SHOTGUN STRATEGY TO SHOOT YOURSELF IN THE FOOT

Unlike Fantasyland, where "when you wish upon a star, your dreams come true," in real life that's a worrisome gamble.

Michelle, twenty-nine, is an example of that. She's been in an on-again, off-again, sometimes live-in relationship with a fellow eleven years her senior. She laughingly describes him as ". . . a chicken. He's a whole other story. Trust me—you'd die if you knew the whole story of him. It would take much too long!"

It's sad to me that she thinks I'd die if I knew more about this man because he is the man she made a human being with—for the second time. The first pregnancy was aborted some three years ago. This one, she indicated, was a "keeper."

She immediately assured me she loved him with all her heart! She then made it clear that she couldn't get him to commit to marriage—which was clearly why she'd "messed up on the birth-control pills."

Ostensibly, she called because she wanted my advice on how to tell him. She professed to be confused: She didn't want him to *not* marry her. She didn't want him to marry her just because she was pregnant. What she hadn't accepted was that he hadn't wanted to marry her when she *wasn't* pregnant. Clearly, the child was a means to end her boyfriend's bachelorhood. And chances are, even according to her, it wouldn't work.

But that doesn't stop us from trying, does it?

THE ERROR OF "JUST GOING FOR IT"

Doesn't stop us from thinking and hoping that if we "wish" hard enough, all our dreams will come true.

The lengths to which we women may go to enforce the wish boggle the mind and hurt the heart.

Women have a desire, a hope, a yearning, a wish, for a kind of lifestyle. These goals are fine. They help motivate and invigorate.

Yet too many women, running on emotional steam, figure that an emotion of the moment means a necessary action of the next moment. Forget long-term benefits of planning and patience and persistence, let's just go for it.

And this leads me to highlighting other such predicaments women get into when they aren't more circumspect about with whom and under what conditions they decide to make babies.

MAKING A BABY WITH A MARRIED MAN

One of the more outrageous cases was the woman who had been having a two-year affair with a married guy who frankly said he would never leave his wife. She was upset because the future child's so-called grandparents made it clear they wanted nothing to do with her or her baby.

Now, morally, I have to admit that's somewhat irresponsible, not to say cold-blooded, of them—but what did she expect? There was never any real possibility that her boyfriend would switch his wife for her. Unbelievably, the wife, knowing about the mistress's pregnancy, stayed with her philandering mate!

REMEMBER, IT'S ALWAYS THE CHILD WHO PAYS

Predicaments? Predicaments!

I'll give you more predicaments. And you'll sadly notice that it is always going to be the child who pays the price.

GETTING LEFT IN THE LURCH—AND FORGIVING HIM

Audrey, twenty-four, had a "boyfriend who got me pregnant, and then split," she complained. Now, what I want to know is, how did he do that without her noticing?

That was about three years ago. During that time she's had a platonic male friend living with her and her baby, being helpful and supportive and acting as a surrogate dad. Now the old boyfriend maybe wants to get back in the picture with her, and maybe not.

She calls to ask, "So, what should I do?"

Doesn't she realize that she is playing games with the child's sense of attachment and security?

A SIXTH SENSE FOR LOSERS

Kathy, forty-one, called with an incredible dilemma.

"My question involves how I should tell my two middle children that they have a different biological father than their older siblings," she said.

She has six children ranging in age from twenty-one to three years, two from her first husband. It's the next two that are the issue.

The third and fourth children were from a seven-year relationship with an alcoholic. "It took me being pregnant twice to realize that I needed to break it off," she continued.

Children five and six are three-year-old twins from her present husband of four years.

The third and fourth children are six and eleven and think that the first husband is their daddy. Their actual biological dad, the sperm donor, was never involved in their lives. Kathy's first husband is listed on the birth certificate and provided emotional and financial support for both of these kids since birth.

"I like this man," I said. "Why did we dump him?"

"Stupid?" she offered, laughing.

One of the rare women to admit to the reality!

She also offered that "life is not always easy."

True enough. So why make it harder?

Why continue to be sexual with guys you know are married, gay, addicts, alcoholics, cruel, noncommittal, not interested in hands-on parenting, violent, etc.?

WHEN YOU WANT HIM TO VANISH—AND HE WON'T

Remember this: When you risk pregnancy with the wrong guy, under the wrong conditions, you'll be dealing with him, or the threat of him, forever.

Ask the women who write me with terrible situations such as having a mean or neurotic or addicted sperm donor chasing after them, wreaking havoc over child visitation and custody. These men don't really want the kids; they are just continuing the sick relationship and escalating it to a higher level of damage and pain.

STOP BELIEVING IN MIRACLE TRANSFORMATIONS!

I've rarely spoken to a woman who didn't admit to "how he was even before." So, please, don't rely on love or hope to produce a miracle cure or transformation. And stop giving in to being scared, weak, or anything else, because that won't stop you from getting pregnant and having to deal with the consequences of that.

Marriage, to my mind, is necessary, but not sufficient motivation or condition to make babies.

ONE WOMAN'S CATCH-22

Brenda, twenty-seven, was "calling because me and my husband have known each other for ten years, we've been married for eight years. My little girl was about nine months when we got married. I got a job at night and came home one night after work to find him with my best friend in the shower. This was eight years ago."

I asked her whether if she gave me the following eight

years of history, would there be mostly things like that to tell?

"Yes," she said firmly. "He's been doing this, and he's been an alcoholic, and he's been treating me bad. I took all his garbage and he said he was going to change."

A month ago, Brenda began repeatedly asking him for a separation because she didn't want him "bothering me and my three kids."

I was thunderstruck! After knowing "what she was living with," she made two more kids with him! Is this the Catch-22 Syndrome of women? You're miserable, so you make kids, now you have kids and you can't get out for the sake of the kids—even though you are miserable with him?

It will come as no great surprise that right after her request for a separation, he professed to be madly in love with her.

That's all it took: All of a sudden, she's confused, unsure about the separation.

As long as he proclaims love, he can torture her to his heart's content. Why do women confuse words with actions? Why do women value words over action?

Because, I think, with these hollow protestations, you get yourselves off the hook from making and expediting brave decisions and behaviors. It always comes back to that!

THE VICIOUS CIRCLE

Many women, as in Brenda's case, continue to make babies as though it were a way of digging in for the winter, to ensure safety and security.

Making babies becomes a way not only of pretending things are okay, but also of trying to force things to be okay, and, perhaps, at least, doing something within this lousy context that *is* okay.

So here we are, though, with children being brought up in a bad situation, which women say they can't get out of because of the children.

Does that really work for you?

THE TIME FOR EXCUSES IS PAST

You must make concrete, rational, intelligent decisions about when and by whom you become pregnant.

No more excuses.

You have the power over your bodies.

I implore you to use it.

8 Stupid Subjugation

LETTING HIM HURT YOUR BABIES

The single most ferocious creature in all nature is a mother whose young are threatened. Ever try poking into a nest with the mother bird close by? Ever experience the rage of a mother bear who believes her cubs are threatened? I don't know how much choice or altruism you can attribute to this behavior. It could be instinct, pure and simple—but just maybe there are love and sacrifice involved, too.

Human beings are the most highly evolved of animals—who have retained only a few instinctive or reflex actions. With our highly evolved cerebral cortex, we can rise above instinct and make choices. That is our glory. And sometimes our shame.

And nowhere is this choice-vs.-instinct issue more evident than in the area of motherhood.

You know, as I write about instinct and choice and the natural inclination to protect our children, I think how mega-totally, how cosmically, I love my own child. If I had to make a choice between anyone or anything and Deryk, it wouldn't even be a choice.

When Deryk was born, I told my husband—the world's most gentle, generous, loving man—that if I thought for a millionth of a second that he might hurt

Deryk, I'd reduce him to sub-molecular particles. He said with a gentle smile, "As well you should!"

I remember those several years when my husband and I were struggling to make a baby. I had major surgeries, hormones, temperature charts, etc. At thirty-five I decided I really wanted the experience of pregnancy and mothering—and when that feeling came it was overwhelming.

One night, before I actually became pregnant, my husband and I were watching a PBS program on philosophy and ethics. They were discussing, among other subjects, lifeboat ethics. If fifteen people were on a lifeboat equipped for twelve, what do you do? Dump three people so that the others are assured of survival? Or do your utmost to keep everybody alive and hope for the best?

So, going along with these ideas, I asked my husband, "If, after we have this child, the three of us were in a boat that began to sink, assuming you could only save one person, whom would you save? The child or me?"

My husband, being no dummy, realized he probably could never win this one and declined to answer!

I thought the answer was easy! I said, "I'd save you. You and I have the primary relationship. I guess we could always make another child."

I guess at that point it was difficult for me to imagine the attachment feelings I might have for the child, since he/she was still only a possibility—too abstract for emotional bonding.

Several months later I got pregnant. Late one night I woke my husband with this very earnest question, "Lew, how long can you tread water?"

The question of my attachment and responsibility was no longer abstract. Here was a life of my life, growing in my body—my son. I instinctively knew that this was, for me, the most special of bonds.

And all this from a woman brought up during the

feminist years of the sixties who'd thought mothering was some kind of cop-out. What a glorious evolution.

Unfortunately, the whole world doesn't always feel the way I do. All too often, our stupid choices smother our natural mothering instinct and—surprise! surprise!—there's frequently a man involved.

WHEN THE MOTHERING INSTINCT GOES AWRY

Along those lines, I've never been able to forget a case dating from when I first opened my counseling practice. The caller was a woman in her late twenties who had a problem with her boyfriend. He liked her well enough but didn't want her two little kids around—at all. In fact, he was pressuring her to give them away. Her question, believe it or not, was "What should I do?"

That there was even a question was incomprehensible enough, but what followed simply stunned me. Naturally, she didn't want to give up her kids, but she didn't want to give up the guy even more.

I talked with her at great length about love and what it meant in terms of attitudes and behaviors—not just hormones or fearful dependency. I further suggested that adulthood and parenthood didn't feel good all the time but that the long-range gratifications from loyalty, sacrifice, and self-reliance were incredible. I assured her they were the stuff out of which real happiness and self-esteem were forged.

Externally, I was behaving like a calm, rational psychotherapist, but inside, I was seething with rage. How could a mother even consider this choice?

We talked for an hour. At the end of the conversation, she still wasn't sure what her choice would be.

And she never called back.

Was this woman so crippled by desperate need that she couldn't take one step forward? What could have happened to create in her such blind terror of loneliness? I'll never know. But I'll always wonder. . . .

TRAPPED BETWEEN ABUSED AND ALONE

Both on the air and in my private practice, I've always used humor to leaven the mood and make callers more comfortable with difficult ideas and realizations. Even so, one particular call was beyond humor:

Celia seemed at once extremely distressed and emotionally numb as she told me she had married for the second time—she had two toddlers by her first husband—to a man who was physically abusing her and the children. She insisted she didn't know what to do about the situation. When I talked about her leaving, Celia said she just didn't think she could do that—because of the kids.

I asked, "Does that mean you believe it is better that they have a guy who beats them than no guy around at all?"

She hesitated, and said, "Yes."

I was dumbfounded.

I wanted so much to help Celia that I risked sounding nasty by asking her to repeat what she'd said—that it was better to have an abuser around than no man at all. I wasn't trying to be cruel; it's just that I know, as a therapist, that when we hear ourselves say something, it becomes more real, more concrete. And it was crucial that she hear herself loud and clear.

She struggled with the sentence for an interminable amount of time. Then she got going with it: "I think it is better that they have a man around who beats them than no man. . . . no! That's not right!" she screamed into my head-phones.

At that point we were both in tears. I gave her a woman's-shelter emergency number and some woman's-support-group numbers, and told her how brave she was. I only hope Celia got the message—and got herself and the kids out of there!

FATAL RATIONALIZATION

At any one time I am talking to only one person. I realize, however, that any one caller represents hundreds or thou-sands with whom I could be having the same dialogue. So to every woman, to all of us, to each of you, I say:

It is never better—for you *or* your children—to be beaten, terrorized, humiliated, demoralized, or violated than to be alone. Remember, in an earlier chapter, I men-tioned how upset I'd gotten at the mother in *Dead Poets Society* who stands by her man at the expense of her son's survival? That's a perfect illustration of such behavior. This rationalization, and that's what it is, comes out of your fears of autonomy and lack of awareness of possible re-sources.

THERE ARE RESOURCES OUT THERE

Granted, a woman may argue that she's trapped by her lack of education, ability to earn an independent income, or the apparent unavailability of social and community support. Arguably, all these alibis have some grain of truth to them. But there is finally no excuse for jeopardizing your children.

Many women in financial difficulty enter into joint living ventures with other women who also lack extended family support. Others enter programs and shelters. In short, there *are* alternatives to the literally perilous path abused women and their kids are treading. First, you've got to give yourself permission to see that they're there. Second, you must face the fact that there isn't always a neat, pretty, simple way out of the situation—but there *are* ways. If you care about your children, if you care about yourself, you'll muster the courage to do what's right.

But the sacrificing needs to be made by the adults, not by the children—as this next episode clearly illustrates.

ADULTS MUST SACRIFICE, BUT THAT DOESN'T MEAN MAKING THEIR CHILDREN THE OFFERING

A nice couple came in for counseling. Their presenting problem was an inability to budget properly. They would begin businesses, do well for a while, and then the business would go under because of their mismanagement of money.

I suggested they'd be better off seeing a business expert, but they insisted on sessions with me. We kept going in circles, and on the third session I suggested that I talk to each of them alone. I had the feeling I'd been skating on the surface of something important to understand.

She came in alone the next week. I asked her what the secret was. I was not prepared for what she said. They'd been married for twenty years or so. When they first got together, he wanted to start a business so that he would work for himself. She was to help. Then she got pregnant. He was angry about the extra expense a child would bring, and the time it would take out of her being able to help him in his business.

They sold the child. And with that money, he started his first business.

She had wanted to please him, keep him, help him. She said that she figured they could always have another baby. They never did. She said that after all, it was probably her fault for getting pregnant, and she didn't want to mess up his dreams. And she didn't want to lose him. She didn't want to sell the child or give it up, but she didn't know what else to do at the time.

So the choice was made.

The pain and the guilt, mostly unspoken, for two decades was so great in both of these people that their self-punishing cycles of business failures suddenly became understandable.

WHO SAVES THE CHILDREN?

Sherri began by telling me that she and her sisters had finally admitted to one another that as children they'd all been molested by their stepfather. Although their mother had divorced the man for physically abusing her and had "had a feeling" that something was going on with him and her young daughters, she had never made a move to find out about it. That marriage had produced a son, who now lived with the father.

Through her stepbrother—who hadn't been abused and knew nothing about what had had happened to the girls—Sherri learned that her ex-stepfather was planning to marry a younger woman with a small child. Sherri's quandary was whether or not she should tell the prospective wife about the man's proclivities. "I just can't bear to think of having what happened to us happen to his new stepchild," she insisted, "but I'm scared of the repercussion to me!"

I told Sherri that this man rapes babies and beats women and that she had an obligation to prevent his doing so again. Of course, the fiancée will suffer, but she's an adult. She has a choice. Her baby doesn't.

DON'T LET A MAN DEFINE YOUR MOTHERHOOD!

Another caller, Carol, is a repetitively dominated woman. She has two children from her twenty-two-year marriage to a controlling type. Now she's married again, to another man who not only is doing his best to convince her she's incapable of autonomy but won't even allow her twenty-three- and nineteen-year-old children to visit. He is emphatically childless.

"Well, honey, it's ultimatum time," I tell her. "If he chooses to continue this behavior, leave and live somewhere where they can visit. . . . You don't let any man dictate your relationship with your babies. And they're always your babies, no matter how big they are!"

Carol is a mature woman, but she's got a lot of growing up to do. I only hope she does it!

WHEN THE ABUSER IS A HUSBAND, PARENT, OR GRANDPARENT

Women sometimes make extraordinarily sickening sacrifices to appease the "god"—your man, without whom you must feel you can just not live—without the attachment or hoped-for approval. And it can be just as scary, even more so, when the man . . . is your father.

A caller named Nadia sticks in my mind because of her extraordinary detachment while relating a horrendous personal history.

She had grown up with a father—to whom she referred as "a dirty old man," although she was irrationally devoted to him—who abused other little girls in the neighborhood. Although he'd never touched her, she knew from her friends what he was doing from the time she was five years old. All the while, her own mother seems to have played—consciously or unconsciously—a permitting role in what went on. Nadia had made a virtual career out of denying her mother's complicity—and almost every powerful emotion she herself had—by becoming "strong in order to survive," cerebral to the max.

Nadia grew up and married, only to find out long after her father's death that he had also molested her daughter—who hadn't told Nadia at the time because she didn't want to hurt Nadia, or affect her sadly unconditional love for her father.

When Nadia confessed she was thinking of writing her story and trying to have it published, I applauded her. For a woman so bound to reason, it seemed an entirely appropriate self-awareness technique.

DR. LAURA: Nadia, that's a wonderful—and needed—thing to do. You need to write to women who put their own children in vulnerable positions with their abusive parents as a way of staying close to that parent. Almost like an ancient sacrifice ritual. You have to do all you can to make sure other women don't do what you did—because of what your mother did before you—letting your need to stay close to Daddy overshadow your maternal instinct to protect your kid.

NADIA: Yes, I think I know that.

DR. LAURA: You need to show them that no matter how intelligent, how "strong" a person believes she is, denial and emotional need can be so great that we put our children in harm's way.

NADIA: Yes.

DR. LAURA: And I think you could do a great service writing it that way. It'll hurt you, make you cry, make you tear your hair out at points, but you could do a great service kicking a lot of women in the butt. And as a consequence of your writing this book, a lot of children might be more protected.

NADIA: Thank you.

THE IRON FIST OF DENIAL

The scary part about talking to Nadia was what she had become in order to be strong and to survive—so removed from her feelings and so unwilling to face the painful truths that she sounded like a therapist discussing a patient. She had actually taken her father's not molesting her as a "sign" of his love, a gift he would never take back.

Surprise, Nadia. The dirty old man appears to be giving with one hand, but he's actually taking with the other.

FOLLOWING IN DANGEROUS FOOTSTEPS

My caller Linda wasn't able to control the cycle of need, hurt, guilt, and rage. They came out in her nightmares—dreadful dreams in which she repeatedly saw her sixteen-year-old daughter dead or dying. Recently, she'd been dreaming that her now deceased mother saves her and her children from a fire, after which Linda becomes a little girl again, with Mother assuring her that everything will be okay. In the dream, Mother protected her, but in real life, she'd done just the opposite:

Linda had recently begun therapy. Why? Because she and her daughter had both been molested by Linda's step-father—although she'd insisted she allowed him access to her child only after having been assured he'd been cured!

DR. LAURA: Linda, the dreams are not the point. They are only the means by which you are trying to come to terms with powerful and frightening feelings and awarenesses . . .

LINDA: Yes, I can see that . . .

DR. LAURA: Let me tell you what I think about the dreams. I think they represent your working through your guilt and anger. You do try to whitewash Mom—who on some level was a complicitor to the abuse. You didn't want to lose Mom—so you bet your daughter.

LINDA (SOUNDS OF RESOLUTION): Yes, I did.

DR. LAURA: You are putting yourself through more hell not acknowledging the truth of your mother and the truth of your tragic mistake out of desperate need. What child of any age would find it easy to accept that neither parent gave a damn?

LINDA: I understand. If I kill off my daughter, if she's "dead," then the proof of my mistake is gone.

DR. LAURA: And you also identify with her in that a piece of both of you died with that adult betrayal of trust and pro-tection.

LINDA: It's hard to be angry with Mom, because she's dead.

DR. LAURA: Oh, let's do it anyway. She put her marriage to that bum ahead of her own babies.

LINDA: Yeah, she did. She swept it under the carpet.

DR. LAURA: You are beating yourself up and tearing yourself apart. In your therapy, be courageous enough to deal with this all openly—so you can heal, and so you can help your daughter heal.

LINDA: Oh, thank you so much.

WHY YOU EXCUSE THE INEXCUSABLE

When needs for attachment and acceptance are so strong that rational judgment gives way to fearfully unexamined emotions, the consequences are rarely minor.

Women have called me because they've had abortions solely because "he said to, and I didn't want to lose him." Women have called me because their boyfriends or second or third spouses have gotten "sexually involved with my daughter. I know he did wrong, but what can I do about it all now? I just can't think about being alone again. And what about the finances?" Women have called me because "he's been really mean with the kids. I try to talk to them and tell them that he really doesn't mean it—it's just his way. I just don't know what to do. I really need him."

THE COURAGE TO DO WHAT'S RIGHT

Those needy feelings create an undertow that can pull with frightening power against rationality, disgust, and guilt. But sometimes—due to instinct, character, spirit, call it what you will—we overcome them and make the only decent choice.

Jackie had been feeling desperately lonely, hoping against hope that she would accidentally run into her old boyfriend. She came from a childhood of threats, name-calling, physical abuse, and here was this guy who treated her really well.

So why, I asked, had she broken up with him? Well, there was this one little problem: He had tried to molest her daughter. She'd actually called the police and had him arrested. Now that her daughter had turned eighteen and gone off on her own, Jackie kept fantasizing about readmitting him to her life. You can imagine how I felt about that!

DR. LAURA: Jackie, he is obviously a manipulative creep who makes people feel a certain way so that he can use them. It's typical of pedophiles to schmooze up the mother to get to the kid.

JACKIE: So he picked me because I had a young daughter.

DR. LAURA: That and because you were vulnerable to hearing those nice things. Because without outward approval, you don't feel special or worthwhile. That's the perspective you've got to change, and it's not done through another person—it's done through you.

JACKIE: How?

DR. LAURA: What have you done lately that gives you the most self-pride? Here's one very important thing. I want to tell you that what you did, putting aside your own "sense of security" to protect your child, is truly noble. I've been a therapist for a very long time, and you want to know how many "kids" I've spoken to whose mother made the opposite decision?

JACKIE: No.

DR. LAURA: Don't even ask. But to talk to a woman like you, who was so hurt, so vulnerable, so needy, who still did the right thing—I am very impressed. And I don't think you are appreciating what a thing you did.

JACKIE: I couldn't have lived with myself.

DR. LAURA: And that's real quality of character and courage. So somebody who is going to accept you for what you are—man, you better make sure the next guy knows the quality that he has to live up to in order to be in your life.

JACKIE: That's so nice to hear.

DR. LAURA: My friend, you need to take on challenges you can respect yourself for, in which you come to realize how much you—and others—can count on you. Give it your best. You are already a special lady—you just need to know it better. Call me again.

JACKIE: Oh, thank you.

NEVER BE DETERRED BY FEAR OF BLAME

Don't kid yourselves, mothers, that your children will accept or forgive your weakness or selfishness in not protecting them. Don't kid yourselves, mothers, into thinking that they will see him as more of a bad guy than you—as the cases you've just read about confirm, as well as this next one.

PERMITTING EQUALS CULPABILITY

I was gripped by this news story from the *Los Angeles Times:*

Zelaya's fifteen-year-old daughter, Flora, had been killed while walking the railroad tracks with her sixteen-year-old boyfriend. Did they commit suicide together? No one knows. Zelaya says, "I just know she didn't do it, she was a good girl." Here's something about the good girl's bad life:

Flora was placed in foster care two years before her death, when she was thirteen, after disclosing that her stepfather had been tying her to a chair and forcing her to have sexual intercourse with him since she was five years old. The stepfather was convicted of three counts of felony child sexual abuse and sentenced in August 1991 to fifteen years in state prison, according to the Los Angeles County district attorney's office.

Zelaya had admitted that her husband frequently beat her and her three children, including Flora, with the flat side of a knife, his fists, and the hose of a vacuum cleaner. But she said she had no idea he was sexually abusing her daughter until Flora went to school officials and told them her stepfather made advances toward her seven-year-old stepsister. According to Zelaya, Flora blamed *her* for failing to stop the abuse, and she chose to stay in foster care.

I will never understand why the mother was not brought up on charges of child endangerment for permitting the physical abuse—about which she admits to knowing.

I realize that some of you are now really upset with me for the word *permitting*. The stepfather is the actual perpetrator of the beatings and sexual abuse. If he was the perpetrator, the mother was the one who allowed him to act. She became the permitter.

WOUNDED CINDERELLAS, WICKED STEPFATHERS

We know that people who have been abused as children may tend in some manner to perpetuate that behavior with their own children. Abused boys can grow up to be abusers. Through denial, fear of loneliness, or romantic relationships with men that are really morbid attachments, abused girls may grow up to be permitters of abuse. Hence the many wounded Cinderellas bonded to wicked stepfathers whose stories fill these pages. But self-pity is simply no excuse for allowing children to be harmed!

None of us can eliminate the reality of evil, but we can, as women, avoid inviting it into our homes and beds and when we've identified it, we can make sure not to keep it there. And certainly, we can avoid letting it hurt our babies.

NURTURE, LOVE, AND PROTECT

Moms, don't let anyone hurt your babies and don't sacrifice your babies to make your man happy or to hold on to fantasies of attachment to an evil parent. Nature has entrusted women with the most wondrous miracle: to be able to bring forth new life. Nurture, love, and protect that life.

Keeping or pleasing a man or sacrificing your babies as a Band-Aid therapy for your own childhood pain is not the fast lane to self-esteem. Valuing and honoring your responsibilities is the express route.

DON'T SETTLE FOR ATTACHMENT

A man who would either suggest or demand you do otherwise is not worth the paper he ought to be smudged on. He certainly does *not* love you. He just wants you there to meet his needs. That he meets yours only means you have some clear-eyed soul-searching to do.

When you're stronger, there are a lot of wonderful men out there. I know. I talk to them every day on the air. So stop being so damn desperate!

The price our children pay is much too great.

For years I have been astonished and saddened with the apparant absence of a mothering instinct. One day, I confronted this issue—not as a therapist but as a woman and a mother. I came close to having my head smashed.

My husband, our two-and-a-half-year-old son, Deryk, and I were having a small weekend vacation in beautiful San Diego. We heard of a lovely restaurant, which was a bit nicer than your usual family-style place. We ordered our dinners. I could hardly wait for my salmon, and Deryk was having a ball decimating crackers and breadsticks. (If he's happy, he's relatively quiet.)

It had been a long day, and we were all pooped, so we weren't chatting much. I was lazily looking around the room, people-watching. A family came in and sat down at the round table next to ours. The dad was very tall, a big strong, handsome type with a crew cut. He looked military. His wife was a soft type, brownish-blond hair, print dress. There were two children, a small boy and a girl around eight or nine. Mom and Dad sat at opposite sides of the table, and the boy picked another middle chair while the girl hovered anxiously close to Mom. I heard the girl gently whining to sit next to Mom. Mom didn't say anything. Dad demanded, gruffly, that she sit at the chair to his right, far from Mom. The little girl insisted. He became more stern. Mom sat quietly.

The obviously frightened girl was walking toward me (her dad's seat was back-to-back with mine) to come around him, between us, to take the chair he demanded she go to. As she passed him he reached out and smacked her face sharply with his very large fingers.

My blood pressure spontaneously went up so high my eyeballs nearly became projectiles.

I could not let this go.

I immediately said to him, "How could you do that? How could you hurt her like that? All she wanted to do was sit with her Mom—and now I know why!"

Now it was his turn at boiling blood.

He rose up and started to curse and threaten me with bodily harm.

That he was a complete jerk was readily obvious. It didn't seem to me that there was any point in talking to him without a bodyguard.

I turned to Mom. Frankly, I was more angry with her. And I said, "He's just a jerk, but how can you let anyone, any man, hurt your babies? These children came from your body—how can you let him hurt them?"

She sat there dumbly while he raged on at me. Then she began to mumble something about, "He didn't really hit her that hard."

I came back with "What difference does that make?"

At this point the manager of the restaurant came over, having witnessed the entire event also, and asked them all to leave. It seemed other patrons had observed this family as I did and had commented too.

They left.

The manager conveyed his approval and that of other patrons.

I was so upset I could barely eat my dinner.

When I went back on the air that Monday, I described the situation to the audience and asked for feedback about my actions. Many people were concerned that this would cause the father to escalate later and said I should have kept out of it.

I suppose that is possible. Perhaps it's also possible that the public outcry may have validated the mom's feelings that her husband's behavior wasn't right, and may have given her the strength to do something about it.

At least, I hope so.

The question is: If a mother isn't going to protect her children, should we simply stand by? Where does our responsibility for preventing abuse begin and end? Naturally, there's no cut-and-dried answer, but I have to tell you, I'd intervene again if the occasion arose!

This whole issue of intervention is one I contemplate often. I hope you will too.

9 Stupid Helplessness

"OH, I ALWAYS WHINE AND WHIMPER WHEN I'M ANGRY."

Girl babies know when they're angry. And they have no problem letting anyone around them know that they're angry. So what happens when they grow up to be women and are confronted with a righteous motivation for anger?

Well, mostly self-doubt, whining, whimpering, self-blame, depression, confusion, and lots of other stuff, which has nothing to do with taking on the problem with any objectivity or courage.

FRIGHTENED BY THE FLAMES

Is this because women really don't recognize their own righteous anger? No, I don't think so. When I've probed, nagged, challenged, and nagged some more, I've gotten to the reality of the anger. The main problem is that women are too scared about the ramifications of expressing anger. So they "do" oblivious, confused, hurt, or depressed instead.

Take, for instance, this letter from a twenty-eight-year-old caller who is planning to marry after a year-and-a-half engagement:

Most things in our relationship seem good except I was wondering about the following: We have good sex. He usually ejaculates too quickly. I usually satisfy myself. He says our sex is great, but he just likes to ejaculate again, so he watches lesbian videos after I go to sleep. He masturbates at least once a day. We make love 2–3 times a week. He has called 1-900-SEX and not told me. Is this behavior good? What could this mean? Help please!

There is so much that is sad about this letter, as well as the sadness it expresses. For example, "Most things in our relationship seem good." Does that convey so much as an atom of enthusiasm? It is such a qualified endorsement. Then, "He usually ejaculates too quickly. I usually satisfy myself." Does it sound as if he's interested in her? No! Just in orgasms—preferably nonpersonal. This is not a guy with a Ph.D. in intimacy.

So she knows she's unhappy and has probably toyed with being angry, but she doesn't do it. Instead, she intellectually wonders what it all means. That indicates that if anyone, especially her fiancé, gives her an apparently reasonable explanation that validates his behavior, she will stuff her feelings of hurt, rage, and dissatisfaction.

Will she then invalidate her own feelings of disgust and perceptions of his selfishness and sorrow over the true lack of reciprocal caring and intimacy? Probably.

WOMEN EXPERIENCE HURT INSTEAD OF ANGER

The central issue here, as I've said, is that women frequently experience hurt when they should be expressing anger. And as long as they are hurt, they don't take any active steps in redressing, improving, or escaping from a bad situation.

HURT MAKES YOU POWERLESS

Hurt is, of course, injury or damage. For our discussion, it is not about a skinned knee or an overworked muscle; it is about emotional pain. The injury is psychic rather than physical. We are hurt by the behaviors of others that are not what we expected or feel entitled to or that demonstrate a lack of caring for us. Hurt obviously indicates a significant degree of emotional involvement and highlights our need, healthy or not, for the other person.

ANGER IS ENERGY

Anger is about extreme displeasure, hostility, and indignation. Our anger can have many faces: irritation, annoyance, resentment, rage, and fury. No matter the face, the common denominator is energy.

DEPRESSION: THE ABSENCE OF SELF-DEFENSE

When we—or the order in our little world—are threatened, we react with anxiety or anger. These are internal mechanisms that help us mobilize to protect, defend, and reestablish our sense of safety and control. In the absence of self-defense, there is depression.

In depression we simply come to accept a situation in a passive-submissive way. It is far healthier to rise up against the injustice and demand redress or change. It is far healthier to walk out in the face of prolonged lack of redress or change.

LEARNING TO ACT ON RIGHTEOUS ANGER

Although healthier, it is not necessarily typical female behavior to get in touch with your strongest feelings.

I was struck by the caller Judy's sadness as soon as she began speaking. In a voice tinged with sorrow, she described a situation that would create turmoil in anyone. About three years previously, when she was in her mid-forties, she had confronted her father with the fact that he had abused her as a child, and he had admitted it. Subsequently, though, he recanted, claiming she was making up the entire experience. And her mother sided with good old Dad.

At that point, Judy had requested that her husband sever all connections with his father-in-law, and it seemed he had—until Judy discovered they had recently spent time together. Now she was feeling "very depressed and down" about things. Depressed and down—but not angry? When I suggested that too often women substitute depression for anger, she agreed she did feel some anger, too.

JUDY (NOW WEEPING OPENLY): I've told my husband before that I think it's betrayal, him seeing my dad.

DR. LAURA: But, Judy, you feel it and you think it and you've told him, and he does it anyway. And the reason you went into depression is so you wouldn't have to face that. Right?

JUDY: That's true. That's true.

DR. LAURA: Well, enough of this depression. You've suffered enough. Do not acquiesce to other people's selfishness!

JUDY: Okay. How do I . . .

DR. LAURA: Well, you could start by telling your husband that he's loyal to one or the other, and he'd better choose right now or he is out. . . . I have a feeling that the disloyalty in this one episode is not something out of the clouds.

JUDY: No, it's not.

DR. LAURA: Okay, Judy. This is a form of abuse, in my opinion.

JUDY: Right.

DR. LAURA: So sit up straight! No more depression!

JUDY: (laughs)

DR. LAURA: Judy, your anger is righteous. It is real, valid, justified. Act out on it . . . and I don't mean you pop him on the head.

JUDY: (laughs)

DR. LAURA: You tell him to choose—or he's history. And I'm sorry about your mom and dad, but not all eggs and sperm come from people with the honor and integrity and courage to really be parents.

JUDY: It's just like—you still want their love.

DR. LAURA: Forget it! They don't have lovingness to give—except toward themselves, if you can call it that.

JUDY: Right. Okay.

DR. LAURA: So, no more depression. Say, "Laura, I'm angry."

JUDY: Laura—I'm angry!

DR. LAURA: Hooray!

THE PASSIVE-SUBMISSIVE PERSONALITY

The ultimate sadness for me is to hear how people refuse to stop trying to get love and approval from bloodsucking, slime-producing, im(or a-)moral, insensitive, unloving, uncaring, self-centered, disgusting sperm and egg donors (aka lousy parents). And the all-too-typical next step, after you're weaned and out of the nest, is to continue that hopeless crusade through a very similar spouse, which is a new, warped definition of *normal.*

That's when I get mail like the following from a fifty-year-old woman whose husband has been blatantly fooling around with a next-door neighbor for eight years!: "I went to three psychologists and two self-help groups trying to fix why I was so paranoid about this arrangement my husband had . . ."

That is an all-too-typical scenario for women: Blame yourself. It's safer, frankly, than putting the blame where it belongs and risking intimacy and vulnerability with healthy people. It's easier, it is believed, than fighting through the fear, pain, and loss to become healthier inside yourself.

DESPERATE ATTACHMENT

In addition to the safety of the passive-submission technique of not risking the pain of change or loss, there is another important explanation to the "it must be me" syndrome of handling someone else's inappropriate behaviors: Sometimes too much of a woman's identity, like that of a child's, comes from a desperate attachment to a male. That means *his* actions are inexorably connected to *her* self-worth.

Sue's boyfriend also calls the X-rated 900 sex lines, and it's making her feel just terrible—about herself.

DR. LAURA: Now, instead of going, "Oh, is there something wrong with me?," I want you to stand back and ask yourself, "My gosh, do I want a guy who does this? Yuck. Do I want this guy to father my babies?" Now, why do you think you went immediately into the "What's wrong with me?" mode?

SUE: Because . . . well . . . I always think it's me that's wrong.

DR. LAURA: You are really not answering the question. Your reaction is always "What's wrong with me?" I'll tell you, Sue, what's wrong with you. You are so desperate to be wanted by a guy that you almost don't even care what kind of a guy he is as long as he wants you. You are not choosing. You are sitting there hoping to be chosen.

SUE: Yes.

DR. LAURA: That's the problem. You are too needy of the attachment.

SUE: Okay.

DR. LAURA: An independent person would have stood back and said, "What a jerk."

SUE: Right.

DR. LAURA: Confronting him about the phone sex is an entire waste of your time. I wouldn't bother doing it. You simply have to say, "I am a mature woman and I have respect for myself." (You might have to fib a little here, Sue . . .)

SUE: (laughs)

DR. LAURA: . . . That's good practice. "Do I want a man who engages in these kinds of behaviors—do I want it? Regardless of whether he wants me—do I want this kind of man?" And then, Sue, you answer that question. That is what an independent, mature woman would do right now. You have the opportunity to be one of those.

SUE: Okay, got it!

GOING ON OFFENSE

Have you noticed how women jump right into the defensive position? If you got into the offensive position, your man would probably know he had someone of quality to contend with. That's assuming he is up for that kind of challenge. Granted, I can't promise you a 100 percent success rate, but I can assure you that the more you practice self-assertiveness, the more natural it becomes.

My caller Sylvia claimed "to have a pattern of getting my hopes set on men who hurt and disappoint me," and she gave me the following example: About a week earlier, she had phoned a man she had first met through her church but whom she hadn't seen in a while. They had a habit of going to lunch after services, so when he said, "I'll see you in church," she figured that meant lunch. But when Sunday arrived, he was there with another woman.

DR. LAURA: Sylvia, you just assumed something. And hopes, dreams, and fantasies have no power. If you want something, you must be willing to express it.

SYLVIA: Yes, I realize that.

DR. LAURA: I'm not sure you do. Because when you say "disappointments," there is a difference between somebody's being concretely disloyal and his not having the vaguest idea what is in your head.

SYLVIA: It does make me see that I've done this before. How do I break this pattern?

DR. LAURA: You say, "I'd really like to be with you in church and go to lunch like we used to." And then he would have to say that he'd like that or that he can't due to a prior engagement or that he's got a new honey or whatever. But you have to say what you want, think, need, feel. You have to be willing to do that.

SYLVIA: I know that this is the nineties and women have permission to do this now. And I have taken the initiative in this relationship more than he has. So I think I have gotten the message that he is just not that interested.

DR. LAURA: Well, you know, not everybody has great taste!

SYLVIA: (laughs) You're nice!

DR. LAURA: Let's hold out for one who does and let's be real clear as to who Sylvia is and what she would like. You have to be assertive in your own life, my honey.

SYLVIA: Okay, I'm trying to learn that more and more all the time! Thank you.

And that's just about a date. Sometimes it is about a whole marriage.

FAMILY FEUD

Lee called me in tears over a family matter. It seems she and her husband had started their own business a few years earlier, and at her husband's insistence, his brother and sister-in-law were hired on the assumption that eventually there might be a second store, which they could manage. And it hadn't worked out—in spades. Not only did the couple have to be let go because of their incompetence, it subsequently turned out that they had embezzled money from the business—although Lee and her husband had decided not to prosecute, for the sake of the family. Now Lee was going to be forced to attend a family Easter celebration with "those people who have hurt us."

I wondered if *hurt* was really the word. It wasn't. She was furious. Furious because she'd been against hiring the in-laws initially but her husband had insisted. Furious that they were able to screw her over, and she'd been too wimpy or careful or timid to handle it up front.

"I'm not sure which it is," I told her, "hurt that they screwed you or anger that you feel powerless to do anything about it because you're afraid to cross your husband." I advised Lee to do something active in terms of confronting them, if only to demand a family mediation session. Because staying in a one-down position wears on you—whether it's with people who betray your trust or husbands who make the decisions regardless of your own feelings and intuitions.

SUPPRESSED ANGER KILLS

According to an article in the *Medical Tribune News Service,* "Suppressed anger may increase the risk of death from heart disease or cancer. Married women who suppress their anger are at the greatest risk of premature death. For wives and women there is a direct relationship between suppressed anger and mortality, more so than for men."

And women do suppress their anger—out of worry about direct confrontations or negative exchanges, about not seeming nice or feminine. You worry about rejection and criticism. You worry so much that instead of showing righteous anger you cry, act injured, sulk, get depressed, exact small, nasty, subtle revenges, and generally suffer. And, according to the above study, get sick and die.

THE ORIGINS OF TIMIDITY

Alicia, forty-seven, is a successful businesswoman, but she has one trait that makes her feel bad about herself: She doesn't "have the courage to tell people what to do." She was even afraid to tell her cleaning lady to park in an alternative space so that Alicia could park in her own garage space. Why? "I would end up feeling very guilty for hurting her feelings," she said.

I told Alicia that she was not "five years old any longer. Your parents are not going to keep your allowance and put you in your room without supper. You see, you are talking from the vantage point of a little girl whose welfare is totally dependent on the goodwill of her parents. Now you are a grown woman, and other people have to count on your goodwill. It now goes two ways. And you haven't updated yourself to the adult stage of this. In your mind you are still the five-year-old girl who is afraid of getting Mommy and Daddy ticked off!"

LOSS OF PARENTAL ATTACHMENT: A CRIPPLING FEAR

And that is just where it is. Women get afraid of hurting people, because people will get mad—and if people get mad, people will reject or punish. And all will be lost! You will be lost!

While I feel and believe that the special affinity women have for relationships and attachments is lovely, too much of a good thing can be bad. When women are afraid of losing any attachment, no matter how insignificant (I know a good cleaning person is hard to find) or dangerous or destructive or unfulfilling—it's gone too far.

And that goes for relationships with parents, too.

As a matter of fact, that's where it all begins. And when it doesn't end well there, it can go on forever.

Theresa, my twenty-seven-year-old caller, was fear personified. She was so frightened, she wasn't even making sense—at first. Once she settled down, I learned she still felt guilty about leaving home to go to college against her parents' wishes and never returning on a permanent basis. Still, she was close to her family and deeply aggrieved (and guilt-ridden) by the recent death of her dad. Theresa had a good job, with potential, and was living with somebody. The somebody turned out to be the problem. She'd started dating him—probably, she suggested, as "a crutch"— around the time of her father's death. Now he was pushing for marriage, but his insecurity and extreme dependence on her put Theresa off.

DR. LAURA: You don't sound like you want to marry him. In fact, you sound like you'd rather he just go away.

THERESA: (laughs) But he is so dependent on me.

DR. LAURA: Like your parents—your family is, too!

THERESA: Yeah, I suppose.

DR. LAURA: Yeah, so you've had all these people pulling on you for their needs—their needs—and you feel guilty wanting and putting yours first. Your punishment for leaving home—your father dying—is getting yourself stuck with this guy who is just like your family!

THERESA: Yeah, I suppose.

DR. LAURA: Why don't you finally be definitive?

THERESA: Yeah, I guess.

DR. LAURA: If you would permit yourself the luxury of being honest right now.

THERESA: All right! I want this guy out! I don't want to hurt him.

DR. LAURA: Theresa, there is no life without pain—and the experience and the survival of pain are often the price of growth.

THERESA: Right.

DR. LAURA: And the measure of you as a valuable, lovable person is not that you don't cause pain. There is a difference between intentional viciousness and the pain others quite reasonably feel when they don't necessarily get their own way—or have to face their own weaknesses. That is just a normal part of life—a necessary hurt.

THERESA: So what do I tell him?

DR. LAURA: That you regret not sharing his desire for commitment and marriage—and the relationship is over. I think you are basically afraid to have your own desires put into action lest you be seen as bitchy or selfish.

THERESA: That's what I've always been called when I do it.

DR. LAURA: Not by me!

THERESA: Okay.

DR. LAURA: I hereby give you, Theresa, twenty-seven years old, who has struggled these many years, permission to assert your individuality, to make the decisions that you wish. You will be more of a giving person if you are in a place where you really want to give. The kind of giving you are doing now is acquiescence, not giving.

THERESA: You're right, thank you.

INCLUDING YOURSELF IN THE EQUATION

There is a big difference between cooperation out of respect and submission out of fear of rejection. Women need to believe—or, until that point, just take as a given—that they, like every other human being (including parents, siblings, spouses, friends), may assume the privilege and power to be a unique individual in their own right. This doesn't mean eternally running rough-shod over others; but it *does* mean including yourself in the equation—and not as a leftover, a byproduct!

So that when people take outrageous liberties, when they betray trusts, when they display ongoing total disregard for your welfare, when they use and abuse you without remorse, when they refuse to accept responsibility for any of the pain and devastation you suffer—please don't just sit there and eat, drink, take drugs, sleep, or work yourself to death to avoid the reality that they don't care.

DOWN WITH "THE BENEFIT OF THE DOUBT"!

It is so painful to witness this denial and pale attempt at giving other people the worn-out benefit of the doubt. Is it really that you are not getting through due to bad syntax? Is it that your voice is modulated too low? Is it that his hearing is damaged and he can't hear female higher-pitched sounds? No! No! No! It is that he doesn't care and he knows he can get away with it!

NEVER AGAIN!

That's where anger becomes important! It sets limits, it puts the other on notice that there are consequences, it says, "Never again."

You must give up the illusion that service to the dominating needs of others brings love. The fantasy of winning approval or love through long-suffering toleration of others' single-minded self-centeredness doesn't bring in the love of others. And it promotes the hate of self.

COURAGE: THE INSTANT CURE

We misplace the anger when we are afraid of seeming inadequate by showing our hurt or vulnerabilities, when we are afraid of anger, disapproval, or punishment. The instant cure is to use your courage to speak up directly and find, to your long-term, infinite pleasure, that you can and will live through it!

WHEN ANGER DOESN'T BELONG

Having said all that, I admit anger isn't always righteous. It can be inappropriate, invalid, wasted, or misdirected—even sought after.

SETTING YOURSELF UP TO BE MAD

Yes! Much too often, women—due to the "I am attached, therefore I exist" utterly nutty romantic concept—actually set themselves up for hurt and anger in their relationships with men.

For instance, showing interest in all his things as a way to catch him. But then, what have you got? A partner? A friend with mutual interests and respect? No way. Then you spend the next twenty years being mad at him because you feel like your interests don't count.

As I've been saying in chapter after chapter, women tend to make a relationship their life, their identity, while men make it a part of their lives. So women are constantly angry at men for not being caring and intimate.

Recently, a caller described herself as "melancholy, nurturing, caring, and sacrificing," and described her man succinctly as "self-centered." Not an uncommon complaint. I asked her if he could also be described as "energetic, involved, active, outgoing," and she answered in the affirmative.

Women, fearful of risk, often pick such men to attach to in order to complete themselves from the outside. Through him, the woman vicariously experiences the qualities she dares not risk. The problem comes when she later vilifies the man for the same qualities that initially attracted her.

There are no two ways around it: Women must have more dimension in their lives than "loooove!"

INVALID ANGER

Remember Janine, who had asked her husband to lie outside with her on the grass and watch the stars? He suggested instead that they watch TV together. She called me because she was "terribly hurt by his rejection." I asked if he had ever been the laid-back or romantic type. She said, "No, but . . ." (I always stop women at the *but,* because it is just an attempt to erase the full realization of the answer: No.) I told her that she married a wonderful elephant and was now irked that he wasn't a kitty cat, purring in her lap. No fair!

That's not an unusual scenario for what I call invalid hurt. Here's another:

GIFTS WITH STRINGS ATTACHED

Vicky, twenty-five, has been married for three years and feels something has changed about her husband's unconditional love for her since she became his wife. "Before," she tells me, "he used to appreciate me. I don't feel he does anymore. . . . Every time I try to do something nice for him there is always, instead of thank you, some kind of negative." She claims she's afraid to do things for him for fear of doing them wrong and making him angry. Now comes the killer example!

In the process of making chicken soup, Vicky asked her husband if he wanted the skin left on. He said he didn't know. But she persevered and nagged and nagged—until he finally started to scream, "I don't care." "I would have screamed at you, too. Nobody likes to be nagged," I tell her, before giving my interpretation of the situation.

Granted, this guy could be a complete S.O.B., in which case Vicky should lose him, but here's what's more likely behind his actions. There is a notion about doing things for someone as a gift and doing things for someone to entice or manipulate him into seeing you in a certain way or behaving in return in a certain way to fill you up. It is a seduction, not a gift. It is a manipulation, not a gift.

THE TELLTALE IMBALANCE

If, over a period of time, a man feels as if you are not really giving but that you are trying to manipulate him into changing or doing something you want, he is going to get more and more resentful. Vicky's husband may be gaining resentment over her behavior. Either that is a valid part of what is going on—or he is a creep.

Either way, the doing-for and buying are certainly indirect ways of asking for something. It is out of our vulnerabilities and weaknesses that we treat others in ways we call giving, and then watch, perplexed, as the recipients' resentment and annoyance mount. That is the telltale imbalance that leads me to say that Vicky's husband is not registering what she is doing as giving but as her attempt to get something in this indirect way, which always leaves him feeling inadequate to meet her demands.

STACKING THE DECK

Jicka, twenty-four, is suffering from the same syndrome. She called to ask how one recovers from being cheated on. She said that her boyfriend had a date, probably sex. I asked many questions, and here's what I learned: They have no spoken agreement for a commitment or even sexual monogamy. In fact, she has made it clear to him on innumerable occasions that she has no intention of marrying him (defensive fib).

When I suggested that cheating in these circumstances was not possible, she was shocked by my answer. She had really hoped to get complete loyalty and fidelity, giving nothing back but guarded distance! Then he proved her worst fears about men: They can't be trusted! Talk about a stacked deck of cards! Talk about testing under totally unfair parameters.

HURT REACTIONS

These are some examples of unfair, inappropriate hurt reactions—which are not hurts in-the-now but reverberations of attitudes and hurts from the past superimposed on unsuspecting subjects.

Inappropriate Anger

Anger can be inappropriate or unfair. Lisa, twenty-five, has been in a seventy-five-mile long-term relationship with her boyfriend for two years. He doesn't want them to move in together and he is not ready for marriage. He enjoys their relationship and has been up-front about his feelings and intent. And Lisa is angry.

I suggested that if he were being evil, cruel, manipulative, devious, or whatever, her anger would be appropriate. As it was, she didn't have the right to anger, since he'd been honest all along. Disappointment would be more appropriate.

In point of fact, Lisa's not really angry with him, she's feeling unfulfilled as a person and imagines that marriage will fix that for her. Therefore, his resistance stands in the way of her fulfillment, safety, identity. So she is livid!

I suggested that her anger toward him ought to be redirected toward her own personal growth. Such a lot of repressed anger, when used to fuel personal growth, could give her the energy to do some really spectacular achieving.

Wasted Anger

Belinda, forty, has been married for twenty-two years and has three kids, six, fifteen, and twenty-one. Since 1988, her husband has been romantically involved with another woman. When Belinda found out about the affair, he didn't apologize for the incident but "only said he was sorry that I got hurt." Even now, every three months or so, the woman's phone number shows up on Belinda's bill. "I feel like he's doing this on purpose," she insists, "to punish me for whatever."

DR. LAURA: Now, that's interesting—for punishment. I think he's doing it because he simply wants to, and he can do it and get away with it.

BELINDA: And I don't want him to be able to do that anymore.

DR. LAURA: What are your alternatives?

BELINDA: I have children, and, um . . . stay or get out.

DR. LAURA: That's right. You're not going to change him; he's not willing.

BELINDA: No, he isn't.

DR. LAURA: So if you want or feel you need to stay, say to yourself, "Self, I'm making a choice to stay for the security of the kids." And then get off the case.

BELINDA: Dismiss it?

DR. LAURA: Well, if you are determined to stay for the security of the family, you might as well accept it. Understand that you are making a choice and a sacrifice—we all have to make 'em in life. When you make them, you have to truly accept them. And you still haven't accepted the choice you've made, because it is the one-down position of no power. I understand that. You are trying to change him instead—forget that. But do use condoms if you continue to have sex with him.

BELINDA: Thank you, Dr. Laura.

Mind you, I am certainly not condoning this man's behavior—I'm trying to save Belinda from a heart attack. And sometimes, when women *really* settle down with the reality of their predicament, they choose *not* to settle for the predicament. Instead, they become more motivated to do something about it. But not when the anger is misplaced.

Misplaced Anger

Sally is five months pregnant and also has a toddler in the house. She called because she is being "so bitchy" to her husband. She wants to know why. First she says, "Everything is just fine." It took me a while to get to: "Well, I'm tired all the time, we're not having fun like we used to, there seems to be so little time for affection and sex."

She is certainly feeling the weight of parental responsibilities and is not dealing directly with the changing needs of her life and how they are colliding with her personal needs. Women often don't like to admit they can't "handle it all." So they act bitchy.

I asked Sally to talk to her husband directly about the fears, the losses, the worries, all of it—and I was certain she would find he shares the very same feelings.

WHY HISTORY REPEATS ITSELF

To recap: Our early childhood attachments, love, and nurturing experiences will teach that we are lovable and that emotional attachments are generally safe and rewarding—or the opposite. If it is the opposite, then we come to expect such things as hurt, loss, betrayal. When we are in that mode, it is amazing how history seems to repeat itself with future adult relationships. And we are constantly hurt. The anger that might have seemed so appropriate to the situation is squelched by the incredible self-doubts, which lead us to feel we have no right to anger—we just aren't worth it.

AMEN

Yet the only way to become worth it in our own lives is to believe in some kind of universal inalienable right to respect, honor, commitment, caring, and love—and then to earn it in our own minds by our courageous efforts in our own behalf in just about every aspect of our lives: work, relationships, and love. Brave choices. Brave actions. Self-esteem earned. Amen.

I want to leave you with the story of Judy, twenty-eight, who is humongously off the mark when it comes to what to be angry about.

She just found out her fiancé has a five-year-old child whom he doesn't see or support financially. Judy is angry that "the relationship can't be that close if he didn't trust me to tell me." I suggested that if she were planning to make babies with him, she ought to be more concerned that he did nothing to fulfill his parental obligations and responsibilities in an honorable way.

She seemed not to react much to that. She was more concerned about her security within the relationship than with noticing the quality of her future husband.

Oh well.

10 Stupid Forgiving

"I KNOW HE'S ADULTEROUS, ADDICTED, CONTROLLING, INSENSITIVE, AND VIOLENT . . . BUT OTHER THAN THAT . . ."

Have you ever noticed how motionless a praying mantis remains, no matter what is going on around it? The only creature capable of equaling that limitless patience and tolerance is the human female—who will invent millions of excuses to avoid getting out of the way of an oncoming bad relationship or permanently escaping from one in which she's already ensconced.

These excuses encompass protestations of practicality and unselfish love, obligation and commitment. Since they are all lofty ideals, they make a good defense.

If you have the courage to dig a bit deeper, you'll find fear, self-doubt, avoidance of discomfort, and ingrained habituated patterns of relating that have been in place since your childhood family dynamics.

THE PRACTICALITY PLOY

Let's start by exploring practicality. Anita called to talk about the balancing act she was attempting to pull off between her pot-smoking husband and the ex-husband with whom she has sex now and then. We discussed the alternatives of personal as well as marital therapy, status quo, or leaving. She didn't like any of those. She had a million reasons why she couldn't/wouldn't change any part of or the whole situation.

A few weeks later an articulate, heartbreaking—and clarifying—letter arrived from her. In it, she explained that she had married her "not-so-good" second husband, the pot smoker, so that her kids could have a full-time mom as well as a dad who provided for them. She stayed with the doper because "a loaded dad is better than no dad at all." If, at this point, you think you're experiencing a sense of déjà vu, relax; the "any dad will do" excuse is one of the major themes you've read about in this book.

She agreed I was right when I told her she needed to find a sense of purpose, but claimed she just wanted to be a good mommy to her girls. Then she continued:

> I've wanted them to have what I didn't have—parental attention, a family home life, some new clothes once in a while, a decent car and house, help with homework, socializing—just the normal things a kid deserves. I am perfectly capable of going out into the world and getting a decent job, but I like being a homemaker.
>
> I am not expecting my ex-husband to rescue me. I think, rather, we are both rescuing each other from a loveless life—even if it is only for a few hours a month. It is a sad thing to live without loving. Sometimes you (ME!) seem to disregard the realities of life and its complications.
>
> For those of you who have done things in the proper order (education first, then career, and children later), the world may not seem so frightening. For those of us who must face the future with many hearts depending on us and being ill-equipped and knowing it, the choices are not so simple. Anita.

I realize that such a letter could make a houseplant weep. Luckily, I'm a totally heartless and cruel therapist who only wants people to get better and be happy, so I wasn't about to fall for it.

UNWILLING TO CHANGE

Basically, Anita isn't being honest with herself. Granted, she wants things to be different in her situation so that she can be more content. But—now comes the "hook"—she is totally unwilling to change anything. Oh, of course, there are excuses and rationalizations, but what it all adds up to is "How do I change this without touching it?" But why?

As I have said at many a counselor training session and civilian speaking engagement, most of our problems don't come from being stupid or insane but from our attempts to solve other problems. It's just that the side effects of such solutions are immobility, frustration, and unhappiness. By now we've built a house of cards. If we remove the bent card, which obviously has to go, the whole structure might collapse. So we stay and feel stuck.

TRYING TO SOLVE THAT OTHER PROBLEM

The situation Anita actually wanted to resolve had less to do with her children's welfare than with her own unhappy, apparently isolated childhood. So she made babies with a fellow who invoked her parents' emotional distance, then sacrificed for the kids in exactly the way she wished her mom and dad had done for her.

That may seem to benefit the kids, but it's sure not good for her.

MAKING PEACE WITH YOUR TRADE-OFFS

For everything there is a price. Your sanity and inner peace come from recognizing, accepting, and paying that price. Therefore, my advice to Anita is this:

You must make peace with your choices and trade-offs. A change in attitude can mark a change in happiness—and this attitudinal change is your only option if you're unwilling to change anything else about the situation.

There are times when such trade-offs—staying in a not-so-good situation for reasons—will be your choice. The point is that you need to make the choice consciously and maturely. If you don't, you leave yourself open to disappointment, frustration, anger, and hurt.

In which case, you are not a victim, you are a volunteer who is not behaving maturely.

CHANGE OR SHUT UP!

Generally, women resent and resist the idea of acknowledging up front what you are in reality accepting and putting up with anyway! Do you think constant protestations of victimization and unhappiness absolve you of responsibility for your choices? Do you think if you complain or whine loud or long enough, things will change all by themselves?

Forget about it!

RECYCLING IS ABOUT GARBAGE

Liz, thirty-nine, has been in what she considers a relationship with a fellow for six years. They have a four-year-old daughter—or, rather, she does, because he split right after that fertilization. Liz is both resentful and confused because the man repeatedly comes in and goes out of her life for sex, money, a roof over his head, some attention, whatever, and then slides right out again when someone or something else more interesting comes along.

Talk about a commitment to recycling!

Liz expressed so much annoyance and confusion at his most recent vanishing episode that I was shocked. Why, I asked her, was she was so "surprised that a gorilla was eating another banana?"

How blinded by fantasy can you be! Get real, girl!

WHEN NOT CHOOSING IS EASIER

Of course, it is the facing of reality that causes the most fear and pain. And sometimes, not choosing is easier than changing. To avoid the pain, you've got to do something: anger, drugs, food, affairs, depression, physical illness, toying with suicide, perpetual recovery groups—something!

However, the real challenge is confronting the realities within you.

ENSURING YOU DON'T GO BACK

So let's say you do that. You face the music and leave. Now what do you do to ease the pain of the emptiness? You fill it with giving and growth, learning and creating.

Without doing these things, as you will see later in this chapter, you'll probably yearn to go back into that bad relationship situation, repeat it with another guy, sit with sadness and regret and imagine you've probably made a mistake.

SHE LEFT, AND SHE'S STILL MISERABLE

For instance, one woman called me on the air yesterday to say she left a rotten relationship because she thought, "I'd be happier once I left. And I'm not." I told her that she left "to have the opportunity to build happiness."

Leaving is not enough. Happiness is not a given, nor is it automatic. It is hard-earned.

DO I HAVE THE RIGHT TO LEAVE?

Now, if you suspect you are in a bad relationship situation and are playing with the idea of getting out, you may be struggling with the question "Do I have the right not to want to stay?" Like Kay.

Kay is a forty-year-old mental-health professional who is married for the second time—to an alcoholic. Whenever she insists he stop drinking, if only for the sake of his two sons from a previous marriage, he insists she's blackmailing him. At this point, she is serious about giving him an ultimatum and leaving if he refuses to get help, but she feels guilty.

Kay's husband is undermining her resolve by tweaking her typically female sensitivity about hurting others and demanding too much. Mix that in with the anticipated discomfort of change and loss, and you have the formula for questioning your right to leave.

Therein does lie an important key: preexisting self-doubts. In Kay's situation, you have notions of repetitive marital failure, the impact of turning forty, and professional doubts about having used the wrong "technique" on her husband.

IS SOMETHING WRONG WITH ME?

Usually, however, the doubt is more basic: Is something wrong with me? That's what Susan wondered.

Susan got right to the point by saying, "My husband has some sexual desires which I don't like and just won't participate in." These activities—in which he was pressuring her to participate—included group sex and watching him have sex with other women and with men. She knew she was at a crossroads in the relationship and would probably end up leaving. So why had she called? She wanted my reassurance that not giving in to his demands didn't mean she was sexually dysfunctional.

What I told Susan is that the sexual issue was actually not relevant. If she was being urged to do something she felt was wrong for her, she had every right to decline. "Susan," I said, "you are entitled to live the kind of life you want. It simply doesn't matter what he says is normal sex. If you're asking me if there's justification for leaving, well, I'd have to say there's always a case to be made for leaving an uncomfortable and unpleasant situation."

THE SELF-DOUBT COP-OUT

"Slipping someone a mickey" of self-doubt is the way controlling people like Susan's husband exercise much of their power: "You'll never find anyone to love you more than I do"; "If you don't want to have group sex, no man is going to want you"; "You're much too (fill in the blank)"; "You'll drive everyone crazy"; etc.

Sadly, the technique is generally a sure-fire winner when used on women, whose sense of self and value is measured too much from outside acceptance. But there is one plus: If you can make a connection between your need to be controlled and childhood trauma in a therapeutic context, it could be the key to understanding and conquering misplaced shame and guilt.

STAYING PUT DESPITE THE PAIN

Without therapy, those personal early-life losses, and the desire not to repeat them, provoke you to question whether or not you have the right to leave.

When you wonder if you have that right, it's not so absolute a judgment as one might think. It really depends on your baseline, or what seems more normal or expected.

For example, a private patient of mine spoke of being physically abused by her husband. She was well educated and gainfully employed, and I wondered why a woman with no children who was capable of financial autonomy would tolerate this situation for as long as a second. She looked at me through her tears and explained, "Well, he beats me less than my father did. So for me, it is an improvement."

An improvement! How sad a perspective.

Unfortunately, this woman is not the exception. There are countless others who are also not even thinking about leaving—but they should.

IT MUST BE MY FAULT

There is Aurora, who for over three years had been going out with a congenital—not to say pathological—liar. Why did she call? To ask if I thought *he* needed counseling! I observed that he wasn't the one who had called, so he probably didn't feel strongly motivated to change. She, on the other hand, was. But Aurora wasn't really hearing me— until, in answer to her repeated attempts to get me to talk about his problem, I responded sarcastically, "It must be your fault!" Then we started to get somewhere.

DR. LAURA: Aurora, this is an issue of your self-worth.

AURORA (CRYING): That's what I've been told by my family.

DR. LAURA: But you don't listen! You want to make this an issue of what is the matter with your boyfriend? Okay, he is sick. And you are overwhelmed by your fear of being alone, of loneliness. As long as you can worry, forgive, and care-take him, you never have to be alone, you never have to grow, you never have to face your worst inner fears.

AURORA: That's true.

DR. LAURA: He's an excuse and a way you hide from yourself, honey. But you are the one who will pay the price.

AURORA: You are right.

DR. LAURA: And you must believe there is a time coming in your life when you will know how valuable you really are. Right now you don't. I'm going to give you a therapist referral. Interested?

AURORA: Yes, yes I am.

DR. LAURA: Great. But, Aurora, nothing will change until you acknowledge that in your benevolent martyrdom to this man—who will always disappoint you—you are only running away from what can become your greater self. Make that phone call!

AURORA: I will!—thank you, Laura.

TRYING TO AVOID THE INEVITABLE

Carol, twenty-eight, has another motive for not even thinking about leaving—when she should be fleeing for her life! She had been married for ten months to a man she described as "this person." She even had a baby by him. Only after the marriage did she find out that he had, as she described it, "a felony record." When I pressed her, she admitted his offenses included strong-arm robbery, petty theft, and "something where he has to register as a sex offender."

DR. LAURA: What? Carol, you just made a baby with this guy. If he rapes and/or molests, then this child and you or others may be in some kind of danger.

CAROL: Right. Well, he says . . .

DR. LAURA: Whoa. You know, when women say, "He says," I get scared. Because that's usually a woman who doesn't want to think for herself.

CAROL: Yeah.

DR. LAURA: That's a woman who, if he says the right thing, makes believe everything is all better.

CAROL: Yeah, well, I also found out that he lies all the time.

DR. LAURA: Carol, why are you still with this creep?

CAROL: I guess I feel like a failure in my marriage.

DR. LAURA: A failure? Your husband is a blot on society, and you feel like a failure. You made a mistake, Carol. That's not the same thing as failing. Failing is staying with him and risking the welfare of you and your child! Use some objectivity here. Now, Carol, do you want to compound the mistake? Or do you want to get smart and get out?

CAROL: I'd like to get smart and get out.

DR. LAURA: Then do it.

CAROL: I . . . I just don't want to hurt him any more than he has already been hurt.

DR. LAURA: Don't give me "You don't want to hurt his feelings"—he's earned whatever consequences he gets. That is so typically female! No matter what horror he perpetrates, you don't want to hurt his feelings by telling him he's hurting you.

CAROL: I'd have to go to my family in northern California. I'd be taking his son away from him.

DR. LAURA: Carol, this guy is a sex offender, not a pillar of the community. You could well be doing your child a favor, at least for now. And right now what you and the child need is the roof, the food, the support. And you need counseling, with some distance to give you objectivity. Go home! Okay?

CAROL: Okay, Laura.

I must admit, after this call I put my head down on my notebook during the commercial break. This much voluntary blindness was difficult to bear. It isn't anger I feel at calls such as this. It is intense emotional pain. And it is out of that pain that this book was conceived.

STUPID IS AS STUPID DOES

Women, in my opinion, aren't in these predicaments out of stupidity. Remember the title of this book refers to stupid behaviors, not stupid women. Women are more likely to get into these predicaments because of their orientation toward life, which has less to do with inner courage, independence, and individual creativity than it should.

HOW CAN I EVER TRUST HIM AGAIN? I'LL FIND A WAY!

Tammy, twenty-eight, is married to a man who's a repeat offender in the infidelity game. Granted, he straightens up and flies right every once in a while—when Tammy threatens to leave. But she stays put, and he reverts to type. She called because the guy had a job that wasn't within commuting distance, "so he's gone most of the week," she told me mournfully. Clearly, her question for me was "How can I trust him?" And there was no response to that. But what she really wanted me to know was she felt she "had nothing, was nothing."

DR. LAURA: You have yourself. That's not nothing. You forgot that, though, didn't you?

TAMMY: Yeah, I gave that up a long time ago.

DR. LAURA: Well, get it back! You know what you're going to do? You are going to get busy on your life. When you make him your life and you fear losing him—and sit there and say you have nothing—that scares me. He is supposed to be a partner—he is not supposed to be you! You are supposed to be you.

TAMMY: Every time I try to start something, he would do something to undermine me.

DR. LAURA: You have to remember that you are not a slave or indentured servant; you are not owned by him. He is not your father; you are not a minor. You are a grown woman and you make your own decisions. You have to get that back in your mind. You need something of your own to feel good and strong about.

TAMMY: Yeah, that's true, but when I first got out on my own before, I had some bad experiences so I more or less hid behind him.

DR. LAURA: Well, don't take that typical female escape route again, because you only end up losing yourself—totally.

TAMMY: Well, he knows if he fools around again I'm gone.

DR. LAURA: He doesn't have any reason to believe you will.

TAMMY: Yeah, that's true.

DR. LAURA: Now, let's talk about your dreams and your interests. I bet we can get a reality-based game plan going. Okay? . . .

HIDING BEHIND HIM

Hiding behind him. Sad. And bad. Aside from the obvious reasons why, think of the kind of man you get when you pick a hiding place. It's certainly not going to be someone desiring an equal, open, mutually respecting relationship—is it? No, of course not. You'll end up with someone who gets off on being one-up.

And the behavior of a "one-up" type is not going to feel that good to you on the receiving end. You do not have any bargaining power at all, because you are so inappropriately dependent. At those times, you have to accept the trade-off.

ISN'T IT HIS MOVE?

Ann, fifty-five, has been married almost three decades. She's always suspected his affairs, but unfortunately, now she has concrete evidence. The pretense of all these years is not so easy for her to maintain—it is just getting too blatant. So she tries to salvage by asking, "Well, doesn't it mean he loves me if he hasn't asked for a divorce?"

No, of course not. This is not a man who loves. This is a man who possesses and keeps power over women in various forms. Ann is struggling to keep the fantasy of a relationship going, somehow. She asks, "Well, isn't it his move to tell me he wants a divorce?"

No, of course not. He's got all he wants. He is not the one dissatisfied. This is Ann's life—she's the one who is supposed to make decisions for it.

She toys momentarily with the notion of a divorce, then thinks about the physical, tangible, practical elements of her life—the money, the house, the "family," and the general social structure—and thinks out loud how she doesn't want to lose all of that. Then she says, "No, I think love is what I want and need."

"But, Ann," I answer gently, "those two things, security and love, will not occupy the same space at the same time in this marriage. Pick one."

And she picks the one she's always picked—security.

So I tell her, "Dump your concrete evidence and forget it."

THINKING YOU'RE A VICTIM DOESN'T MAKE YOU ONE!

I just don't consider Ann a victim, except of her own unexplored, undeveloped, and untapped inner self. And that is a tough concept to get across to women who proclaim to be hungry and open for love and intimacy while camping out in a barren desert.

So many women call with this complaint: "If it weren't for him . . .", as though they had no choices! If you want Chinese food, it seems foolhardy to me to go to an Italian restaurant and scream for years at the chef about why there are no dim sum on your plate! Right? Right!

THE PROBLEM IS NOT THE MAN

Women, look within. The problem is not the guy—it is the way you have chosen to solve the problem of your fears about intimacy—by not really risking any. And this self-protective, predictably disappointing predicament is whitewashed with "But I love him."

DESPERATE DEPENDENCY

Please. You are not talking about love—mutual regard, admiration, respect, thoughtfulness, openness, acceptance, honesty, etc.—you are talking about desperate dependency, a sad attachment of familiarity.

Familiarity can be a deadly trap. The convenience, the routine, the time invested, the daily structure, provide an intense pull. Combine that with a fear of the unknown both in the world and in yourself and you have a recipe for quicksand. You're just not going anywhere.

What motivates moving on? For some, the pain of where they are just gets too great. For others, it is the glimmer of hope and the attractiveness of new possibilities, provided by role models and books like this.

HAVING A MAN WON'T HEAL YOU

Having a man won't heal your hurts, resolve all your self-doubts, and protect you from life's challenges. The kind of man you pick while you're in that mode is not one you would recommend to your best friend. Admit it. Face it. Do something about it.

Or you may end up hurting more than yourself: Like

Aurora, Carol, Tammy, and Ann, Sandra is too afraid to think about leaving—but she should!

UNDER HIS THUMB

Sandra began by saying she was thinking about putting her son into therapy because of the havoc wreaked by her marital relationship. What she really wanted was to get her overbearing husband into treatment, but the man, who is in total denial, claims he doesn't need it, that everything will be peachy keen if "I just listen and obey him."

And I tell her: "Whoa! You need to tell him that that's all well and good, but right now you are dealing with certain things in your interactions, which have nothing to do with doing things correctly, that are diminishing your feelings of love and attachment. Ask him if that is of any concern to him.

"Tell him you need him to come work on these things with you. The ultimate reality is that if he refuses, because he doesn't take you seriously or is too scared and therefore stubborn, that this goes to the extreme—leaving."

Sandra must stay focused on her personal perspective—as a responsible adult, not as a little girl under Daddy's thumb. Her marriage is in deep, probably irreparable, trouble. Sending her eleven-year-old to therapy will be relatively useless unless his home situation considerably improves. Whatever old patterns are being acted out through her being dominated, Sandra—with professional help—must learn to take charge and make changes, for the good of her son and herself.

SOMETIMES YOU DON'T WANT TO SEE

A call to action. Finally! So why didn't all those women see clearly that they were in the wrong place? It's not a question of not seeing—it's not *wanting* to see. Let's face it, change is difficult, painful, scary. The devil you know is always better than the one you don't.

THE DREAD OF LETTING GO

This brings us to the dread of letting go and moving on. There are many styles of this literally paralyzing anxiety. Here's a sampling of them:

The People-Fixer

Fixing a man is the way some women try to affirm a self. Holding on to a man is the way some of you basically define a self.

Barbara knows what to do—but she is frightened. It is sad how women can let being scared become the predominant force in their lives. She has been going with a very dependent guy, who's pressing for marriage—despite the fact that he has never made love to her and doesn't plan to. Far from wanting to marry him, Barbara really wants to end the relationship—but she is a "people-fixer." She seeks out the needy in order to avoid fixing herself. It's time she got to work on that and stopped even considering sacrificing her own happiness for someone with a serious hang-up whom she doesn't even want around.

Saved by the Tooth Fairy

Suzy has been separated for two years because "he won't let me go." I laughed and told her that this was not the reason she was still separated but her excuse. Some women stay connected just in case they can be saved by the Tooth Fairy, or whoever. Suzy's husband is an alcoholic with a bad temper. He doesn't get any help, just comes back and forth with promises and disappointments. But Suzy keeps hoping that next time will be gold.

After a while she stated the real fear: "What if I can't find another man?"

I guess it would be the end of the world, gravity would cease, and the entropy of the universe would go for broke.

Fairy Tales Never Come True!

Linda's husband has always had affairs, even during her pregnancy. She spoke to me just before she was to give birth and had gotten the resolve, finally, to file for divorce. The divorce, with the substantial financial settlement, will be final in two weeks. Now he is being, in her words, "perfect." She wants to know if she should stay out or not. I mean, it would be nice if fairy tales did come true. Let's face it, ladies, seducers are good at their job—with their wives and all their other women. They know how to tell you what you want, what you need to hear.

He's a Louse, But I'm Lonely

Bobbie, fifty-two, has been harassed for many years by her drunken ex-boyfriend. She sounds as if she is angry with his recurrent attempts to connect with her. But then she admits that she becomes open to him because she gets lonely, and welcomes even this sick attention. To her, I say: "You're never too old to get a life. Go do it, and you'll find yourself shedding your neediness."

The Dancing Yo-yo Master

Heather, twenty-four, has been in this relationship for ten months, during which time he yo-yos her with closeness and carries on with at least one other woman. He gets called on it or caught red-handed and cries. She is beguiled by the tears. I told her to keep focused on the behavior between the tears—it counts more. It's the tears that give Heather the momentary longed-for belief that he wants her.

She is too hungry for that moment.

But He's Not All Bad!

Lisa is also feeling very conflicted. She's been separated for one year and has two children, five and six. That makes the picture muddier. She admits he is a good dad, a good worker, and has been faithful. As our dialogue continued, it became clear that he didn't make a good partner.

His insecurities led him to be so terribly controlling that he lost all sight of compassion. His neediness was destructive. It was hard for her to stay out because of his "good qualities" and entreaties that he had changed.

Lisa's brother has a terminal illness, and several members of the family want to take him on a trip to Europe before he dies (which will be soon). Her husband, emphasizing all the changes he has made, had demanded she choose—the trip or the marriage.

I thought that made the decision to stay out easier.

So did Lisa.

ONCE YOU'VE MADE THE MOVE . . .

So let's move on to what happens once you've made the decision to leave.

You've had the good sense and guts to stay out. And, then, within days or after many years, you have those terrible second thoughts: Maybe you've made a mistake. What might make you think that?

MAYBE I'VE MADE A MISTAKE!

Pat had broken off a relationship five years before, and now she was having second thoughts. Under my prodding, she revealed that the guy hadn't wanted to get married, was unemployed and on drugs. So why in the world did she want such a no-goodnik back? Well, it seemed he'd gotten his act together and was doing well. She, on the other hand, had done nothing with her life and had a job that she found unfulfilling.

DR. LAURA: You look back at this guy, see that he pulled his act together, and you go, "Oh gee, maybe I should have stayed." You were intelligent to leave when you did, but you haven't done anything with your life. So you are looking for some guy whose nest you can go into.

PAT: Right.

DR. LAURA: And then what? You think that alone will make you happy?

PAT: No.

DR. LAURA: Yes you do! You think that will save you and make you a fulfilled human being.

PAT: So I should just make myself happy, right?

DR. LAURA: Go make yourself feel like you have purpose on this earth. Go feel like your existence makes the world different. Go do something that gives your life meaning. Your choice in men will improve. We only go after, and we only accept, what we think we deserve. Go back to school—go become yourself. Dream, reach.

PAT (WEAKLY): Okay.

DR. LAURA: You sound so unmotivated. And you tell me *he* didn't want to make a commitment? You aren't willing to make one to yourself! You are asking for somebody else to do for you what you won't do for yourself!

PAT: I realize that.

DR. LAURA: I know it is scary and tedious, but go do something. . . . The rewards are great.

PAT: I will. Thank you.

Pat made the right decision leaving the wrong man. That step is necessary but not sufficient for a fuller and happier life. It's like cleaning out the cobwebs—now you've got to paint! The leaving gives you the room you need to grow—now you've got to get into the process of growing, learning, taking on challenges, and taking new risks as you work toward your dream.

And, frankly, a guy who "pulled himself together" wouldn't be too interested in a woman who didn't do the same!

I KNOW I SHOULD HATE HIM, BUT . . .

Janet, forty-five, also made the smart move of leaving and, like Pat, is having second thoughts. This time the reason is that she doesn't know any other way of relating to a man other than being his "mommy."

Janet's is a twelve-year live-in situation with an alcoholic drug addict who "borrows" money (sometimes with permission) but never repays, and who doesn't keep any responsible work.

"I should just hate him, but I just sit here and cry," moans Janet. "I know I did the right thing by throwing him out. . . . I just keep wanting to call him."

Janet's challenge, now that she did the right thing by leaving, is to be brave enough to grow from where she is in her own mind and heart: believing that being someone's mommy is the only way to ensure some security in the attachment with a guy.

If she, at forty-five, is too scared to deal with that, she'll continue to have these second thoughts.

For Pat and Janet and too many of you, second thoughts become a welcome relief from change.

WHEN STAYING CAN BE THE RIGHT THING

Finally, I want to mention two reasonable, major motivations for not leaving, even though it would seem, at first glance, the right thing to do.

For the Sake of the Kids

Lisa, thirty-one, admits that marrying was a "business arrangement." He got a mother for his two kids; she got the financial security she desired. She has been having some sexual flings for "emotional and sexual" satisfaction—he knows all about it.

Then this call took a twist! "I don't want to leave the children. We are very close. Their mother abandoned them completely and I don't want to make them go through that again by my leaving. I love them," she related.

I was most impressed. Here is the moral trade-off point. The benefit of being a parent, of nurturing and experiencing the wonderful feelings of a warm relationship with children, was her number one priority. She was willing to accept the reality of that trade-off for what she felt were the unbeatable gains.

I told her I admired her.

That's one important reason to stay when you ordinarily should leave. Kathy has another.

When the Problem Is Partly Your Fault

Kathy has been married for almost eight years. She relates going from one dependent relationship to another, like a rebellious child. And here she is again. She says her husband is critical and controlling. She realizes that her dependency made her pick him—but now, she says, she's been changing and growing and no longer needs nor wants his "type."

She has been totally withdrawn from him, communicating and sharing nothing of her thoughts or feelings. He's read her journal to find out what's going on with her, and Kathy is furious.

I told her that she went into a game with him and now changed the rules. I would suspect he's quite hurt and feels rejected. If someone married me for the qualities I had and then decided later that these qualities were despicable and withdrew from me, I'd feel hurt and sick and nervous too!

"So you need to have some compassion for his position," I said. "Instead of looking at him as your enemy, a controlling S.O.B., you need to look at the reality that you didn't want to make choices in your life—you wanted to make someone else responsible, and that was what you opted for. You owe him frank discussions about what is going on, to see if he could also evolve. He's not the enemy. He's not the one who has been keeping you back your whole life. You were!"

So Lisa is staying for the children—for their personal

benefit and for the satisfaction it gives her. Kathy should at least stay long enough to have one experience in which she does not behave like a rebellious child as a means of showing or experiencing independence.

ALWAYS FOLLOW YOUR SMARTS, NOT YOUR FEARS

I have often said on my program, "Water and self-esteem seek their own level." That means that when you are with a man who does bad things (violent, negative, controlling, addicted, illegal actions, etc.), your mixture of compassion ("He's really got a good heart underneath") and reticence ("Oh, I'm just too scared to leave; maybe it'll get better . . .") demonstrates that you don't think much of yourself or your possibilities in life.

Well, women, the only way out of that is to follow your smarts and not be led by your fears. Do what you would recommend to anyone else—leave, grow, change, take on challenges. Do something obviously constructive. That's the way you impress yourself into better self-esteem. Stop resting on the wilted laurels of being an adult child of (fill in the blank). That just keeps you weak.

Follow a game plan with courage, grit, guts. That's the way any of us finds satisfaction, ultimately.

Do the right thing . . . and don't tell me you don't know what that is—I know better. Don't let fear, laziness, or cowardice be your Pied Piper.

I know you can do it. Hey, I'm counting on you! So get ready, get set, and go take on your life!

P.S. Here's an extraordinary item from Ray Richmond's television column in the *Los Angeles Daily News,* which highlights the lack of conviction in too many women:

"If you watch tonight's edition of the syndicated *Night Talk with Jane Whitney* talk show, you'll see a North Hollywood couple named Marla Young and Kenneth Makley participating in a theme show about 'Men Who Won't Commit to Marriage.'"

Young called to note that she has issued Makley an ultimatum: Commit to get engaged by Christmas Day or else.

Or else what?

"Or else . . . I'll get upset," said Young. "But I won't leave him no matter what," she added.

"Now," concludes Richmond, "there's a woman who stands by her convictions!"

Epilogue

THE BIRTH OF THE SMARTS

So what do I hope you've gotten out of this book? Simple. I hope it's jump-started your courage; that it's made you aware that you must stop acting stupid, that you must get smart and come up with unique solutions to your personal situations. Your behaviors have to change, and that means taking leaps and risks that are, I admit, scary. But look at the alternative. After all, you've been living with it.

Recently, I've listened to far too many women callers absolutely marinating in their history, writhing in misery because nothing has changed—even though they've had the Therapeutic Insight or attended Adult Child of Whatever meetings for a year. The real key to growth, as these women know but fear to face, comes from within, not without. It is doing something new and different for yourself, something that will challenge you to rise above where you're at now in your soul.

In May 1993, I gave a talk to a group of working moms and received only a 50 percent approval rate. In fact, the room seethed with hostility as I endorsed the absolute necessity of babies being with mothers and/or fathers who attend to them and provide the love and positive feedback they need to grow and mature in good emotional and physical health. A good number of the audience members who attacked me, it turned out, were women who had made babies with bum husbands who then left them, one-night stands, men with no intention of committing, married types, guys with serious hang-ups, etc. The so-called victims of these turkeys claimed I just didn't understand that society, social services, etc., weren't set up to allow them to be proper mothers, to "do the right thing" by their kids. According to my detractors, all I was doing was laying guilt on them.

"Well," I countered, "I'm not about to take responsibility for the stupid, irresponsible behavior that landed you in your no-win situation in the first place—or for the rotten luck that undermined your best-laid plans. I am, however, willing to discuss the need for creativity and determination in finding a way out of your pain."

Just a week ago, at another public appearance, I was approached by a young woman who had attended my Working Moms lecture. She had, she told me, been among the angry ones, but she had subsequently realized that her resentment was really about trying to affix blame on someone beside herself. Since then, she'd taken my advice to heart, gotten smart, and created a gourmet-lunch-delivery business, which, since it operates out of her home, allows her to be with her child. She had started out resenting me bitterly. Now she was thanking me sincerely. Truly, that touched my heart.

I assume that many of you who have read this book are also angry at me.

Yes, I know that females who are sexually abused or who have been raised by single/never-married mothers often become sexually active too early and end up being single moms themselves—in a desperate attempt to repair hurts and make a special connection. My hope is that, if this profile applies to you and you've made it through this book, you are now motivated to shift gears and move in a positive new direction toward self-determination and fulfillment.

The current feminist agenda mostly accuses men or society in general, thereby ignoring the pivotal role played by women themselves in their life predicaments. What I'm asking of you is to acknowledge to yourself that all persons on this earth confront challenges—willingly or unwillingly—and that some of these challenges are uglier than others. Let's face it: There is no destiny outside of what you give up or take on.

With this book, I passionately want to help you face your inner and outer demons and lay claim to your own lives. I want you, through your courage and compassion, to begin to build a better, richer existence. Once you take the first step, you will experience a "ripple effect" in which more strength brings better choices, which leads to greater satisfaction for you and for those whose lives you touch.

This book, to me, is the first pebble thrown into the brook to make those ripples begin.

REFERRALS

Twenty-two first steps for women to take when they decide to get smart

TOLL-FREE HELPLINES

Attorney Referral Network
800-624-8846
24 hours

National Council on Alcohol &
    Drugs
800-475-HOPE
Information on local treatment
    centers; literature

Child Abuse
800-422-4453
24 hours
Information; referrals to local
    agencies; crisis counseling

National Council on Child Abuse
    and Family Violence
800-223-6004
Information and referrals
    on child abuse, family
    violence

Credit
800-388-CCCS
Information on local credit
    counseling services

Domestic Violence National
    Hotline
800-799-SAFE
24 hours
Information and referrals
    for women abused verbally,
    mentally, or physically

Eating Disorders
800-382-2832
24 hours
Information and referrals

Mental Health (National
    Clearinghouse Family Support/
    Children's Mental Health)
800-628-1696
24 hours
Information and referrals

Pregnancy
800-238-4269
24 hours
Information and counseling to
  pregnant women; referrals to
  free pregnancy testing; foster
  and adoption centers

Sexually Transmitted Disease
800-227-8922
Education; information on
  sexually transmitted diseases

Youth Nineline
800-999-9999
24 hours
Referrals for youth or parents
  about drugs, homelessness,
  runaways

HOUSING RESOURCES

ACORN
202-547-9292
nonprofit network of low- and
  moderate-income housing

MISCELLANEOUS SELF-HELP ORGANIZATIONS

Rational Recovery
916-621-4374
Helps achieve recovery from
  substance abuse and other
  compulsive behaviors through
  self-reliance and self-help
  groups (nonreligious)

Women for Sobriety
800-333-1606
Helps women achieve sobriety

Debtors Anonymous
212-642-8220
Recovery from compulsive
  indebtedness

Gamblers Anonymous
212-386-8789
Recovery from compulsive
  gambling

Sexual Compulsive Anonymous
213-859-5585
Recovery from sexual
  compulsiveness

Compassionate Friends
708-990-0010
Support to families bereaving
  death of a child

Share
513-721-5683
Recovering from violent death of
  friend or family member

Abortion Survivors Anonymous
619-445-1247
Recover from impact of abortion
  on self and relationships

Survivors of Suicide
414-442-4638
Helps families and friends of
  suicide victims

Widowed Persons Service
202-434-2260
Peer support for widows and
  widowers (associated
  with AARP)

10 STUPID THINGS COUPLES DO TO MESS UP THEIR RELATIONSHIPS

Dr. Laura Schlessinger

HARPER

NEW YORK • LONDON • TORONTO • SYDNEY

To Deryk and Lew,
who make both the lows
and highs worthwhile.

Acknowledgments

I am grateful for those who stood by me in times of pain and turmoil, including family, friends, colleagues, and my listening audience.

Thank you to my Chief of Staff, Keven Bellows; the President of Premiere Radio, Kraig Kitchen; and the special folks who work with me on my radio program, Cornelia Koehl, Michelle Anton, DeWayne McDaniel, and Dan Galanti. My radio program is the engine for my foundation for abused and neglected children (The "My Stuff" bag program), and Janine Holmes is the conductor of that train of mercy.

I am fortunate to have friends of substance and loyalty, without whom life would be a more difficult trial. I especially want to acknowledge Rabbi Moshe Bryski and the entire Chabad network for keeping me connected to my Judaism—sometimes in spite of myself.

My editor and publisher, Diane Reverand (aka The Reverend Diane) has been with me through six books. I respect her so much that I am quadruply enthralled when a sentence doesn't get the red pencil treatment.

I thank Hashem. In spite of the fact that the mission sometimes seems too big a burden, I am grateful for the gifts and for the opportunity to do something of value. I hope I live up to Hashem's expectations.

—Dr. Laura C. Schlessinger
April 2001

Contents

Introduction

Ten Stupid Things Women Do to Mess Up Their Lives was published in 1994, and *Ten Stupid Things Men Do to Mess Up Their Lives* hit the bookstores in 1997. It is now January 2001, and by my estimation, things have only gotten worse. It is my observation, from talking to tens of thousands of men, women, and children over a span of a quarter century on my syndicated radio program, that these last few decades of the millennium have been horrendously destructive to the ability of men and women to relate, commit, and enjoy building and being a family.

This book is not about documenting the ugly and relentless attacks on the healthy expression of the unique qualities of masculinity and femininity, marriage, family, and parenting; I've passionately done that in *Parenthood by Proxy* (later published in paperback as *Stupid Things Parents Do to Mess Up Their Kids*). This book is about the problems men and women face in finding "peace in love" in an American society that is anything but conducive to spiritual bonding and the joyful mutual commitment to obligations which are, as everyone ultimately admits on his deathbed, the very foundation of a meaningful life.

American society is best defined by the nature of its children and young adults. Our children believe that chastity is defined by oral and anal intercourse—as long as there is no vaginal penetration. (Thank you, President Clinton.)

Our children believe that commitment is temporary at best, so why marry at all—just shack up. (Thank you to many of their parents.)

Our children believe that relationships are not for them to cherish, but, as slaves, to serve them; and when the relationship just doesn't "feel good" anymore—move on. (A thank you to their parents who leave "to find themselves" or for "true happiness"—generally in somebody else's undershorts.)

Our children believe that children are not very important. If they were, why would parents leave, marry someone else, make new children, and not see them anymore? If children were important, why would their mommy and daddy only see them just before bedtime? If they were important, how come they don't even know who their daddy is?

Our children don't know what they're supposed to do with respect to being a man or a woman, a husband or wife, a mother or father. There are no definitions and no scripts; not for healthy behaviors, anyway. There is hostility to anything masculine and there is victimization mentality about anything feminine; no one really needs to be married; parents are replaceable by hired help and technology.

Our children don't know how to face a future with all these uncertainties and chaos typifying our society. The focal point for the current confusion, resentment, and stupid behaviors of people today in their relationships with the opposite sex are the new *norms*, which are devastating.

Sexual intimacy doesn't have to mean anything.

Commitment is dependent upon your current feelings or circumstances.

It's not only okay, but necessary for you to be sexually experimental, including a variety of techniques, partners, and genders. College campuses like Penn State U. and the State University of New York at Albany now have student activities, under the guise of health, which promote S&M and other vulgar displays. In other words, nothing you do is wrong, your actions cannot be judged; people need to be free to express themselves in the basest of ways.

I think we've lived and played with these notions long enough to determine whether or not this experiment is a success or a failure. Results are in. This experiment is a failure. The reason is simple. Human beings have needs—not only temporary curiosities and desires—they have needs. The profound human need for the consistency and safety of a loving, bonded relationship is not met with the free-for-all mentality that promises only the moment, not tomorrow.

Recently on my program, I had a call that so neatly clarifies this truth. A young woman in her early twenties talked to me about the pain of two betrayals. She is visiting the United States from Australia on a three-month "educational experience." Her boyfriend of three years just e-mailed her that he's already in someone else's bed and body. Her comment to me, "Well, that's okay, but my friends are still hanging out with him." Can you believe that! The "love of her life" just started "doing" someone else during her brief absence, and all she says is, "okay," but the real pain is the lost loyalty of her friends?

First of all, I told her she was in denial to merely accept that her boyfriend didn't care enough about her and their relationship to sustain himself through his "inner sexual pressures." I explained that when young men experience free and easy sex without commitment, just for the feeling of it, that it is a spigot not easily turned off. Fidelity is about commitment to a person and to an ideal—one absent from their lives. She admitted this to be so.

I then answered her question about whether or not she was being unreasonable to presume that her friends would be loyal to her because "he did her wrong." I responded, "Yes, you're being unreasonable." She was really shocked here. I explained it this way: "You and he had no commitment. You expect your friends to react to your relationship as though you had one, and he had breached a vow. There was no vow, no promise, no covenant, no commitment. There was only familiarity and sex. There is no foundation for your friends to have to choose. They are living in exactly the same way as the two of you and realize that they want the freedom he took."

So, here it is. This young woman wanted to feel loved, cherished, valued, and special. She wanted to be in a safe, loving, warm commitment. Yet, she did nothing to ensure that because none of that is the *norm* any longer. She wanted to feel supported by her community when the sanctity of her unsanctified relationship was broken. That support is not there. In other words, today's societal norms *do not* provide for or create or support romance and a place for valued, safe, and truly intimate relations.

Men and women of all ages, religions, educations, ethnicities, socioeconomic realities, backgrounds, and experiences call me every day about their problems in life. It has become more and more clear that the core issue for almost all of these problems is a basic lack of moral standards by which important decisions are made. Why are these people astonished when it doesn't work out "right"?

For example, let's look at "courtship." That's a term most people don't even know, much less use in their lexicon or life. Courtship used to be a special time for people to get to know one another. It had rules, chaperones, support, and advice. Courtship provided an opportunity for men and women to develop a friendship, an understanding, a true knowledge of one another. It was a time of flirtatiousness and of chivalry, it was also a time to discuss religion, work, children, families, homes, philosophy, and to see how the respective families could function together. Courtship was about taking time to learn about another in enough depth to decide whether or not to become intimate.

Courtship is gone—instant "intimacy" is in. "Hooking-up" is the catchword of the day. That means having sex before you actually even know the person's middle name. Hooking-up and shacking-up are not about being in love with the ideals, goals, and promises historically inherent in such proximity. Hooking-up and shacking-up are about having without true giving. And when it stops giving, don't worry, just go someplace else and hook-up and shack-up all over again, and again, and again.

Eventually, they call my show. They're wondering what went wrong. They're hurt or angry, and definitely confused. They feel what one would expect from losing a loved one, yet have trouble admitting that their own behaviors created the loss. Hook-ups and shack-ups have no depth, no promise, no attachment, no contentment, no meaning. They do not demonstrate assumed value of the participants.

The saddest calls come from women and men who, after years of shacking-up (and maybe a baby or two), want to marry, only to find the other person enjoys this perpetual state of uncertainty.

The most annoying calls come from men and women who, after years of shacking-up, decide that this really isn't "the one," and it's time to move on. They call about whether or not they should keep seeing the others' children and wonder whether or not this is going to hurt the kids. I'll admit, I go crazy. It flabbergasts me to this day how cavalier people are with the psyche, feelings, and well-being of children.

When folks start out a call telling me about shacking-up with somebody with kids, I ask them directly if they think this teaches children something positive and hopeful for their futures. They almost always say, "No," but continue on as if those children don't matter, only their own feelings do.

Next to the chaotic, amoral, ultraliberal, current social *norms* that currently dictate our behaviors, hyperindividuality is the worst problem people have in relating to one another. Basically, if anything goes, and I'm not obligated by G-d to people in any way which doesn't serve me, then what I want/need/desire/do at the moment is my life's philosophy. If everybody lives that way then no one lives for anyone else, and none of us are safe from each other's whim or mood.

Welcome to modern America.

Twenty years ago, I would likely hear women callers complain about not being able to find a man who would commit. Now that's a rare call. Today, I more generally hear from men not being able to find a woman serious about marriage, family, and mothering. And, it would seem, it's getting more and more difficult for a man to find a woman he can respect.

Herb, one of my listeners, wrote in June of 2000.

"I was listening to your radio program when I heard you say something to the effect that you still believed in chivalry and that modern men don't see it in the same way as in the past, because the feminist movement paints that behavior negatively.

"But there is another side to this. In a modern world where a substantial number of particularly young women behave as boorishly, vulgarly, and sluttily as uncouth men do, falling on one's sword is not a logical reaction from men. The concept of even acknowledging, not to mention protecting, a woman's honor is about as foreign as the lunar landscape. What honor? Where?"

One "very concerned mom and grandmom" wrote in on the same day:

"What have these women become over the last forty to fifty years? Personally I think they're all brain-dead when it comes to their well-being, self-respect, children, etc. They have sex outside of marriage without thinking of consequences. It's the in thing. The feminist movement believed this would bring women on an even level with men. . . . Real men respect women who respect themselves. The feminists have encouraged women to give it away for free. Guess who ends up getting 'screwed' again!! (excuse the pun). And, in the process, they hurt innocent children, families, etc."

I receive thousands of letters from young men and women in their twenties and thirties trying desperately to untangle themselves from the nonsense they've been sold by a popular culture which cares nothing about people's true spiritual needs. Young women, who are born-again-virgins, want some meaning to their physical intimacy. Young men and women, who profess to hold virginity dear until their wedding nights, are mocked and dismissed by their peers, teachers, and other adults. Young women who, after having children and taking the six weeks of maternity leave, realize that they have to take career leave in order to properly parent and bond with their children. And young men don't know where to look for that old-fashioned girl with values.

Karl, one of my listeners, weighed in at this point.

"It seems that the feminist movement has done a marvelous job in alienating cooperative and warm relationship dynamics between men and women. A majority of American women now have fallen victim to the doctrine that devalues fatherhood, equal relationship dynamics, and a devaluation of men in general. This doctrine promotes single motherhood and that a/the father is not a necessity, actually a hindrance to actualization. Materialism and career-egocentrism are central to a woman's happiness and

that is all that matters. And yes! Dr. Laura, . . . children have become a 'cool fad' like SUVs and other yuppiedom possessions.

"Unfortunately, this is the prevailing atmosphere in the dating scene for those of us in our thirties and forties. But not to be dissuaded, there is hope for those of us men who long for a cohesive family that is based on love, devotion, and family values.

"If the fruit of a tree is poisoned, go to another tree. In my professional travels, I met a delightful and wonderful woman nearly my age. She is what we polite, well-mannered, loving, communicative, devoted, and supportive American guys are longing for. She is brilliant and talented, yet is interested in a warm family with two parents and knows that one parent alone does not work in raising children, or for the fabric of society as a whole. Plus, she appreciates my holding the door for her, and having a warm and balanced relationship. We plan to have children not dumped off to day care and we both know that our larger family will be important.

"So to all the chivalrous and sincere men out there, there are plenty of loving women around, stick to your principles. Don't give up."

I know what you're thinking . . . that I am blaming women alone for this current social mess. I do put more emphasis on women, because I see them as the ones with the ultimate power. What women don't allow, men can't and won't do. I learned this from my now deceased father. The notion inspired my first book, *Ten Stupid Things Women Do to Mess Up Their Lives*. He and I argued about responsibility, and he made the point that the upward or downward trend of the morals and morale of a culture was dependent upon what women did and permitted. He believed that men, rejected by women, would not continue the behavior that got them rejected in the first place. From womb (mother) to vagina (sex), he said, men are judged and approved of by women. Men behave badly when women accept it—simple as that.

In my then feminist mode, I argued bitterly with his point

of view, angry that he was blaming women for men's bad behavior. Now, I have come to see that he wasn't blaming, he was explaining, and he was right.

The feminist movement has become hostile to heterosexual relationships in general, marriage, mothering, modesty, and religious values in particular. Young women are surrounded by this liberal muck and are stumbling around "relationships" grateful for the morning-after pill and the abortion pill to get them out of one jam after another. Years later, I get the letters of shame and regret.

One sixteen-year-old girl called my program recently to "confess." She'd been at a party at a friend's house with drinks provided by her friend's parents, and had been making out. I asked her about whether her parents knew or would have approved.

"No," she said.

"So after getting sloshed on the booze, you started necking with him in the open, where others could see? Not very dignified, was it?"

"Well, we were a little off to the side."

"Then what happened?"

"He started to take me up the stairs to go into one of the bedrooms and have . . ."

"Is this a guy you're going steady with, or something?"

"No."

"Is this a guy your parents have met?"

"No."

"This is just a guy at school who happened to be at the party getting looped and touchy-body with you?"

"Yes."

"Did you end up having sex upstairs?"

"No, my friend's mother saw us going upstairs and said we couldn't use those rooms and sent us back downstairs. We started to neck again."

"What's your question for me?"

"Well, I feel bad about what I did and I want to know what I should say to him when I see him at school."

The so-called old-fashioned rules usually included parents who were responsible with their own kids and those of others. When adults are permissive about drugs, alcohol, and sex, children feel empowered by what is ultimately an inappropriate expectation. This teenager certainly did, as peer pressure extended to irresponsible adults.

I commented to her about how easy it is to do one stupid thing after each added stupid thing: drinking . . . necking . . . intercourse, and how this could have landed her in an abortion clinic, an adoption center, a welfare office, a STD clinic, or a counseling office. I suggested she tell the guy, "I made a mistake, I am ashamed, and I won't be doing that again."

I also told her to tell her parents.

My point is that our children lack direction, because we adults have lost direction. And the lost adults get older and older. One of the more frequent subjects callers seem to be struggling with is errant "grandparents." Can you believe it? Young married couples with children call me wondering what to do with their shacking-up and/or affair-leading parents: "Should we let them see the kids?" or "Should their 'honey' be introduced to the kids?" or "How do we work family holidays?" and so forth. Man 'o man, it's just all falling apart. The role models are dropping. Age is not bringing wisdom anymore. Decency is under attack from everywhere!

Yet, ultimately, people come to understand what they need is a warm, happy, secure nest. Susan wrote to my website (www.drlaura.com) that it is the truth from the past that brings us back to what is good and true about life and love:

"I met my prospective husband in July and married him in Sep-

tember. My mother had always told me, 'Be sure you know a man through all four seasons before you marry him,' and boy was she right! Three months is nowhere near long enough to discover someone's character. My (now ex-) husband claimed to have left some very nasty habits behind him when we started dating, but, as I said, three months isn't long enough to see the truth. Within two weeks of our wedding, he returned to using marijuana, which he had claimed to have quit for good. A little over a year later, two months after the birth of our son, he returned to using heroin, which he claimed he had been clean from for quite a few years. Apparently marriage and fatherhood were too much for him to cope with and the only coping tools he knew were drugs.

"I am sadder and wiser. My wonderful second husband and I knew each other for several years before we even started dating, both of us believing that a good friendship is a good basis for a good marriage. Through friendship we were able to really get to know each other's character, long before that tricky little devil, lust, got in the way of our clear judgment. Dr. Laura, I teach both my sons (ten and twenty-two) that anything truly important for a long-term, successful marriage can be learned through good solid friendship, even before a first kiss takes place. That's when you can still think with your brains instead of your libido. I also tell them, 'Know someone through all four seasons before you marry them.' Hmmmm . . . where have I heard that before?"

Grateful for the contributions of my twenty million listeners—via calls, e-mail, faxes, and letters—I offer this book as a guide for those fateful four seasons.

Dr. Laura Schlessinger
January, 2001

1

Stupid Secrets

*"Dr. Laura, when, if ever, should I tell a woman
I'm dating that I used to own and run a whorehouse?"*

Believe it or not, that was a recent question from a caller on
my syndicated radio program. Though this specific question
may stimulate snickers and outright laughs, the basic question is an important one: What, if any, information from
your past are you obligated to reveal during dating, engagement, and marriage? And what if the past is only last week?
And on the flip side, is there any danger in "the whole truth,
and nothing but the truth"?

Is Everything Private a Secret?

The first issue to think about when deciding "what to tell"
is to be able to distinguish between *secrecy* and *privacy*. This
is not a small issue or insignificant distinction at all. I
recently asked my listening audience their opinions and
experiences with secrecy and privacy in intimate relationships and got the largest and most immediate response I

ever received to an on-air question. Here are some of those responses:

➤   "Privacy is something you 'give' someone out of respect. Secrecy is something you 'withhold' from another."

➤   "Privacy is when you want to go to the bathroom or pick your nose without your spouse looking—or try to buy them a gift without their knowing. Secrecy is when you feel guilty about something that you can't tell your spouse."

➤   "For spouses to be secretive, they would also have to be separative. Secrecy builds lack of trust, reservation, guarded intimacy of the heart, and resentment—all of which lead to bitterness. Private is personal only to the individual and should not include anything that affects in any way both parties or the family."

➤   "In my opinion, privacy in marriage is your own personal space. In this, there is trust and respect. The other partner is aware of this space and respects it without intrusion. We all need a little private time to ourselves, otherwise we go nuts! I think secrecy is destructive in marriage—it is a lack of trust and respect. This is something the other partner is unaware of, and in essence, it is a lie."

➤   "Privacy is something we value within ourselves. It is something we decide a little at a time to share. My thoughts are private and I will choose to share bits and pieces. Secrets are wrong if they promote dishonesty, distrust, and compromise morals and integrity."

➤   "Privacy is having some quality time or spiritual time alone. I think secrecy in a marriage could be a form of deceit."

➤   "Privacy is the withholding of information concerning yourself, the disclosure of which would be of no benefit to the partner, and which you do not wish to share. Secrecy, on the other hand, is the withholding of information that may have an effect on the well-being of the partner. This effect may be financial, spiritual, physical, or mental. Privacy is acceptable. Secrecy is not, unless it protects the partner from harm."

➤   "Privacy is using the bathroom (especially when smell is involved), plucking your eyebrows, picking your nose, popping zits . . . all the ugly little things that are bad enough doing yourself let alone being involved with your spouse. Secrecy is not telling your spouse about a special surprise for them . . . definitely not something which would hurt the marriage or the spouse."

Whenever I receive a call about "telling" something to an intimate, the issue of what is private and what is secret is always the first part of the discussion. I not only want people to have integrity in their treatment of others, but it is vitally important for their well-being that they have compassion for themselves and maintain reasonable dignity. Too many folks seem to believe that they have to filet themselves wide open on the cutting board of their new relationships in order truly to be cleansed. These are the folks who have no sense of personal privacy at all. Others are filled with so much self-disgust that they want to hold everything in for fear that there is no forgiveness and no moving on. These are the folks for whom absolutely everything becomes a secret.

Being able to accept one's limitations, historical warts, and problems while being willing to risk truly being known by another is a definite sign of positive mental and emotional health, without which, quality relationships are not possible.

Fear of Privacy

There are flawed and sad elements in everyone's life and there are people with profound insecurities. These are the people who have to know everything you're doing, saying, thinking, reading, writing, and with whom. If they don't have this constant reassurance of information (their attempt to control the world and make themselves safe), they immediately imagine the worst and exaggerate and misinterpret everything and anything—leaving a wake of arguments and frustration.

Our cultural environment propels otherwise reasonably secure and well-meaning people to question the sincerity and fidelity of their dates, fiancés, and spouses like never before in history. Why? The answer is as simple as it is destructive:

➤   The general societal approval of out-of-wedlock sex has led to an epidemic of experimentation, casual sex, promiscuity, and a diminished "meaning" of physical intimacy. This produces a long line of prior lovers, who are still present at work, in the community, or in families—or who just can't let go.

➤   Pop-psych has called much of infidelity and promiscuity and perversion a *disease*. Men and women are ignoring their families to have internet affairs because of an *addiction*. Men and women are cavorting with extrarelational dalliances because of an *addiction*. This puts the victim of bad, selfish behavior in the position of being unsympathetic to their philandering partner's illness. Oh, puhlease!

➤   Our culture has supported the moment-to-moment quest of immediate satisfaction and gratification by making divorce no-fault and by saying shacking-up is equivalent to marriage. This puts people into positions that historically would have offered security (marital vows and social pressure), but now the social pressure is for individuality at the expense of vows, spouses, children, marriage, and community.

➤ The family courts do not support the sanctity of marriage, nor do they recognize the absolute needs and welfare of children. Spouses can up and leave for virtually no good reason, take the children three thousand miles away, shack-up with one or more new sex partners, and still retain status as good parents.

Rome is burning and most people are getting scalded—yet there are no alarms being sounded—just faint fiddling. It is no wonder that there is an increase in fear and cynicism about making a commitment.

Putting these extraordinary pressures aside for a moment, the fact remains that where there is no trust there will be no respect, and where there is no respect there will be no ultimate security for the relationship. Where there is so much insecurity in one person, the healthy, necessary, and natural line between privacy and secrecy will be squashed as the unhealthy partner will interpret reasonable privacy as a dangerous attempt at keeping evil secrets.

On the other hand, insecure people, so fearful of judgment or rejection or losing control, make absolutely everything private in a kind of desperate attempt to hold themselves together. In other words, they make everything a secret as a way of hiding, ducking, avoiding hurt.

One listener wrote in with her firsthand experience with a spouse who had such fears.

"Even though we wed too young, we made it through very rough years and hung in, based on our learning of this key element, privacy vs secrecy. At the beginning, my husband had huge

issues with privacy and felt very invaded, since he was no longer able to keep everything about himself to himself. He has learned to let go and let me in. I have learned that some things should be private, because telling the truth about absolutely everything can be quite destructive. For instance, my husband is the only sexual partner I have ever had. Before we met, my husband did have other partners. So, he has chosen to be secretive about the particulars since telling me will not be productive to OUR relationship and will most likely bring about a twinge or two.

"Learning that there is room for privacy without it being considered a destructive secret has made all the difference in our marriage. He feels secure, now that he has shared so much of himself with me, and I feel much more secure since I realize there is no need for me to know all."

Wow! What an accomplishment for them both. He changed by trusting her with his secrets, becoming secure in her affection and acceptance of his basic, true self; she changed by trusting his love without needing perpetual details which she now could allow him to keep private. That's the balance everyone should strive for.

People must be able to keep a sense of self as well as share their lives.

Keep It to Yourself!

There are times on my radio program when I yell directly at the caller, "What were you thinking!?! Why would you tell them that?!" I just can't believe it when, for example, a question will come in like:

"Dr. Laura, I'm looking to get some insight from you. I had a girlfriend when I was around eighteen years old. Now I am married with a beautiful ten-month-old son. Recently I became unhappy in my

marriage for an unknown reason. I got back in touch with my ex-girlfriend. I very quickly became depressed. I finally told my wife that I missed my ex-girlfriend. And it has understandingly hurt our relationship. I have told her that I am over it now, but she still brings it up when she gets mad. I was on the internet checking my e-mail today and I found a message from my ex-girlfriend asking me to give her a call. I don't know what I should do. I love my wife and son, but I don't know why I still have feelings for my ex-girlfriend. I don't know whether it is her friendship I miss or if I still love her."

He told his wife about his fantasies for another, real-life woman? Oy! This is definitely the realm of private. When we treat our spouse like our shrink or confessor we make a huge mistake that is often impossible to repair, even if the relationship continues. This is a time when we go to a real shrink or to real clergy. It's a time where we struggle with the natural impulse to avoid the difficult (marriage, mortgage, children, bills, busted water heaters) and escape to the easy (new or old sex/fantasy partners).

Such private struggles are the struggles of all human beings. These struggles enter the realm of destructive secrets when we return that call or e-mail.

As one listener wrote:

"Privacy deals with thoughts or ideas that are personal. Often situations that occur in nightly dreams are better not shared. Recounting laundry lists of ex-boyfriends is unnecessary and private. Ideas that take shape, but are just ideas, that might not be productive to the marital relationship are private. Privacy ends when thoughts, situations, or ideas are acted upon and impact the relationship and could damage the marriage.

"Frankly, I don't want to know what went on in his life when we went to separate colleges before we were married. Moreover, I'm sure he doesn't want to know my thoughts when I'm premenstrual or when I had the dream about the sexy stranger. We share

our future goals, funny jokes, most thoughts, our daily lives, and most importantly, our love for each other. I think we both stay away from situations that we would have to keep secret."

If that last comment isn't perfect! I'm suddenly remembering the caller who said he had a wonderful Harley motorcycle. His wife, whom he loved dearly, had no interest in bikes. One day he put an extra helmet on the back of his bike to use whenever he gave a ride to a pretty, young, female coworker who was thrilled at getting motorcycle rides. He called because his wife was upset. She noticed the extra helmet when he got home, and he told her what it was for. She was hurt and angry. He wanted to know if he was out of line. I suggested that unless he were suicidal, stupid, or disingenuous, it was inappropriate for him to spend vibrating bike time with a single woman while he was, and wanted to stay, a happily married man. I reminded him that he wouldn't have kept it a secret if he had really believed it was acceptable.

After the Fact

Sadly, sometimes there are predicaments and situations that can't be remedied and the truth or information has to be revealed. Other times, what seems like an obvious secret should be made known, because there's time left for an important lesson to be learned so that history won't repeat itself.

One young woman wrote to me wondering about keeping something a secret or making every effort to make sure the "involved" party was informed.

"I had been seeing my boyfriend for a year and a half. Two weeks before my eighteenth birthday I got pregnant. My parents and I decided that the best thing was to have an abortion. So ten days after my birthday, I had an abortion.

"He was totally against abortions. So, he does not know I had an abortion. I told him I was not pregnant. Am I obligated to tell him eventually? I feel it is my personal business, between my parents and myself. I know if I ever told him I had an abortion, he would be so upset. Should I tell him or keep it a secret?"

The truth is that this is not an issue between the young woman and her parents. It is an issue between her, the father of the child, the terminated child, and G-d. Her parents expedited the termination and preserved her secret, but there is more to the story.

If this were ten years or so after the event, my answer would be not to impose pure ugliness and hurt on someone who has gone on with their life. This situation is in the present, and this boy-man must know that unmarried, unprotected sex resulted in his first child being eliminated. While the young woman has the power to make the decision about terminating the life of her child, he has the responsibility to behave in a way that would never endanger his potential offspring. He needs to know, in my opinion, because he needs to learn something which will direct him to make better choices in the future.

The Right to Choose

When it comes to people having informed consent, I'm very pro-choice; that is, people need to take the time to learn enough about their potential partner, making a true choice—not just a response to fantasies, hopes, dreams, desires, or desperation. It takes a certain amount of maturity to slow down to do that, and the honesty of the other person willing to reveal important issues and factors that might "break the deal." Of course, since no one wants rejection, it's easy to understand why people fake it or keep secrets that shouldn't be kept. Ultimately, secrets are revealed—and it's rarely a happy ending.

One listener wrote:

"My husband chose not to tell me that he had a mental break-down and was in a state mental hospital six years before we met. Needless to say, it all came out. After almost three years of marriage, we had a baby. During my pregnancy I watched him change and become someone I didn't know. He said he didn't tell me about it prior to our marriage, because he thought I would leave him.

"Shortly before our baby's birth, he injured himself on the job on purpose, the same job he was begging me to let him quit even though our baby was due within weeks. Oftentimes he would only get out of bed minutes before I came home. I spent two months with him maxing credit cards, gambling it all away, buying a truck with payments higher than our rent, and getting into physical confrontations with drug dealers.

"My husband was finally diagnosed by a counselor as manic-depressive. When he was hospitalized, I found out several secrets and things he had done since day one. We were forced to file bankruptcy, and I had to go to work. Needless to say, this has wrecked our marriage. I've spent enough time praying to God for the strength to forgive him for his lies and what I feel was his betrayal—praying for the strength to honor my vows and keep our home intact for my children.

"He never told me, because he was afraid I wouldn't marry him. Maybe I wouldn't have, but I wish he had given me the chance and respect to make that decision."

If he had been willing to share that secret, it would have built trust, because it would have demonstrated his willingness to face truth and reality with her, not operate against her. If he had been up-front about his problems, she likely would have helped him on his journey toward functioning better with medication and therapy. Instead, he and his family (who bear some responsibility here) tried to protect him from hurt, not considering how he would hurt his wife and children, and that he would end up abandoned and rejected and in ever-growing psychiatric distress.

Bad secret.

Another woman had a similar experience with problematic secrets of her husband.

"I have been married to my husband now for twelve years and we have a nine-year-old son. I met my husband and we clicked immediately and things moved very fast. He gave me a ring after two weeks of dating, but we did wait for eight months to marry.

"I thought I knew everything about him. I had talked with his parents and siblings and became part of the family very fast. After we were married I started seeing a side of him that I had no idea existed.

"First of all he would spend many, many hours on the computer. Then I noticed some feminine things about him. He would, supposedly as a joke, ask me to put makeup on him. He would put on my clothes and pretend that he was playing it as funny. It went away, or so I thought, for a few years, and we had our son after two years of marriage.

"He was traveling with his job and staying in hotels where he dressed like a woman and went out in public. I decided to leave. I came back because my father said to give it another try.

"It has put a lot of distance between us. My son loves his dad dearly and doesn't know any of this. The thing that really got to me about this is that his parents and siblings knew and never said a word to me! I have sat and cried and wondered why I was kept in the dark. How could anyone keep something like this from someone that would affect them the rest of their life?"

The answer is selfishness, plain and simple. Their collusion with her husband to keep this secret from her suggests that this man's parents and siblings probably are ashamed and somewhat in denial; that's when if you don't look at it, don't see it, and don't speak about it, you can pretend it no longer exists. Her husband is more willing to give in to this compulsion than seek treatment. These emotions and motivations were dealt with selfishly as he and his family wanted everything to appear normal, at the expense of this woman and her children, if need be.

The ultimate moral to this story is that there is *always* something wrong when impulsiveness (love at first sight, engagement at first date, sex at first lust) and instant intimacy present themselves. The romantic, childlike part of ourselves always loves such made-in-heaven or soul-mate moments. But, reason and patience and a willingness to get "real" must prevail. There are always going to be predators; most of the time the victims are volunteers; innocent vulnerability is a definite liability.

Getting to Know You

Self-interest is normal and natural. Self-interest at the expense of truth and the welfare of others is just plain evil. One of the reasons I nag people via my radio program to take time, at least two years of getting to know someone, before taking steps which minimize or eliminate objectivity (intimate sex, shacking-up, marriage) is because it takes time to get past reasonable, much less unreasonable, attempts to put one's best foot forward and not to reveal information or traits which might jettison us out of someone else's heart and life.

My experience with callers concerning secrets in dating is that they are more upset about the lack of openness, the deceit, and manipulation than they usually are about the issues being hidden. Sometimes that makes sense—sometimes it doesn't. I am disheartened by what some people are willing to tolerate just to be able to say to themselves that they have somebody.

It is obviously self-defeating to tell lies or mislead a potential loved ones about yourself. If they stay in your life and "love you," they're not really loving *you*—just the pretend you. Your goal of really being loved for yourself is never really met. You haven't really won anything.

One listener wrote me about how her boyfriend's deceit was a deal-breaker:

"He and I had been together for seven years. Partly as a result of becoming a listener to your show, I was no longer content to be a forty-year-old part-time shack-up honey. I told him I was uncomfortable with this arrangement and wanted to become engaged. He proposed to me in August, 2000, and presented me with a lovely ring. Intuitively, I sensed there was more behind the ring than he was telling me. He was vague about where it had come from, and elusive when I asked. I didn't want to be rude or seem ungrateful or materialistic, so I let the matter drop—even though I wondered why he had selected a ring that I never would have picked for myself.

"Three months later the truth came out. When he decided to propose to me, he asked his mother if she had a ring he could give me. She gave him an old pendant she had inherited from an aunt, which he made into a ring. The irony is that receiving a ring that had been in his family (whom I adore) would have been the best engagement present he could have given me.

"Before you think I'm being petty—the fact that he had not been forthright about the origins of the ring, had carried this secret for three months without fessing up, and moreover went on and on about how much he spent on it turned me right off. I gave the ring back to him and told him that I would only start our married life off on a note of complete honesty.

"The deal-breaker was when I found out that he had sucked his family in on the secret—asking them not to let on. His mother told me she had urged him to tell the truth, but his fear of either

looking like he couldn't afford a ring—or his unwillingness to actually spend the money—clouded his judgment and made a liar of him, a fool of me, and dupes of his family.

"I learned more about his character than ever at this point. He turned the whole thing around to make me somehow at fault: I would have thought him cheap, nothing is good enough for me, I'm making a mountain out of a molehill, etc. Everything but take responsibility.

"Though I am disappointed to no longer be engaged—I am grateful that his character was revealed to me before it was too late. Well, actually, after seven years I have had ample opportunity to see other signs of weak character—walking in on him in bed with another woman, giving me half-burned-down candles in a Ziploc bag for my birthday, smoking pot with the boys—but I chose not to see that. This was the last straw, because I realized I need and want a husband with a healthy relationship to money, truth, and integrity.

"While privacy should be respected, there is no room for secrecy. As we say in Al-Anon, you're only as sick as your secrets."

There it is—some folks are just more sensitive to the concept of secrets than they are to infidelity, disdain, drug abuse, cheapness, lack of respect, regard, or love. It's as though the devil they find out they don't know is not as acceptable as the devil they do know.

Here's where some laws of physics do apply to human relations. Once an object is in motion, it tends to stay in motion unless confronted by equal or opposite force. Well, the same goes for some people. Once they're in a relationship, being sexually intimate, shacking-up, or having sent out the invitations, they're loathe to use their best judgment and withdraw from an obviously bad situation. There is denial and there are excuses and there are the promises and there are the hopes that it will all just miraculously get better or spontaneously work out.

That equal or opposite force quite often is the rude awakening that occurs after ugly secrets are found out.

One listener had been in a relationship for three months when she became suspicious, because her questions about financial topics were not answered. She called in a private investigator. She found out that he had been married one more time than he had admitted to. It turns out he was financially responsible for three ex-wives.

"He said if he told me the truth that I might reject him. I told him I can deal with the truth easier than a lie. He was not completely honest about his financial integrity either. My trust has been broken and I feel like there is probably more I don't know and don't know when to believe him. It is very important to be honest when building and laying down the foundations of a relationship. I was lied to to cover up past and present mistakes, so I feel misled about the person I thought I was in love with. I was on top of the world when I didn't know about the lies and now I feel at the bottom of the barrel, but I am glad I know."

The secret is out: People who hide and manipulate truth in order to get or keep someone in their lives do not love that person, they just want that person. Love for another person consists mainly of caring about their well-being and welfare. Unfortunately, the victim of the lies too often takes an inappropriately sympathetic approach because the deceiver gets all pathetic and pleads fear of rejection. The victim too often gets mushy and forgiving and "feels their pain." Instead, the victim should be running for the hills. Forgive the deceiver if you want, but steer clear of them. Forgiveness does not mean you have to continue to put yourself at risk—nor are you obligated to struggle with the other person's issues. Better the deceiver learns from a true rejection and grows into a better human being for the future.

Me, me, me is the main motive for lying and keeping

secrets to get and keep someone. It isn't love, love, love or relationship, relationship, relationship—so don't kid yourself and don't be beguiled. One listener wrote about her one-year involvement with a man who had been involved with another woman when they met. My listener told him in no uncertain terms that she would not see him if he were so involved. One month later, he informed her that his prior relationship had been resolved. She later found out that this was a lie. He had been sexually intimate with both of them, with neither of them aware of the other. When my listener caught him, he said that it was easier for him to lie to keep her in the relationship than risk losing her while he was still "working through his issues" with the other woman.

She responded to him with:

"So, let me get this straight. You lied to me to keep me in the relationship. And you lied to her to keep me in the relationship. And you were intimate with her to keep me in the relationship? How perplexing. What, did you do a handspring from the bed one night and cry, 'Eureka! I've got it! I will be intimate with both of them and this will sure win X's love for me?!'"

She then went on to tell him that his secret was not only stupid and deceitful, but that it was playing with two people's lives. His attempt to keep her lost her, and his deceit was cruel and reprehensible.

I was gratified that she was an exception to Newton's First Law of Motion—she used human good sense. What people do IS who they are.

The Past Is Right Here, Right Now

There isn't one person reading this page, there isn't one person existing on the face of the earth, for that matter, who doesn't have stuff they'd rather keep in the past. Who wants to dredge up and have to explain some of the bad and dumb things they once did for which they now have guilt, shame, or embarrassment? More horribly, who wants to relive the pain of vicious victimization or unwittingly struggle with a serious psychiatric problem? It's true that some people just won't understand; some will judge; some will be repelled; some will be rejecting.

As I've said earlier in this Chapter, what good does it do you to be "loved" and "accepted" when you know there's more to the story?

When we get to know someone new, and it seems to be getting "serious," are we obligated to tell all? Is each new relationship experience a forced confession? How many times are you expected to reveal deeply private concerns before it begins feeling as if you're volunteering for psycho-logical/emotional rapes? How much depth of detail is neces-sary? At what point in the relationship should you open up this much? At what point in the relationship do you take this risk? These are vitally important issues. Let me use some listener examples to answer these questions.

Unfortunately, sexual abuse (molestation or child rape) is a frequent "secret." Here's what one listener wrote with respect to talking to a prospective partner about sexual abuse:

"It was not very smart to go into a relationship with someone when you haven't dealt with this issue (sexual abuse) yourself. You think you can hide and pretend it never happened, but in real-ity lots of things are centered around what happened to you. You can't be your true self and be comfortable. You always feel as if you are hiding something, and you present signals you are not even aware of, like feeling guilty or uncomfortable with holding hands or kissing.

"You are afraid you will be rejected because you are 'used.' You are afraid someone may think you are weird or not normal. You didn't ask for these things to happen to you, and when you realize

that and get help with related issues, you don't feel like you are hiding something from someone you love."

The calls I get on my radio program are not only from women wondering about whether, how, when to talk to their boyfriends or husbands about their experience being molested as a child, they are from women who found out too late that their husbands were molested and were still suffering with the guilt, filled with shame, afraid of intimacy, confused about their sexuality and about having children—lest they do to others what was done to them. Additionally, the calls come in from men, loving and protective of their girlfriends and wives, but now angry, frustrated, and confused about what to do when there is a sudden revelation about their partners' molestation, and a clearer explanation of such strange behaviors as moods and negative issues about sex.

We all realize that withholding of this information isn't done to be mean—it's an issue of self-protection. The unknowing partner is still deceived, and disallowed to make a choice about what they wish to take on and deal with in their married lives, and the partner is not given the opportunity to work with the secret holder to make things better.

I've had callers say, "I don't really need to talk about it—I'm fine with it and it doesn't impact my life at all in any way." My answer is generally, "Then it would be wonderful for you to share how resilient you are. That's a positive quality that would make you valuable in a marriage!"

The answer to that is silence.

I don't think it's at all correct, much less necessary, to bare your soul, psyche, and history when you're casually dating. I believe that people do this compulsively when their history has become their sick identity. Then, it's kind of a provocation, a test, a manipulation, an immature game.

When it seems clear that this person is a likely "keeper," it's important to talk about the more profound issues that have forged and challenged your life. After all, what we all are today is largely a response to all we've gone through. And, don't kid yourself, it shows. It shows in the reactions you have to things today. It shows in the effort it takes to conceal. It shows.

Waiting until after marriage is not fair and not the way to build a secure foundation. As one listener wrote:

"I kept this horrible, sick secret from my husband and his family, praying that no one would ever find out my deep and harrowing shame. Finally, after three years of marriage, my conscience could take no more. I knew that in order to protect my marriage and my sanity I had to be honest with him at all costs. We were both exercising in the workout/computer room; I finally got up the courage to let him know everything. He forgave me for not telling him before he married me. But it took a long time for him to be able to trust me again.

"The lesson of this is that I should have told him the truth in the first place. Yes, there was a chance that he would dump me.

"I was finally able to find someone who accepted me as I was—and by not being honest with him from the beginning, I almost lost it all. As it was, he did forgive me and we will be married for nine years as of February 2001."

Are you thinking, "How dare he or anyone else get on his high horse and claim injury, just because he didn't know something?" Think about it some more. When you commit to someone, don't you want to feel that you are the one person in the world he or she can trust, rely on, come to, be open with? Of course. Add to that the fact that secrets of the magnitude of molestation are corrosive to the individual hoarding them as well as to the openness, comfort level, and teamwork of the marriage.

Punch line: Secrets about the past always have an impact today. You can minimize the negative effect of the past on the present and future by dealing with problems therapeutically and spiritually (that means opening up to a professional or clergy), and by letting your beloved in. This way your partner can understand you better (and can deal with some of your behavioral characteristics without taking them so personally) and can be helpful in supporting your ongoing growth.

Rejection Is a Good Thing!

So far, I've only given you happy endings, but sometimes a sad ending is its own happy ending. One listener wrote of learning that lesson:

"I was nineteen at the time and dating what I knew would be my future husband. I had a secret that was haunting me, and I really wanted to tell him before we were married. I posed the question like this: 'I have a deep dark secret. I'll tell you my secret if you tell me your deep dark secret.'

"He told me, 'No.' I took that as, well, I tried, and he can't say later that I didn't.

"He was a virgin at thirty-three and he knew I wasn't but what he didn't know is that I had lost my virginity through incest. Well, eight years later I told him anyway. The words he told me which hurt the most, and I wanted to avoid, were, 'I would have never married you if I knew about the incest.'

"The secret was stupid because in my mature nineteen-year-old mind I thought that he was the man for me—that this deep secret wouldn't affect my relationship/marriage, but it did."

This is exactly the point I make to so many callers: If this (wo)man can't deal with such truths, how do you expect to be able to count on this person with the challenges of life in the future: illness, finances, children, and natural disasters . . . ? Unfortunately, we think too much in the box of mirrored walls: "It's just about me," we whine and worry.

Wrong! It's also about him (her) and his (her) character, compassion, and strength, and it's about you two as a team, handling problems together.

Dealing with these secrets is an important way to find out if this is "the one." Too bad the usual approach is mainly based on romance and orgasms. Too much of more significance is missed.

Another listener confirmed this. She wrote:

"When I was in college, I was raped, became pregnant, and gave the baby boy up for adoption. I did not tell my boyfriend, who eventually became my husband, because I was afraid he would look on me as damaged merchandise. Had I done so, his reaction to the information would have been the testimony of how HE really was. Therefore, I would NOT have married him. It wasn't until after the wedding that his true selfishness came to light."

You really come to know people when you deal with the difficulties, not just the fun stuff. Remember that.

Secrets Keep You Stuck

In addition to finding out if the two of you can really take on life together, there is still the important issue of personal growth and change. The profound impact of our past unfortunate experiences often follows us through life as we "defend" against the pain and the truth. Here's what one man had to say to confirm that:

"The stupid secret that I hid from my ex-wife was in the end the reason for our divorce. My ex-wife attributed my outgoing and sociable personality to a kind heart. The reality was that it was a front for much insecurity and behavior that was directly connected to sexual and psychological abuse in my childhood and early teenage years.

"My ex-wife was almost 100 percent right in separating several times and then leaving, for my behavior was grossly disrespectful and wrong. Examples are: flirtation with women as a way to regain the manhood that I believed was 'taken' from me, harsh criticism of my wife, and misplaced loyalty to a dysfunctional family and 'mother.'

"I fought the separation, but with time embraced my time alone in a rooming house. For one year, I read books on the subject of child molestation and abuse, and emotional incest. Listening to your radio program, and Rush Limbaugh's, I heard the philosophies which were later the catalyst for the changes I made to my character. The abuses would no longer have a stronghold on my mind.

"In retrospect, if I had told her about the abuse in my younger years, all the bad moments could have been avoided. Now I work on releasing the guilt from a failed marriage, so that I'm open to relationships as God intends and work on my character every day.

"If there is a message for men and women who are abused it is this: You must deal with it—not keep it a secret from those you love and who love you. You must deal with it, it is the only path to freedom—or else you continue to reinforce the power the abuser once had."

Another listener learned the hard way about how secrets keep you stuck. She met a young man in church and married him some eight months later. These short courtships generally are an attempt to "make something be" rather than "allow things to evolve." There's generally immaturity and insecurity involved.

What she hid from him, her secret, was that she was bulimic and had struggled with depression.

"I didn't intentionally try to fool him, because I kept thinking I would get better and stop doing those things to my body. I wasn't even honest with myself. I think a big mistake we made was we were not honest and open in our conversations when dating, and were just blinded by the 'lusty' side of attraction.

"*After we were married for about a year he slowly found out what a mess I was inside myself. We fought a lot and ignored each other a lot, and he felt that I had deceived him.*

"*Now we have been married over five years. I did get medicine for my ongoing depression, and I stopped the bulimia one year ago. We are yet to have a romantic relationship—it is more of a partnership.*

"*I think the moral of the story is, wait to get married. Be friends first. Talk a lot. Talk about your faults and insecurities more openly. I put on a facade for my husband before we were married, that I was 'perky and perfect,' but I was not. I had problems.*

"*We are still married and will stay married—we both believe very strongly in working things out and staying together, but the journey has not been fun at all. But I think as things improve, and as we both grow and mature over the years, things will work out.*"

To Know My Journey Is to Know Me

I can't tell you how many callers, ashamed of some past action or behaviors, suffer forever because they can't forgive themselves. Part two of that lack of forgiveness is a terrible fear of being hated or rejected by a loved one as part of that perpetual punishment.

I remind these callers that true repentance means that they have taken responsibility, experienced true remorse, done what's possible to repair, and are committed to not repeating. Once these 4 R's have been accomplished they are to move on!

It is so difficult for some people to give themselves points for progress—to realize that they have changed, would never repeat the "bad thing," and that they have the right to be happy and be respected for their courageous journey.

One listener wrote about making such a journey:

"Had I kept secret a long past abortion from my pro-life boyfriend, only to have it surface after several years of marriage, it could have been catastrophic. I told him about it, and how much I truly regretted it. He was able to understand that I was no longer that person who was so stupid and irresponsible. He told me that he loved me. We now have two beautiful boys and have been married seven-plus years."

Virginity: Private or Secret?

Considering the impact of the sexual revolution of the 1960s and the impact of condoms being handed out in public school classrooms in the 1990s, there wouldn't seem to be much necessity to discuss virginity. Happily, there is, since it's making a comeback as a virtue and as a protection against unwanted pregnancies, abortions, sexually transmitted diseases, low self-esteem brought on by meaningless intimacies, and an ultimately empty feeling.

One listener had converted to the Mormon religion after years of secular free sex.

"In the Mormon community, when you marry you assume you are marrying a virgin, because you are taught from a very young age to abstain from unmarried sex. I knew in my heart that if my future husband did not know about my past it would be unfair to him, and he could not make a clear choice about whether he should marry me. With all my strength and fear of losing him, I told him. He loved me anyway, and my sharing my secret brought us closer to one another."

And you thought sex was the ultimate in intimacy.

But, here is the important point. What do you tell? How many? What positions? This is where people get into trouble. Clarifying where you've been in your thinking and being is a way of getting close. Giving details is what you do when you're selling your story to some disgusting tabloid newspaper sold in grocery stores.

One listener had this very question:

"Do I have to tell my husband the truth about how many sexual partners I had before we met? I told him five because I thought it was an easy number to maintain in my lie, but the truth is that it is more like ten. I told him this lie to keep from looking like a slut.

"In my younger years I made some choices in order to be accepted, and later I came to realize that in fact I was only alienating myself from everyone and everything that was valuable. Should I now tell my husband the truth and risk hurting him? He may not be very understanding as he has only had one partner prior to me, and his values are very old-fashioned."

Okay, here's the answer. He needs to know everything from "In my younger years . . ." to ". . . valuable." That is what will tell him about you. That's what he really needs to know: that you were lost and suffering and used sexuality to try to be found and achieve peace. You've grown from that into the wonderful woman you are. This is what's valuable about your story for him. This is what should not be a secret. The number of guys is private—keep it that way. It doesn't add to the story, it takes away from it.

If It Ain't About Sex, It's About Money

It's probably true that the two biggest secret categories are about sexuality and finances. As one listener wrote:

"I have read a million times that finances are one of the main reasons for relationship troubles. I am a twenty-four-year-old female, on the verge of getting married. My boyfriend does not know yet, but I have a horrible, horrible credit record from when I

was eighteen to twenty-two. I know I should tell him. But I have never needed to. I have a car, and we currently rent a house. It's going to come up and be a problem when we want to buy a house. I live in dread that an old creditor will find me and reveal everything, perhaps on the answering machine or something.

"I carry this secret around like a big, black, dead weight in my gut. I know this is something that will highly impact him in the future; once we are married our 'credit rating' will be as one. . . . He thinks that I am just as responsible with my money as he is. I am okay now but that's because no one will give me credit so that I have no current debt—just a bad old debt record."

It is really stupid and useless to imagine you are going to keep secret something that is public record. All you do is add deceit to what was a problem to be handled. Since this young woman has "changed her irresponsible ways," she has a positive story to tell. And that's the key in telling the other person your deep, dark, ugly, yukkies: Find the positive story.

I'll give you another example that seemed hopeless. Another listener wrote:

"Not telling my husband about the incredible debt I had incurred before our marriage led to many problems that entangled the entire family. Avoiding my debt, instead of sharing with him my problem, made him angry and bitter—especially after our tax refunds were being withheld in order to pay for my debt.

"He said it would have been better to come clean from the beginning. Now, the refunds that should be going to the family savings for kids' activities and family holidays are going to pay my debt.

"So—no secrets when it could impact the family in a negative manner. You're not just lying to yourself and your spouse—your kids suffer too."

So, what could have been the positive story? How 'bout this: "Honey, I've been living with one set of priorities, but now that I've met you, that's all changed. I used to think about having stuff in the moment as a way to feel good about myself and bring happiness to my life. So, I spent too much money and worked up a debt. Now, since I've met you, I see that love, commitment, family obligations—you know, caring and living for others—is the right way to feel good about life and to be truly happy. Problem is, that I have debt from my stupid way of thinking. I want very much to marry you and have your children. I want you to trust and respect me—so, I'm going to take the necessary time to pay off these debts before we marry so that you can trust my intent and maturity."

I bet that would work!

Secrets Are Often the Symptom

When there are sad and serious problems in a relationship, secrets are sometimes the means by which people try to hide from that truth. Instead of facing the problems, getting help, trying to change, or realizing the sick futility of their predicament, people will use the glue of secrets to shore up the dam. It ultimately doesn't work.

As one listener wrote:

"I know a person who has to sneak stuff into their own house. Perhaps it is clothing, or a new CD, movie, or even a book. They keep it a secret instead of facing the fact that their relationship must be unhealthy, not allowing them to be an individual with responsibilities, rights, respect, and discipline. Secrets usually are kept to avoid a confrontation."

Clearly, this is not a relationship of loving, equally sharing, caring adults. This is a relationship of fear and domination—deceit and manipulation. Not much chance for improvement, repair, or relief when the truth is hidden. Secrets in this case replace dealing with truth and reality.

Another listener came to understand how she shifted into secrets to protect a fragile relationship:

"After having come out of some pretty serious problems in our marriage, I guess I took for granted that things were okay again. So, one day as I was doing the checkbook and paying the weekly bills, I realized an error I had made to the tune of $200. I then took the same amount from our savings to make up for the deficit. I planned not to tell my husband, because I didn't want him to know I goofed and I wanted to avoid a fight. When he inquired about the savings account one day, I lied and said it was the amount it had been for a long time.

"This morning he found the savings book and saw what I did. He demanded an explanation. But, as I gave him my reason, I began to see just how stupid it sounded."

When you're working on improving a relationship, making sure you look good or don't get caught making errors or seem always to be right, are not the means to a healthy, loving relationship. First of all, they're all about you—not about him or her or us! Keeping secrets about mistakes in judgment or action is a form of lying and can do serious damage to the relationship by hurting your credibility and trustworthiness. Probably one of the most important elements of a relationship is the confidence you have in the other person's fundamental intent never to hurt you or the relationship.

In order to gain that credibility and trust, you must never give your spouse an indication that you would be deceptive to avoid a confrontation, keep out of trouble, be held accountable, look bad, be wrong, or not be in control. The "us" has to be more important than that.

On the flip side, instead of making sure you look good, it does little for the long-term health of a relationship to protect your spouse from him or herself. One listener was, unfortunately, doing just that.

"My husband is very touchy about making sure bills are paid

on time; this would not be an issue except that he also wants to overspend on things that are not necessary to survive. As a result, I have been keeping an $800 credit card debt (in my name only) a secret and trying desperately to get it paid off without calling attention to it. The $800 was accumulated here and there to pay utility bills, etc., it was not used for unnecessary spending. It was a result of his using the checking account to buy tools, leaving us short on the bill money. He would always get mad if I stated that we couldn't afford something and demand to know why, leaving me to sometimes say, 'Yes, honey, go ahead—we have a little extra money this week,' when we don't, and then use the credit card to pay for the phone or electricity.

"I hate to have any secrets between us."

If she had called my radio program, I would have told her to put the finances in his hands. She needs to get him one of those electronic checkbooks, so that he can know exactly what groceries, utilities, and so forth really cost. This way, he's being the petulant child, not caring about what there is, just about what he wants. The secret makes her live in fear and keeps him childlike.

Secrets Keep You Alone

The saddest aspect of secrets in a marriage is that you are alone with your fears and problems. Obviously, that is counterproductive to intimacy. One listener wrote about her marriage. She described a year's courtship and engagement filled with agreements on such important issues as religion, family, work, and monetary priorities. While her husband was completing his final year at the university, she became pregnant. That's when everything seemed to unravel. She found large sums of money were missing from their savings account, he had gotten failing grades at school, and then faked that he was going to school at all. Instead, he hung out at the mall, leaving her home with the twins.

Though she was determined to divorce him, they went into Christian counseling first.

"Building back trust takes a lot of work, and there are still some awkward feelings which I do not hesitate to tell him about! My husband had one terrible secret: He could not handle the pressures of going to school, working, and my difficult pregnancy. His mistake was covering up the fears with lies. Lies begat more lies and so on. This destroyed trust . . . one of the most cherished things in a marriage. We have worked hard to rebuild our marriage. I sense that he did not feel like he could tell me he was under pressure. He knows and regrets what he did. People can learn a lot from our story. He withheld information from me thinking that the truth would destroy our relationship. It was not the truth, but the secrets that almost destroyed our relationship."

Whether your spouse is the best-looking, smartest, most successful, most fun, sexiest, most agreeable person you'd ever hope for or not, that person has vowed to face life with you. That is the counterpoint to being alone. We are each distinct, separately contained entities. It takes a leap of faith to touch and care about another person and to allow them, invite that person to take care of you. It means lowering your pride and ego, and raising your arms in an embrace of trust.

We all deal with adversity better when we deal with it together with our loved ones. None of us is loved for being perfect—if we are loved, it's for compassion, vulnerability, kindness, thoughtfulness, humor, sensitivity, and trustworthiness. It is never better to have some stupid secret pop up—it is always better to swallow pride, admit the truth, and work it through together. What makes all relationships strong is standing up together against some outside threat or challenge.

One listener summed it up:

"I kept my feelings secret from him. I allowed him to think everything was fine with me when it wasn't. When I realized I was hating him, I got scared. Once I stopped keeping my feelings a secret EVERYTHING started to change in our relationship. With hard work and faith we are still married heading into our fifteenth year. We both realize what damage an unspoken secret can cause."

We cannot love when we do not trust. We cannot be close when we hide. For the most part, secrets have little place in intimacy. Intimacy and secrets are like poles of magnets—they repel each other.

Good Secrets

All this said, there are times when truth becomes cruel and destructive. Perhaps we could call these "good secrets." For example, you should never tell your spouse that you're turned off because of receding hairlines, ripples in thighs, sagging, postpartum breasts, crow's feet, graying hair, slower gait, a few extra age pounds, and so forth. We all need to age gracefully and accept the aging and imperfections of our loved ones graciously.

You also should never tell your spouse that you've had sexy feelings about anyone real. Instead, you should remove yourself from that temptation and hike up your attention and affection with your spouse. It's amazing how being more attentive gets more back in return than just fantasizing in anger does.

To the ire of some listeners, I have told some callers that they might consider taking to their graves the secret of a brief dalliance, IF AND ONLY IF they were truly repentant; the impact of full disclosure on the marriage and family might be terminal and the children only stand to suffer. If the behavior is repetitive or long-standing, I generally recommend not keeping that a secret, since it implies more of a serious character failing than an "event."

When the Secret Is You!

One of the more unusual responses I received from my radio listeners on the subject of secrets was from a woman who had recently been introduced to a fellow to whom she was very sexually attracted; when asked, admitted that he had a girlfriend. They ran into each other a month later.

"I had no intention of having sex with him knowing that he had a girlfriend. However, that night, as we were lying in bed, we ended up having sex. It has now been four weeks, and he says he doesn't plan to be with his girlfriend forever and doesn't want to ever marry her, but he hides me from her, and I can't stand it that I am a secret.

"Is it good for me to be involved with him?

"If I stop seeing him, do you think he will give up his girlfriend?

"Do you think he would be good for me if he did this?"

I guess she thinks being a secret sex toy is a compliment and the beginning of a beautiful relationship. Well, here are my answers: No. Who cares? Not likely.

This letter makes the point that sometimes the worst secrets are the truths we keep from ourselves. It's generally downhill from there.

2

Stupid Egotism

> "How many egocentric folks does it take to screw in a lightbulb?
>
> One.
>
> She just holds the lightbulb up to the fixture and waits for the world to revolve around her!"
>
> —April, a listener

That quote was April's *P.S.* The first part of her letter was a blunt confession of the main problem with egocentrism in a relationship; basically, that it's an oxymoron:

"Being an Aries, I have a big, inflated ego which I have to keep in check. Now I am married and I love it more than anything, but when I was younger I had the 'everyone for him/herself' mentality, which is egocentric thinking. I now know that EACH PERSON IN THE RELATIONSHIP NEEDS TO BE BRINGING SOMETHING WORTHWHILE AND SPECIAL TO THAT RELATIONSHIP. WE HAVE TO THINK OF OUR FAMILY MEMBERS AND BE AWARE OF ACTING IN THE BEST INTERESTS OF THE FAMILY/RELA-TIONSHIP . . . EVEN IN THE DAYS OF EXTREME PMS!

"If we are egocentric in our relationship we are being stupid because nobody wants to be with someone like that! Do you? I

don't. We all need to grow up and see that the universe does not revolve around only us."

I'm sure that as you read April's letter, you thought to yourself, "Well, yeah, that's obvious—so what's the big deal?" I agree. The idea should be obvious. Too bad the practicing of it seems to be so troublesome to so many. The problem doesn't lie in any epidemic of genetic mutations that have produced self-centered, inconsiderate, selfish, self-protecting-through-hostility, insensitive, frightened, or confused people who don't know how to "become one." There have always been some folks with personality styles incompatible with healthy intimacy. But there is something new under the sun: the societal emphasis on individuality and the determination toward SELF-fulfillment, SELF-actualization, and PERSONAL happiness, as separate from obligations, commitments, and sacrifice.

As one of my listeners realized:

"Trying to be 'my own woman' has hurt my relationship. I found that the more I became my 'own' self, the less I was part of 'our' life. I started thinking more about individual needs instead of family needs. I was lucky enough to have a husband who brought me back to reality. Now, I have my 'own sense of individuality' within my family."

Jim, another listener, came to the same conclusion:

"I am man enough to give up my 'rights' and 'individualism' for the benefit of my family. It works because I think of them first and their needs before I think of myself. And, when they see that in me, they give up their rights for my sake. It's a win-win situation.

"But, know this, I can't do this on my own, but through the power of God alone can anyone think of another before they think of themselves. In our own power, we are too selfish and self-centered."

Jim's letter points out a highly contested issue in our society today: Can one be "good" or "moral" without G-d? Senator Joseph Lieberman, while running for Vice-President in

2000, got caught in that maelstrom when his religious Orthodoxy at once won him a title of "very moral and having profound character," and an attack (from his own side) that he'd better not be saying that religiosity and morality had to go hand in hand. Whew! Make up your mind!

The reality is that secularism is pragmatic and spirituality is transcendent. Our society has become one in which collective values and virtues are secondary to individual and self-proclaimed group claims, protests, angers, irrationality, radicalism, intimidation, and outright terrorism. In other words, special interest groups will say or do whatever it takes to satisfy their agenda, regardless of fairness, goodness, or truth. Those individuals who stand for traditional (religious) values are scoffed at, demonized, and marginalized.

The result of all this societal transformation is a population that is frankly egotistical. Historically, one would more likely hear, "Ask what you can do for your country," today the slogans are, "Yeah, but when do I get mine? You can't make me! I'm entitled! But I want it!"

G-d Is Dead—Long Live ME!

Lately I've been reading a lot of nonsense published in the mainstream press about how believing in and respecting "G-d's Commandments" is unnecessary to compassion and morality. As proof, we are given the actions of animals. One example I read recently was how ants will sacrifice themselves by forming a bridge of their bodies over water to allow other ants to live. You actually believe the ants sit around and philosophize about the morality of sacrificing the few for the many? Of course not! Their behavior is built into their genetic wiring—it's called "instinct." Instinct isn't reasoned, it is reflexive.

When you see adult male brown bears moving into an area with mother bears and their cubs, killing the young, and mating with the females, you're not viewing sociopathic behavior. You're witnessing the genetically hard-wired, instinctive behavior to make the new male's genes go forward, not those of their competitors.

When you see a human firefighter, rush into a burning, collapsing building to rescue someone else's children, you are not seeing instinct (that would be to run away!), you are seeing commitment, compassion, responsibility, heroism . . . and . . . maybe the rush of the thrill of facing danger. Interviews with heroes usually give little information other than that the person was taught it was the right thing to do. That's morality. That's uniquely human, and definitely tied into the spiritual quest to be more than our animal instincts.

Family Values . . . Yucch!

The predominantly liberal press has a field day with the notion of "family values." Instead of a respect for a construct that connects, supports, nurtures, loves, and motivates each one of us, this institution is the object of perpetual derision and condemned as an exploitation and domination of women, a Victorian kill-joy of sexual pleasure, and an unrealistic and oppressive brake on the natural tendency toward polygamy.

The loss of the respect for obligation to family has inevitably produced a self-centered population struggling to find something by which to make life meaningful.

What I have witnessed growing over these years is not a celebration of freedom, but a sadness, loneliness, and confusion as the promised land turns out to be of sour milk and fetid honey.

Family values are about sex, marriage, and children. Let's take these issues one at a time.

Sex

The sexual revolution promised sex free of commitment and responsibilities, promiscuity without judgment, and intercourse without conception (the birth control pill with an abortion chaser)—just self-centered pleasure seeking. The feminist movement taught us that this was all a good thing. When women, it said, are freed from the shackles of morality, modesty, and marriage, then orgasms would be more frequent and more explosive. What actually happened was the loss of courtship, romance, chivalry, falling in love, commitment, and marriage. It does not appear that most women are particularly happy that the price for this liberation was so profound and personally devastating.

Sex has become a kind of sport for both men and women. Where once, a pregnancy precipitated assuming responsibilities, today men easily walk away as women are left with their freedoms of abortions and unmarried parenthood. It is ironic that there is still such an emphasis on criticizing deadbeat dads for walking away, when an aborting mother is not seen as a deadbeat mom, though her decision actually brings death upon the scene. What's the big deal about deadbeat dads when women can get sperm from a bank or an unsuspecting sexual partner and, like many movie and TV celebrities, just be a "single mom" with no criticism? Sounds like woman are speaking out of two sides of their mouths.

And what about "safe" sex? There isn't any. The epitome of intimacy, the union of men and women in pleasure and procreation is anything but safe because it is a leap of trust. Forget the STDs, abortions, and the unfortunate illegitimate children, and think of the repetitive hurts of "serial monogamy" and the ultimate loneliness and emptiness that follow sex without context.

Marriage

At best, marriage is now seen as a fragile promise. The young people I talk to are afraid of "commitment" because they have seen so little of it from their parents and peers. How can we expect young people to give their hearts and be willing to trust and love, when their own lives have been traumatized, sometimes by multiple losses of family cohesion and stability as their parents marry, divorce, shack-up, move on, again and again?

Consequently, these frightened but lonely, needy, and somewhat hopeful young adults are shacking-up. Contrary to their hope of finding the right one through this trial period, the statistics show elevated depression and anxiety, infidelity, violence, and a greater rate of breakup inside or out of a marital relationship. Unfortunately, too many children are born into these even more fragile relationships, only to suffer the loss and hurt along with their parents.

In the past, callers to my radio program who were contemplating divorce, did so out of great angst; alcoholism, abuse, affairs were the triggers. Nowadays, divorces seem more and more to come out of a sense of entitlement for perpetual glee and satisfaction on all grounds.

The most surprising trend is looking at marriage as barely a home base for one's individual endeavors. A number of women, for example, have called my program proclaiming their spouses "controlling" because the husbands were not overjoyed at their leaving the country for months or years to complete some course of study or take on some "once in a lifetime" job opportunity. What?

Another example of callers who make it clear that marriage will not stand in the way of their personal endeavors is the man who wondered if it would be okay to place their several-month-old child with their in-laws for a year and a half or two so that they could get on developing their careers. What?

Marriage used to be about folks finally learning that the greatest value in life is to be a part of something greater than yourself: family and children. Marriage today is about having some company, for as long as you like it, while you get on with your life. Pure egotism.

Children

There is hardly a more profound teacher about generosity, selflessness, bonding, mission, compassion, or love than parenting. For most of us, life becomes more serious and meaningful when we become responsible to others.

Even this has been thwarted by a "me" and "career" and "acquisition" oriented society which falsifies reality (thanks to certain agendized sociological and psychological groups) in order to tell parents that their children do not need them other than to earn money and be happy. Full-time, evening-time, sick-time, vacation-time, anytime childcare is promoted as a boon to individual, adult freedom. There have even been "studies" purporting that mothers at home with their children hurt their children intellectually and socially. How low can a movement go to justify itself? Obviously, very low.

The responsibilities of, and participation in, marriage, marital sex, and child rearing are how an individual not only lives for others, but lives for the future of others and humanity. Obviously, that is the opposite of the narcissism, the demand for immediate pleasures, accomplishments, and satisfactions which predominates today.

Feminism

"I was sorry to hear that Barbara Hall would be giving a love interest to Maxine of *Judging Amy*. Maxine is an independent and self-sufficient woman. There are lots of ways for her to continue to be self-actualized on her own . . . a hobby, or other pursuits in which she can help society. I thought feminism had progressed beyond the age-old theory that women need to have a man. . . ." Jan Winning, West Hills, California (*The New York Times*, Letter to the Editor, April 9, 2000).

What saddens me the most, in addition to the fact that this was written by someone in my neck of the woods, is that it is an attempt to deny a basic biopsychological reality of healthy, normal women: They desire and enjoy bonding with a man. Hobbies, work, and other pursuits are a wonderful, creative, and necessary aspect of any human's life, man or woman, but the drive for connection is normal, natural, and important too. It makes me mad that feminists would deny this undeniable reality and, in so doing, cause substantial harm to so many women.

"I am . . . a reformed feminist. I am twenty-two years old . . . and once thought that I could basically do whatever I wanted in a relationship because I was a strong, young woman. I didn't want to do something special for my 'man.' I would often be defensive . . . because I was filled with this BS feminist nonsense, and I did not want to have to cook a dinner or have a relationship with him. But now I see that you should do things for your partner to make them happy. I cannot stand it when I see these women on

talk shows who do not work and say they feel like slaves because their husbands want them to clean and cook for them after the man is out working all day . . . it is crazy. You have to make certain sacrifices in a relationship, but doing your part isn't a sacrifice, it's just how things are supposed to be."

Wow! Now, that's an important revelation for the feminists. ". . . doing your part isn't a sacrifice, it's just how things are supposed to be." It's an issue of teamwork—not oppression against ovaries. I also consider myself a "reformed feminist." Having been at University in the 1960s, I was "enlightened" to believe that marriage and mothering were conspiracies to eliminate my power, worth, and voice. I carefully watched every word, nuance, attitude, suggestion, expectation, reaction, and behavior for proof that "he" was trying to dominate or disrespect me as a woman.

At the same time, I wore pretty clothes and makeup, expected to be asked out by the man, waited for him to open the door and pay the check, and played coy at the door after a date. How crazy-making was I? Looking back, though, the point is that there was a disconnect between social pressures and natural tendencies. I have learned in the many years since this time that femininity, modesty, and domesticity are not horrors, nor are they the assassins of freedom and individuality. They are elements special to life, values, and relationships. They are not "instead," they are "in addition to."

As one listener wrote:

"I grew up with a feminist mentality that no man would rule me. I am just now beginning to realize how this has put undue pressure on my marriage. I think the biggest problem comes by 'straddling the fence.' There have been times when I want to play the damsel and my husband the knight: 'Save me, dear husband,' one moment and 'How dare you expect anything of me,' the next. I have been arrogant and pompous at times."

Having a feminist mantra of distrust of the masculine and disdain for the feminine has been at the crux of a lot of confusion and dismay for women who guiltily like the idea that woman is different from man.

I received this letter from one of my listeners:

"The first year of our relationship was hell. I was trying to be myself, a strong and independent woman. I rarely asked him for permission to do things or spend money, especially if I thought it was okay myself. I am somewhat masculine in that I like to do hard work and wear jeans and T-shirts most of the time. I rarely wear makeup or perfume or jewelry. Well, apparently that is not what he wanted. He would get upset that I didn't dress up more often, that I didn't ask him about big decisions I made, that I refused to play the 'weaker sex,' and that I was working at a man's job (I was an assistant for a horse vet, which required heavy lifting and hard work). It really floored me at first that this man actually WANTED a woman like that.

"I am the daughter and granddaughter of a pastor. . . . I knew that the Bible says to submit yourself unto your husband, but I didn't understand at first what that means. It DOESN'T MEAN 'LET YOUR HUSBAND WALK ALL OVER YOU,' it just means consider him first, and let him be the leader in family decisions. I learned that the compromising that is marriage isn't just going to a Mexican restaurant when you are in the mood for Chinese. It is compromising your life and yourself because you love someone. Sometimes I would purposefully ask my husband to lift something heavy, all the while thinking I could do it myself, because it makes him feel needed. Sometimes I dress up just for him because it makes him feel wanted.

"I haven't given up my SELF for him (I still plan to be a vet and work with horses on my own ranch). I've merely modified myself in exchange for a deeper love and peace in the household. I think it is worth it."

Frankly, in my feminist years I would have had a fit over

this letter because she appears to have given in, she is pretending for his ego, she has caved in to sexist roles. How foolish I was to ignore the realities of man and woman—the subtle means by which men and women relate in order to please and connect.

During the late 1970s and 1980s I found myself, as a licensed Marriage, Family, and Child Therapist, counseling many couples struggling with how to relate in this new society. Whether they were dating or married, it often came down to an important piece of advice: To men (women) I would say, treat her like a woman(man), not just like a brain, a human being, a buddy, a partner, a neuter. The astonishment and resistance was huge! Nonetheless, I stayed with the program of reminding people that IQ and extraordinary talents notwithstanding, we are ultimately male or female, with a brain and endocrine system organized in unique, somewhat polarized ways, which require respect and attention.

Without acknowledging and responding to the masculine and feminine in each other, with the respect, admiration, and attention these aspects deserve, I saw that marital partners would be more demanding, less patient and understanding, and less solicitous and thoughtful—in other words, more egocentric. When I emphasized with them that they both needed to express what was uniquely male/female, it opened up part of their relationship previously ignored or inappropriately devalued. They both would become kinder to each other.

Why is it that women can complain about a man not expressing his emotions and talking and sharing with her so that she can feel involved and useful but a man cannot with equal respect complain about her not needing him for the trouble-shooting and problem solving and protecting and providing that is more typically in the male personality? Feminism, of course, and the desire to feminize men.

Here's an example of that short-sighted hostility:

"I remember as if it were yesterday his statement that I didn't really need him because I could change the oil in the car, mow the lawn, and build a deck. It was like a baseball bat to the brain— the revelation that he did not understand emotional needs . . . but only those other needs of defined male/female roles."

Well, how 'bout that she didn't understand the physical and practical needs? Why is it this competition rather than cooperation? Fortunately, this next listener "got it":

"I was raised to be 'independent.' 'You can accomplish anything you set your mind to. Don't rely on others to make yourself happy.' Being 'betrayed' by an adult from when I was nine to fifteen years of age, and being on survival mode for those years, has contributed to my 'independent' quality.

"After an argument the other night . . . his last line of the fight was . . . 'You don't need me, you don't rely on me for anything. . . . You do whatever you want without thinking of me.'

"He was right. This has been troubling me because I so much love this man and he puts me and our son above everything else in his life. . . . Well, it does do damage to have that mind-set of 'being my own woman.' It is alienating my husband, making him doubt his own ability to be a husband."

Early on in my therapy career, I was taught various techniques for dealing with controlling people. First, I was made to appreciate the fear that went into the need to control: fear of loss of self, security, love, change. The issue of control, therefore, was neurotically centered.

Then feminism put a whole new spin on control: It's something that happens automatically in a relationship with a man, and if you don't control everything in your life yourself, then you are pathetic, neurotic, powerless, and vulnerable to the whims of a despot spelled "h-u-s-b-a-n-d." Whew! How confusing. Here, I'll make it simple: If men control, they're bad; if women control, they're good. There. Now you're clear, right?

As another listener learned, it's not "right":

"My husband and I got married when I was twenty-four and discovered I was pregnant. I told him upon our 'agreement' to get married that I was going to continue to work . . . and we were going to keep everything 'separate and equal.' I had my own checking account and he had his own. We even filed separate tax returns. There was no way I was going to be 'dependent' on any man. After our little girl was born I came to the realization there was NO way I could go back to work and leave her with a sitter or a day care. I didn't come right out and tell my husband . . . how could I admit this 'weakness' and then on top of that be 'dependent' on him. So, instead, I got resentful and angry . . . hated him for existing. I hated the fact that I wouldn't have my own money and I wouldn't have any power in the relationship because I wasn't contributing financially to the household.

"I was going to be a mom and dependent on a man . . . everything I was indoctrinated against. I went back to college and took up another degree . . . you see I needed a job where I could make good money, take care of my baby, and not be dependent on my husband. During nursing school I spent less time with my husband and daughter.

"Today I truly believe God had different plans. It was during my drive to and from nursing school that I discovered the Dr. Laura show. My priorities changed. I realized that my behavior and attitude toward my husband wasn't God directed—I was going to break up my marriage and take my daughter away from her daddy in the name of my independence . . . because of my stupid pride.

"I love my husband . . . I love my children . . . and I am loving being 'dependent' on him. I pray that I can be a better example for my daughter and son. I have turned into the woman that my friends and I were trying to liberate during our rallies in college . . . and I am so very glad."

Many women are angry at the bill of goods the boomer generation and the 1960s and 1970s sold them. *"They really screwed with our heads. Let women be what they want and respect them for their choices,"* is what one exasperated listener wrote. It is a paradox, that the very folks, the feminists, who espouse CHOICE, CHOICE, AND MORE CHOICE, only mean, as with most radical groups, their style of choice and then demean all others.

A major eastern women's college, for example, permitted a radical group to yank references to the high marriage rate of successful graduates from their recruitment brochure. Why? They said it was discriminatory against those who preferred not to marry men and sexist in its obvious reassurance to parents that their daughter's education would not undermine their ability or desire to marry. It struck me as awful that "choice" did not include what has been a normal, natural and desirable, and G-d commanded activity since humans walked the earth: the bonding of men and women in holy matrimony, creating the stability and love in which to raise children. Tsk, tsk—how insulting can we be?

I Want to Be Alone . . . Move Over

I am struck at how the totality of liberalization of sex, cohabitation, and childbearing have caused massive confusion and devastation in personal relationships by emphasizing the "me" over the "we."

This is probably one of the most frequent issues to come up on my radio program as callers grapple with what they should be allowed to do in spite of being married and what they're spouses shouldn't be doing because they're married!

"Single while married," is a recurrent problem because our ego-loving society doesn't seem to put any reasonable demand on people, no limits, no boundaries. Hence we had eight years of a President who finally admitted to infidelities, lying, and perjury; we have civil rights leaders admitting to the very out-of-wedlock births that plague their communities. Some role models. And, there is little corresponding outrage or significant consequence. So, what's the average person to deduce? That it's all ultimately okay, and there exists no behavior that would make you a bad person, or wrong, or immoral (unless you count criticizing such behavior on religious grounds)—just temporarily embarrassed. I hope that the election of George W. Bush is signaling a significant spiritual, philosophical, and behavioral move away from that destructive way of thinking and acting.

Too many people find themselves on the receiving end of "single while married," and they don't like it:

" 'My right to stay out all night with the guys while you are pregnant is more important than your feelings or needs.' Boy, it was the last thing I needed back then, waiting up all night for the 'father' to come home. I learned great lessons from that: A man who loves you will stay with you and watch movies even if you only have the sniffles. That 'father' disappeared six months after our son was born . . . must have been important to maintain the nights out."

I have always contended that no woman should marry a man she doesn't believe would swim through shark-infested water to bring her a lemonade. Likewise, no man should marry a woman who doesn't have a patient sense of humor about guy stuff.

There are some clear-cut ways people determine to be single while married: money and spending, hobbies, addictions, internet "relationships," and outside activities.

"My husband is currently doing something stupid in our relationship. He spends money on big items, mostly motorcycles and parts, and recently purchased a newer Camaro without talking to me about it. He feels he deserves it and doesn't need to discuss

large purchases. We can't afford this. I feel he has betrayed me and after numerous times of buying, hiding the purchase, and me finding out, our marriage is doomed."

I just love that excuse, "I deserve it." Where does that immature sense of entitlement come from? Spoiling from parents? A society which measures success in acquisitions? No matter how you look at it, it is egocentric. When we marry, as I remind listeners and callers, we give up the privilege of doing whatever we want whenever we want simply because we want. While to many that is a major catastrophic reality, most of us see this as a welcome tradeoff to have someone care about our well-being, to have something to live and work for outside ourselves, and the comfort of companionship. Happiness is not perfected until it is shared.

One female listener owned up to her selfishness about "friendships" outside of marriage.

"During my nearly eight-year relationship with a very wonderful man, there have been lots of stormy times that have at their root my determination to do what I want to do . . . have friends I choose to have . . . go where I want to go. This attitude that I have brought into our relationship out of fear that I would become my mother and allow him to steal my soul has done nothing but alienate him and cause him to be even more insecure and controlling.

"For example, at one point in our relationship, I had a coworker named David whom I was very fond of. I would come home and talk about things he said or things I liked about him, without giving any thought to how that made Russell (my fiancé) feel. My only thought was, 'He's not going to tell ME whom I can have for a friend.'

"I finally got the point that Russell said it was hurtful and caused him to be suspicious and jealous. I have since realized that to be good to him, and thereby good to us, I cannot have friends of the opposite sex that I gush over in our home. I cannot forget that the person I should be praising and adoring is the one I chose to be with and the one I love."

I'm often asked, generally quite angrily I should add, why married folk should not have close friends of the opposite sex to talk with, do things with, share, and so forth. I try to explain that we should not engage in behavior that brings unease or suspicion into our marriages. We should not use another person outside our marriage for intimacy and revealing of personal information about our partner (save for clergy or therapists in counseling). It is generally a lie to suggest that there is no aspect of man/woman stuff going on or that could potentially go on. At least one of the two likely has "designs," which is what motivates them to be so "understanding" in the first place. No married person should repeatedly put themselves in a situation with romantic potential. Religious people, for example, are never alone with a member of the opposite sex—they realize that how it looks and what it could become should be avoided out of respect for vows.

As another listener writes, some people will hold on to their addictions more tightly than they embrace their vows—denying, of course, that they are addicted—protesting instead that they "have a right!"

"My husband is determined to be his own man, and it is hurting our relationship almost as deeply as infidelity. My husband is an alcoholic. I consider it to be his best friend and mistress. He must be his own man. He gets angry so quickly instead of merely talking things out. Then, if I dared to defend myself from verbal attacks, I get the silent treatment for the next couple of very long days. I just love to pieces that man he is when he is not drinking, but when he is his own man, and does what he damn well pleases (drinks), I would rather be any other place on earth."

Another listener's husband has a hobby. Hobbies are good to relieve tension and experience creativity in a nonstructured way. However, some married people pursue a hobby as though they were single. One listener wrote me that her husband loves to hunt. She recalls that when they were first together, he would be away for many three- or four-day weekends. This was okay with her because, after all, they were dating and not married.

"We have now been married seventeen years and have three wonderful daughters and his hobby now takes him away from us a minimum of two to three weeks a year and on some weekends. The fact that he travels on the average of three days a week for business means he is away a significant amount of time during the year. He does not listen to my pleading for a cut in time spent hunting until the girls get out of high school He believes he has the RIGHT to do this, and calls any attempt on my part to communicate hurt feelings, as attempts to control him."

I hear from and about a lot of men who believe that their work or hobbies are some kind of inalienable right, against which responsibilities to family pale. That's why I was so glad when one of our editors quit working on my magazine, *The Dr. Laura Perspective*. It seems that he was working late every night at home on articles. One night his wife and children did not come home or call. He was frantic. When he finally reached them, his wife wondered why she should come home early in the evening when he wasn't really there. He quit the next day so he would have quality time with his family. I miss him desperately, but I so respect his correct decision.

Too many men and women get ferociously arrogant about their work and neglect their families while identifying themselves as some kind of heroes. One woman caller recently told me she was a great schoolteacher and thought that the numbers of children who benefited from her work far outweighed the sacrifice of her own children suffering through day care. I reminded her that the notion that being such a good teacher was more important than parenting should have come before pregnancy. However, now that she had a child, G-d blessed her with that responsibility that she must fulfill before she gets her professional ego massaged. I suggested she wait until the child was ready for kindergarten, and then start teaching while Junior was also at school.

Last, but not least, is the new phenomenon of cyber affairs. Frankly, this is pathetic. I have dealt with this subject on my TV and radio programs, as well as in *Perspective,* and I am struck with the complete lack of humanity and depth existing in folks who have cyber-relationships. There is no touch, no sight, no truth, no depth, no reality, no nothing of value. It is truly the epitome of getting an ego stroked. However, this passion for really being important to someone and finally getting needs met (no responsibilities or obligations are part of this fantasy, of course) has destroyed an alarming number of homes and marriages.

"My now ex-wife found it necessary to try to find her own self. Little did I know that our new computer was transforming my wife of fifteen years into a person I would never recognize as my wife. One day she asked for a divorce. I found out that she was actually having an online affair with this person that she was willing to give up everything for. Two months later I had convinced a judge to grant me custody of our sons (fifteen and twelve) and she left the state, and her sons, and moved to New Jersey with her new cyber-boyfriend. I was left with trying to explain to the kids why their mom had left."

I, for one, can't understand the degree of selfishness it takes to abandon, on a whim, all that has been built up and all who depend on you, for a flighty fantasy of sex and freedom. I can imagine imagining it! I just can't imagine actually doing it. It becomes easier and easier for people to behave this way since society has stopped condemning, judging, punishing, and shunning. I expect that the cyber-affair woman's family is probably hostile to anyone who says an unkind word about her—after all, family is family. Even when you abandon yours?

One man, a listener, sums up all this "single while married," mentality:

"I found that fighting for my rights or individuality is being selfish, shows lack of concern for others, and gives the wrong message to the kids. It is necessary for me to set the example. If you have self-esteem, you don't have to fight for your rights, you know who you are and there is nothing to prove. If I give up my rights or individuality to be there for others and receive the blessings from God in return, so be it!"

If There Is Only Me . . . Then You Can't Hurt Me

Some of what makes people self-centered in relationships has to do with immaturity, lack of experience, poor role models, personality styles, habit, self-protection, and some combination of the above.

For example, as one listener wrote:

"Being on my own for so long I got very used to taking care of myself and if I was hurt or in any type of bind, no one else had to know about it and it really just wasn't their business anyway. When I became engaged this affected our relationship greatly because it took me a while to realize that I can't become one with someone and still behave like the Lone Ranger. I had to share my thoughts, what I had, and very personal information. That wasn't easy, but I have to thank God for a patient and tolerant man who is now my husband. He taught me a lot and helped me realize he was there to help, not hurt me and I didn't have to do everything on my own."

As many people who have gone through decent therapy have learned, it is not unusual for people who have suffered to take it out on their spouses—a kind of "I suffered at the hand of another so now you owe me!" mentality.

This was (heavy on the *was*) the perspective of one listener:

"I grew up in a sexually, emotionally, and physically abusive home—my father molested my sister, brothers, and me . . . as well as many of our friends and cousins. Because of our rough home life, my brother turned to drugs, my sister and I became promiscuous. I am astonished at how stupid and self-centered I used to be and how far I've come. At one point, I thought that because I was a wounded bird, that the world owed me something. When one approaches life as a free-for-all, there are no standards of behavior and nothing to live up to and for. I have built a decent, respectable life by having a foundation of values by which I live—with family."

While it is not unusual for people hurt as children to react in such a chaotic way, pushing away values and good people and good experiences out of unresolved historical anger, a fear of hurt or loss, or a discomfort with normalcy after so much chaos, the solution always is love, bonding, commitment, purpose. The solution always is getting back on the soul train someone threw you off.

That "pain" isn't always from childhood, although those experiences do have an impact on how you handle challenges along the way. Some people have had terrible experiences, which they generalize to all relationships.

"I had come out of a very bad six-year marriage when I met my second wife. The first wife was very controlling and I did not like that. So, I decided I would not let that happen again. I never allowed my new wife and myself to grow as a couple. I decided that work was more satisfying to me than my marriage and family, in spite of the fact that marriage and family was always what I wanted. At the end of the marriage I was very lonely. My independence caused that. It's been a year since the divorce."

Self-protectiveness is alienating and lonely. Somehow, the person has chosen safety over risk, and without risk there is no gain, and without gain there is no intimacy, and without intimacy there is no peace and safety that comes from being known *and* loved.

I Hurt . . . Therefore, I'm in Charge!

When I talk to people on my radio program about their "life-long" problems and they go into their history to explain the origins of their issues, I remind them that there are two parts to ongoing behaviors: The first is the precipitating events (abuse, abandonment, etc.); the second is what are called "secondary gains." Secondary gains refer to the benefits of maintaining the problem. Here are two examples, one having to do with pain, the second with overeating.

"When I say something to her and when she does not complete a task I've asked her to do, she gets mad and starts yelling—then she starts crying and talking about how bad her childhood was and says no one loves her, no one cares about her. I do get mad at her when she won't do anything. The only reason I don't leave is I feel sorry for her, because she claims that she was abused, molested, neglected, and never taught morals in her childhood. I don't want to spend the rest of my life trying to fix something that will never fix."

I have talked to many women over the years who admit to holding historical pains up as a banner declaring themselves off-limits to demands, expectations, and responsibilities. It's a tough one to give up because all the sympathy and permissiveness makes life so easy at times; they feel righteous and in control. The perpetual suffering, pity, and aggravation are too big a price to pay.

Obviously, this is a "spite your face" type of behavior, because you end up not respected and not competent at anything that will be satisfying. One woman listener wrote about how her father made a big deal about her weight when she was a teen. He had put pressure on her to lose weight at that period of time when she was just going through puberty and it was a truly normal growth spurt. She was not overeating.

"To claim control of the situation, I began sneak eating. Fast for-

ward nineteen years later, I'm married to a decent guy, whom I always promised I would get myself fit and healthy for. Twenty years, thousands of broken promises, and unused exercise equipment later, I was still eating . . . out of spite. That was how I claimed my 'right' to my body. I am in therapy now, having realized that I need to claim responsibility for my spiteful eating. My spitefulness has hurt my marriage, but it has hurt me, too. I was determined to prove to my father/husband that they could not control my body. I do realize whom I have been hurting all along. Me."

Carrying over old problems into marriage and family is a selfishness borne of unresolved anger and hurts; nonetheless, it is a self-centeredness: me, my hurts . . . you won't get me!

Each individual must bring his or her healthiest, most trusting, and least hostile self into a relationship. Using others today, simply to heal from or vindicate past pain, is self-centered and destructive.

Bored Means Boring

It is amazing to hear from people who criticize their marriage or partner as boring. Actually, it means that all relationships can get boring. But it's often not the usual suspect (the other person) that is the problem. The fact is that bored people are usually boring. They just blame it on others and circumstance.

That's why people get so shocked and annoyed when I tell them that if they're bored they better become more interesting rather than demand that of their partner. It works, trust me. Here's an example:

"I am married for nine years. About three years ago my marriage was in serious trouble—mostly due to my being stubborn. If my husband wouldn't give me what I needed, then I sure as heck wasn't going to give him what he needed. We rarely talked, did

almost nothing together or as a family, we never hugged, touched, or kissed. I wanted him to love me first the way I needed, and then I would love him back, the way I felt he needed. He was a potato.

"I went to a minister for counseling. He told me to think of what I could do each day, special, just for my husband so HE would know he was loved. The entire session became about what I could do. It was about what I could give. My marriage is a complete turn-around. After just a few days of being 'my husband's wife,' he began to try to find ways to make me happy. I can't tell you how much the selfishness I had was the problem. Now I have the man of my dreams."

Another listener had the same revelation:

"I really thought my wife was no fun anymore. I saw a book about ten thousand ways to say 'I love you,' and realized I was really a selfish person. I started on the simple things like picking up after myself, fixing her dinner after a long day, leaving notes of appreciation. And wow! Things started happening. The gates of communication burst open and the sex and communication have never been better.

"GEEE, I never knew that giving lots gets so much back . . . I wish I would have known this many years ago . . . and how many years I wasted dreaming of leaving and finding the perfect lady when I had her all this time and I was too selfish to figure it out."

You Mean, There Is a You?

When babies are born, they are the center of their own universe; even their mother's breast is seen as an extension of themselves. It is a wonder and a shock for them to discover that there are other people, with opinions, desires, demands, expectations, power, and personality. When we grow into adults we supposedly have learned to navigate in the world of "others" and to get along with people, using skills we've developed along the way.

Sometimes we get stuck in the "me" mode and forget there is a universe of others out there. Sometimes all we need is a little nudge as a reminder. Sometimes we need a big smack upside our heads. Here are some expressions of that lesson learned:

➤   It's not that you're always wrong, it's that I'm always right: *"When I married my husband nearly eighteen years ago, our first three to five years were pretty rough. We both have our own faults, but it wasn't until I quit criticizing and trying to change him that our relationship really came alive."*

➤   We're not fighting, you are!: *"I have a very quick temper and seem to take it out on everyone around me at the time. We recently split up, because I was so tired of all the arguing. This all could have been avoided if I'd realized what I was doing then was being a self-centered, spoiled brat and needed to grow up. It takes two and I have to ask myself what I am doing to contribute to this arguing?!"*

➤   If we all do everything my way we'll all be very happy: *"I thought that if he could see that I was right, then we could do the right thing and all would be well in the marriage. I did not see that there were times when the right way or answer was not mine but rather what was right for us BOTH."*

➤   It's my life, isn't it?: *"I used to believe that it only mattered what I felt in this life since it is my life. Now I realize that this world does not revolve around me. The world is full of people who are in need that same way I am."*

It seems such a difficult task for so many to realize that happiness and love are not gotten by force of will, nor are they automatically granted simply because you show up. The greatest amount of getting is through giving. If you take care of the ones you love, even when you're hurting or not in the mood or they've done something to annoy you, it not only shows love, it primes them to be more giving.

Everything Except Each Other

The struggle against selfishness is difficult and never-ending. That is because we all want. We all need. We all have impulses. Self-control, as opposed to selfishness, requires effort and sacrifice. This includes making time for each other a priority. That means apportioning time for work, play, hobbies, children, extended family, religious activities, and community service. I sometimes weary at the complaints of those who are exhausted and stressed by their "obligations to students, worshippers, clients, patients . . ." I remind them that there is both choice and ego involved. The ego part is about the gratification they get for being so "wonderful" and "necessary." The choice involves the denial that they are acting on ego.

Perhaps a thousand cheering fans is more exhilarating to some that the grateful hug of a son or a husband (or wife)— but I'm not one of them. The legion may be sincere, but it still lacks the depth of the one-on-one at-home experience with spouse and children.

As "One" in the Eyes of G-d

One of the most profound truths is that G-d made us incomplete; and, it is not a Ph.D. that completes us. What completes us is a joining with our gender counterpart. One husband and listener wrote this:

"As far as being an individual, when you marry you are no longer an individual. That's why you are referred to as Mr. and Mrs. at the wedding ceremony. The people who have problems with losing their individuality were most likely insecure to start with. God said that the two should become as one. So, the answer is that you lose your individuality only to gain a new, and complete one."

Another listener completed this thought with the following observation:

"It's amazing how honest you tend to be with each other when you imagine God literally in your house as your 'boss.' We appreciate that we are each our own man and woman. But, when we come together as one we are unstoppable and inseparable."

That's it in a nutshell. When it's me or you, it's a fight. When it's you and me in the sight of G-d, it's a festival.

Selfishness not only cuts out your partner, it cuts out G-d, and without G-d, there is only "me." And "me" is ultimately alone.

3
Stupid Pettiness

"After all my years in combat, I've learned something I've carried with me throughout my civilian life. When I get angry about something, or at someone, before I act I ask myself, 'Is this the hill I want to die on?'"

—(RETIRED MARINE MASTER SERGEANT, A LISTENER)

I swear, on my radio show I think it would be much easier to talk someone out of outright murdering another person than it generally is to talk someone out of being *mad* or *hurt* (same thing, really) at some imperfection or perceived slight or personal style. And, forgive me, we women are worse than the men when it comes to being petty.

Last time I went through airport security we couldn't figure out why I kept setting off the alarm after I'd removed my belt, wallet, jewelry—everything but my fillings! The culprit was the wire in my bra! I mean, really, how high can you turn up the sensitivity on that machine before it gets silly. Same for women in general. Perhaps it is because we women are simply biologically fine-tuned (sensitive?) to interpersonal nuances, because we are the gender that gives birth, tends children, manages the neighborhood and family social interactions. How many times have you heard the story that when the matriarch dies, the family glue is lost? Often. How many times have you heard the story that when the patriarch dies, the family glue is lost? Never.

Whatever its evolutionary plan and benefits, the sensitivity to the actions of others is definitely set on max when it comes to women. Like airport security, moderate sensitivity is good for detecting problems to be handled, but maximum sensitivity actually causes problems.

This is not to say that men can't be hypersensitive or nit-picky—it's just not as general a rule for men as it is for women. If it were, so many women over so much time would not have had the age-old complaint of a tuned out, not-paying-attention, insensitive, clueless spouse or boyfriend.

Let me give you an example from a recent radio conversation with a woman caller. She complained that in November, at a neighborhood gathering, her friend-neighbor had invited her to a Christmas Night party at the neighbor's home. The woman also told her that she'd be away for the weeks before the party, having to travel to visit with family. Fine? No, of course not. Our caller was on the phone with me in January, complaining that the neighbor was rude. Her question for me was, "Should I confront her or just ignore her from now on?"

"Why," I asked, "why would you have to do either? What's the problem?"

"Well, when she came back from her trip she didn't call me to tell me exactly what time the party was. So, I didn't go. Then, I found out from another neighbor that she did have the party. She's a liar."

"Huh?" I answered dumbly. "What are you talking about?

You were invited. You knew she had numerous family obligations and then had to prepare for her party rather quickly. Why didn't you go? Why didn't you call and ask to help her? Why didn't you . . ."

"Well," she came back angrily, "she should have called me."

"Let me get this straight. If I invite one hundred people to a party telling them when and where, I am expected to call all one hundred just before the party again to assure them they're still invited?"

"Well . . . I was expecting a call."

"You know," I retorted, "if you were a guy you would have been over without ceremony and with a keg of beer on your shoulder. Guys don't get all bent out of shape about the details. They don't spend serious time mulling over the details of tone, innuendo, timing, intent, facial expressions, and the rest. They just get on with it. Why can't we?"

"I don't know. So, should I confront her or just ignore her?"

"I give up."

Generally, it isn't the large bombs of life that do the most damage, it's the gnawing away of serenity and good sense by pettiness that is the most destructive force of intimate relationships in general, and men-women relationships most specifically.

Save Me From a Sensitive Mate!

"Don't hang around with or get into relationships with sensitive People!!!!!," writes a listener who got out of a relationship with one of the few overly sensitive men on the planet. *"Thanks to being raised by a straightforward mother, I was not too sensitive. I was once involved with 'a sensitive man' and, as if that weren't enough, went into business with 'a sensitive woman.'*

Dr. Laura, I wasted too much time apologizing for things I did not say or mean. Thankfully now, both are out of my life, and I did learn that valuable lesson."

Frankly, her rule is a good one. I generally tell folks to avoid dealing often or in depth with the hypers—it's a you-don't-ever-win situation. It is impossible to get along with the overly sensitive for very long before you become completely paranoid, worrying and wondering if or what or when they're going to feel hurt or angry or something (and, of course, not deal with it openly at the moment—overly sensitive types suffer on for a while) and when they're going to blow up and accuse you of all sorts of things you don't even remember and didn't even mean.

When Petty *Is* Important

All that having been said, there are also too many times when people discount as petty issues or circumstances that deserve respect. Petty sometimes has a point; as my Rabbi, reminding me of a famous quote, said, "G-d is in the details."

One of my listeners makes this point:

"I am one of those people who can handle any kind of crisis but the everyday trivial little things set me off. Little things like not putting the cap back on the toothpaste, not cleaning up after oneself, not erasing the messages off of the answer machine, etc. I just feel if each person in my household did these little things instead of leaving them for me, then I could reserve my sanity for when they really need me. It's usually one person in every family who gets stuck with it all. How much do you think one person can take? Think about that the next time you're about to walk away from something that you usually leave for someone else to do. Give a helping hand."

In all fairness, that's a very good point. When I was in private practice counseling folks with similar complaints, I would ask them, "Yeah, it's usually one person in every family who volunteers to get stuck with it all. Why did you volunteer? Why not leave it there long enough for someone else to eventually volunteer?"

Letting small things pile up by not pitching in is setting up the more responsible or compulsive of you to pick up after you. That's instigating a problem. Though it is true that the responsible person has a choice in doing it for you or leaving it alone, does the family or relationship really need two sloppy, irresponsible, childish folks?

When you look at it that way, it seems unfair to regard a small issue as stupid when the other person considers it a big deal. One listener had an example that illustrates this:

"My husband does not like it when I leave my closet door open because it is in view of people who may visit. While I may feel this is not a big deal, I try to respect him, but I would never tell him that is stupid. After all, everyone makes a big deal over small stuff, whether you want to admit it or not. What's important to one person may be viewed as stupid or petty by another. However, we should not voice that opinion but respect the other's view."

It is true that a loving relationship is in the "small stuff." Keep that in mind, and bend a little bit to comfort and please your partner. As they say, "It's not much skin off your nose."

When Petty Is Really Very Important

I get calls from men and women who ask me if they're being petty—when they definitely are not! It's always interesting, and sad, to hear some level of serious incompatibility or insult, followed up by, "I know I'm just being petty. How do I get over this?"

"Sometimes I catch my husband looking at other women and it makes me feel like he needs more to look at than just me," one

listener writes. Well, gee, feeling a bit bent out of shape when our honey makes a quick gaze at a pretty body is just one of those realities of life. However, a quick look is one thing. What follows in the letter is another:

"I feel like this is such a petty pet peeve in the scheme of things. This just bothers me and when I have asked him not to do this, he says he likes to stay aware of his surroundings and challenges me that the girl is not going to jump him in the store, is she? I have tried to overcome this, but it irritates me!"

The truth is, this is not a petty peeve. It is the reasonable hurt of a wife whose husband throws his awareness that there are girls prettier than she in her face. This is abject insensitivity bordering on mental cruelty. My advice to her for the moment this happens? I have suggested that women (a) say aloud for all to hear, "You're right honey, she's gorgeous and sexy looking—I can see why you're hot for her!" or (b) move forward toward the woman/girl and offer to introduce them, again out loud. Trust me, the behavior stops. But we're still stuck with a spouse willing to hurt.

What a lot of people dating seem to forget is that those "small things" are just the things one is supposed to assess for potential long-term suffering or joy. It still amazes me that dating is seen more as a conclusion than an investigation. One listener complained that her new boyfriend, while nice when he's around, lies about smoking, and never shows up to dinner on time (work . . . maybe) and spends half the week traveling (work . . . maybe). She chides herself for being petty, especially after the hurt of a divorce.

I ask them, point-blank, "If you were not dating anyone, and I suggested a blind date with a guy who smokes and lies about it, isn't around half the week, and can't be counted on being anywhere when he says he would, would you want to go out with him?"

"No, of course not," they wisely say.

"Well, then don't," I respond.

"But, I'm not being petty? I mean, aside from that, he's terrific with my kids."

"And that's the problem—he solves only part of the problem. The rest of the problem is going to be left unsolved? Is that the life you want to volunteer for?"

This is a worrisome issue to me. It is disturbing when folks cannot or will not distinguish between genuinely bad behavior and whether or not they're being petty by being hurt or saying/doing something about the genuinely bad behavior.

Sometimes petty is just downright meanness.

"I'm a thirty-six-year-old male married for twelve years and have three children from two to eleven. We both have full-time jobs. My daily routine consists of getting the girls up, dressed, breakfast, lunches, seeing them out the door while my wife showers and gets ready herself. My wife always complains about something, especially if things aren't going her way, like getting to work on time. She will constantly blame everyone for her lateness. I usually get home early to clean the house, feed the kids, and interact with them, but it seems that the house is never clean enough."

On my radio program I recently reported on a study from England which concluded that the largest cause of the overwhelming divorce rate is the bad behavior of women! Feminism once stood for a belief that career aspirations and social roles should not be limited by gender. Today, feminists are applauding women engaging in stereotypical masculine misbehaviors: aggression, self-centeredness, abandonment of marriage, pornography, and promiscuity. More and more women decide they're entitled to their happiness no matter the cost to children, families, or society. The listener's wife's constant barrage of petty complaints is a symptom of a larger problem of this growing selfishness and insensitivity in general in our culture, and, more frighteningly, in women in specific. When the gender of nurturance, regeneration, and sensitivity becomes crass and coarse, the field of hope becomes barren.

"My husband is a good man in every way," my listener writes. Well, if that were true, we wouldn't have more to the paragraph, but we do. *"But he can also be brash, sarcastic, easily exasperated, and cutting. We were married for eighteen years and I felt constantly bruised, a condition that made it hard to love him and hard to feel love. We went to counseling, and our therapist made an off-handed remark that stuck with me. All those things about my husband that drove me crazy—she called them his 'style.' I knew then that they had very little to do with me, and everything to do with his style. Somehow, this perspective enabled me, finally, to take his comments in stride."*

Let me get this straight, if someone's bad behavior is something they do all the time, and they do it to everybody, not just you, then you're not to be upset because it's not about you personally? But that means you're supposed to take it and they're not obligated to change their style? This works?

Evidently not, because her physican put her on Prozac for an intense and worsening kind of hypochondria and depression. I guess we just needed to understand that it was "his style" to cope with being *petty* about his nasty personality.

"He thinks I wear my feelings on my sleeve," was the beginning of the letter from another *petty* listener. Turns out her new beau (she is fifty-three, he is fifty-six) gives her short shrift on the phone, he's moody without explanation, he spends almost all Sundays worshipping football instead of attending church, and lives with his ex-wife to save money.

"I know it sounds fishy . . . ," she writes, but she still worries that she's being too petty. Oh, puhlease.

To summarize the points so far: Hypersensitivity is annoying and destructive, people will call you petty when you're not, only to avoid taking responsibility for their own misbehaviors. You shouldn't bury reasonable concerns by dismissing yourself as petty. Good. Now, let's get on to types of, reasons for, and how to deal with pettiness.

Ya' Don't Even Know You Are!

I remember a story one of my psychotherapy mentors told in class which says it all about how habit, experience, and familiarity can make us petty and we don't even realize it.

He said that early on in his marriage he came down with a terrible cold. He lay in bed, suffering "terribly," wondering when his wife was going to bring a huge glass of orange juice, just like his mommy used to do when he was a kid.

The orange juice never came. He was getting annoyed at her lack of sensitivity. Trying to prime the pump, he hinted: "Ahh, could I have some OJ, please?" She complied, cheerfully.

He looked down at this shot-glass sized orange juice and became more upset. "What?" he yelled, "Can't we afford a real glassful of OJ?"

His wife was thunderstruck at the sudden rage and criticism that came with her doing exactly what she thought he'd asked for.

It looked as if he were being petty and overreacting, when he'd been playing out an old script: boy sick, momma bring lotsa orange juice, equals love.

He felt unloved when the OJ didn't come, and then slighted further when it came in a small container. Old script. New life. They don't match. That's where communication comes in.

Old habits die hard—harder still when they're attached to sensitive emotions—but easier when the individuals have character.

One listener had such character:

"Before we were married, I had been on my own raising my two boys for twelve years. I figured I knew how to do pretty much everything there is to do better than most anyone (read: husband). All my life I have placed the utensils in the dish drainer with their business ends up—it keeps the part that touches your food out of any standing water, which makes much more sense to me than doing it the other way (read 'wrong' way, aka 'husband's' way). We argued over it and he finally saw it my way.

"We recently moved into a house with a dishwasher—my first. The other day I bent over to remove the clean dishes from the dishwasher and impaled my hand on a steak knife that was loaded—of course—business end up. I thought about hiding what had happened and clinging to my petty, but hard-fought victory. Instead, I chose to go to my husband and say to him, 'You know that argument we had when we first got married about whether the knives go up or down in the drainer? Well, you were absolutely right, and I will never question you about it again. Please forgive me.' He bandaged my hand with a smile, without comment, and with the utmost gentleness. And I love him all the more for not rubbing my face in it."

Coping with adult and childhood experiences teaches lessons. Sometimes these lessons result in behaviors that generalize from the one stimulus to almost all situations, relevant or not. That's when we get into trouble. For example, swinging at a ball when you're at bat is reasonable; swinging at almost anything that comes at you without distinguishing between a slap or a kiss, is not reasonable.

"My sensitivity to slights causes me to feel unloving toward my husband, which is not good. In my teens and early twenties I could be reduced to tears with just a look. Now I realize that most people are involved in their own problems and slights usually have nothing to do with me. I grew up in a home with a very grumpy, critical mother and a father that ignored or tried to ignore the unhappy climate in his home.

"In turn, I grew up very sensitive to any sort of verbal or nonverbal slight, real or not. There was a time when I blamed my mother for everything that went wrong in my life. Now I see she did the best she could in her own way, and I am responsible for changing the way I handle my perception of daily life. I choose to be happy."

The listener who sent this letter realized that her relationship with her mother, that of walking on spiky eggshells, was not what had to be with everyone. That is a remarkable, brave, and life-affirming revelation.

Familial patterns are tough to break. But they have to be broken, if destructive, or adjusted, in compromise, when you make a new family with a person from, of course, his or her own distinct familial pattern. One listener was brought up in a military family where accuracy and appearance were everything, and criticism was common.

"I did everything in my family to be perfect and avoid criticism. Then this guy came along that made teasing remarks and didn't get raving mad when I complained about his criticism, who even welcomed a healthy argument with me, someone I could argue with without being put down or iced out—I couldn't believe it! He knocked me off my 'miss prideful perfect pedestal.' He showed me there were other ways to look at something sometimes besides 'my way.' He gave me grace a lot sooner than I gave it to him. He is now my husband of sixteen years."

What a wonderful lesson, when we chose to learn one.

ASSumptions

Listen, I'm not sniffing my nose at sensitivity. Without it we all become concerned only with ourselves. It is sensitivity that tunes us in to others. When that sensitivity is turned on maximum, we sometimes become concerned only with ourselves. The surefire way to modulate that necessary sensitivity is through communication. I still am ferociously amazed at how willing so many folks are to react, condemn, and annihilate, and how many of those same folks are absolutely struck dumb when it is suggested they actually check to make sure their reactions are warranted. "Don't shoot 'til you see the whites of their eyes," could be translated into "Don't shoot 'til you hear it from their lips."

Here's a sensitive example of what I am talking about. This listener's father was diagnosed with cancer. She wrote cards to him and called him on the phone.

"I was unable to visit and I was told not to worry about it. A couple of months went by and I didn't hear from him. I tried calling again, no response. I stopped calling and sending cards of encouragement—I figured it was of no use to continue. My feelings were hurt that he didn't respond. I also thought that my father's wife just didn't want my father to hear from me. I had all these thoughts going through my head. In the meantime my father is going through chemo, surgery, etc., and his wife is with him all the time. The problem is I should have continued with the letters and cards regardless of my feelings. I wasn't the one in pain physically, and I wasn't the caregiver. My parents were going through so much. I should have done more and reached out instead of looking for someone to console me."

Bingo. One of the most significant dimensions of being an adult is to recognize that the world does not rotate around you or me or any one person as an axis. We are all on the spinning globe together. Everyone else has a life. Communication is the only means we have of bridging that natural gap. Without communication we only have assumptions. And you know what assumptions usually make of us? Check out the first three letters of the word *assumption* for the answer.

When I was talking about the communication vs assumption problem, a listener responded:

"How funny that you have this topic today. My fiancé and I had a very petty fight today—the fight seemed important to me but not to him. I had my feelings hurt because he spent my day off with his friend. He is a farmer, so I can ride around with him, but the miscommunication was that he didn't know I wanted to spend the day with him and, therefore, he assumed I wanted to do other things."

Sadly, the writer continues her complaint about his not seeing this, what she calls "miscommunication," as a problem. It wasn't a miscommunication—it was no direct communication at all. She wanted him to "just know," whereas he's treating her like an adult not an actress in a romantic fantasy. This isn't a petty fight. It's a serious problem when one person expects the other to mind-read and gets angry when he doesn't.

Communication is the most important key to just about every interpersonal problem. Perception, that is, how a person uniquely sees and interprets an event or comment, can make or break a relationship.

One listener wrote about the stupid issues he and his wife fight over. The prior evening, she had asked him to take his dishes into the kitchen after they had dinner in the living room. It wasn't, he admitted, that big a deal, except that he perceived her to be in a nitpicky mood, and he had wanted her to be loving toward him as he had had some amorous plans in store for the evening. He took the comment as her trying to treat him like a child and told her that he didn't need to be told to take his dishes into the kitchen. While it didn't actually start an argument, it put some emotional distance between them.

After thinking about it, he realized his perception of her parent-to-child request was an extension of his guilt for not having cleaned up as he usually did earlier in the evening. It was his own guilt, reflected through her innocent statement.

So why hadn't he cleaned perfectly? He'd put himself in

the little boy–mommy scenario. He had to struggle to put himself in the man–wife amorous scenario after that.

These sorts of inner struggles are normal, natural, and not unusual. If you are honest with yourself, as he was, you get by them. If you're honest with the other person, you get by them together.

Not all communication is done the "right way." And, not everything that comes out of your mouth, under the supposed banner of communication, ought to come out.

"Some of the best advice I can give friends now, after five years of marriage and dealing with many petty slights," writes a listener, *"is that old saying, 'know how to pick your battles.' I tell them that because life is entirely too short—don't waste it arguing with the person you love the most in the world. I tell them, 'If it's a petty issue or not, that's when you need to not argue and instead, communicate the most!'"*

Herein lies an important point: What are the limits of communication? The limit is when you get abusive, hurtful, nasty, sarcastic, cutting, threatening, and . . . well . . . you know from the experience of being on the receiving and giving end how that can go.

You need instead to communicate with information, praise, helpfulness, coming from a place of love, not from a place of selfishness or pettiness.

And while open, honest, and sensitive communication is a necessary antidote to building a mountain of resentments from a molehill of petty complaints, sometimes the river of frustration can't be permanently dammed up.

"My wife has these supersensitive antennas up 24/7. In some ways, this has been a positive for our relationship because it's taught me to be more aware of what comes out of my mouth. Also, any controversy tends to be dealt with immediately, thereby keeping things from 'festering.' However, I can tell you there is a tremendous downside, which does affect our relationship. It has to

do with that thing called 'perception.' When someone is this sensitive to everything around them, then they either perceive things to be more serious than they are, or they totally misperceive the message. This is complicated with a blended family of wonderful kids, but a constant monitoring of 'who said what' and 'what did it mean' is exhausting. I love my wife dearly and am devoted to her forever, but this is a real problem for me."

This is an opportune time in one's life to seek professional intervention. When our personality and behavior is destructive and repetitive, it is time for us to take some responsibility; not just because we're driving someone else crazy, but because who needs to live each day with that constant trickle of paranoia? In fact, we have an obligation to bring our best selves to our marriages—that may require a diet, spiritual guidance, more baths, and psychotherapeutic treatment.

What's My Problem?

Over the years, callers and listeners have communicated their stories and have shared the conclusions of their self-examinations to me. I am ever impressed with the courage it takes to face the demons within—in many ways that's much harder than the demons without.

There are a significant number of wellsprings for hypersensitivity and pettiness, some learned from history, some from the power that criticism or hurt feelings give us, some from attempts to survive.

Feelings of Inadequacy

Many people have been picked on above and beyond the average. All kids are singled out for things ranging from the superficial, like hair color and freckles, to the meaningful, like handicaps or heritage. Not dealt with well, these leave scars; and unlike scars on skin, which have diminished sensitivity, emotional scars leave the person extrasensitive and alert to slights not only on that subject, but in general.

Here are some more typical examples:

➤   *"I was always small for my size. Through grade school, because of my size, I was passed by for the sporting events and always picked last. As I grew to adulthood, I believe I carried some of that resentment with me to my personal and professional life. At home, when my wife 'infers' that I have done something wrong or not to her standards, I get the feeling that she does not value me. I will return the inflicted pain right back to her and we have a fight. And the thing is, she doesn't mean anything by it—I just 'feel' she's picking on me."*

➤   *"I am twenty years old and married for eight months. I have noticed how petty and supersensitive I really am. Nearly 99 percent of our disagreements are because I took something he said to me too seriously and consequently became offended. I can see this potentially causing a huge rift in our marriage as soon as he quits trying to talk to me. Why am I like this? I moved when I was nine years old from Denver to a small private school in Bothell, Washington. My entire grade consisted of sixty students. With such a small population there were really two groups of kids, the Popular and the Jocks. Well, I was neither one. I endured constant ridicule for five years. I began to think that everything everyone said to me was meant to hurt me. I really hate the way I am, but I'm not sure how to control it. It's an automatic reaction that was developed during the most impressionable years of my life."*

➤   *"Having grown up in foster homes, I had a huge chip on my shoulder. I was going to prove that all from foster homes were not trash. I was very defensive. I lost my friends and husband over how bad my behavior was. I would not let him criticize or parent our child because she was going to be the best and brightest of all children, because I came from foster homes. I took offense at everything because I took it as a statement that I was less because I was from foster homes."*

➤   *"I was raised in a competitive way and I was teased a lot because I was not as verbal as my sisters. Consequently I didn't see that teasing could be affectionate, I saw it only as making fun of me, a rejection. I really have to struggle all the time with the 'they don't like me' feeling creeping in."*

➤   *"When I feel the least bit slighted I tend to take out my insecurities on the people closest to me. I got this way from growing up with an emotionally unstable mother who drank and developed poor communication skills. I have become more aware that I do that and stop myself before I do, but I still have a hard time with it. When I am not doing things to tend to my spiritual needs (getting out of oneself) I find that I am more negative, ungrateful. I have come a long way from what I used to be like. I still have a ways to go but my communication is much better, my child is much happier."*

Therein lies the key. The solution, the saving grace for petty behavior in general—and especially the petty behavior that comes out of the scars of childhood emotional trauma—is "getting out of oneself"! The focal point of hypersensitivity is the notion, the incorrect notion, that everything is about you! As I tell people on my radio program, "Oftentimes when people don't acknowledge you or behave in a friendly, positive way, it's because they have intestinal gas pains, not because you are in the center of their thoughts in a negative way." This makes the point.

That's why I suggest that people solicit the other's well-being instead of assuming "bad intentions." For example, when you see someone not being as friendly as usual, before you get into fits of rageful hurt over being ignored or treated poorly, go over and say, "I notice you're not your usual self today, is something wrong? Can I help with something?" Get out of yourself. Try it.

Jealousy

When we offer our soul, spirit, body, and life to another, we are quite vulnerable. It is a definite time for hypersensitivity with respect to any threat or loss of that love. We can minimize such a threat by being psychologically healthy, picking someone psychologically healthy, communicating in a generous way, and behaving in a loving manner in general. Short of that perfection, as we all are, there is wiggle room for worry.

It is one thing to overreact anytime our partner talks about or to another person; it's another thing to react appropriately to real challenges to our intimacy (such as private meetings and communications) which need attention. It's yet another to react to the past.

I've had callers and listeners tell me about feeling threatened about their spouse or their intended going to a funeral of their ex. A funeral! Being jealous of the dead is too great a leap from reason for me. "If he loved me, he wouldn't go, because it upsets me," a caller would say.

Well, how 'bout this: If you loved him, you'd support his mourning and supporting the loved ones who are grieving.

How sad is it to be jealous of the dead.

Typically, though, it is jealousy over past relationships. When our partner is in constant contact with past relationships, the word *past* no longer applies—and there is a problem. Lately, on both my radio and television programs, I've been getting a lot of questions about a partner keeping old photos and letters in a "locked box, in a trunk, in the attic." Probably, there are more such questions because more folks are making, breaking, and moving on to multiple relationships, more so than ever before. And, with the evidence of past loves, one worries about becoming another inclusion in that memory bin—with good reason.

As one listener wrote:

"Although our relationship was going really well, I was overcome with curiosity one day when I was at his house alone. I am not sure why I did it (looked through a box filled with cards and letters from his past relationships), because I never wanted any details of his past relationships. He always made me feel special and loved. Then I started feeling insecure about our relationship, because I realized how strongly other women felt about him in the past. He told me that he was planning on throwing them away, anyhow, and if there is anything I want to know, just ask. I would never want him to leave his past behind. I want him to carry along all the lessons that he has learned thus far in his life. I want him to share those lessons with me."

Making someone you supposedly love erase any evidence of a past is a petty, annoying, and destructive behavior which alienates them from you—it doesn't solidify your importance in their lives. Only you do that.

On the other hand, I am reminded of an audience member on my television show who thought retaining pictures of an ex was healthy; so healthy, indeed, that he carried a sexy picture of his ex-girlfriend with him all the time—in spite of the fact that he had a new girlfriend. That's worth being petty over!

Manipulation

In "therapy school" we learned about "secondary gains." Those are the "perks" of having a problem. As the joke goes in my home, there are a few days a month when I get to whine, be grumpy, and eat Oreo cookies with impunity; hooray for menstrual cramps! That is a secondary gain; it's the "good news" part of the good news/bad news joke.

It's not unusual for people not to want to give up their problems totally because of secondary gains: sympathy, power, and a release from responsibility. The same goes with the annoying behaviors of petty hypersensitivity.

As one listener admitted:

"I used to display ultrasensitivity as a means by which to control and manipulate the men I would date. There were frequent occasions when I would sulk, pout, storm out of a room, or become offended at the slightest provocation for the intent of soliciting sympathy from the male-du-jour. It would work for a short period of time, but eventually my boyfriend would tire of it and beat a hasty retreat out of my life. It wasn't until a particularly painful breakup that I began to make a more honest examination of my actions and motivations."

On my radio program I generally describe this personality style as melodramatic—focusing on being the center of attention and controlling by displays of pain and hurt. Another listener wrote about her style of pouting or ignoring the person until she got the right reaction—which was for that person to

". . . plead with me about what was wrong, and apologize and finally ask forgiveness and show regret. I was good at this. It met my need to feel 'in control' and 'wanted.' I wanted everything to revolve around me as most petty and supersensitive people do. I made people feel nervous and uncomfortable and stifled—not knowing what would 'tick me off.' I lost a lot of friends and dates who gave up trying to meet my emotional needs. I finally know that I am just me, not the center of everyone's thoughts. It has been hard admitting this."

I have often said that there is no love where there is fear. I might add here, there is no love where there is intimidation. Making someone feel constantly responsible for your emotions, having them frequently groveling for forgiveness for some perceived (and clearly unintentional) slight, and making them feel like a bad person for hurting you so often and easily, is intimidation.

Perfectionism

One of the most painful personality traits is perfectionism. The biggest problem with perfectionism is that perfect is not possible, therefore no goal is attainable. For so many people, such ultimate and perpetual disappointment breeds constant frustration and a lack of ability to enjoy the journey of life. The process of experience and learning is painful, not invigorating.

The ugly part of perfectionism is the beating others often take at the hands of a perfectionist. As one listener revealed:

"My husband, the poor guy, feels like he can't do anything right. I think it is because of my nitpicking. I have always been really picky—especially with myself. I am a huge perfectionist. I tend to have high expectations for myself and for my relationships. I think that sometimes my expectations are unrealistic, and that it's unfair to impose them upon others."

Perfectionists experience being human as a great insult, inadequacy, and failure. They are generally all too ready to look at harmless comments as proof of their worst fear. One listener who was going to school full-time while her husband supported them constantly felt as if she were not doing enough. She commented to her husband that she was proud of herself for going to class when she didn't feel well (heroism) and her husband responded with, *"Yeah, it's always good to go to class, especially since the reason you're not working is so you can do really well in school."* She took his comment as a criticism and demand that she be perfect in school, because it's all she has to do. Her husband was devastated by her hurt and wrath, because he thought he'd just been seconding her statement.

They cried over their problems together. She talked about feeling pressure to do well. He talked about feeling pressure to take care of them. And, she got it!

"Although I was still tempted to be a total brat and say that people didn't like to be reminded that someone was making a sacrifice for them, the thought suddenly struck me that all he really wanted or needed was a 'thank you'! If I had looked at the big picture from the beginning, none of this would ever have happened. I expressed my gratitude to my husband, and I know I need to remember this lesson if I want to continue to make my marriage work."

Imagine the following: You are looking through binoculars at a distant small entity. That is you seeing only your pain, perception, feelings. Now, pull back the focus and take in the rest of the surroundings. That's you looking at the bigger picture. If you take the time to do that before shooting from the hip, your relationships will work better too.

Self-Protection

One listener wrote about how her being petty was an attempt to protect herself from possible hurt. As I have said on air, putting steel windows up to keep out the dust also keeps out sunlight, the sounds of birds and children playing, and the fresh smell of the flowers. It's overkill. So is shooting first, and asking questions later. Yet, so many people, people who have suffered in the past, use pettiness as a steel window.

"I used to pick fights with the guy I am with now just because I was not used to a man not beating me or arguing with me. I lost him once but we are back together now. I realized that I didn't

have to argue or be beaten to be happy. Life is so much better for me now."

While this listener's letter sounds extreme, it actually is quite representative of a relating style that is prevalent: not admitting or showing too much affection, keeping the other person off balance, not letting the other person know how needed they are, or picking fights so that you don't have to be intimate and vulnerable. I find that many people stay in relationships with people who commit adultery, are violent, abuse drugs or alcohol, or are just immature and ratty—but decide to leave after the person "gets better." These are the folks who can't tolerate the risks of love.

Revenge

Being petty is a favorite way for some folks to get their anger out—anger with their partner or somebody or something else in life.

"I find that I become petty as a result of other 'more important' marital problems. For example, if my husband spends too much time playing games on the internet and not enough time taking care of household tasks, I become very petty and overly sensitive to everything real fast. After an argument, and once we both recognize the source of my pettiness, we are able to resolve the main issue and move on."

Of course, it would be better to communicate about the main issue up front and avoid all that ruckus.

The revenge is not just about venting, it is also about tit for tat. One listener wrote:

"I find it easy to be sensitive to just about anything when I am looking to bicker in the relationship. For example, I may feel that my boyfriend has been spending a lot of time without me, and I

become unhappy and even more insecure. Next time he's with me, I hunt for something to complain about, thus leading to a petty argument, still avoiding the original problem. It makes me feel like I'm back in control. Not being honest with myself and not trusting his love for me—leads me to see that I am simply protecting myself from being hurt."

The revenge motive doesn't necessarily have to be precipitated by your current relationships. It is sadly not unusual for people to take out on their spouse the hurtful rage from other, less safe places—like family, friends, neighbors, coworkers, and bosses. This is the experience of one listener who came to understand that destructive formula:

"The conclusion I came to (after a screaming match with my honey) is that I have put years of hurt and anger concerning wrongs done by family members years ago on him and created unrealistic expectations. I have resolved to do a few things . . . first, is to treat my honey like I would treat a good friend, with the same respect. Second, is to take care of myself in a more constructive and compassionate way—and start forgetting those ancient hurts."

This is a good news/bad news moment. The good news is that your dearly beloved is someone who will ideally love you warts and all—so you have the privilege of being open, vulnerable, truthful, and painfully real. The bad news is that sometimes we abuse that privilege to protect our image on the outside by not dealing with the people and the situations which put that burr in our shorts in the first place.

Getting Un-Petty

Many of the letters in this chapter have outlined the means by which people have gotten a grip on their pettiness. Here is a summary of their ideas and a few more of mine:

➤ Pray more often. Prayer is not only calming, it is humbling, and reminds you of your obligations to others. Since much of pettiness is ultimately anchored in a self-centered view of the world, spirituality helps you broaden your awareness and perspective. Pettiness as a self-focus which is the opposite focus of religion. G-d's laws are about compassion, understanding, obligations, consequences, patience, meaningfulness, and holiness. These concepts are bigger than any one of us and require giving of oneself in humility. So many people find this approach enlightening, exhilarating, and transcendent. It helps you with the bigger picture.

➤ If it's that important to you—you do it! I have told many people that instead of nitpicking others to death about how something must be done, do it yourself. Take responsibility over those things that you cannot seem to be flexible on. Perhaps if you then find yourself so overburdened, you'll realize that doing it yourself, because it has to be your way, is not the best or only way to go about things. Consider that it isn't a choice between just "your way" or the "wrong way"; it's "your way" and somebody else's "your way," which is just a different way; take the "wrong" part out.

➤ Teamwork is part of the blessing of a relationship. It is a far, far better thing you do to find ways to solve problems and grapple with issues as a team, rather than alone. It's this teamwork that solidifies relationships; the mutual dependency will make you close. People too often forget that mutual dependency breeds a familiarity of affection that cannot easily be broken by gray hairs or an interloper.

➤ Risk not being perfect. When I was counseling people, I often sent perfectionist types to a coffee shop and told them to order Jell-O and just pick it up in their hands and squish it. Why in public? Because perfectionists care about how they look. Why squish Jell-O? So they could have fun being silly. Frankly, I was amazed at how effective such a simple experience was in helping some folks loosen up.

➤   Communicate. Communication is the most important element in relationships. Communication avoids assumptions and misunderstandings. Ultimately, it is better to know the truth of where you stand and how others experience you (as painful as those truths sometimes are) because it gives you the power to grow and it gives them the knowledge they need to love you more.

➤   Stifle yourself. Sometimes it's wise just to shut up. This is probably one of the more difficult anti-pettiness techniques—I know it is for me. When your stress level is high and you have so much to do, it's tough not to lash out at anything that appears to add to your strain. Learn to use that moment to solicit support, not strike out in frustration.

Basically, the cure for pettiness is working harder to treat your loved one as though you loved him or her. This one is self-explanatory.

4

Stupid Power

"Sometimes it's not even that I need to be right,
but that I DO NOT want to be wrong."
—A LISTENER

As I've said many times on my radio program, "I love juxta-position!": when two faxes arrive from entirely different people from entirely different places and so naturally play off each other—for example, one makes a philosophical point for which the other is the living example. Juxtaposition confirms for me a sense of cosmic intention.

Juxtaposition happened two days ago. Right after I finished organizing my material for this chapter, having about an hour before dinner, I sat down to find a movie to watch for relaxation. What does the television turn on to? *Bus Stop*. What is the main point of this movie? Stupid Power. Whew.

The two lead characters are Cherie (Marilyn Monroe) and Bo (Don Murray). Bo is a very young, rich, spoiled, egocentric, overbearing, pushy, demanding, insensitive, but innocent and very cute guy who has come off the isolation of the huge ranch he was brought up on to find a wife. Cherie is a not quite as young, sexy, dim, definitely not innocent, honky-tonk stripper. Bo, having drinks in a good ole boy's joint, takes one look at Cherie through his drunken stupor and decides that she is the angel he's been looking for.

Cherie is used to guys coming on to her for "favors," but this guy wants her, on sight, to be his wife. He's boorish, loud, and very embarrassing. She resists. He demands. She resists. He kidnaps her against her flailing and screaming will onto a bus to go off to his ranch.

A snowstorm forces the bus to stay overnight at a bus stop. Here she plans to make her getaway. Bo roughhouses her into submission. The bus driver, stating he has the authority of the "captain of a ship," takes the young Muhammad Ali wannabe outside and gives him a beating.

At this point, Bo's old caretaker/sidekick really lays into him about how other people have their own feelings, desires, opinions, and wills, and that he has no right to treat the whole world as though it were an extension of himself. He tells Bo that this was a whipping he needed and that he owes everyone, especially Cherie, an apology.

At this point, the beaten, injured, and humiliated Bo can't imagine even showing his face.

The next morning, with his elder friend's urging, Bo does apologize to the bus stop keeper, the bus driver, and finally to Cherie, who, in fine codependent style just melts into his arms (after all, he's all changed, isn't he?) and off they go to the ranch to live happily ever after.

At least he did not get the girl until he was sensitive, gallant, and respectful . . . if only for twenty minutes. In real life, too many people don't even wait for that twenty minutes, or even a promise; they melt on the basis of their own hopes. Unfortunately, these kind of hopes are generally only postponed disappointment.

It Gets Bad

The following two examples of Stupid Power will give you a picture of the spectrum of this controlling and critical behavior, from the ridiculous to the unbelievable.

The first example came from one of my callers, a thirty-four-year-old man who had recently married. He called to ask me if it were okay for him to put a picture of his great aunt in his wedding album.

"Was she at the wedding?"

"Yes."

"Was she in the wedding pictures?"

"Yes."

"Is she someone important?"

"Yes, she virtually raised my mother and myself."

"Well then, what's the problem about having those pictures in the album?"

"My wife absolutely refuses to include any pictures of my great aunt."

"Why is that?"

"Because my great aunt did not RSVP in advance, but at the last minute showed up and my wife was angry that she had to arrange for another plate of food and setting at a table."

"You're kidding."

"No."

"Your wife knows how important this woman is to you, and she wants to punish this woman for being a last-minute yes-show by cutting her out of wedding photos?"

"Yes."

"I have two things to say to you, fella. One, make for yourself a second album with all the pictures. Two, good luck—having married a petty, vindictive, controlling person as you describe your new wife to be is going to be quite a challenge."

The second example is an episode I had with a young married couple when I was in private practice as a Marriage, Family, and Child Therapist. Her complaint was that he worked a long day, came home, and went directly up to his home-office and worked some more. They had two children. She was a stay-at-home mom. There was virtually no family time.

Well, it is easy to get into a knee-jerk dislike-him mode. After all, how selfish can one get? Wait, there's more.

When I queried him as to his schedule, it became clear that he had the work ethic in the extreme. It was not enough to do his best in the time he had. For him, there was an imperative to do it all and perfectly in whatever time it took. What he didn't finish at work he felt obligated to finish at home. He was his own prisoner.

It gets worse. She told me how critical he was of her, her child-rearing, her house-cleaning, and her appearance. It seems that he would walk into the house after a long day's work and run his hand over the top of the refrigerator to check for dirt. She was his prisoner.

Instead of getting mad at him for being such a controlling jerk, I thought about how terrible it must be to be him, much less be with him. He can never let himself off the hook, he can never let himself feel satisfied for a job well done, he can never let himself enjoy the love and comfort of his wife and children. For this man, there are never fruits of his labors . . . just labors.

In the first example, we have a woman who cannot adjust to change. Her discomfort turns to petty vindictiveness. In this second example, we have a man who cannot adjust to a full life. His discomfort turns to compulsive effort. Both of these people are to be pitied, because they are their own prisoners; both of these people cause tremendous pain to their spouses and children. Both of these people make lousy partners.

P.S. The young man did well in therapy. Eventually, he was able to agree to only an hour's work at home with his children at his feet. After one hour (sharp) his wife would give him a neck rub and some homemade cookies. She was happy to do that for him. He became better able to allow her to do this for him. His basic personality style was pretty resistant, but he could use manual overdrive and temper it a bit. Evidently, a bit was enough for her.

Oh yes, the rule was that any appliance he checked for dirt, *he* had to clean. Amazing how that behavior stopped dead!

Stupid Power Is Corrosive

"My impatience," writes one listener, *"coupled with a lack of sensitivity to our differences, has led me to this type of behavior. I've responded to what seem like 'dumb' questions (either the reply seems obvious to me or the question has been asked so many times I can't believe he doesn't remember) with a condescending attitude and tone of voice and, over time, this has eroded his confidence and our relationship. I think sometimes I'm just busy and frustrated with what seems like a 'bother and unnecessary' to me. I need to remember that he and I are different, and if he needs to ask things several times, that's okay."*

This letter makes a very important point. Differences in energy, style, personality, and experience are often met with exasperation. Think about it. What you grew up with seems so natural, so obvious, so clear. You have to resist showing annoyance and displeasure at what is new, different, and unfamiliar to someone else, because, unless you marry your own sibling, you're getting together with somebody with a whole different set of experiences and habits. Remember, they have to deal with you, too!

When I speak to callers, it seems so obvious to me that a core issue is the basic lack of communication between people. People are either afraid of laying things out and admitting certain desires or vulnerabilities, or they just reflexively believe that there is no need to communicate because they know all the parts without hearing them.

Stupid power is when you need to be on top, in control, in charge, one up, and so forth; you only need to hear enough from the other person—if you're willing to hear anything at all—so that you know where to go in your argument. That is, instead of listening to learn or connect, you're listening for strategy to attack.

This is exactly what another listener wrote to me about:

"My wanting to 'one up' or 'be right' in our eleven-year-old marriage creates a broken bridge in our relationship. There cannot be effective communication if I'm not listening to what he is truly saying, trying to be ready to counterattack with a one-up or a comeback. I know this is a defect in character of mine and we work at it by giving five minutes when he is allowed to 'talk' without my interrupting. I'm glad I have tools to work with now, so I can love better."

This last letter came from a woman who grew up in an alcoholic home. To protect herself from the irrational and self-centered ragings of alcoholics, she learned not to listen and to have a self-protective response. Unfortunately, this early unhealthy training ground led to self-protective behavior when it wasn't even necessary, simply because it had become habit. Her five-minute quiet and listen tool is a great way to break a habit.

On the other hand, when the perpetrator of Stupid Power is not so enlightened, it is hell for their spouse.

"My husband is one that practices one-upping on a daily basis. The result is his actions have made me a very different person. I no longer respond. A typical conversation consists of my saying something, him responding negatively, and then my shutting up.

The unfortunate thing is he doesn't realize how this behavior affects me. His needing to be the boss has me holding back and not saying exactly how I feel. Many times in the past, I have written him a note explaining how this affects me, and upon reading it, he took a red pen and started picking apart my thoughts. You're right, it's not a healthy marriage at all. Some day he may wake up, probably not, but it probably will be too late."

That's so sad. There is no winner here. He may be exerting his power to put her down so that he can feel up, but it's artificial. His being "up" is an illusion, and he knows it. He is just so terribly afraid of finding his flaws and potentially losing her love because of them. That's the irony. He's supposedly hiding his flaws, and still she doesn't love him anymore.

Sometimes people work it out. One listener admits her Stupid Power has stressed out her relationship—stressed out, but not destroyed it, because they have "an understanding."

"He knows that I do not like to admit that I was or am wrong. Because of this, he avoids certain subjects altogether. The way that I am dealing with this is to practice saying, 'I am sorry, I was wrong.' It is not the easiest thing to do, but I know that it is very important so that I do not drive my husband crazy. Thank God for people who are willing to work through these difficulties."

Not so bad. He knows her weakness and he doesn't go there. She knows her weakness, and she tries to control that instead of him. Not so bad.

Mine Enemy

I've often said on my radio program that the person you marry should be the one person in all the world with whom you can share your deepest, innermost, uncomfortable, shameful past and problems. Instead, many marry treating their partner as the enemy, not the ally.

"My husband and I both went into our marriage with very specific ideas about what our marriage was not going to be about. I grew up with an extremely domineering father who treated women like they were servants, not people. My husband, on the other hand, grew up with an extremely domineering mother who ran the house with an iron fist. So our ideas consisted of this: I refused to ever be run by a man again, and he swore no woman would ever control his life again.

"This is hindsight, of course, we had no idea this was the case when we said, 'I do.' We began to fight about everything. It basically boiled down to one underlying problem. He didn't trust me, and I didn't trust him. We both saw the other as the enemy.

"To make a long story short, I began to read my Bible and things concerning marriage began to pop out all over the place. I realized that being my husband's helpmate did not mean that I had to become a meek, trod-upon waif. Instead, I could stay the strong woman that I was and still prefer my husband over myself. Once I began to trust my husband not to run over me, and I understood that I wasn't going to become a doormat, he responded in kind. I started trusting him with my life instead of being in complete control. Amazingly, the same thing happened to him as he began to trust me with his life."

Where this revelation and metamorphosis does not take place, there is either all-out war, unilateral surrender, or an uncomfortable détente. The latter is a state in which nothing is shared because sharing is evidence of a loss of control.

"My children never witness their parents sharing hobbies, views, ideas, or common goals. We simply don't trust the other person not to try to take control. I believe it stems from a basic lack of trust in each other. I believe that it will someday be the straw that breaks this camel's back. I love my husband and I know that he loves me, but. . . . But, I also know that love cannot survive the two of us as we are now."

This behavior reminds me of a *Twilight Zone* episode where, after a global war, it appeared that two people were left alive: one man and one woman. Unfortunately, they were on opposite sides of this war. At first they simply tried to kill one another, as good, loyal soldiers would. Then, realizing the ultimate uselessness of this effort, he tried to make civil contact and have them cooperate for survival. It looked for a while as if they would connect; they were both young and attractive—the romantic possibilities were obvious (as was the parallel to Adam and Eve). Then, war posters would remind them of their identities, or some action or words would be misunderstood. In the end, there was no real, lasting trust. In the end, there was the end—of humanity.

And so go many relationships. Because of family wars, dating wars, and inner wars, the end is too often the tragedy of not being able to connect with comfort, with trust.

"In my life, I have been 'walked on' by many different people. As I grew into adulthood, I determined that I would not let anyone else 'walk on me' again. I took that determination into my marriage. I would always have to be right, because at all costs I would not be my husband's doormat. Then, one day, I listened. Instead of trying to be right, I shut my mouth and listened to my husband. Then, I listened to God. I began to realize that I needed to let God use me as the bridge between my heart and my husband's heart. A bridge MUST be walked on. So, now I have begun to make a commitment to be walked on, not stomped on. I desire a loving, godly marriage, and if it begins with me, then so be it."

I was so touched by this letter from a listener. It proves that change is possible, that the first change must be in ourselves, in our attitude, and perspective, and reactions, and that trust is a decision—one without a guarantee, and that's what makes change a brave thing to do. These acts of supreme risk give us the most potential return.

Power struggles may leave you "on top," but they also basically leave you alone. There is no real intimacy where power and control are exercised. While it is true that bad experiences with violent or untrustworthy or philandering partners can leave you armed for bear in making sure this doesn't happen to you again, it is also true that shooting before you see the whites of their eyes (or the black of their hearts) leaves your relationship dead.

Heterophobia: Men Are the Evil Empire!

In 1999, a longtime feminist, Daphne Patai, wrote a book, called *Heterophobia: Sexual Harassment and the Future of Feminism*, coining the term *heterophobia*. The premise of heterophobia is that the feminist mentality shifted from expanding choice for women to an outright visceral and frightening antagonism toward men, wherein heterosexuality itself is to be considered oppressive. I found this thesis true and the author brave to make it, as severe antagonism and retribution are generally directed to any women who break ranks to criticize anything female or to compliment anything male.

Over the years, many women have written to me feeling betrayed by the feminist movement, unsupported in their "choices" (like at-home mom), and synthetically manipulated to be angry at men—or the "patriarchy."

"Feminism has done little more than subdivide me into a fragmented image of a women," writes one listener. *"First, feminism divided me from men by making me afraid of them. A teen in the seventies, I was bombarded with messages of how I would be used by men and never treated with any respect. I was terrified and angry before the first poor guy ever looked crosswise at me. How do you even approach a marriage when you are convinced that what was once 'giving' is now 'being robbed'?*

"Then, feminism divided me from my sexuality. It told me that indiscriminate sex was my birthright (power)—that I should be able to sleep with whomever I chose whenever I chose and without feeling anything in particular. Funny, now I see that as endorsing the old male stereotype of sexuality and actually setting me up for the exploitation those same feminists had warned me against in the first place."

I have received thousands of letters repeating the same story about being warned about men as a fundamental part of the feminist mantra.

"I grew up in the midst of all this 'women's lib' nonsense, and actually bought the thought that fathers are not necessary. Though married, I did not stop and think what marriage was really about . . . working together. This is an art form I did not learn easily. I thought I was protecting myself and my boys by never depending upon my husband. If he did not see things my way, I did it my way anyway. When he became angry, I would threaten to leave with both boys because 'I have already been on my own and could easily do it again.' "

Fortunately, unlike so many others, this story has a happy ending. After she walked out on her husband, he was persistent in trying to talk with her. He got her to think. She realized that if he had treated her as she treated him it would have been ugly! After counseling, they are doing better.

P.S. Her son, then eight years old, came and asked her one day if he had a stepmother. My listener, confused, told him "no" and explained that a stepparent is the person who marries either the mom or dad after a divorce. It seems that most all his school chums had divorced parents, and referred often to stepparents. He just wanted to know if he had one. He was relieved to know he didn't if a divorce was what it meant. Perhaps more than anything else, that was the glue that cemented the notion of commitment, trust, and sharing for my listener. She didn't want to hurt her child. No better motivation in the world, I think.

But I Want a Controlling Guy/Gal!

It just doesn't seem possible after all these examples that any-one would choose somebody controlling with whom to part-ner up. But, every day on my radio program, I get calls from, largely, women, who complain, complain, complain about the very controlling behaviors they opted for when they picked the guy in the first place. In my first book, *Ten Stupid Things Women Do to Mess Up Their Lives*, I point out how some characteristics can seem exciting or tolerable while dating, because some people refuse to see the leaves, just the forest. In other words, they want to be married, protected, sup-ported, or rescued, or they overestimate their ability to change a person's basic personality and consistent behaviors.

One listener wrote me describing how she fell under the spell of a controller:

"Prince Charming came into my life and promised me the world, and ripped mine out from under me. You see, the power of the controlling type, which he was, is the daily therapy that you receive from him. The words that he speaks to you are program-ming you, like a robot. Because of my fantasy, weaknesses, desper-ation, and insecurities, I became pathetic and he fed on that."

Another listener related how she married a controlling guy, just like dear old Dad, regardless of the fact that her mother ended up remarrying a wonderful man. Some kids will go to strange lengths finally to have that father-daughter relationship, even if it is with a bad father, and the relationship is painful. Perhaps she thought that with her, as opposed to her mother, it would be different. Well, her handsome, romantic Prince Charming went from the so-called compliment of jealousy to the punishment of violence.

When people have been victims of a cruelly controlling par-ent, they learn very early that to fight back they have to either beat 'em, join 'em, or be beaten by 'em. A child can't really beat a parent, except by indirectly causing them pain by illegal and immoral activities. Many are simply beaten down by that parent, and become depressed and passive. Some come to believe that there are only two modes of existence: to be the victim or to have the power. So, they take the power.

That's exactly what one listener wrote:

"I grew up in a home where my father has never lost an argument. He has always portrayed that his opinion is right and always reminds us of how we hurt him. I am finding sometimes in my relationship with my husband that I get on a Stupid Power trip. I think I know more than my husband in some areas. And I will get loud . . . like my dad . . . beating a dead horse to try to get him to see my point. I admit that I do that . . . and am able to control myself sometimes, and certainly recognize it and apologize to my husband for it. My father hasn't changed. At least I am really trying."

Other callers have told me that they needed a "daddy" to take care of them because they weren't doing too well at it themselves. For these women, having a cooperative relationship of equals would require them to hold up their end of the bargain—something they either can't or won't do. Hence, the opening for the controller. As one caller said, when I questioned her about agreeing to a relationship with a guy who seriously controlled finances, "I did at the time because I had a ten-year-old son, and felt secure. I was grateful for the relationship, yup."

Another caller, married for twenty-four years and with three teenage children, just got an inheritance. Her question? "How do I explain to my husband that I need control of my inheritance without throwing him into absolute cardiac arrest here?"

"Why don't you trust him to work with you on whatever new money is in the family?" I asked, innocently.

"Because he has taken control of that."

"I don't know what that means."

"Well, he always has had pretty much control of the money. I let him have control. I have heard you say before that anybody that has the responsibility has the power. I've let him do that. I've let him take care of the books and do the investing and that type of thing without my input. His attitude basically is that I've not carried my weight financially in the marriage and whoever makes the money should spend the money."

Because of this inheritance money, she wanted a change so that she could be in control. I reminded her that since she had agreed to a certain style of marriage, as with certain ground rules in a game, if you suddenly want to change the ground rules to have an advantage, the opposition doesn't react well. Her worry was well founded.

It is important to reexamine the match-up mentality in the first place. When people have deficits, some things they really ought to work on, they can either try to correct their weakness, or just get those characteristics *from* their mate.

"Exactly, I guess that is what I did. And he did the same thing."

"Yeah," I responded, "but your direction is chaos. His direction is control and accomplishment. What qualities of yours would he take on? He doesn't respect your characteristics."

"No, he doesn't, and he makes that clear."

"And that is precisely the point. Your characteristics are a contrast. You know what he got from you? A sense of superiority. Both of you have inferiority issues, you because of a lack of skills, he because of a sense of never being good enough. In marrying you, he is automatically good enough, even superior. You married him because he fulfills all the things that you don't need to do. Now, you have the money, and in your home, money is power."

I explained that money didn't make her competent, and the money being hers didn't make him inadequate. Nonetheless, they would both react that way, and possibly destroy the marriage. In situations like this, a very clever and competent therapist is necessary to help both these people move simultaneously toward self-esteem. She needs to exert the effort, to train herself, and to be confident. He needs to let himself be loved in spite of not being perfect. They need a therapist with the wisdom to see that she is not a victim and he is not the perpetrator. They've been an unhealthy team, ultimately each with the intent of protecting themselves and being loved. Unfortunately, Stupid Power games like these mutually eliminate love. There is generally only resentment and disgust and fear and loneliness.

Basically, the inappropriate exertion of power, Stupid Power, is an attempt to be something we're not, to protect ourselves from former or imagined enemies. It is proof that we still see ourselves as we did in infancy—as the center of the universe.

The King of Pain

When in private practice, I was impressed by how many couples fought over who suffered the most, therefore was entitled to the most. This competition was an Olympics for pain. One listener recently sent me a letter in which he named this strategy the King of Pain.

"When my wife and I argue, particularly about money, we often resort to what we call the King of Pain strategy. I'll talk about how I'm working two jobs, sixty to seventy hours a week, and she'll one-up by talking about how much more stressful her job is. Then I'll come back with how I'd love to have just one job, no matter how stressful—if I could have weekends off. We end up trying to show who is more

stressed . . . and lose sight of the money question that we started with. We found that by naming this phenomenon the King of Pain Syndrome, we are able to get back on track with the discussion that is important, rather than the one-upping. It allows us to laugh a bit at the silliness of our fighting, and lightens the mood enough that we can have a meaningful and useful discussion about the checkbook. Now, if only I had a crown. . . ."

The problem with jockeying for power in decision making is that competition is bad for intimacy. Competition always means somebody loses and feels demeaned or unvalued.

The irony is that when the King of Pain strategy is employed to get some kind of appreciation from the other person, it is only by trumping their pain that you win. When their pain is dismissed, they don't feel like being too nice to you at all! So, basically, it's a stupid strategy.

Here's some proof:

"Not long after we married, the contest began," writes one listener. *"I make more money and for some reason believe I am entitled to more praise, pats on the back, and other ego-boosting affirmations. After work, on a daily basis, the typical question of, 'Honey, how was your day?' turns into a battle of who worked harder, whose feet hurt or are the most swollen, who got the least amount of sleep, who worked the longest amount of hours, and who had the hardest day overall.*

"For just once, I would like to hear myself not buy into the game and just kiss him on the cheek and say, 'I had a great day. How about you, Hon?' But that is not my life. I make myself miserable. Tomorrow is a good day to start. Better yet, tonight is a good night to start."

What would she lose if she were comforting and interested in her husband? Status? Clearly, trying to be the one to get all the attention isn't working—it never does. There is terrific reward in being caring. If two people do that together, everyone is cared for without these Stupid Power manipulations.

At least this listener learned the lesson:

"I was constantly one-upping my husband to prove to him how valuable I was. The harder I tried, however, the less respect I had for him. Years after we divorced, I finally learned that it had nothing to do with him. I had never had any respect for myself, and therefore, I was trying to force it out of him. Sadly, I didn't learn this through therapy. I learned it the hard way. But, boy, did I learn it. Now, as a strong Christian, I have self-respect, self-worth, and a wonderful future."

"Being Right = Being Lovable"

One of the most remarkable revelations I ever had when I was counseling couples came from a session with a young couple with marital problems. It seemed that he had to be right . . . no matter what . . . every time . . . regardless of what he had to do to make his wife say that he was right. I'll admit, this guy was not easy to like. I really had to dig down into my therapist mode of thinking to be helpful. What I would tap into was the notion of "finding the pain." That is, I always assumed that the reason behind a person's awful behavior (unless they were evil, or sociopathic, or psychotic) was some pain. When I would register that flight plan, I could set aside the reasonable disgust that arises when confronting someone that annoying.

Sure enough, the pain was there. His father was an overly strict, martial-like disciplinarian and only showed affection toward this young man when he had done something right or gotten an answer to some challenge. Well, here's the formula for misery: the notion that if you can get your partner to see you're right, then he or she will be affectionate and love you. Problem was, he would figuratively beat her into submitting that he was right, and then couldn't understand why she wasn't affectionate and loving. You'd think something like this would be so obvious. With such early and severe training, he literally could not see what he was doing. When I tied the past and the present together for him, he was just stricken.

It was actually a nice moment; she reached over and comforted him. I pointed out that he was getting affection for being real, not right. It got quiet in that room for the rest of the session.

Differences Are Not All About Superiority/Inferiority

"After almost fifty years of marriage to an extremely sweet man," wrote a listener, *"now that we are retired and together daily, I find myself very annoyed with his misunderstanding of news reports and other topics. I find myself correcting him frequently and enjoying it. When in school together, I was always the better student of the two of us. I graduated high school at sixteen, he was nineteen. I love him, but feel guilty at what I'm doing to us."*

It is not just at retirement that we note the differences between us and our spouses—it is all the time! Differences should not be an opportunity for Stupid Power. Differences should be an opportunity for affection, humor, respect, patience, and even learning. Instead, I usually find that folks use differences as motivation for one-upping each other in moments of inappropriate gratification. Often the conflicts are over knowledge, opinion, ideas, perspectives, goals and dreams, reactions, and even something as mundane as putting dishes in a dishwasher or as sacred as playing with a child.

I get frustrated with the folks who really, seriously believe that because their partner does something differently from the way they are in the habit of doing it, that their partner is wrong. I often ask if the difference is dangerous, destructive, or illegal. The reaction I get back is one of puzzlement. I proceed to tell them that if it isn't a difference that is dangerous, destructive, illegal, or immoral, simply different from what they are used to—SHUT UP!

Wow! Does that ever get a surprised reaction! I continue by explaining that for the sake of a difference in how to make a sandwich, either somebody is hurt or everybody goes away hungry. I ask, "Is that your goal?" The answer is inevitably, "Well, no, of course not." To which I answer, "But that's what you are doing every day with the people you say you love the most!"

One listener confirms this when she writes:

"I used to constantly one-up my husband. It could have been anything. I one-upped him when he loaded the dishwasher by huffily reloading it the PROPER way after he had already done the job.

"I didn't want him in the kitchen at all because he was incapable of keeping it organized to MY STANDARDS.

"I didn't want him to cook dinner because what took me thirty minutes usually took him about an hour and a half.

"When he drove, I informed him of the superior way to get where we were going, and became frustrated knowing that if I were driving the trip would be much less stressful.

"Eventually, I found that I was CONSTANTLY IRRITATED with him. My irritation and constant nagging resulted in him not feeling needed, wanted, or even capable. I had broken him down. Many of the reasons I married him in the first place were the exact things I made disappear.

"While he was feeling less capable than ever, I was feeling more overburdened than ever. I had to do everything around the house to make sure it got done my way. I then complained that he didn't help enough.

"One day I was thinking about how things were going and I thought, 'Mary, all this seems to be stemming from you. You're

the one spending valuable time just trying to get things done. You're the one spending valuable time being frustrated over inconsequential things.' So on that day, I vowed not to one-up him anymore. It's truly been a challenge to keep my big mouth shut, but well worth it. The truth is, maybe the dishwasher isn't loaded very efficiently, but it's loaded and I didn't have to do it.

"Stopping one-upping allows you to feel love and respect for a person that you previously blocked by having negative feelings. Our relationship is now much more relaxed and rewarding."

Just keep in mind that you were not put on this earth for the express purpose of pointing out all your partner's mistakes. When you see a flaw, a difference in technique, or a characteristic which you don't prefer, sit back, breathe deeply, and thank G-d for having sent you somebody to love and to love you.

When It's Way Over the Line

There are certain circumstances which are either so destructive or outright dangerous that something serious must be done—be it psychiatric intervention, legal intervention, or a dissolution of the marriage.

Perhaps you remember the movie *Sleeping With the Enemy*. The rich, handsome, wonderful husband turns out to be a monster. Not only does everything have to be perfect (labels on cans all turned outward, cans categorized, towels folded just so, and so on), but he cannot tolerate any hint of negativity from her about anything, nor will he permit her to have any part of her life to herself. When she resists, he becomes violent. Scary, very scary. And not that unusual.

I get too many letters from women describing their boyfriend or husband's physical and verbal abuse. One woman wrote to describe her husband as very compulsive:

"He has done many strange things to get his point across or to teach a lesson. Because the girls were not in the mood for broccoli for dinner, he brought out about ten bags of scraps of food that he had hidden in the freezer under my frozen stored foods and sat those bags on the table to let them know how much we were throwing away. A lot of this was discarded food that he did not eat and was not put away. But some were scraps left over from meals. I store leftovers in the refrigerator. We do not waste that much food. To think that all this time he was hiding garbage in the freezer scares me. I think there is something wrong with someone who goes to that extent. It makes me wonder what else he will do. I am at the end of my rope. We tried counseling together, but that didn't work. I never know what is coming next, and that is scary."

Another listener wrote me that her husband of seventeen years lets nothing get by him, just in case he misses an opportunity to correct her. Before bedtime, he will check all jars to see if they are closed completely and properly. If one is not, she writes:

"He turns on me like an attack dog. He makes such a big deal out of it and it usually leads to a fight because he treats me like a child. He forgets about the whole thing in about two minutes, but I resent him the rest of the evening. Then when it's time to be intimate I push him away. I tell him why I'm pushing him away and he calls me petty. It starts all over again."

It seems that for some folks, domination and humiliation of their partner is a kind of aphrodisiac. That power makes them feel potent. Or, in some other cases, it isn't even "personal." It's just that being in control, alert, and on top of things (even if it means on top of loved ones) is satisfying enough to relieve life's anxieties and let them relax into sexual intimacies. No matter how you frame this, it is ugly and it is sick and it should not be tolerated.

In Conclusion

The power struggle cycles are exhausting. It is difficult to live a reasonable life with someone who is constantly or unpredictably angry, and it is difficult to live a reasonable life being angry about the small stuff. This approach to life is to relegate yourself to the slavery of impulse and the picayune.

One of the most interesting ideas I studied in my personal religious journey was the one of slave and master, and I believe it is relevant here. I try to be a serious Jew, and in doing so, have to take upon myself many "rules" (*Mitzvot*, in Hebrew, Divine Commandments). Some people have told me that having all these rules, like Kosher rules about food and Sabbath rules about not working on Saturday, make me a virtual slave.

They have it backward. Instead of being a virtual slave to my impulses and appetites, I make conscious choices. Because I wish to lead a more holy life, I choose to not eat bacon or cheeseburgers that are scripturally prohibited (with some Rabbinic input). I am not a slave to my appetite, I am a master of what goes into my body. What slave can say that?

The Sabbath is to be a holy day, wherein one is reminded that G-d created the universe and that G-d, unlike man who makes physical objects and land "holy" or sacred, has made "time" holy and sacred through this day. No man can control time—that is the one venue over which we have no power. As a religious Jew, I choose not to work on the Sabbath and to keep it holy. What slave can do that?

So that when you say, "I can't control myself—I can't help what I'm doing," you are basically saying that you are a slave, and not a master of your identity, actions, or possibilities. As I have said many times on my radio program, an irresistible impulse is simply an impulse that hasn't been resisted. You can choose to be the master. You can choose to say something nice instead of a criticism or complaint. You can choose to shut your mouth when you feel a nag or criticism coming up. You can choose to not rearrange what your partner has done, simply to "do it right." You can learn to sit with the discomfort of not having things your own way. The discomfort will pass once you get used to it—and then you will be the master.

Finally, in the words of a listener, you can learn to value the relationship as greater than yourself:

"Reflecting on a failed marriage caused me to question just how much it has ultimately benefited me to have put the emphasis on my needs, wants, ways, and schedules. It is clearer now that not a few of the struggles were power struggles. I am in a new marriage now, and I found a process to help me protect this relationship.

"Step 1: Deciding, once and for all, that this relationship is worth protecting from myself!

"Step 2: Becoming keenly aware of the feeling that starts consuming me and my thoughts when a power issue or situation is in the early stage and I am on the verge of saying, 'I'll show you!'

"Step 3: Pausing, saying nothing, and thinking for a moment, 'What would I tell my daughter, someone whom I love and value and want the best for, about the situation to protect her true needs and the relationship?'

"Step 4: Finding something much more beneficial and appropriate to do than I've generally done before.

"I had to work at it, but it works. It is my cure for out-of-control power-tripping."

There it is. It is simple. What makes it difficult to give up Stupid Power is the fear of what one is left with. If one picked a partner wisely, the answer is that it leaves you with peace and love.

5
Stupid Priorities

"At that time, we realized that the most important things in this world are our kids and each other."

—A LISTENER

Believe it or not, there are times on my radio program that I am, for microseconds, flabbergasted into silence. There are other times when I am so enraged that it's good I'm on radio so that folks can't see my eyes bulging with the incredible restraint it takes not to go through the microphone and throttle the caller. When are these times? Well, the flabbergasted moments are when a caller is so obviously the clear and present architect of his or her own pain; and the second, when I feel the impulse to throttle, is when the caller is so obviously the clear and present architect of a child's pain. Most of these circumstances have to do with Stupid Priorities.

One example of a flabbergasting moment was a call I got from a young man complaining that he and his wife were not close at all anymore. It seems that the time they do have together, short and rare, just isn't filled with that oomph that they had when they met. I queried him about their schedules. They both have full-time jobs and go to school full-time and have various friends and functions that they maintained from before they were married. He said this all with pride at how active, involved, growing, successful, and important they were.

"Ahh, I'm confused. You're complaining about the lack of intimacy, sexual and otherwise, yet you speak with enthusiasm about a schedule I would find anywhere from enslaving to punitive."

"Yeah, maybe, but that's what we like. We like being active. We're both smart and accomplished folks."

"That may be true, but it sounds to me as if you're not penciling each other into your schedules. What's important to the two of you is not anything that has to do with the two of you. I'm not surprised you don't have much of a relationship left. What I don't get is that two smart people just don't get it. A relationship and a spouse is not a bed you just crash onto at the end of the day. A relationship and a spouse needs to be a focal point of one's life."

"Well, I don't know about that. We each have goals and plans and are very supportive of each other's reaching them."

"Yes, I believe that. As you each support the other's selfishness, your own is supported automatically. Of course that works. But it doesn't give any warmth, texture, or meaning to your lives."

"That's not what I called about. I just want to know how, considering our goals and commitments, we can feel closer."

"Sir, damned if I know."

That's when I'm flabbergasted. Now, the throttling moment is merely an extension of the flabbergasting thinking. I remember this caller, again a young male, as though it were now. He called to find out if what he and his new wife were planning was "okay."

"How can I help you?"

"Well, my wife and I are married. We're finishing college and have plans for graduate school."

"Okay."

"Well, we also have a three-month-old child."

"Aahaa."

"And we work to support our bills and to pay for school."

"Mmmm."

"And we wondered if it were all right to have her parents raise our daughter for three or four years while we work and get our schooling done?"

"Are you kidding? Are you pulling my leg?"

"No, I'm serious. We thought, that way, the child would be well taken care of and we could get our education and careers under way. What do you think?"

"I think that this is one of the most morally vacant, self-centered, crass, cold, insensitive . . . (Now I'm mad!—I'm throttling!) . . . inhumane, unbelievably horrible suggestions ever made to me on or off this program."

"Why? If we get a good education and good careers, then we have a lot to offer our daughter. And, her parents did a good job with her—why not with our daughter?"

"I'm even more crazed now that you come back at me so 'innocently.' It is phenomenally sad to me to see even more profound evidence of the decay of reason and responsibility in our society—when a seemingly decent person like yourself can offer up a plan in which the bonding, nurturance, care-taking, loving, living, and being with your own child can get so easily put aside and rationalized as being in the ultimate interest of that child.

"Your suggestion is disgusting. If your in-laws raise that child, they will be the bonded mom and dad, and you folks will be the too busy aunt and uncle. You then think you will take that child away from her home and the only mother and father that matter as though she were a parakeet or an adopted hound? You think that those things in the future that you can offer her will be anything but meaningless indulgence—a payoff for your conscience? You think this will teach her the meaning of mother and father, family and commitment? You think this will make her think that she is important? You think this will help her move forward into life with confidence and hope for a loving family of her own in the future?

"Get off it, sir, and grow up. You guys got pregnant when you didn't want to, you got married 'cause you thought you should, but you're both living lives as single people with no obligations. I recommend you put that child up for adoption into a two-parent, mom-and-dad, covenantally married home, where they believe your daughter has intrinsic value. Thank you for your call—I hope I can get over it soon."

"Oh."

This call would not have been half as bad were it not a symptom of the prevailing societal values with respect to marriage (shack-ups and serial monogamy are now common), child-raising (nannies, day care, and baby-sitters the norm), and priorities (success is everything). And there is no shame for any of this.

As if in direct response, one listener recently wrote to me:

"My priorities were all backward, and so I lost the things that really meant the most to me . . . only I didn't know that at the time. (Well, really, I did know that, but I figured that once I was a 'success,' everything would be okay. So, I spent all of my efforts at being 'successful.' Well, I did not have much luck at being successful, and even worse luck at being happy, or making those around me happy.

"Today, I am an older person, with a disability (with which I am okay), but my former wife (who divorced me) has nothing to do with me; and my adult daughter doesn't have too much to do with me either, although she makes some effort.

" 'SUCCESS,' and the pursuit of it, have left me lost and lonely. If I may offer any suggestion to others, I would counsel them to consider what 'success' really means."

Show Me the Money!

I remember a fascinating moment in Synagogue during the 2000 High Holy Services. In seeming contrast to what this listener wrote, the Rabbi's sermon included a hope that all of us would become very rich. He wished us massive financial success as part of his blessing for the upcoming year. I could see that many in the audience reacted with discomfort— after all, a major part of anti-Semitism is the belief that Jews are avaricious. Understandably, there would be an initial negative reaction (albeit a silent hope that his blessing worked!) to a suggestion that money be a goal of "worship."

I know the Rabbi well, and understood what he was building to. He wished us all prosperity, not for our own benefit, but that we would have the power and the resources to help perfect the world. Money may be the root of all evil in the hands of many people without a spiritual basis. However, money is the possibility of great good for a great many. When money is a goal in itself, success is empty; when money is a means to a more noble end, success is a G-dsend.

The emptiness of success as "the" goal is highlighted in this letter from a listener who figured this all out, the hard way:

"My husband and I have been married ten years and have two children, six and eight. When we first married, we were living outside Seattle and both working in rewarding careers. We worked for the nice house, new car, designer clothing, exotic vacations, etc.

"When we had our second child, we realized that we couldn't continue the way we were going. There just wasn't enough of me to go around. Plus, all the money I was making was going to pay for

day care, parking in town, car payment, insurance, plus multiple meals to go, since we had money but not time.

"The wake-up call came when our three-year-old was molested in her day care by the owner's son. At that time, we realized that the most important 'things' in this world are our kids and each other. The material possessions don't mean squat in comparison.

"We quit our jobs and moved to a small farming town, budgeting down to one salary. Six years later, our marriage is now flourishing and so are our kids. I love being home and involved in our kids' school. We have home-cooked meals and eat dinner early, so we actually have an evening. The housework is done during the day, so when the kids go to bed I have time alone with my husband.

"We found that by rethinking our priorities and concentrating on what's really important, we were able to make life changes that strengthened both our marriage and our family."

I fear too many of our young adults today don't understand this family's decision. They'd probably just think of a lawsuit and a new day care. They are the product of rampant selfishness and devaluation of vows, obligations, and sacrifice for some greater good. They are the generation who watched their parents' infidelities, divorces, drug and alcohol abuse, selfish pursuits, materialism, and basic immaturity. For many, this kind of thinking is the norm, not the anomaly it should be.

As another listener reminds us:

"I just think that the 'ME' generation in our society needs to take another look at their priorities. That 'ME' generation are all going to end up in nursing homes because they are raising a generation of children that do not know an example of selflessness . . . only selfishness. Thank you for your time."

I loved the polite salutation about "time." Time is the one thing we humans can't buy, create, or control. Time is our gift from G-d. Time is our gift to each other—the most supreme gift—for it is only in the medium of time that we have the opportunity to connect, to love, to support, to bond, to nurture, to caretake, to heal.

Work Is #1

A mother from Dallas, Texas, called me on my radio program recently to complain about an event in her high-school son's "Career Orientation Class." According to the caller's son, the teacher, a feminist, disdainfully chided the girls in the class, reminding them that "they'd better pay attention to this class and decide on a career now, because if they didn't they would find themselves at-home moms wiping their snot-nosed kids."

I kid you not.

Thankfully, her son raised his hand and commented that he didn't see himself and his five siblings as "snot-nosed kids," that his mother stayed home with all of them and they were all good kids who appreciated having a mother and father who took care of them.

I told the mom to go to war with the school, calling on my Dallas radio affiliate to assist them to get parents organized to fight this corrosive and disgusting attack on motherhood, marriage, and family, and contributing to the growing confusion and ambivalence many men have for women in general, much less women who want to raise their own children.

I have been sickened by how many women call me, who have "seen the light" and want to stay home with their children, who have husbands, brought up by working and single mothers, who actually threaten them into working so that they can afford the goodies "they" always wanted. Men used to measure themselves by their ability to take care of their families—now they want their families to take care of them! Sad.

One woman listener pulled her act back together after a "near death" realization:

"My husband and I began our marriage as career-oriented people who understood the importance of personal advancement in our professions. He is a teacher/coach and I am a professional nurse.

"We both worked hard to earn a living and advance in our careers. After a few years, and with a young teen at home, I had the opportunity to advance to an upper-level management position. In order to meet the demands of the job, I had to work sixty to seventy hours per week.

"I prioritized a professional title, success, and money above spending time with my husband and son. As a result, my husband and son became very independent from me, and my husband became frustrated with spending evening after evening at home without me.

"The stress at home and at work resulted in health problems for me, including chest pain and hospitalization. Fortunately, I realized the damage that was being done, both psychologically and physically, to my family and me, and resigned from what I thought was the position of my dreams.

"I couldn't be happier. I don't have a prestigious title now, and I gave up income. But nothing is worth sacrificing my family over."

"But Honey, I Do It All for You"

When I was in private practice, as a Marriage, Family, and Child Therapist, it was amazing how many men, primarily, would justify their horrendous work schedules by saying, "But, honey, I do it all for you!" That, of course, would make the women grimace with annoyance and shrug with some embarrassment, as they weren't able to think of an apt comeback. For sure, they had nice things and would rather not give them up. Yet they were tired of feeling so not a part of their husband's lives.

Sadly, it now swings both ways; women as well as men creep up the ladder of their solo dreams, shouting down to their spouses, "But, honey, I do it all for you!"

"Bull," I would say to the protestor. "You'd do exactly the same if you were single. Yes, your spouse is benefiting with things, but they'd rather not make the sacrifice of relationship for things. You are the one determined to make that sacrifice, ironically in the name of sacrificing yourself for him/her. How manipulatively clever. How ultimately disastrous, unless, of course, you've got some honey in the wings who is all too ready, willing, and able to adore you and to let you sacrifice the relationship so he/she can enjoy the things."

One of my male listeners confirmed this mentality:

"I am twenty-eight years old and an avid listener to your radio program. I am the King of Stupid Priorities. The following are all the things I put before my wife and child: a two-to-ten shift job, my lawn-mowing service, the Navy reserves, and a full load in college with music and art projects.

"I love my wife and child, but I feel like I'm not a very good provider sometimes. I know what you would say, nothing should be put before your wife, but I do not feel like a man unless my family's needs are met. Also, I feel dead if I'm not doing something constructive. I'm not proud. I know I'm probably doing more harm than good, but I feel I'm in too deep and I can't give up on my dreams for fear I'll lose myself. I know this must make you sick, but, it's the way I feel."

He's right. It makes me sick. It also makes me terribly sad. Not only has he already lost himself, he'll likely lose his wife and child. When somebody feels dead without perpetual stimulation, they need psychological help. All people need challenges and stimulation—that's a normal part of being alive. When stimulation is the goal of one's life, and one is "dead" without it, one is already dead in the spaces that truly make us human—those are the places that derive joy and triumph from giving, sacrificing, loving, protecting, and simply "being with."

Work is not the only priority venue that can occupy folks to the extreme and hurt or destroy their relationships. Cleaning is another source of problems for some couples. Listen to these two comments:

"I used to think that a spotless house would make my husband 'feel' important, cared about, and proud. Come to find out that it is not as important as spending quality time with my husband. My husband and I work opposite shifts so that someone is always home with our fifteen-year-old, so now I clean when he is at work and my son is doing his homework or some other activity, and save my weekends with my husband and son without worrying about such a clean house."

And the second:

"My husband of one year is expressing that I prioritize all other obligations below his needs and the needs of the relationship. But, I must admit, I feel everything in my house MUST be in order for me to feel intimate. Confusion and chaos take the mood away. I need help in reconciling my thoughts and being attentive to his needs only."

The sad reality for people who need constant challenge and stimulation or everything in order before they can get to their relationships is that they really can't get to their relationships at all. The work and cleaning are merely screens, behind which they hide their fears of imagined, or in some part real, problems, weaknessness, inadequacies, secrets, anxieties, and so forth. The work and cleaning are how they make themselves feel intact, stable, and in control—all of which they fear will go away if they cease activity or become vulnerable and open in an intimate relationship. In other words, they feel safe and competent with a computer or a mop, not with the arms of their spouse or their children. This requires introspection and professional intervention and explains why they hang on to their determination not to give up what they're doing in spite of the obvious problems in their relationships.

"I'm Ready for My Close-Up!"

One of the tough realities a growing child has to face as he/she matures is that they are not the center of the universe. It's easy for a small child to feel that he or she is the center of the universe when every gurgle and scribble is oohed and ahhed about by parents and relatives. The first time that their kindergarten teacher tells them they can't take that crayon away from Mary, or that Johnny gets to go first, or that their drawing needs work, children recognize that life is a cooperative effort.

Some don't give up being the center of the universe easily, and getting attention and becoming the focus of others takes on many forms—some healthy, some not. It's all a matter of degree and balance. Some become entertaining, or even entertainers. Some become "needed," some become utterly dependent, some become perpetually ill, and so forth.

All in all, the "I must be in the spotlight" mentality generally brings darkness to the family.

"I have spent the last year and a half as a drama/debate coach at our local high school," writes one listener. *"I was able to go to the state level in almost every area in which we were competitive. I directed three plays (one being a full-length musical with a cast of one hundred). Both parents and administration thought I had done very well for their children. I thought that I had done very well until I realized that my son was about to be one. I lost his first year of life. My daughter was potty-trained by others.*

"I was so intent on being seen as the best that I became the worst mom and wife."

It is important to watch that ego! The ego-trap is an easy one for people to fall into. Being good at something makes one feel important—that too often leads to a sense of entitlement—that moves right into a sense of superiority—and that collapses relationships.

Work Is Not Everything—It Is the Only Thing

Too many folks get their primary sense of value and connectedness from their work instead of apportioning it between their work, their marriage, their children, their friends, their family, their community, and their inner spiritual life. If "all work and no play makes Jack a dull boy," then all work and no family and marital bonding makes Jack or Jill have a life without texture, beauty, meaning, and purposefulness.

This is exactly what one listener expressed:

"I worked fifteen years for a company and thought I would be there forever. It was a family-owned business. I put everything I had into my position. When I was pregnant with my first child, I worked right up to the delivery day. I went back in four weeks. It pained me to leave my baby, but the company 'needed me.' I was making good money but never able to go away for even a weekend, much less a vacation.

"Before I knew it my child was twelve. The owner of the company gave the store to his son and I was the first to go. In the beginning, I was devastated. But blessings really do come in disguise. I was hired in a totally different profession, make exactly the same money, work much fewer hours, and I'm off every weekend. My husband, daughter, and I are really enjoying all of the free time we have together making lasting memories.

"It doesn't make any difference how much money you make, or

how high you climb that corporate ladder, if you can't be around to enjoy the people you love and care about the most. The only regret I have is that I didn't lose that job ten years ago."

It is interesting to me how many of these letters about Stupid Priorities report a disaster as the way folks learn "the hard way" what balance and what priorities are essential for a quality, happy, and successful life. We can't be wishing disasters on folks in the hopes that they wake up and save their relationships with their spouses and children. This is the prime motivation behind this book—maybe you, or someone you love (but are starting not to like) could benefit from the stories of others.

Sometimes it's not simply that folks are totally selfish or insensitive of the needs of others; there are strong pulls, like the tide, which draw us along—much too far—before we start paying attention. What always surprises me is how easy it seems to be for us to "get with that flow." In addition to neglecting others, that we don't even feel a need for that intimacy ourselves. I often wonder why we don't miss it more, and how it really is possible to feel warmed only by success or power or money.

This listener got caught up in the flow, but eventually pulled himself out.

"I took a job as a gas station attendant in New Mexico. After a month or so, the current manager quit so I took the station over and became the manager/owner. I was determined to make it and began to work 105 hours per week—seven days a week—363 1/2 days per year for four years.

"I was offered several outs by God, or so I believe, but turned them all down. After all, I was the BIG owner—the BIG Kahuna (I was also the guy who cleaned the toilets).

"I only saw my kids and wife when they came down to watch me work—and I missed several years of my babies' lives.

"After all my EGO and posturing, the actual owner of the property put the land up for lease bids and I was outbid by three times.

In an instant I was ruined—absolutely nothing to show for the work.

"My firm philosophy now is 'WORK SUX.' Now it's family first. What matters is now I see my family and enjoy them."

Well, I guess G-d had to get very direct to wake this listener up!

"It's My Divine Obligation"

Speaking of G-d, in 2000 I was privileged to speak to a room full of Rebbitzen from all over the Bronx, Manhattan, and Brooklyn. Since these women, wives of Orthodox Rabbis, were from a traditional world, I was certain I would not be addressing the usual, more secular concerns about work and family.

I was wrong. It seems that along with the caretaking of generally a lot of children (the Orthodox value large families as blessings to and from G-d), they felt compelled by responsibility to the needs and demands of people and families in their Synagogues. Unfortunately, they found it difficult to balance doing for others, with having time for their children and their marriages. Rabbis have the same dilemmas.

I acknowledged that this was a real and serious problem, because they, in fact, did have responsibilities based on their commitment to being spiritual leaders. However, there are two points to keep in mind: one, being role models was a powerful way to serve their community, since making their families the fundamental priority was a way of teaching others how to structure their lives and deal with the pulls and pushes of others; and two, that they may be underestimating how much of sacrificing the family for "religious obligations" was really serving their egos—after all, it's always easier to be a hero on the outside than at home.

One listener amplifies these points:

"The biggest mistake in priorities I have ever made came a few years ago. I believed that God had put a ministry in my hands and that it was something that He wanted me to do. The ministry took on a life of its own . . . my family took second place, and often that second place was well down the line of things—because the ministry was so big and intrusive.

"My family and personal life became chaos. I THOUGHT that I was putting God first; in the end, I realized it was me that was first—that I was taking my own past, and trying to make a difference to absolve my own feelings and try to 'earn' God's favor. This goes back to my family and how they have made me feel over the years. I simply thought God was just like them.

"Now, I am out of this ministry, and since I home-school, I have really placed the priority on family. God has really blessed me."

Not that all caregivers in the name of G-d are egomaniacal, or attempting to repair ancient hurts and guilts, but those that are should heal themselves or get out. We each have to be careful to examine ourselves to see if our serving is self-serving. One way to tell the difference is to see who and what you sacrifice to do the serving and whether any of the serving targets include the folks you are the most obligated to, your marriage and family.

I believe the most successful ministers of spirituality hold family first. One perfect example is the Reverend Robert Schuller. He has an incredible ministry and an elaborate Church/School complex. I have the privilege of knowing his entire family, and not one of them has ever paid a price for his ministry, since they came first and became a part of the projects. His ministry is literally a family affair.

My local Rabbi, Moshe Bryski, is an amazing success with the development of Chabad Houses, adult education, children's Jewish Day Schools, and international networking for Jewish Outreach. He has some tough rules. He's always home for dinner and to help his many children with schoolwork, and don't bother to try to find him Sunday, that's family day.

These are men I respect because, as accomplished as they are, neither they nor their work has become a god, and their families come first.

"A year ago, I was never at home," admits another listener from the clergy, *"and my three kids were in day care from 6 A.M. until 7 P.M., only to be picked up and dropped off at a baby-sitter or family member's home until 11 P.M. There were days when my family did not even see me. The weekends were worse. I was gone all day Saturday and most of Sunday.*

"By now you are probably asking yourself just what in the world I was doing! My answer may shock you . . . I was serving the Lord!—or, at least I thought I was. I praise God that He woke me up to realize that I serve Him by serving my family first. This is a lesson that I am happy to say that I learned in time."

There are two issues here—one is clearly ego gratification, but the other is learning how to set boundaries and to say no, which again has some basis in ego. We all want to feel needed and important. When I was in "therapy school," we were warned against developing the "Messiah Complex." That was another way of reminding us not to get too big for our britches—not to develop an inflated notion of our own power and importance. It's easy to slip into that when people are looking up to you for help, answers, advice, and guidance. There's nothing more sobering and reality getting than the truths about ourselves we all get at home with our spouses and children! Boy, that's humbling—and humility is required to be a good helper.

One woman listener wrote to complain about how her "hero" husband used to be with just about anybody that called on him for help.

"Soon after I married, I noticed that he was everyone's favorite person to call for an emergency. Actually, looking back, I could see

it was happening while we dated—I'd just been blind to it. Even people who were casual acquaintances could call on a moment's notice and convince him to cut short a date with me, or our kids' birthday party, to deal with their needs.

"For several years I just lived in frustration, and without even realizing how dysfunctional I was becoming, began creating an occasional 'emergency' of my own just to keep his attention. When I saw our children learning to do the same thing, I realized something wasn't working right.

"We got counseling. Over time, my husband realized that his constant response to 'emergencies,' at the cost of family time, was just his way to feel better about himself. When he really listened to the kids and me talk about how neglected we felt, he realized that we should come first and things improved greatly and our family is much happier for it."

When our priority is our own ego, we can try to camouflage it as G-d's work, or what we have to do for the family, but the reality is always that we have Stupid Priorities, self-serving and ultimately destructive to our soul's and our family's life.

"I Don't Want to Grow Up!"

Sometimes people don't really want to grow up. Some of those people still get married—and some of those people have babies. All of those people hurt the ones they've vowed to protect.

The "I don't wanna grow up" types believe that being married and having children should in no way curtail their fun times. Sometimes it's their hobbies. (*"He has always been an avid hunter and spends great amounts of time, money, and energy on bow hunting. Often I felt as if I was low on his list of priorities after work, hunting, and fishing. When does it all end?"*) Or, it's hanging with the buddies. *(". . . Maybe golfing with the guys and returning drunk or four-wheeling with his pals. Our divorce was final and he hooked up with a twenty-year-old who moved in with him and got pregnant right away.")* Or it may mean just opting out of the picture altogether. *("He informed me that being with me and the twins would be like being in prison. I loved him with all my heart. I wanted the American dream. He wanted to go out with friends, and just not grow up. You know, it took him four days to go to give blood for our son, because he was too busy. I do believe that his priorities were a little messed up.")* These immature types choose their own immediate gratification over their obligations and well-being of their (supposed) loved ones.

It's very difficult to reach these folks. I remember that when I was counseling couples, the childlike member felt entitled to the fun . . . because: Their spouse was a drag and never wanted to do anything, the house was a mess, the children were a problem, they were entitled because they worked so hard, it's what they always did and he/she picked them knowing that, life is short, this is a free country, and on and on.

The bottom line is that these types do not live to give anything, hence they make bad spouses and parents—and they show their spots when you're dating. Some of you wish to be blind because "you're in love" or you're desperate, or you think it'll change, or it seemed cute at the time. Here's one letter from a listener who ought to jump ship—how obvious can it get?:

"My boyfriend is a full-time college student and also has a full-time job. He doesn't save his money because he wants to buy all of this 'new, fool stuff.' He has a car that runs pretty good and he has no ambition to move out and be independent of his parents. I, on the other hand, have been on my own for five years and I have a newer car, a decent job, and make the same amount of money he does, but he has a total lack of responsibility with his money. He wants a brand-new car that's about $20,000. And he can't

afford it. He doesn't want to move away from home either. His priorities as an adult are all backward and it drives me nuts!"

It drives me nuts that she even calls him a boyfriend. Clearly, there is no evidence that he will be a committed, responsible, trustworthy, or competent husband or father. He must be cute.

The Circus Juggler

Hopefully it's clear by now that a mature, responsible adult makes choices, and that those choices are made based on a value system that dictates priorities—and I do mean dictates!

Either just for the sake of curiosity or as a direct challenge, I'm often asked how I juggle a radio program, writing books, a charitable foundation, making jewelry for charity auctions, and being a wife and mother.

Actually, I tell them, it's really very easy. There are just so many hours in a day and just so many days in a week. From Friday sundown to Saturday sundown we observe the Sabbath—that means no work; which brings me down to six days a week.

Monday thru Friday, our son leaves for school at 6 A.M. I have to be at the radio station by about 11 A.M. to prepare for broadcast. That leaves me five hours to work on a book or column, or do the television show (which, by the way, was determined by me in contract to happen in the A.M. or not happen at all), or work on jewelry, or read a novel, or exercise, or whatever else occurs to me. Sundays I might work on a book until 12 noon, at which time the family takes little day trips for family time.

Every day I am home by 4 P.M. Our son gets home from high school (Orthodox Jewish) at 6 P.M. We have dinner together every night and then hang around to help with homework. After homework is completed, the "boys" (dad and son) watch a game.

I choose not to work at night—except in an emergency—because that's family time. I literally squeeze my career and interests into whatever is left over from family time. I travel very little, and when I do, the family comes with me, unless our son has to be in school; then, dad is with son at home for the one or two days I may have to be gone to testify for a bill in some state, or lecture about morals in advertising to an ad council.

Bottom line? I don't juggle. When you have to keep balls in the air, you make very little contact with any of the balls, and one always falls. Sadly, that one is usually family. It is easier to push aside family than it is to push aside a boss—a boss will fire you, while your family is expected just to tolerate what you do. Most of you find it infinitely easier to disappoint your loved ones than risk the same with work.

Many listeners have written to me about this juggling nonsense:

"I know firsthand how putting work, school, and hobbies as the top priority can hurt family relationships. About ten years ago, when I was a radio broadcast student, I was juggling my school, work, and family life poorly. I never turned down an opportunity to work extra airshifts or make personal appearances on behalf of the station. The result was no time for my wife or kids. I was trying to sleep evenings when my wife was working second shift to help support us while I pursued my dream of being a 'radio star.' The result was our children being on their own when I should have been there for them. Add to this an affair with a young lady who was also in radio and you can see how I let my ambitions and selfishness tear my life and my family apart.

"Fortunately, my ties to the church (albeit weak) kept me from finishing off the disaster. As I started to attend church more fre-

quently, I saw the error of my ways. I quit the jobs that didn't properly provide for my family. Life today is so much nicer for all of us because I finally figured out that family was a 'we' situation and not a 'me' thing. They have become my reason for living. They help me to be who I really am . . . dad and husband."

The family as "we" versus "me" is probably the most important concept under Stupid Priorities. Too many people marry and produce children not understanding or submitting to the notion of obligation and commitment. When you take on the care and raising of a spouse and children you, with grace, give up the privilege of doing whatever you want, whenever you want. Your family is not an inanimate object, like a bed, which you just come up and flop into after all the really important things in your life are taken care of. Yet, that is sadly how so many people treat family—and, it is an attitude supported by society.

Just yesterday, I received a call from a large city newspaper in a state from which the Governor was assigned an Ambassadorship, leaving the Lt. Governor to be promoted to the number one position. The Lt. Governor is a woman. No problem there. However, she is about eight months pregnant with twins and lives 150 miles from work. I was asked my opinion about the situation. Though it does appear that the dad may be the stay-at-home parent, these children are clearly going to have little to do with their mother for the next however many years she reigns as Governor.

My comment? It is a far, far better thing we do to parent our own children, and let those so unencumbered do the state politics. Choices have to be made. And here is yet another vivid example of how personal opportunity and ambitions are put before the needs of newborn, dependent, innocent children. And here is yet another testimonial to how family and children are less important than the "me."

And here is yet another opportunity for a strong, woman role-model to demonstrate how children don't really need mothers. Sickening.

And that is exactly what this listener remembers struggling with:

"I am the mother of three fine young men. When they were younger, however, I was influenced by the likes of Phil Donohue, etc., that told me I was not a whole person unless I worked outside the home. I went back to school and got a nursing degree, worked night shift so I could be home with my children in the day and wound up dependent on pills to slow me down because I could not sleep. I was always worn out. In hindsight, I did not help my family or my husband and did much to the detriment of my own health, because I thought I needed to be something. Since then, I have realized that only the peace of God, the love of my family, and the ability to do for others, not a career per se, is what is important.

"If I had to do it over, even with the loss of income, I would never have missed one day of enjoying all the joys that motherhood and the sweetness of a great marriage bring."

As Adela Rogers St. John is purported to have said, "You cannot wheel two pushcarts at once." This was in reference to her choosing a career over motherhood. In *Parenthood by Proxy* (in paperback called *Stupid Things Parents Do to Mess Up Their Kids*), I wrote about a female Army General who quit because she realized that her ambitions had robbed her children and herself of the mother-daughter bond.

It's not that woman can't or shouldn't work. I work. But, working should not be done at the expense of marriage, parenthood, or family. Priorities need to be set, decisions must be made and kept to. It gets easier and easier to say "No" to requests that would polish your image everywhere but at home.

As you've probably noticed, the folks who make the transitions from "me" to "we" seem to have a strong religious base. I don't think that's an accident. I believe when people "know" that they are part of something beyond themselves, and that there are divine values, they more naturally move from "me" to "we" because it is in the "we" that they truly satisfy the "me."

In conclusion, I received from one listener this warning to all the "women's libbers" out there who think they can have it all—while their all is mostly at work: *"I remember that one woman I worked for (house cleaning) made a speech to women's libbers about how she could keep her husband and her children happy. Well, while she was at work, her kids were at home taking dope and her husband was chasing me around her kitchen and her dogs were doing poo all over the house. Then, she came home and threw a frozen dinner in the oven. Where do these women get the idea that they can do it all?"*

The Stepford Parents

Every now and then, in between dealing with the hordes of parents who are too indulgent or neglectful of their children, I confront parents who are in overdrive with respect to their parenting—to the point of neglecting their own health and that of the marriage. Sometimes it's because they are more comfortable relating to a child than another adult, who has expectations and demands and the ability to be critical or rejecting, so they make the parent-child relationship their first—strike that—*only* priority. Obviously, this shuts out the spouse. That's the paradox—they're afraid of being vulnerable to their spouse, so they focus on the child, and in doing so push away the very person they're afraid of losing.

Other times, it's overzealous parenting. *"It took my husband and two kids and seven years of marriage to realize that we had*

gone overboard in our parenting. In our quest to become the per-
fect parents, we forgot that our love is what started this family in
the first place!

"*I am a stay-at-home mom and have been for six years, so my*
days are kid-centered and so is my thinking. When he would say,
'*Let's go out,' I would think that was not being a good mom and*
dad, and our relationship was starting to suffer. You are a better
parent for letting your kids see that the love and respect you two
share is what keeps the family going, and you should take care of
it just as you take care of them—with all your heart."

This realization is even harder to make when the child has
special needs. One dad who wrote to me has several children
with a rare disease which will cause them all to die somewhere between the ages of sixteen and twenty.

"*Well, Dr. Laura, we don't do it so well. Our lives are totally*
focused on the survival and quality of life of our children. I believe
that when they die, the 'reward' for our years of self-sacrifice and
dedication to our kids at the expense of virtually everything else, will
be our separation and divorce. There is just nothing left between us
outside managing our children's disease and our lives. I have tried
on many occasions to get my wife to invest in our relationship and
have been told point-blank in every instance that she is overbur-
dened by life and that she has no intention or desire to add another
load."

This is not an unusual scenario when there is an ill or
handicapped child. It is remarkable how the normal responsibility to one's children can become exaggerated by guilt
and a sense of martyrdom. I was caught in the crosshairs of
this mentality because of a call I took with a woman whose
son is seriously impaired behaviorally by autism. This boy, in
spite of all efforts, is so terribly out of control that he
becomes violent. Family members have asked them to come
visit sometimes without their boy, so that there can be some
peace during the visits as well as some peaceful time for the

parents. I gently supported that option. Boy, from the letters, calls, and faxes from irate mothers of autistic children (who, by the way, had not heard the call, but were e-mailed angry comments from one listener), you'd have thought I said to euthanize them all! Telling someone she's entitled to some free time and that the marriage deserves attention was considered an evil act.

The truth is that when our children have problems of any kind, of their own doing or not, parents are often consumed with guilt for having "created" the problem. That inappropriate guilt has them lash out at any attempts to do other than "fix things," or at least sacrifice themselves on that altar. Additionally, some folks gain their value and identity from sacrificing themselves on that altar; the most extreme version is Munchausen's Syndrome, where parents, mostly mothers, actually make their kids sick for the resulting attention and to fulfill a need to be important.

A friend of mine is struggling with his three-year-old son's cancer. He realized that he and his wife were surely turning this sweet little boy into a monster by letting him get away with things, because of their compassion, and that they would self-destruct if they didn't ignore the inappropriate guilt feelings and spend time on themselves and each other. They made the necessary adjustments as best they could under the circumstances. Being basically centered, strong and in love with each other obviously helps a lot.

My Mother or My Spouse? Hmmmm

"I think that now that I am older and married, I realize how at the beginning of my relationship with my husband, I would drop everything at the tone of my mother's voice, or, if my dad would call. My husband would do the same with his parents. Now, the

two of us realize that the only way that our marriage is going to work is if we make each other our #1 priority.

"When people are married, the parents have to step back, and the couple needs to step forward, away from their parents into their own space."

Yes, indeed, but I can't tell you how many calls I get from guys whose wives won't move away from Mommy, won't stop calling Mommy several times a day, won't stop Mommy from just dropping in uninvited whenever she darn well pleases, and who won't stop checking in with Mommy for an opinion on everything the couple is deciding. Now, obviously, this kind of woman is a very dependent personality, and any guy who picks her is looking for a cushy pillow instead of a partner. The mistake these guys make is in thinking that she will automatically change from her Mommy's cushy pillow to his with a ceremony. Surprise!

This is no different when the guy is a "Momma's Boy." Women who pick these men actually want a guy who jumps through hoops at the mere mention, much less the sound, of a whistle. And they too think that the guy will take the whistle from Mommy and give it to Wifey. Wrong!

Some of these situations are blunt and explained in advance:

"My husband has always made it clear that his parents and brothers are more important in his life than I am. I have heard his parents say, 'Blood is thicker than water,' more times than I can count. I have also heard his Dad say, 'We are family, everyone else is an outsider.'"

Other situations come into view over time:

"I've been thinking a lot lately about how my life has not turned out the way I wanted it to, and not at all how I planned it. I just turned fifty this year, and I suppose you could blame my state of mind on a Midlife Crisis, or some such psychobabble. I think, though, that I just didn't set my priorities in the right place as far back as I can remember. I was always the 'good' little girl

who didn't want to disappoint her parents. At this late date, I can see that I just never grew up enough to set the priorities that were right for me. Guilt can be a terrible thing, especially when it is misplaced, and not at all appropriate. I went back to work for my workaholic parents twelve years ago—conforming to their desires and expectations, instead or mine or my family's.

"Your parents gave you life, but you shouldn't allow them to set your priorities after you've 'grown up.' "

People are often confused about their obligations to their parents compared with that to their spouse and children. When they call me, they ask about the Commandment to Honor Thy Father and Mother. For an extensive analysis of this Commandment, please read my book *The Ten Commandments; The Significance of God's Laws in Everyday Life* (Cliff Street Books/HarperCollins). Honoring your parents does not include dishonoring your vows or obligations in marriage. Honoring your parents does not mean that they get to, at their preference, make decisions in your life. It does mean that you must show respect and make sure they have the necessities of life—but it does not mean that you must sacrifice your family to do it.

Let me give you the basic concept of a proper parental relationship with an adult child through this story told to me by a wise Rabbi. There was a great flood, and the rains continued. The poppa bird was caught in the storm with his three baby birds. He wished to take them all to safety. Not knowing if there was time to take them all to safety, he picked up the first baby bird and carried him over the swollen, raging river. As they flew, the poppa bird asked, "Baby bird, will you always take care of me? Even when you have your own baby birds?" The baby bird, looking down at the swift current, answered excitedly, "Oh yes, Poppa, anything you need at any time, I'll be there to take care of you, don't worry about a thing, no matter what it takes."

The poppa bird dropped the baby bird into the river and flew back to get the second baby bird. The same dialogue occurred, and the second baby bird also was dropped to his death.

As the poppa bird flew over the flood waters with the last baby bird, he asked him the same question, "Baby bird, will you always take care of me? Even when you have your own baby birds?" This baby bird said, "Poppa, I can promise you that I will take care of my babies the way you have always taken care of us." This baby bird was carried to safety in its father's beak. Why? Because it is the order of things that when you leave your parents' nest, you take what you've learned from them, apply it to your own family, and that is the best way to honor your parents.

Catering to the whims of a weak or demanding parent is clearly a perpetual motion machine and causes the direct destruction of your psyche and your marriage; it is a display of disrespect for your vows, commitments, and obligations to your spouse. Where there are serious needs, as with a seriously ill or dying parent, those needs must be met with honor and compassion and compromise.

Neither spouse should put the other in charge of his or her own responsibilities to parents. Since each spouse is obligated to bring his or her healthiest self to a marriage, where there are clear problems with inappropriate attachment to the original family, mental health assistance should be used.

A Success Story Where You Least Expect It

I never cease to be amazed at which relationships do ultimately work out in spite of how horrible they seem. It impresses me how incredibly resilient and creative people can be when they are motivated.

One listener letter illustrates my point:

"I was twenty and he was twenty-six when we exchanged vows . . . and we were young and stupid. I wanted the fairy tale . . . he wanted his mother. Our sex life went downhill fast, and we blamed it on our priorities. He was spending all of his time on the computer, playing games and collecting photos of other women . . . while I was watching TV and blaming him for my unhappiness. I blamed his porn habits for my insecurities, and he blamed my poor housekeeping for his lack of interest in sex.

"I eventually packed my bags and moved home with my parents. After a month of internet correspondence with my husband, I went home. Things have never been better between us. We now talk each day . . . really talk. We make time for each other. We do things together and enjoy each other's company. My husband's porn habit is over . . . he trashed everything. I now clean the house and try harder to please him by doing simple things that don't really take much time, but mean the world to him (bake him cookies, rub his neck, cuddle with him on the couch).

"It was a matter of organizing our priorities and realizing which ones were important and which ones were selfish and stupid. I love him and want our marriage to work . . . and for once in three and a half years, the sun is shining on us."

It's the priorities, stupid!

6

Stupid Happiness

> *"My mother has been trying for years to find happiness.*
>
> *First she tried to find it in my father.*
>
> *Then it was in a bottle of beer.*
>
> *And then she felt she could buy it at a department store.*
>
> *She spent time in a mental hospital,*
>
> *And she finally got her 'happy pill (meds).'*
>
> *To this day, she doesn't get the message."*
>
> —A LISTENER

As I finished my breakfast this morning, on the very last page of the very last section of my Sunday newspaper, which I was reading before sitting down to work on this chapter, I found an ad for clothing. The model, middle-aged, with gray hair and glasses, is wearing a plain black, ankle-length shift, with a red, buttonless cardigan. She is smiling with great glee, and the only caption, outside of the designer's name, says "Practice happiness."

I immediately called my husband over to see this remarkable juxtaposition of "message" and the substance of this chapter, which I was about to write. It made me happy to experience such a coincidence largely because, as a religious Jew, I no longer believe in coincidences—they are events of meaning, assuming one is open to receiving the message. It made me happier to sit down and write—a process that makes me happy just by itself.

Why am I going on about this? Because it is for the lack of attention to and respect for such seemingly insignificant "happifying" experiences that too many of you jettison a perfectly good relationship, figuring that you'll find happiness in some other bed.

I know, because I hear these stories all the time on my radio program. It used to be that a man or a woman would leave a spouse because of violence, alcoholism, no support, serious character deficiencies, infidelities—serious issues. Now, I hear from both men and women alike, even with pregnancies, small children, or numerous children, how they just feel like it's time to leave, because they're not "happy."

What does that mean? And why should relationships end over a temporary and largely self-induced mind-set?

Is somebody under the impression that a quality, long-term marriage is supposed to make you perpetually giddy, or that happiness is a quality that must only be experienced emphatically, not subtly? You know, like Big Bangs versus a cool breeze?

The ad says it all: "*Practice* happiness." Happiness is a conscious decision, a determined attitude, an openness to nuance, requiring action and understanding on your part. Generally, and ironically, those people who say they are "unhappy" for reasons unknown, are generally behaving in ways which wouldn't bring any joys to anyone around them either, the same way that bored people are usually boring people.

I remember one particular day when I was in graduate school

in Manhattan. I was sullen and unhappy over stuff in general. As I was walking toward some subway stairs, an old black man, sitting in a chair holding out a cup, caught my attention when he said to me, "Hey, you're too pretty a young lady to have such a frown on your face. Smile. It's a beautiful day."

Yikes, was I ever embarrassed. Here was an old, crippled man, begging for coins, who looked happier than me, a young, healthy, woman, attending an Ivy League graduate school, on the way to a Ph.D. I've thought about that moment many times in the thirty years or so since it happened. Sure, there are things to be upset about, disappointed over, and frustrated by—but they don't ultimately have to determine happiness.

For the rest of that day, I *practiced* happiness—walking with a bounce, smiling at people, and making some positive plans for the day. Amazingly, I felt happy.

One of my listeners wrote to me about her realization that happiness is mostly a behavior, not a mysterious occurrence:

"I was married for the first time at the age of thirty-four, assuming that with my great career and self-confidence, I was ready to make mature and unself-centered decisions. After having two kids, I began to resent my husband. I did everything I could do to prove he didn't care and began treating him very badly. We fought over everything. I was sure this marriage wouldn't last and became very depressed and was irritable (unloving, resentful, and disrespectful) toward him all the time.

"He just wasn't making me happy anymore.

"This was about the time I started listening to the Dr. Laura program and learned that no one else is responsible for my happiness, and 'so what if I'm not happy,' I have a commitment and responsibility as a wife and mother.

"I started behaving differently toward my husband, and slowly but surely, I started feeling differently about my husband, marriage, and family. Now I am a 'committed' wife and mother, and

a very lucky lady to have a husband who was willing to endure the toughest first years of our marriage."

Here's a woman who realized and accepted that, 1) the "feeling" of happiness must not be the priority our society appears to put on it as "the" criterion for determining the value of our lives and our relationships; 2) fulfilling our obligations, and behaving in ways which are loving and positive, make us happy in and of themselves; 3) when we create pleasantness, in spite of our mood, we create an atmosphere in which others flourish and feed us back even more positively; and finally, 4) that feelings have no conscience or IQ—they are not to be revered over obligation, morality, and common sense.

Women Talk, Men Shovel Snow

A woman caller was relating the terrible experiences of her last two years: Several close relatives of hers and her husband's had died and their child had leukemia. She expressed being exhausted, anxious, drained, and generally bummed out with life. Her primary concern at the time of the call was that her husband just didn't make her happy anymore. "He doesn't comfort me," she lamented.

"What do you mean, he doesn't comfort you?"

"Well, he doesn't share his feelings or listen to mine. I'm thinking of divorcing him, because I'm just not happy in this marriage anymore. He's not giving me what I need."

"Well, what you need is a complete break from stress and terror—but that's not coming soon, is it?"

"No, it isn't."

"And you're thinking that what you really need is to break it off with him, because he doesn't understand, doesn't care, and doesn't make you happy, right?"

"That's about it."

"Well, you're wrong—he shovels snow."

"What?"

"Your husband shovels snow to show you that he cares, understands, and wants to make you happy. Two things are going on here. First, is that bad stuff is happening, and it's difficult, if not guilt-provoking, to try to be happy in the midst of all this death and illness. Second, is that you are like a radio turned off; your husband is broadcasting 'caring' and you're not receiving the message."

"No, that's not so. He just isn't helping. And, what do you mean, shoveling snow?"

"When we women want to comfort somebody, we make them hot cocoa and talk for days. When men want to comfort their woman, they shovel the snow . . . symbolically, that is. Men *do* something to try to make things better—they don't ruminate—they do!

"I'll bet you can think of at least three things, under the category of shoveling snow, that your husband has done even in the last twenty-four hours to try to make things better for you— that's how he's trying to comfort you. Tonight, when he comes home, throw your arms around him, list off the three things, and thank him immensely for comforting you."

At this point I ended the call, having my screener take down the woman's phone number so that we could call her the next day after the "experiment." The caller was not all that receptive to my suggestion—in fact she was a bit hostile.

The next day she called back, glowing in gratitude and "happiness." She did exactly what I ordered: She threw her arms around him and thanked him for what he was doing to make things easier for her; he melted, she melted, and a great lesson was learned.

"Dr. Laura, you absolutely saved my marriage. I just wasn't willing to see happiness when it was there."

When life is causing us great misery, there is no one to

"get back at." That's why spouses often get the brunt of our rage, hurt, and sense of powerlessness. We imagine that they are a safe place upon which to vent frustrations, get even with life, and finally have some power. Sometimes we take it even further, imagining that if we get rid of them, we simultaneously get rid of all our troubles.

I remember once in "therapy school," at USC, reading an extensive research report suggesting that most folks who divorce regret it afterward realizing that it wasn't the panacea they thought it would be. The number of callers who did such, only to find themselves in similar predicaments with other people, realized a little too late that the main problem was that they took themselves with them wherever they went.

Happily Ever After

Keeping in mind that very few people live the concept of *practicing* happiness, it is naively assumed that a marriage *in and of itself* will be a wellspring of happiness. One of my recent website (www.drlaura.com) questions for my listeners asked, "Did you get married for all the wrong reasons?" One particular answer summarized many people's basic problem:

"I'm not sure what you mean by all the wrong reasons, but after ten years, I can see how naïve I was then. I thought (then) that marriage would be more 'happily ever after.' Sure, we both worked, but car troubles and minor accidents, financial strain, living far from our families, and a miscarriage in our newlywed period made me realize that marriage doesn't protect you from life like I thought it would.

"After all this time and two children (six and one), I'm glad we're best friends. We still struggle with finances, but because I stay home and we moved back to our hometown, we're doing better.

"We now look at life and marriage as a team sport, with each player trying to give 100 percent, not 50/50. This way, if one of you can't give your all, the other person more than makes up the difference. Overall, it's been nothing like I expected, but more than I could've hoped for."

How touching is that last comment? Hers is a philosophically brilliant insight: A quality, successful, happy married life can be gotten in spite of your expectations and demands and self-centeredness (which is a natural tendency that must be overcome). The key to enjoying the fruits of such an insight is encompassed in the Tenth Commandment, against coveting. The concept here is simple: If you determine to see value and feel gratitude for what you have, you will not be consumed by envy and disappointment. Instead, you will come to see your portion as different from that of others, but no less special, and no less significant, and no less worthy of respect and enjoyment.

Falling in Love

At a more innocent time in our culture, the notion of "falling in love" was the key in choosing a mate. Although falling in love is all about infatuation, projecting our fantasies on another person before we even know who they are and what they're about, it was assumed that this sexual and emotional high was sufficient motivation for marriage. This probably worked more often than not, even considering the predictable demoralization that occurs when you get that infatuation haze out from in front of your eyes (and good sense), because of the societal notion of commitment. Commitment is the bridge over all sorts of troubled waters; it gives people the substrate upon which to build a real relationship.

In our current less innocent times, infatuation is not necessary for sexual intimacy (just being around is sufficient motivation for some) nor as a reasonable condition for shacking-up and making babies out-of-wedlock. Of course, with the commitment part as denigrated as it now is, when the infatuation (synthetic happiness) goes, so do the people, right out of each other's lives.

Another listener wrote me about her experience with infatuation, and what she plans someday to teach her daughter:

"Our mass media is successful in portraying marriage as a 'mindless' institution, something to be entered into only if certain clichés are met (i.e., being weak in the knees, having butterflies in the stomach, and being obsessive about the other person).

"When I married my husband (now of six years) I felt none of those things. I was not nervous about our impending nuptials, felt no butterflies or any kind of obsession— Instead, I was thankful for the blessing of God and the opportunity to enter into a covenant with a man whom I knew would be my life partner.

"My feelings for my then fiancé were more than simple 'love' stuff. I knew he would be an active husband and father, that he would provide for his family and guarantee its security. I respected his mind, admired his achievements, and understood his motivations.

"When the day comes for my daughter to marry the man she believes she loves, I will simply tell her this: Marriage is the beginning of her love for her husband, not the result of it."

When I talk to men and women in sick and abusive situations, I ask them why they're there. Inevitably, I get back the answer, "Because I love him/her." I challenge that predictable excuse with, "No, you don't. Love is about awe, admiration, respect and appreciation. Do you have any of those for him/her?"

"No."

"Then, it isn't love. It's a sad kind of dependency and a

fear of life and autonomy. You are misusing the term *love* to describe unhealthy attachments and needs."

"Yeah," comes the next predictable response, "I know . . . but . . ."

If you're looking for true happiness with another person, you first need to be reasonably mature, psychologically sound, and able to deal with truth and reality. This understanding is the impetus for me to suggest to all clergy that no marriage should be officiated by them unless the couple undergoes premarital assessment and counseling. The fate of too many children, much less the growing instability of our society from the divorces, is at stake.

With premarital counseling, people must face their differences to determine their compatibility and ability to cope with differences; they will push through the infatuation stage and become more pragmatic about the qualities that truly are valuable in a prospective life partner and coparent of children. If I had the proverbial penny for everyone who has called me complaining about his or her spouse and who knew about some character and behavioral problem in advance, but who said, "Yeah, but I thought it would get better," I'd be a zillionaire. Practicing happiness also means taking responsibility for choices you know are not wise or healthy.

I'm Happy If You Like Me

Women, more than men, (probably because of inherent biopsychological differences), pin their happiness on being wanted by the opposite sex. In itself, that is not a problem—it is a healthy extension of the need for humans to bond and mate. What does become a problem is the indiscriminate way in which too many women play this out, and the superficial association too often made between sexual intercourse and true intimacy or love.

"I am a forty-eight-year-old divorced (six years) mother of one thirteen-year-old daughter," wrote one listener. *"The first thing I thought I had to do to find happiness after the divorce was to 'FIND ANOTHER MAN.' It's funny how women search for something so seemingly elusive as Happiness, most for a large portion of their lives, and it is usually right there under their noses. When my mother became terminally ill, she gave me new insight as to what my real purpose on this earth was; that in order to find happiness, I had to see how wonderful my life, my health, a happy, healthy child, being able to work, and so forth, really was. Suddenly, I realized that I was not going to be happy with any man, or anything, until I developed an appreciation for these wonderful opportunities and experiences of life."*

It's not that a husband or a wife can't make you happy—of course the addition of a kind, fun, loving, challenging, interesting, loyal partner, with whom you share values, ideals, and goals in common, is very happy-making. It's just that nothing, no one, no thing, will ultimately make you happy unless you learn the fine art of appreciation and gratitude for what you have, for what he or she has to offer, for the opportunities for giving, and for life itself.

This last concept, that of an "opportunity for giving," is an important one—maybe one of the most important concepts about happiness in life, much less in relationships. I have a charitable foundation—The Dr. Laura Schlessinger Foundation for Abused and Neglected Children. People from all over the country make blankets and clothing, donate toys, books, toiletries, jewelry, water bottles, and so forth, to fill "MY STUFF" bags which are delivered by the thousands to children rescued from their abusive homes, who have nothing but the shirts on their backs. Obviously, getting one of these bags means the world to a child with nothing, including hope.

I can't express to you how incredibly moving it is to get a letter from people who sacrifice much in time, money, and effort to contribute to this project, who THANK ME for the opportunity to give.

Giving makes us happy. Too bad we mostly think of getting things the way we want them as the primary key to happiness. Giving and behaving generously to a spouse under stress, for example, is a far better remedial concept than confrontation and demands.

I remember one man calling to tell me he was no longer happy in his marriage, because his wife always came home from work grumpy. He was thinking of a confrontation and/or a divorce. I suggested that he get a dimmer for the bathroom lights, fill the room with lovely candles, make sure there was a hot bath with bubbles and a glass of wine awaiting his wife at the door the very next evening. He thought I was nuts, but did it anyway. She was shocked, surprised, and a bit uncomfortable, but after the bath, very grateful. This small act of giving put his wife in a whole other mood and mind-set—and they were happy again. Giving. Try it.

Instead, too many, especially young people struggling with issues of identity and existential angst, get caught up in sexual and drug escapades, trying desperately to feel happy. One listener has been to that hell, and has lived to come back from it:

"I thought happiness depended on some guy loving me or thinking I was special . . . I didn't realize that happiness just happens when you follow God's plan for you. I am so fortunate and blessed to know, understand, and live happiness now. I am sorry I didn't listen to my parents as a teenager—I would have saved myself years of self-hatred, agony, and loneliness—not to mention the health risks.

"My pattern began as wanting and needing love and feeling special, and thinking that giving a guy my body would make him

love me—and then I'd be happy. I would plunge heart-first into new relationships, placing everything I had (heart, soul, mind, and body) into that guy. I would talk myself into caring for him so completely, when in reality, I didn't really care for him in particular. I was just so lonely and confused."

What is so sad is that in this hyper-liberal era, dripping with sexual exploitation in even prime-time television, the notions of modesty, covenants, sin, and shame have largely been obliterated, making meaningless sexual and romantic escapades all the more accessible as a false means to an end: happiness.

There is hardly a person alive who hasn't struggled with fears, weaknesses, spirituality, immature choices, stupid experimentation, and the like. Frankly, the more structure there is in our lives, imposed by family, religion, and society, the safer we ultimately are from our weaker selves during these difficult times.

Out of Weakness

Many of you have gotten into, and stayed in, relationships that you knew from day one were wrong. A feeling within you told you that this man or woman, though he or she had some good qualities, was someone you'd be better off without.

Why did you stay? Simple. You wanted to be happy. And this situation and person were available. You hoped it would work out, because if it did, you'd be happy. And, in between the ugly parts, you think you are happy.

I have found it astonishing how hard people will work with the wrong person in order to be happy—when they are so willing to throw out the right person when times are difficult. Why does the former individual struggle when he or she shouldn't, and the latter person not work at it when they should?

The answer, I think, is a paradox. In both cases, you say you want intimacy and happiness. But, in both cases you are avoiding real intimacy. In the first scenario, trying to make a round peg fit into a square opening ultimately doesn't work. Trying to make a bad choice work doesn't work. No happiness results, of course, but there is no real threat to one's ego either. In other words, the reason you're not "close" is the other person. You are now absolved and alleviated from the responsibility of personal responsibility and growth. Struggling to make things work with someone not psychologically available for intimacy is a noble struggle, giving you superiority and an external excuse for your problems.

In the second scenario, dumping the good spouse for "happiness," instead of working as hard as in the former situation, is yet another way of preserving ego: You are not happy because of your spouse. If you stayed and worked harder, you'd have to face the fact that you are contributing to your own unhappiness and problems, with either/or behavior/attitude. That's too uncomfortable, so, bye-bye.

In neither situation do you have to change (read: grow, mature, become healthier). That you are ultimately unhappy is your sacrifice to preserve your rickety sense of self.

"Out of loneliness," writes a listener, *"I settled for over a year, until my mother opened my eyes. She told me how it was not so bad to be without a boyfriend. So, I broke it off. And, as a good preacher once said, 'Don't try to look for the right one, BE the right one.' And that is what I'm doing now."*

That's right. I've told many a caller that the match they make for themselves is a reflection of themselves. In other words, the more you complain about your spouse, the more you telegraph your own weaknesses. For example, when you're not happy because the other is "controlling" (a favorite of women who want to be saved, and of men who don't have the strength to deal with their own dominating families), it's because you were willing to give up happiness (a healthy balance of teamwork in the marriage) to hide your weaknesses.

" 'Stupid happiness' is taking care of my boyfriend—I guess way beyond what you should have to do. I am a person who believes in taking care of a person. I put my all into my relationships, including my kids as well as the man in my life—because as long as he was happy, I was happy. Finally I realized I was not happy. I've learned my lesson: If he can't take care of himself, he won't take care of me," wrote a listener.

Instead of finding a nice, caretaking kinda guy, she believes for some reason that she cosmically doesn't qualify for such a good guy, and caretakes a selfish kinda guy, in the hopes that he'll get the message. But, takers are not givers or sharers. This listener obviously figured out that this seduction didn't work to change a person, or get her what we all need to be happy—someone who is loving, caring, and giving.

Some people tolerate the most horrendous behaviors, believing that happiness is ultimately out of their reach. "I was married to a man for seven years who had an obsession with pornography. I do not know how far it went, because he was a pathological liar. Even though the intimacy was gone, and in my heart I knew he was doing something deviant, I thought it must be my fault. Somehow, I was not attractive or thin or sexy enough . . . I let him have control of my self-esteem."

Other people settle for—as I described to one woman I was counseling about her bad relationship choice—the bits of cookies hidden in the pile of manure.

"He was possessive and overbearing. He'd make me feel sorry for him. As time went on, I discovered that he drank excessively, and at times he would threaten me and become violent. I kind of began to get a little frightened of him, but of course, he was always sorry afterward, blaming the alcohol. So I let it go. I know this is stupid, because I am really unhappy. Why do I stay?"

Some people have more clarity about what motivates them toward Stupid Happiness.

"I was divorced twice and feeling 'fat, old, and ugly.' So, I thought if I dated a lot of men, and then younger men, it would make me feel better about myself. I thought having so many men who 'wanted' me was an indication of my desirability. I even thought I was having a good time. I thought I was happy with my life. I thought I was getting over my failures.

"All I was really doing was degrading and disrespecting myself. I wasn't really happy. I thought I 'felt' good, but I was miserable because I was not 'being' good."

Abusing yourself, disrespecting yourself, allowing others to abuse and disrespect you, not living by deeper values, may make for some fun moments, even some satisfying moments, but you will not be happy in any more profound, long-lasting sense.

Living for the Moment

Looking for happiness in all the wrong beds and relationships is bad enough; trying to have a happy life by not thinking of your actions beyond the moment in which they happen is downright destructive.

Stupid Happiness is, in part, the talent for trying to create instant joy from the acts that normally do create lasting joy in most people's lives (love, sex, marriage, and children), but without the maturity and thoughtful consideration that needs to go into the who, when, why, where, and how these acts ought to occur.

What motivates such thoughtless precipitousness? Again, our weakness and fears. Our relationships have no hope when they're constructed of weaknesses. Believe it or not, our culture breeds a special kind of weakness that undermines our hopes for quality relationships. How? By its hopelessness about serious, covenantal marriages. Here's one listener's experience:

"When I look back on my life, I see that I was living for the moment and not concerned about the future. I also believe that I was not able to value a marriage relationship, let alone a marriage bed. Our culture no longer teaches us to have that respect.

"Both of my parents are on their third marriages, and both lived with their current partner before marriage."

Fortunately, this listener, after following a few steps in her parents' footsteps, and with the complicit wink and nod of a society that has become proud of tolerance for the vulgar, realized that this was Stupid Happiness. She married a wonderful man, with whom she shares a religious life, and will be celebrating their twelfth anniversary.

"My Husband and I LEARNED to have respect for marriage," she concluded. Such lessons are hard-won in a society which celebrates hyperindividuality and promotes marriage as a kind of oppression.

That our society is so indulgent with respect to sexual behaviors in general has actually made it more difficult for people to rise above Stupid Happiness, because it virtually gives permission, and lots of opportunity, for the basest instincts and impulses to be exercised.

"I thought this lifestyle (stripping) was a good way for me to make a lot of money with a schedule that worked around school. I got paid to party and, at first, most of the drugs were free. I didn't use drugs that much in the beginning—but in time I developed a habit that went right along with my job and eventually it became a part of my daily life.

"I managed to sort of keep things straight for a couple of years, but gradually my life slipped into a downward spiral of drugs, drinking, promiscuous sex, and associating with all kinds of

degenerate, lost people. Once you are in it, it is almost impossible to get out, short of an act of God. The money is too good, and your habits are such that it becomes nearly impossible to fit back into the mainstream world. At first it seems fun, harmless, and almost glamorous."

This party scene may sound extreme, but I have been amazed how, to some extent or other, so many people fall into this ultimately vicious "fun cycle," marry, make babies, and then realize they are not with someone who is taking life seriously. This is because too many people mix up "fun" and "happiness" as though they were the same or that fun made one happy. That which makes us truly happy does not involve immorality or illegality, nor does it put us in places and with people for which we will eventually have shame. The activities contributing to happiness are those we'd want to pass on to our children, and point the way for our friends. Fun can, but doesn't always, fall into that definition.

Rushing to Fix Disappointments

Sometimes people eject out of perfectly good relationships because they want an instant fix to some serious pain. One of the saddest and most typical times for people to lose each other is when they've lost a child. One listener wrote me that they lost a child at birth due to complications, and found out that they were medically incompatible and would never have biological children.

"Instead of considering the alternatives they have out there like adoption, I decided to throw away our marriage. Then I met another man six months later and I have the most perfect little boy in the world, but I am still not happy because I want to share this joy with the man I love (my ex)."

Another listener started an affair when she felt her husband was ignoring her. She admitted not doing much to confront him.

"[I] lived in a huge world of denial, a corporate wife, big house, new cars, gifts of guilt, all the while living with this very mean and ugly man. I eventually started looking for someone to be nice to me. I had an affair for about one and a half years—and realized that I was no more a love for him than a good lay. My life was such a mess that I was just grasping for straws. I guess my point is that when you are hurting so terribly from one catastrophe, it is not wise to jump right on into another to make the first better. The happiness that you may get from that is only momentary."

Another listener, feeling unhappy in his marriage, in retrospect realizes he was stupid and selfish. He had an affair with a married woman, whose husband beat him up severely for it.

"A broken nose, cheekbone, and a concussion didn't wake me up. I still saw her until after her divorce. I still 'wasn't happy' and saw other women at the same time, drinking and partying and ignoring my kids.

"To make a long story short, the consequences of my search for happiness is: two STDs (one incurable but not deadly), my kids are in a single-parent family, my oldest son became a father at fifteen because of my influence, my oldest daughter had drug problems, and my youngest son had a run-in with the police.

"Because of your show, I started going to church and was bornagain. I now have custody of my kids, and I have not been involved with anybody for three years, because I don't have time—my kids need me."

In his "giving" to his kids, he's now happy; trying to get happy through sex didn't work. Big surprise?

Sex = Pleasure
Love = Happiness

Why is it that I now get calls from men and women asking me if they're too weird because they're still virgins? They tell me that people make fun of them and dates tell them that they won't be interested in them for long, and nor will anyone else, if they don't have sex as part of the dating exercise. They worry and wonder if they're missing out on something, or making too big a deal over something that is so "natural."

One listener wrote that at nineteen, she gave up her virginity, because she thought it was time. It was a one-night stand—like the one her mother had that produced her. She wrote that it would have been nice to hold her husband on their wedding night some seven years ago, and know that he was the first.

"Sex is NOT love, no matter what the other person tells you. 'If you loved me,' you would . . . puhleeze! If YOU loved ME, you would . . . wait. It feels great to be loved, but it feels worse to be used and tossed aside like a used tissue . . ."

We too often put aside our morals and good sense, because we think that the sexy, fun-at-the-moment (pleasure) will equate to happiness. It might, but it's a risky way to go about it.

One young man wrote to me of his experience with sex as a teenager. He describes beginning a relationship with mutual interests. Then, slowly, it became less about caring, loving, and nurturing, and more about getting those few minutes alone to do sexual things.

"In time, I forgot why I had cared about her in the first place. I lost interest in protecting her, and only wanted what was pleasing to me.

"I was blinded by what I thought I wanted. There are two things I want to say about the situation of teen dating. First is that it is dangerous to pursue any physicality at all without the commitment of marriage. It feels good while you do it, but it can and often will hurt far more than the pleasure it gives. Second is that I hope teenagers would consider putting off dating until they

are older. When we date while we are in a position where we couldn't possibly marry that person, our relationship is shallow and meaningless. Plus, there will be the inevitable pain with the dissolving of the relationship."

I have included this letter, albeit about minors, because the mentality is sound for all ages. Sexualizing a relationship before its time (marriage) and being intimate without an ultimate point (marriage) does not bring happiness—although the temporary pleasure is seductive.

One man called me about whether he should give his "girlfriend" a second chance. It seems that recently, during one of their "problem periods," she had sexual relations with about five men. She's told him she's sorry. He tells me she's repentant.

"You can forgive her, then dump her."

"Why dump her? If she's repented, isn't that enough?"

"That's enough for saying, 'I forgive you,' for whatever that's worth. But when someone evidences behaviors that demonstrate such impulsiveness, superficiality, immorality, and poor judgment, she ought to be considered high-risk for failure as a wife and a mother. What she has told you in advance, in my opinion, is that when the going gets rough, she gets undressed in some other guy's bed. If you want to play, she's your woman. If you want a wife and mother for your children and a stable life, she's not your woman."

The caller couldn't easily get past the notion that he "loved her" (fantasies and unfulfilled hopes) and that their sex was wonderful (and that's an omen, isn't it?) It also made him "happy" to be so forgiving. The reality is, that when someone's sexuality is so tied into pleasure and self-medicating, they become a liability in the commitment department. Choosing not to read the handwriting on the wall, or failing to heed its message to keep the "dream" possible, is Stupid Happiness.

Happiness on the Sly

"Anything that's a secret—can't be good," were wise words from a very dumb movie I watched recently. That philosophy goes for happiness as well as illegalities. One of the most disgusting new advances in Stupid Happiness, brought to us by the miracle of the Internet, is cyber-affairs. It used to be that fantasies were about singers, movie stars, or some real people at work. Now you can destroy the lives of your whole family on a fantasy.

As one such listener wrote: *"I put the fantasy of a fairy-tale on-line 'perfect' relationship before the commitment of my marriage of over ten years to my husband and my beautiful family. I allowed myself to have an emotionally intimate relationship with someone through my modem, and it, of course, had a shattering effect on my feelings toward my husband. It was stupid of me to believe that sharing my innermost feelings with someone other than my husband wouldn't mess up what I have with him. Thankfully, I saw the huge mistake I was making and I willed to correct it. I adore my family and nothing is more important than the time and energy I direct toward them. I have found that the fairy-tale has been right here, in my reality all along."*

The Stupid Happiness part of this sort of behavior is obvious: Nothing and no one is perfect—and if he or she was, we each know better than to think we're a match! Thinking that happiness is only available and effective when everything is wonderful is to condemn oneself to unhappiness. How does one reconcile wanting our spouse to be a little different, for things to be a little better, for us simply to feel perkier and pleased more often? Frankly, for the best of us it's always a struggle.

And here is where practice comes in. You need to make strenuous efforts to attain joy. Celebrating what is merely mundane is to reframe life in a more positive way. Even putting nicer place settings on your table for a meal—if only for yourself—is uplifting. I listen to oldies, classic rock, on the way to work and sing along (albeit badly) with the lyrics from a more innocent time. I admit that nostalgia is a bit of a whitewash, but so what if it jump-starts our joyfulness at living. Living, with all its pains and challenges, *is* the ultimate in hope, because it brings opportunity.

If you don't use the opportunities of life wisely, you may very well find yourself using the secret shortcuts unwisely.

"I have been involved with a married man for seven years. I know he will never leave his wife. I am overweight and feel that no one other than this substantially older-than-me married man will have anything to do with me. I feel like a hypocrite at church when I say that I am happy to be single, when the reality is that I am having an affair. The affair makes me feel good in the moment, but when I am at church, I am riddled with guilt."

She's not any more fit, she's not any more healthy, she's not any more married. In fact, she's deeper in the hole than ever before. Once it was just that she was "fat" (which is a sorrowful enough excuse to damage or destroy some other woman's marriage and family), now she's still fat but she's also in an immoral relationship. That gives her a lot less to use to appeal to a nice guy; lotsa fat, little character.

Voyages on the starship Stupid Happiness generally lead nowhere, because they are ultimately self-centered; true joy comes from sharing.

Money Can't Buy Me Love

The thing that's attractive about money and what it can buy is that it's under your control, it's immediate, there's definite gratification, and you don't have to hassle with anybody over it. It's easy to feel good about yourself when you have buying power. Buying and possessing a thing is a lot easier than the effort that goes into making a good relationship work. There is a tremendous amount of positive feedback for having lots and lots of things. After all, there is a program showing you the lives of the Rich and Famous—is there a program showing you the lives of the Happily Married and Spiritual?

"When my husband and I first met, I used to do volunteer work in our community as many hours as I worked at my full-time, paying job. I started making more money and working more hours.

"I became consumed in my newfound HAPPINESS of material things. That was four years ago. Since that time, there has always been a piece of me missing, not completely happy. My problem was that when I gave my time and myself to helping others, I felt fulfilled. I realized that I was not here on earth solely to acquire things. By working to make each day better for others, I have learned my greatest lesson: True happiness is KNOWING the only thing I need is to give back to someone else."

This is also the main lesson of good marriages. These days, I hear more about what someone's husband or wife is not giving them, and nothing about what they aren't giving to their spouse. Oh, it's easy to say that you would be giving if only they would be/do such and such. The reality is, waiting around for happiness to be created for you in the fantasy of the perfect spouse (who, after all, has moods, stomachaches, worries, bad days, and so forth) is to stick a knife into the heart of your relationship.

Problems

All G-d's children have problems. Big problems or many problems certainly cut into our sense of feeling happy. Even then, sharing burdens with our spouse, rather than taking out our unhappiness on him or her, is, of itself, a kind of happiness. Perhaps the perspective we most need in times of strife is, as one listener wrote, to realize that even this seeming major catastrophe is *"a small bump on the road to eternity."*

In conclusion, neither you nor your relationship is or will be perfect. That should not stop you from doing the caring, thoughtful, brave, and compassionate things you need to, to bring pleasure into the lives of your family. And that should not stop you from enjoying the value of what you are privileged and blessed to have—if you would only see it that way.

If you're not happy, try behaving as though you were—see how that lightens life up for you and your family, and how that feeds back, lighting up the world.

7

Stupid Excuses

"I hear the word 'but' a hundred times a day!
An excuse always follows the word 'but.'
I think if we add an extra 't,' it would describe
most of us!"

—A LISTENER

"I asked my now nine-year-old son when he was two why he drew on the wall. His response was, 'I did it because I liked the color it made on the wall.' There you go—that simple!" writes a listener in response to my website (www.drlaura.com) query about Stupid Excuses.

It would seem that the truth ought to be that simple for people. After all, aren't we a country that brings its children up on the story of George Washington and the cherry tree? Don't our children learn about honor, integrity, honesty, and responsibility from stories of such heroes?

Actually, no, not any more. Now we bring our children up on politically correct revisionist history lessons (where there were no real historic heroes—just victims) and the nightly news from which they can know that a President is a proven liar, perjurer, philanderer, and was shamefully influenced by friends and family in granting Presidential pardons.

The so-called Village perpetuates the notion that there are darn good reasons for being dishonest, and that these excuses exonerate the wrongdoer. Scandals over what is considered a disability, requiring special treatment at work and remuneration from the government, reveal a degenerating system in which even laziness can be demonstrated not to be a personal responsibility. Even commercials on mainstream radio and television for a DUI attorney service chant, "Friends don't let friends plead guilty." (Remember when the chant used to be, "Friends don't let friends drive drunk"?)

It is no surprise that innumerable surveys demonstrate that young adults not only have become ferociously less honest, but have what they think are reasonable explanations for their lack of integrity and a lack of shame for their lack of integrity. These excuses cover the ideas most parents of our grandparents' generation would have given us a spanking for uttering: "Everyone is doing it," "You're at a disadvantage if you're honest because the cheaters get a leg up," "It really doesn't matter how you get to college because college is your ultimate ticket in life," "I have too much pressure," "I'm too busy to do the work," and so forth.

Of course, these attitudes seep into the personal arena. Again, recent polls indicate a growing acceptance of affairs, shack-ups, children out-of-wedlock, promiscuity, divorce, day care (modern child abandonment), and destroying relationships between the noncustodial parent and child because of a desire for a new sex partner or address.

These days, notions of honor, integrity, responsibility, and obligations are considered oppressive and retro. Excuses abound to alleviate each of us from our responsibilities to others. There have always been excuses. That so many of

these excuses are being considered understandable and ultimately acceptable is new.

The reality is that without honor, integrity, responsibility,
and obligations we are each so unrestricted that we're each ultimately alone, adrift, afraid, isolated, cynical, depressed, and
grasping because there doesn't seem to be anyone or anything
to trust. I know this is true, because I get the letters, calls, faxes,
and e-mails telling me so from all over North America.

A lot of folks tell me that they learned the bad lessons of
Stupid Excuses at their parent's knee.

It's Genetic?

No, of course it's not genetic. Being an apple off the wrong
tree can be a problem, as one listener revealed:

*"It would be easiest to state that as a child I was damaged by
my mother's constant verbal abuse and derision . . . that I am
unable to help my behavior. This is not true! What is true is that
my mother did respond to all stresses by screaming, yelling,
throwing things, and threats. This is what I grew up knowing."*

And that became her excuse for blowing up—that it was
just her nature.

*"At the same time, I know that constant rage, angst, and anger
are unproductive and self-detrimental. I have had to learn that I
am capable of that behavior the hard way: There is nothing worse
than seeing the tears in your children's eyes when your anger
explodes and watching your husband stand bewildered that one
minute I can be fine and the next in a fit.*

"But, I had to accept that ultimately there is no excuse."

It is that last bit of honesty which paves the way for
growth. Callers often ask me how they can possibly break
such habits or behaviors, and break the habit of excusing
away such bad behaviors. My answer is that it happens in

the reverse order. First, you stop excusing it and begin apologizing for it. Taking responsibility should have as its core remorse for the hurt you've caused. Without that remorse, the "sorry" becomes its own repetitive excuse as the behavior continues. Actions then need to be taken to repair damage—where possible. Then comes the plan to make sure you don't repeat the bad behaviors.

One of the best techniques for this last phase is to anticipate situations and feelings somewhat in advance of the usual ignition point. For example, when you start feeling frustrated, pinned down, against a wall, angry, confused, or some other triggering emotion, either say out loud, "You know, I need to take a break for a minute—I'm starting to feel out of control/nuts . . ." or just excuse yourself and leave the room to calm down or refocus or reconsider. Or ask someone for help (counselor, minister, your mother!, Dr. Laura), or develop an "instead-of behavior" that you put in the place of the behavior you're trying to stop.

Whichever technique you employ, it admittedly isn't easy, as this listener's letter reports:

"There are so many times that I want to start yelling and yelling and yelling. However, I did enough damage the times that I succumbed to the feeling. I am trying hard to make sure that I control my temper. I try to use humor whenever possible . . . then I feel lighter because I know I am able to control myself . . . and ultimately not behave like my mother."

Making Excuses Is Very Human . . .

Human beings, like all mammals, are gregarious creatures and spend a tremendous percentage of their lives being dependent upon parental caretaking. This natural dependency upon family and community leads to "how to get along" behaviors. In other primates we see hierarchies set up and grooming behaviors and mock fighting, all geared to help the individuals in the group "get along" for the cohesiveness required to ensure daily functioning and survival.

Although human beings are not as instinctively programmed as lower animals, we do have typical behaviors that serve some of the same functions—a significant one is avoid doing anything to look bad and risk rejection and punishment. If you do bad, finding a way to hide or deflect that truth is the backup position to avoid disdain and consequences; whence come such behaviors as lying, blaming, deflecting, and attacking back (best defense is a good offense), strategies to preserve the image or power.

This behavior is very typical for kids who worry that their misdeeds will lead their parents not to love them anymore and who, understandably, want to avoid punishment. This habit of making up excuses gets severe in situations where parents have been hyperperfectionists or overly punitive.

Of course, the families who teach honor above all, and that integrity is essential to intimacy, attachment, and affection, help their children grow up into adults who will admit to shortcomings, mistakes, bad judgment, and bad deeds. Ultimately, those are the behaviors that lead us to admire and trust another.

. . . And "Owning Up" Is the Most Honorably Human

Maturity is partially defined by the willingness to be held accountable, without excuse, for your actions. Immaturity is partially defined by the unwillingness to do the same. As one listener admitted: *"I guess you could say I have tried for way too long to hold on to my teenage attitude—and I'm thirty. I was a really bad teenager and I always had an excuse for everything I had done. You wouldn't catch me taking blame for anything. Even it you watched me do it and I saw you watch me, I could still come up with a million reasons why I didn't do or why I did it because someone else made me.*

"I have taken this attitude to my marriage and it has caused major trust problems. I have been married for ten years and I want everyone to realize that it is hard when your mate looks at you wondering if you are telling the whole truth or making excuses."

The reasons for holding on to behaviors which so obviously are destructive are many; however, prime among them is the backward notion that if you're seen as wrong or bad then you won't be loved. The irony is that the excuses make others lose trust and respect, which in turn cuts into your being loved. In other words, you end up creating the very circumstance you're trying to avoid. However, it's hard to give up old patterns when you're under stress because you'd rather not take the risk. You'd better, if you don't want to mess up your relationships.

Some folks never learn and some folks don't care to learn because they wish more to protect their image with themselves and their power over others. So, the excuses never stop.

"The World Owes Me"

Anger and hurt often motivate self-protective maneuvers as well as vendettas. Sometimes these actions are aimed at those who hurt us, while more often such actions are aimed and fired with a shotgun approach. This listener admits to such an attitude:

"During my nine-year marriage, I became the queen of excuses. I'm the ongoing, reigning victim of the world. I had a difficult childhood, the result of a one-night stand, a mother married seven times, and

physical, sexual and emotional abuse by her as well as a number of her husbands.

"All that said, I decided in my mind that this world owed me something. I was always quick to announce my war wounds. But never, ever was I willing to address them. I received far more attention by whining about it. I was married to a wonderful man who did everything possible to assist me in addressing these issues and seeking professional help. But, I rejected all efforts. Instead, I used these things to excuse all my immature, selfish, and immoral behaviors, which I would blame on my past, my rough life, my pathetic childhood, and my absolute inability to trust anyone. Eventually, the poor man gave up.

"I continued my self-destructive and selfish behavior for ten more years. Had to hit bottom, and I did. It has been an amazing and scary and painful journey. But I have to learn who I am—and that is some-one who has responsibility in life, and not a constant victim."

As this listener revealed, the main reason people don't eas-ily change behaviors is that they are scared. They are scared of the truth, their weaknesses, other people's power over them, the unknown, change, vulnerability, and losing con-trol. Sadly, these fears often override the good sense to move forward into responsibility; consequently, good relationships are damaged and lost.

And other people are just brats, narcissists, sociopaths, or downright evil. That's material for another book.

Oh, Puhlease!

It would be impossible for me to categorize all the types and styles and subjects and techniques of excuse-making which compromise the integrity of relationships. Under the title of "Oh, Puhlease," here are a cross-section of the most typical, some laughable, all irritating, many obnoxious excuses people have given to my listeners and callers and, probably, to you!

➤ In response to being queried by his wife, who has been ten years sober, about why he's been slugging down vodka in the closet for two years when they were both supposed to be clean and sober, the husband said, "Because I didn't want to be an influence for you to start drinking again." How noble! This excuse explains the closet, but not the vodka—nice dodge.

➤ When his wife asked him why he sneaked a female friend on a day trip for boating and camping with the children instead of bringing her along, he answered, "Because there wasn't room in the truck for you and she was splitting for gas money and entrance fees for the lake and was providing lunch." I see, affairs are now merely money and room-saving efforts?

➤ "My husband's excuse when I asked him why he couldn't just jump in the shower each morning instead of rinsing his head in the sink and getting dressed is, 'I've just got a lot of stuff going on right now!'" I guess soap and water are not among the "stuff going on" right now or ever.

➤ When this woman's husband of twenty-three years decided to have an affair and leave her for another woman, his excuse to her was, "This happens all the time and it's all your fault and it's because of the kids." I guess this woman and her kids were also responsible for his infidelities with his girlfriend too?

➤ To explain his not paying child support ($195 per month) and not seeing his son (except for the rare times when he does father-son things with his buddies—and a kid is required), this listener's ex-husband says that "I work twenty-four hours a day, seven days a week, and my boss won't give me any time off. And, I don't have enough money." Wow, I thought slave labor had been abolished!

➤   One woman listener has been shacking-up with a guy for fifteen years and has a twelve-year-old child with him. She keeps wondering when he'll marry her. He says, "When we have $5,000 in savings." Whew, I'll bet he budgets carefully—spending just enough to be under $5,000 in savings.

➤   One married woman is frustrated that her husband lies to get out of work—when he works at all—to get more money, to get out of doing something displeasing, and to get what he wants at the moment. They are seriously in debt, and when they almost got evicted from their home, she asked him why he bought the four-by-four pickup and toy RC cars and other unnecessary stuff. He countered with, "I deserve these things because I work hard for it." I guess he considers spending his life's work.

➤   One twenty-seven-year-old woman has been for one year dating and sexually intimate with a thirty-seven-year-old man, who has been divorced for six years, and who has two children, sixteen and eighteen. He tells her they will marry but he won't tell his children or anyone in his family that he's even dating much less planning to marry her. When asked why, he says that, "The divorce was such a shock, I just don't want to shock anybody more." Huh?

➤   Another woman wonders why after twenty-one years of marriage, her husband doesn't "get it." Evidently, what he doesn't get is that he shouldn't lie and hide important things from her, like giving loans to folks he hardly knows for business arrangements over which he has little control, and like going out of town for job training with a woman "colleague." His answer to why he doesn't tell her things in advance is, "You'll be mad." Duh, really?

➤   This woman's husband has been a truck driver for only four years. Evidently, he often acts like a jerk and when she calls him on it, his excuse for rude, obnoxious, or frustrating behavior is, "I'm a truck driver. We have an image to protect. We are supposed to be rude and obnoxious." Where is the Truckers Anti-Defamation League when you need them?

While these excuses may sound amusing, and some might sound awfully familiar, they are all too typical examples of the lengths people will go to ignore their responsibilities and obligations, to justify selfishness and insensitivity, to deny weaknesses and serious problems, to justify hurting the ones they're supposed to love, and to not grow, mature, and do what they need to do to preserve and protect their relationships.

Sadly, one of the most familiar uses of excuses is in the arena of one's own denial of fear, weakness, and laziness in taking steps to face the truths of a problem relationship—without doing so, no relationship can flourish or even survive.

I Know It Walks, Talks, Smells, Acts, and Looks Like a Duck—But, Maybe It's Not a Duck . . . ?

A prime example of this behavior was evidenced by a call I recently took from a forty-one-year-old woman, dating a thirty-seven-year-old man for less than a year. She'd been divorced for twenty years and has a twenty-one-year-old daughter. The conversation was long, and frankly entertaining, for although she was in serious denial about the realities of her situation, at least she had a sense of humor.

"Has he ever been married or engaged or does he have any out-of-wedlock kidlets?"

"No."

"Really? No? At thirty-seven?"

"No."

"You are engaged to him after dating him for how long?"

"Ten months."

"What's the problem?"

"Well, he's given me an ultimatum."

"Really . . . which is what?"

"Either complete the fourth step at Al-Anon or he cancels our engagement."

"Why are you in Al-Anon?"

"Because he is a recovering alcoholic."

"How long has he been clean and sober—assuming you know the truth? Users generally lie about such things."

"Ten months."

"What? You're engaged to marry a guy who's been a drunk for a long time, supposedly sober for the months you've known him? My understanding of AA is that they prescribe no serious relationships while they're struggling with sobriety and then the underlying issues. Not drinking, my dear, is only part of the picture. Why, after waiting two decades to pick a man, do you pick a drunk?"

"Well, doesn't everybody deserve a second chance?"

"For what? For friendship? For employment? For club membership? Why would you think of taking a relatively unproven second-chancer into your bed?"

"Well, I'm not perfect either."

"Since nobody is perfect that means that nobody is entitled to a healthy partner?"

"Well, no."

"All you're telling me is that you believe this is the one chance you imagine that you have at forty-one—he's younger? sexy? good in bed?"

"Oh, I'm not going to talk about that (giggles tell it all)."

"Well, my dear, if you really thought this was a good idea, you'd be doing Step 4 of Al-Anon, and you wouldn't be on the phone with me. Something told you this probably wasn't a smart idea. Tell you what, let's compromise. If, in five years, he is consistently clean and sober and has dealt diligently with his psychological problems underlying the drinking, his life, and his personality—I'll dance at your wedding."

The demise of many relationships is often in the denial that brings these people together in the first place. You imagine, hope, pray, ignore, believe that wanting someone will make him or her be more or different from what they are. Think about this though: Since you are not bothering to deal with reality, why should they be stronger or more motivated than you?

I was particularly moved by a listener's letter concerning her termination of denial (albeit twenty-six years into a long and ugly story). Her husband was in and out with lovers. Although the pain was excruciating, she believes that she learned her greatest lesson—from a child:

"I do not want to play the martyr anymore. One evening, after I dramatically told my husband to leave if he wanted his lover, the scene was dramatically played out, and the pain was so unbearable, so intense, that I went into a blank daze. My adolescent daughter walked over by me, crossed her arms, looked down at me, and asked, 'Mom, why do you think Dad keeps coming back?' I answered, 'Because he loves us and is confused.' 'No,' she said to me. Then again she asked, 'Mom, why do you think Dad keeps coming back?' 'Well, because he loves you kids, only right now he

is feeling ashamed.' 'No,' she said, louder. Once again she asked the question. This time I was quiet for a few moments as I stared into the fireplace with great thought and reflection. Finally, I felt like a bolt of lightning hit me, and I began to cry. I looked up at her and said, 'Because I let him.' She bent down and hugged me. I then realized that my husband was not to blame for my current state—it was me. I had lost all my self-belief and I was blaming him for tormenting me and our children. In my way of thought, I had no choice because I loved him. But just the same, I did have a choice.

"Painful as it was, I filed for divorce. After four and one half years, I realize that I clung to a false hope, excusing anything to deny the truth. I was so afraid of losing him that I accepted being treated as no human being should ever have to be treated. My own fear was my great excuse. If I had perhaps not been so afraid to speak up earlier in my marriage, this situation might have turned out differently. No one likes to be verbally criticized or degraded, yet due to his threats of 'If you're going to cry and continue to nag, I'm not going to stay here . . . ,' I always shut my mouth. If I had, many years ago, stood up and replied, 'Then go, until you can calm down or speak to me with respect . . . ,' maybe, just maybe . . . he would have, or maybe not."

Her last comment points to the issue of excusing the behavior of your "loved ones" when that behavior ought to be dealt with. The excuses she made for tolerating bad behavior had her living in hell for almost three decades, concluding with her abandonment. At least her young daughter learned this important lesson: Stupid Excuses mess up your relationships because when you ignore ugly, unpleasant, unacceptable, harmful realities, those realities stay and grow bigger and uglier.

These Stupid Excuses for tolerating bad behaviors (and not mobilizing to improve the situation) include:

"No one else was banging down my door for a date, so what was left?"

"I felt indebtedness to him because he was older and had done wonderful things for me."

"I didn't want to make him angry because I wanted to be loved."

And, sadly, *"I am ashamed and unforgiving of myself for my past. Even when I try to believe more in the trust and forgiveness of God, I don't feel worthy of His grace."*

Yet, one listener wrote in that on the verge of marrying a man with whom she could not be open or comfortable, she found her courage and stopped the Stupid Excuses:

"So many times he said things, did things, and did not do things that I made excuses for. I was constantly worried that I would make him angry. Despite all of this, I planned a wedding that as the weeks passed was becoming a death shroud, not a joyful event. Finally one morning my soul woke up and started to scream. So I took a deep breath, sucked up all that fear, and called it off. I had felt betrayal, humiliation, fear, anger and despair. But it is NOT okay to live your life this way. Don't cower or turn a blind eye to faults that should never be accepted."

Excusing bad behaviors doesn't get you love, acceptance, safety, or a quality relationship—it gets you servitude under your own fears of losing what in fact you don't really have in the first place. Don't excuse bad behaviors when you're dating because you throw away what opportunity you have to improve that relationship or, if necessary, what opportunity you could have to find a better, healthier partner.

I Have a Darn Good Reason

The Past

When people call in to my radio program, it's usually to complain about what someone else is doing. If I suggest that they are somehow kidding themselves about the intelligence or ethics of their actions, or show how they are being provocative or petty, the dialogue generally gets tense. That's okay, because the hardest thing to do is to look into a mirror with 100X enlargement—nobody cares to see their pores that big! It takes a lot of courage to face that, and I applaud my callers, even when it's likely that they won't face up till sometime after the call.

One listener wrote to excuse her constant mistrust of her husband *because*—

"My first husband lied to me constantly for seven years. His lies caused great pain to me and others and even got him in serious trouble with the law. My current husband is very honest, and I know deep down I can trust him totally, but when he answers my questions my immediate thought deep down is I wonder if he is telling the truth. He has proved my fears wrong time and time again. How do you stop your immediate feelings?"

Obviously, this woman does not want a déjà vu experience—but she creates it in her mind with the excuse that she's been there and doesn't want to be there again. That's the irony—*she creates* her worst fear. So here she is, finally married to a good guy, messing up the relationship because she is stuck in reverse gear.

How do you stop your immediate feelings, she asks. You don't, is the answer. When you choose to not act on them by questioning him, checking up on him, being hostile toward him, or punishing him, all for nothing, then you automatically diminish the power of those feelings.

One of the prices of the new sexuality is that people are now dating, being sexual, shacking-up, getting hurt, leaving, and starting the cycle all over again. Unfortunately, instead of being a great liberating experience, mostly people are ending up hurt, negative, cynical, suspicious, and less trusting. This leads to more superficial intimacy (as you function to protect yourself from hurt) which leads to more hurt.

Money

While I often decry on my radio program the dearth of real men—men who sacrifice their dreams and desires to do what it takes to provide for their families—sometimes "providing for" is misused as an excuse to be neglectful of family for the sake of the money. One listener believes that his marriage is back on track and that he is truly his daughter's dad because of my radio program:

"The problem started back in August. I had just taken a new job as a manager for a restaurant. My wife stayed home after our daughter was born. At the time, money was tight, and we were living hand-to-mouth. My attitude deteriorated to the point that I was ignoring my family and working nonstop to make the extra buck and to get ahead. This went on until December when she finally told me she had had enough and put me out the door. Since that day, I have left that job and took a different one that lets me be a husband and father. Your advice saved my marriage, Dr. Laura. Thank you."

While financially supporting a family is essential, pursuing money can too easily become an end in itself, because you can buy lots of great stuff, feel powerful, gain status, and get a fat head, while starving your essential lifeline to a meaningful life: your family relationships.

Weight

Whether or not you like it or think it should be so, our appearance, including hygiene, posture, dress, weight, and fitness, matters in our relationships. It is all a sign of respect for ourselves and our obligation to the relationship.

Certainly, it is difficult to keep up with aging and gravity. Certainly, it is difficult to exercise and eat only the stuff you "oughtta." Certainly, it is difficult to carve time out of busy lives to do body maintenance. Certainly, one needs a mature outlook in balancing the physical with the spiritual and relational (so much for the cosmetic surgery junkies who take an important concept to the extreme). And certainly, one should never feel loved or not based on a bit of flab. A decent partner learns to graciously and lovingly accept the realities of aging in their spouse without comparing.

It is our individual responsibility not to take our relationship or partner for granted with lazy excuses:

"My husband recently announced that he is unable to participate in marital relations with me because of my weight. I am obviously overweight—I used to be 150 pounds and now I'm 200 . . . but I'm saying to my husband that size shouldn't matter and that dieting isn't easy; that if it were easy, weight loss wouldn't be the big business it is. He's just drawn the line and won't budge unless he sees some attempt on my part to lose weight."

I believe it is fair for him to say that he needs to see "some attempt . . . to lose weight," because it demonstrates on her part a respect for his point of view and the physical side of their relationship. It is flabber(pun intended)gasting how many people demand that their spouses be totally turned on to them and pleased no matter how much they abuse their bodies.

One other listener wrote: *"I guess that's my excuse. If he loves me, what difference does the weight make, especially since I am so totally wonderful otherwise."* It's not that the appreciation for all that you are is lost, it is that as you lose interest in pleasing your partner with your best self, so will your partner.

Feminist Propaganda

One woman caller recently spoke angrily about how her husband, who works out of town Monday through Friday, comes home on Friday night and expects her to be dressed in something sensual and to be "playful." She talked about how she is all week long with the house, the laundry, and the kids, and how dare he expect her to be his sex-kitten just because he's home. I reminded her that he's not been at a weeklong party either, and he misses his family and the loving warmth of his wife.

She was stuck in playing martyr and clearly hostile about his supposed freedom. I told her that in spite of her determination to make it be so, hers was not bigger than his—just different. I asked her two questions: One, what was wrong with his wanting her intimately when he got home? And two, what was wrong with her wanting him intimately when he came home?

My interpretation of her excuse for not being a loving, available partner was that she interpreted intimacy and sexuality as demands on her (instead of an opportunity for pleasure and bonding) and that she seemed to need to suffer in front of him as proof that she's worked hard too and that what she did was meaningful. I told her that these issues were standard feminist propaganda, that her husband was not tuned in to any of that, and that she'd better not mess up her relationship with them.

Booze

"I don't need an excuse to drink, because I don't have a problem. I enjoy drinking and I like the taste."

That comment from a caller about his problem with his wife's determination to get him to stop drinking is the most typical excuse for abusing alcohol—the outright denial that there is a problem in the first place. Of course, the pain in the eyes of spouse and children, the DUIs, the ill health, the money, time, and effort dumped into drinking, the sneaking or the grandiosity of "my right to do what I wish" are swept away with, "I don't have a problem."

Contrary to the moneymaking medical community's protestations of alcohol abuse as a disease (insurance payment for fees, lucrative programs), I still see this issue as one of character. Bad habits, even those that have a serious impact on the body and create states of compulsion, are still only influences over which you have a choice how to behave. There is not one ex-drinker I've spoken to in the span of twenty-five years of radio conversations who has said other than that a decision to stop drinking (usually with the connection to G-dliness) stopped the drinking—no other disease is cured that way—through will and grit and character.

I get very angry when spouses call feeling guilty for wanting to get out of bad relationships with folks with such seriously bad habits, the abuse of drugs and alcohol, pornography, and promiscuity, because the medical/psychological community calls them diseases (addictions) and not character failings (not nice to judge). This nonsense has trapped many a decent person in a situation of inappropriate obligation, imagining he or she is not being sensitive in making a judgment to leave. That's cruel, unfair, and wrong.

Pornography

"I didn't think this was a problem for you. We haven't had a lot of intimacy lately, so I'm just looking at pictures to remind me of what I am missing, that it is still there and someday I'll have it again. I am not contributing to the porn industry financially or the exploitation of these women, because I am not paying for the paid sites of magazines—it's all free. And, it's human nature for men to want to see naked women, it's socially acceptable. Besides,

why is it that you don't see it as just something to 'pass the time' or 'have as a hobby'?"

These were the remarks of one husband to excuse his preoccupation with pornography on the Internet.

My point of view is that, in all its incarnations, attention to the body or life of another person when you're in a committed relationship is abusive and threatening to the integrity of that commitment; it allows for attention and emotion to be directed away from family and loving obligations. No excuses change the truth.

You know, it's bad enough to not be willing to admit to skuzzy and hurtful behaviors. It's even worse to treat your spouse as dim, inadequate, stupid, not with it, or actually responsible for the bad behaviors.

YOU Made Me Do It

One of the most insidious excuses is to blame the victim of your behavior for your behavior. For example, "I'm not stubborn. You just don't understand."

One listener wrote: *"I keep my mouth shut when he is talking to me. Otherwise, I would cut him off or act defensive, because I'm so stubborn as to my point of view."*

Another blaming excuse is "I'm not vindictive, you've hurt me!" This latter excuse destroyed one listener's marriage:

"This behavior of vindictiveness was one of the things that caused the demise of my first marriage—I now have to struggle to keep it from taking root in my current marriage. If he doesn't do one of the things I think he should, like wash my car, I'll purposely not do one of the things for him, like cook breakfast on Sunday. All of this is in my mind and he has no idea that I'm even mad."

Obviously, these are issues of assertion of will, and an unwillingness to communicate or absorb the reality that you are now "two" and must take into account someone with a different history and point of view and will.

The most direct way of assigning blame to your partner for your behaviors is to do just that:

"Sometimes when my husband calls me names (f . . . g bitch) he tries to take the blame off of himself and attach it to me. He says that if I wouldn't such and such, then he wouldn't have to say it. He actually says it's my fault that he had to say it."

Folks who are physically abusive use the same excuse. I always remind both sides of that argument that anyone can provoke, intentionally or not—however, provocation does not dictate one automatic response. If there is an automatic, reflexive, typical response, it is a measure of that person, not the person who provoked. Ultimately, we are each responsible for our own choice of action, and don't let anyone convince you otherwise.

Tit for Tat

"The most stupid excuse I've heard (and used) is: 'I did this because you did that!' My husband and I wasted years playing the 'tit for tat' game when we could have better spent that time nurturing and loving each other. Fortunately, we figured it out and began 'acting' to each other as opposed to 'reacting,' and as a result, the last couple of years of our twenty-year marriage have by far been the best."

The tit for tat game is obviously childish and clearly destructive. Why then do we adults do that? Because of hurt feelings. When our beloved does/doesn't do something that contributes to our sense that they love us, we hurt them for hurting us—imagining that that will make them love us better? I don't think so.

Sleight of Hand

Magicians are really experts at distraction. They subtly move your attention away from the action that creates the illusion that magic has happened. Little children do that when they point to something in the distance as they desperately try to conceal the cookie-before-dinner crumbs on their chins. When we grow up, we're supposed to face our wrongdoings and our agonies in a more courageous manner—especially with that person we're supposed to trust more than anyone: our husband or wife.

One listener wrote about her horror in finding out as an adult that her father was a child molester.

"This has destroyed me in many ways. I have been directing my anger at my husband, because he is an easy target and it keeps me from having to face the anger I feel for my father. I called a therapist and I am now in the process of fixing me. I believe that our spouses take a lot of the blame for the problems that have to do with other people as well as ourselves."

She's right. The irony is that because we feel the most safe with our spouses, we excuse our mistreatment of them as we blow off steam and rage meant for less safe persons or places. When she faces her dad, she will have to give up much of her past—taking it out on her husband avoided that.

Oftentimes it's not an issue of deflecting from a third party, it's the inability to assume responsibility for your own misdeeds.

"One behavior that I am not happy about and even dislike is when I get angry at my husband, and during the argument we are having, I begin to shout and yell. It is usually when I am right that my husband in an effort to win the fight begins to push my angry buttons. My husband is provoking, to say the least, and my excuse is that he pushed my angry buttons and got anger. He thus doesn't have to acknowledge any wrong or any correction that

may be needed, because he's been able to prove that I have some-thing to work on also."

Although that sleight of hand is clever, she has the tools to take it away from him: Disarm her angry button; then, he's stuck with himself.

It's Never Over

"I'm sorry that I allowed my unresolved anger to nearly destroy my marriage, however, I am glad we were able to rise to the occa-sion and move forward."

That was the happy ending to a story that doesn't gener-ally end that way for many people. The scenario was that her husband had done something hurtful, had repented, and wanted to improve the marriage. However, *"I was really angry thinking about what he put me through and that he 'owed me' big time for the hurt."*

I always remind couples and individuals that having hurt that lingers after an assault on the marriage and the partner is normal and expected. Once you make the recommitment to accept that person back, and determine to work on the rela-tionship, issues of punishment have to be put aside or the end result, an improved relationship, won't be forthcoming. Using the "I've been hurt excuse," though valid, is destructive to rela-tionship reconstruction plans. At some point, you've got to give up the rage and the behaviors it stimulates.

It's Not an Excuse—It's My Values

"I am a Vietnam vet. I have been married twice. At one time I was very promiscuous—not during marriage. I am seeing a lady that I am very fond of. I listen to your show faithfully and agree on most

subjects. I am in my fifties and feel that your warning about sex outside of marriage applies to everyone, not just teenagers. My lady friend disagrees. She pointed out that we are adults. . . . My reason for following your advice is because of my own personal convictions. She expects an answer soon. She thinks morality is a stupid excuse."

Note: It's not a good plan to have someone in your life who dismisses your core values as "excuses." Values are never an excuse, they are valid reasons. The man's lady friend is disrespectful, controlling, and selfish (Proceed directly to Chapter 9: Stupid Mismatch!).

8
Stupid Liaisons

"Recently at a company party I got heavily intoxicated and had a near-sexual liaison with my boss's nineteen-year-old daughter.

I am fifty-four, very happily married, with a son, who is, incidentally, the young lady's boyfriend.

I don't consider it too serious as all that happened was she performed oral sex on me a couple of times, while all I did was gently fondle her.

What bothers me about the whole liaison is, I think, that it could have become a very big mistake.

I almost cheated on my wife, nearly betrayed my son and boss, and came close to making a drunken idiot of myself with a young woman, whom I consider a very dear friend of the family."

—A LISTENER

Let's see, he got drunk, had sexual relations with his boss's daughter, who is also his son's girlfriend, betrayed his vows with his wife, and he *thinks* he only got *close* to doing something wrong? How Clintonesque! How grotesque. Sadly, these days, how *not* unusual.

In today's moral climate, where the air is thinning by the day, not by the altitude, many folks describe what used to be seen as outright affronts to their vows as "mere" or "almost" or "innocent" or "misunderstood" or even "reasonable" or "necessary" or their "right." Also, as this warped thinking goes, they rationalize not having really done anything wrong by splitting a definition into submolecular particles; if it wasn't intercourse to orgasm, so this argument goes, it wasn't sex. Oh, puhlease!

The point needs to be made that even putting yourself in a compromising situation *is* a breach of your vows which brings hurt, confusion, and mistrust to what should be a safe place: your marital relationship.

Instead, I get calls about women going drinking and dancing in bars at night without their spouses, husbands and fiancés who go to stripper-joints and participate in lap-dancing at bachelor parties, lone spouses traveling and socializing evenings with members of the opposite sex under the banner of "business," spouses car-pooling with either unmarried or unhappily married members of the opposite sex, married men/women spending family time (and secretive time) "helping" unmarried women/men with their home or feelings, perpetuating friendships with "ex" lovers, developing hobbies and activities with others outside of the marriage, having on-line "friendships," spouses flirting and gawking in plain sight of their husband or wife, taking vacations with buddies to a singles resort, and a host of other behaviors that, in spite of denial with the intensity of a pit bull bite, are clearly disruptive and destructive to intimacy, trust, and ultimately, love.

Beyond that, these behaviors are downright cruel. Even to attempt to rationalize away behaviors that cause your spouse pain, is to virtually spit on him or her. I just love it when some guy or gal calls about their impossible spouse, who is just hypersensitive about their innocent friendship. When I challenge what is basically the choice of a person who supposedly doesn't really matter over the person he or she is supposed to love, cherish, and protect, their response is generally a frustrated silence or a protestation of rights (to play) over oppression (of marital vows and obligations and downright thoughtful decency).

This is the point at which the offending spouse gets even more ugly. Adding sulfuric acid to injury is the typical behavior when confronted by their hurt and confused spouse. When callers tell me of their spouse's misbehaviors, it's usually in the form of: "I just want to know if I'm being fair or unreasonable. Is it okay for him/her to . . . ?" referring to one of the above behaviors.

Generally my answer is, "No, that behavior is grossly inappropriate for a married/engaged person. That should be obvious to you. Why do you feel you even have to ask me or any other third party about it? Why are you not trusting your own point of view?"

"Well, because (he/she) says . . ."

"Wait! Let me guess. (He/she) says, 'You're wrong,' or 'It means nothing,' or 'You're hypersensitive,' or 'You're insecure,' or 'You're controlling,' or 'You're immature,' or 'You're not happy with yourself, and you're trying to drag me down,' or something like that. Right?"

"How did you know? You sound like you're hiding somewhere in my house."

"Because, my dear, that's exactly how all people intentionally hurting their spouses talk. It's their way of alleviating themselves of any shred of guilt, to make you back off, shut up, and let them do what they selfishly want to do—which they've somehow convinced themselves they have a right to do."

Of course, it's not unusual for these do-badders eventually to collapse in a heap of begging for forgiveness for "losing

their heads" and "getting off track," or, my favorite understatement and misnomer, "making a mistake."And then I get
the sad calls: "Am I obligated to take (him/her) back?" or "I
took (him/her) back but I can't trust, can't warm up, can't let
go, can't feel love. So, what do I do?"

Here are the choices: Stay and suffer, stay and go crazy,
stay and pray, stay and demand things to change, stay and
take the risks, or leave.

Love Shouldn't Hurt

How can you say you love and care for someone when you
bring that person pain, uncertainty, embarrassment, anxiety,
and insult? Wait—I know the answer to that one—you don't
love them! Justifying actions that clearly hurt and demoral-
ize your spouse is self-serving, not loving, and is psychologically abusive. Here's a tip: If your actions hurt the one you
love, they are the wrong actions. Period.

Love is an action based on the conviction of commitment,
not on the ebb and flow of emotion. The emotion of feeling
overwhelmingly drawn to someone, sexually turned on to
them, or fuzzy all over when they walk into a room or the
thought of them comes to mind, is intermittent, fragile, and
too easily pushed aside by such other competing emotions as
boredom, depression, health issues, financial circumstances,
familiarity, annoyances, and so forth. It is the sense of obligation due to the seriousness of the commitment that provides the impetus for appropriate behavior in spite of
momentary glitches in "that loving feeling."

And, most importantly, it is the *behaviors* of loving that
help stimulate and perpetuate those "loving feelings." That's
right! Your behaviors largely determine your feelings. If you
require proof of that, remember all those times when you

felt down, but spiffed up your dress, stiffened up your lip, and marched into the fray—the very act of behaving un-depressed and confident put you in the position to reinforce those healthier feelings. The same works for intimacy; behaving in a loving way taps into those stored-away posi-tive feelings for your spouse and generates positive reactions from his or her feedback and makes you feel even better and closer.

Yeah, but I Want Those Feelings Quick and Dirty

"I was a new mother and in a marriage that I felt was killing me. I set my sights on a person that I knew would bring me the excite-ment I wasn't getting in my marriage.

"It took me three long years to realize that the grass was not only greener, but much more bitter. I'm thankful that my daughter has a father who was insightful enough to see that her mother would come around."

This listener's letter is very typical for both men and women who find that being married and having children is not the fantasy experience they imagined. With maturity, commitment, and communication, people learn to make the best of life's challenges, difficulties, and disappointments. Without maturity, commitment, and communication, peo-ple look for ways simply to feel better rather than make things better.

For some, drugs and drinking work. For others, it's walking away from the scene—thereby creating the crime. For still others, it's the clandestine affair which makes them feel those fantasy feelings again. Not all in this last category acknowledge what they want. More often, the perpetrator convinces him- or herself that this is just an innocent flirta-tion or friendship through which they can relax in a way they can't at home with colicky babies, a tired spouse, or a busted washer-dryer.

No matter how you spin it, it's self-serving, wrong (check out Commandment Seven), doesn't solve the true problem(s), and risks everyone losing everything.

I recently took a phone call on my radio program from a guy who admitted that he hadn't been acting mature in the marriage. For several months, his wife and child were at his in-laws' house. He said that their separation absolutely had the intent of a time-out and that they would get the marriage back together. Evidently, they'd been talking on the phone daily about their problems. It seems they were both (immature and superficial) party types before they married, and then before their child. She grew up to face the challenge, and he'd been annoyed that she wasn't "fun" anymore. He continued to have "fun" going to bars and being with his buddies. She left. He wants her back.

He called, because he'd been lonely for female companionship so he connected with a woman and has had her to their house (!) for dinner (she cooks) and sex. When I challenged him on the fact that he indeed hadn't changed a whit during this time-out period, in that he still demanded immediate gratification, he then told me that he wanted to end it, but the girl wouldn't get the message. Here it comes: The girl had arrived at his house minutes before he decided to call me. He let her in.

I told him that I was stunned that he had engaged in these activities in the family home and that even now he let this woman into the house. He seemed "helpless" to know what to do now because "a relationship" had begun with this woman. I suggested he lead her to the door, tell her not to contact him anymore or he would file a report with the police for harassment. I don't know if he did that last part or not. I told him also that he had no choice but to tell his wife about what he'd done—especially because this woman was not going to let go.

This sounded like the plot to *Fatal Attraction*.

If it isn't a lover who won't let go, then it's a pregnancy, attempted suicide, extortion, sexually transmitted disease, public humiliation for your spouse and children, disruption of generations of family ties, legal and financial battles, demoralization of your children and the loss of their foundation of safety, trust, and respect for you and for marriage. It's dirty, face it.

In Your Dreams

From my experience on-air, it is definitely a more female tendency to dream and fantasize about an old lover when the realities of life and adult responsibilities hit minutes or years after the honeymoon. One caller said, "Um, I have a question. I've been married six years and I am still, um, every once in a while, seldom, like probably once every other month, having dreams about an old boyfriend I had."

"Okay. Now, when did it start and what else was happening in your life and/or marriage?"

"Oh, um, probably, I don't know—ah, six months after I got married for probably five years now."

"Six months into your marriage you learned something about life, about marriage, about love that you didn't like. What was it?"

"Well, freedom. The freedom was gone and, and um, just that, you know, the excitement is over after six months. Or, the newness of it all. And I think that I just wanted that newness again. Or that flirting. I was wondering if I should write in my journal more to try to figure out my feelings?"

"That's your question? If you should write in your journal? This is a typical female behavior, and I'm a woman so I can tell you that daydreaming, writing in journals, talking to your friends—all make you believe that you're doing something, but truly these behaviors are to avoid dealing with the core problem."

"So what is dealing with it?"

"Good question and the real point. Dealing with it is to realize that in the beginning of your marriage you were doing all this fun stuff and now real life has hit and you have to go out and buy each other Kaopectate and you have to do bills and you have to do all this stuff which is not as much fun. By the way, it obviously can never be the same unless you get divorced every six months from everybody you've married. You've gotten lazy in this relationship and have been waiting for feelings to carry you away or for him to create a mood. What have you done to make this marriage warm, loving, and meaningful—other than write about how unhappy you are and fantasize about Prince Charming?"

"Right. I didn't look at it that way."

It is normal for relationships to have to struggle with reality. What is becoming normal, albeit unconscionably wrong, is to ignore commitments and vows in order to "feel good." I have suggested walking around on a Prozac drip to many people who think the epitome of a good life is always to feel perky. Truth is, real happiness is a more moving experience than feeling perky—but it's only earned over time and with depth. Don't be one of the too many these days who looks for the omnipresent nipple of your infanthood. Much of the value, meaning, and purpose in life comes from giving . . . not feeling.

Back to Yesterday

A listener writes:

"My husband has and sees no problem being friends with ex-girlfriends and ex-wives . . . from twenty years or more. Should I not

get upset and let him go to dinner with these female friends? Also, for your information—this is my third marriage and his fourth."

Do you realize that these two people have seven marriages between them? Do you realize that these people will likely increase that number in the next few years? Here's why: She's afraid of the vulnerability of intimacy so she married men who can't be intimate—then she doesn't have to look inside when she's got something so real and obvious to complain about; he's afraid of the vulnerability of intimacy so he maintains innumerable superficial female friendships which lead him to be able to say that he doesn't have a problem at all. As for his ex-lovers' club, some people are human flames—they crave the constant presence of hovering moths around them. What they don't experience in depth, they make up for in numbers. The women who participate just love the flattery.

A match made in purgatory.

Not all "going backward" is about superficiality of intimacy. Sometimes it's about restoring our egos, which often goes hand-in-hand with a special kind of revenge.

"When I was in college, I fell in love for the first time. Our relationship got out of hand, and it turned sexual. He graduated and left me with the impression that he'd come back for me. Years passed as I waited for him and didn't date anyone else. After several years, he told me he was involved with one of my friends and that we had no future together. But, stupid me, still holding onto a fantasy of romance. After graduating I met a very nice young man—handsome, kind, honest, intelligent. Then, it happened. My old boyfriend called me. He wanted to be friends again.

"I said sure, but had other plans in mind. I wanted to get him to love me again, and then I'd break his heart and leave him like he left me. My new love hated my having a relationship with him and told me he loved me and that he wanted to marry me but that I was compromising the security of our relationship by continuing to have contact with my ex.

"The game was over. I sent my ex one last e-mail and told him not to write or call. Now that I have a stable, healthy relationship, he thinks that I'll just drop it all for him—no way! That was that."

Actually, this listener came awfully close to losing the healthy part of her life in order to "heal" her damaged ego. I've seen so many people fall into this trap. They sacrifice their current moral growth and maturity for the option of erasing a rejection from their past: If they can make that person love them after all, well then, they'll be all right, perfect, wonderful, or whatever. Truth is, the involvement, or lack thereof, by some one person is not an indicator of anyone's worth. And self-esteem is harder won than that— and that's why people choose easier ways. Mind you, the easier ways are always substandard, and exact a terrible price.

Be Careful—and Stop Being So Stupid

I just love it when folks try to soft-sell me that their extra-marital intentions are truly honorable—and that this honor is worth the destruction of their marriage? "Well, no . . . but . . . ," is the soppy answer.

Here's an example that is all too typical. Fortunately, it has a happier ending than most.

"I started noticing how much stuff my husband was doing for my friend's family, and NOT doing for his own. I started noticing what kind of parent she really was and how she dressed and acted around my husband. She was no friend of mine! She was the kind of person my mother always warned me about. That person who likes what you have so they try and take it from you. I told my husband what I was going through and that we needed to dump her like a sack of rotten potatoes.

"Well, of course, he said I was losing my mind. A few weeks after I tell him all this, she has decided to move closer to her ex-husband for the children. Yeah, right. Anyway, my husband says he'll help her move. Fine—the faster the better. Okay, here's the BEST part. He comes home mad as heck. She had put the moves on him. He was disgusted and very sorry for not believing me. At last, she is booted from our lives without a tear being shed."

I seriously doubt that he didn't see what she saw. I believe that he enjoyed the hero status he got from the "friend" for helping out, while at home helping out was simply what he was supposed to do. I believe the flirting made him feel masculine and desirable, whereas at home the mood hardly struck. I believe he was moving toward the "I never really meant for anything to happen . . . ," excuse, but in the end, his conscience got the better of him.

The moral of this story is that you should never put yourself in a situation that could remotely lead to compromise. This specifically includes being alone with a member of the opposite sex for friendship, business, just talking, just eating, just sharing, just driving, just anything. It is simply a fact that proximity is dangerous in and of itself because it allows opportunity for inappropriate feelings to evolve. To show respect for your marriage and your vows, you should never let that happen.

This might be at great sacrifice—but what price your honor and your marriage? In 2000 there was a widely publicized event that dealt with just this issue. A military officer, experienced and decorated, refused to be confined to close quarters with a woman also in the military. He cited his religious beliefs (Catholic), and his vows to his marriage as reason to ask for reassignment or to serve in this assignment with another male. Political correctness being as powerful as it is, he has been severely punished and his record tarnished. This was an outrageous conclusion to a situation that could have been handled with respect. Then again, in today's culture, the only allowable intolerance is toward religious belief.

His character, conscience, and marriage stayed intact. Incidentally, if this were standard military procedure, fewer women would have to be excused from service due to pregnancy.

I Need to Be Needed—I Need to Be the Good Boy/Girl

Sexual or romantic fantasies are not the only motivating force behind Stupid Liaisons, the immoral or unhealthy outside relationships that damage marital intimacy. The unilateral need to feel important in a generic sense propels many people into situations that substantially detract and distract from marital commitment and activities.

As one listener explains:

"When I was married, we decided that I should stay at home to raise our children. I gave up my career and my life to do so. During this time, I lost contact with those I used to work with for years. Our life was different now. One of my friends, another at-home mom, was an alcoholic. So, needless to say, I thought I would fix that one. I would take care of her daughter. I would lie, cheat, and steal from my husband and children. I would say I was home when I had been over at her house trying to help her stop. I would give her gas money or pay for groceries when we hardly had any. I would cheat time with him to give her. Worst of all, I would blame him for not supporting me in doing this wonderful thing.

"My female friend and neighbor across the street made her way into my husband's bed. The worst thing is that I knew it was going to happen. I thought I was worthless, because I could not get my friend to stop drinking. My nonstop drinking friend had taken the life out of mine and the friend across the street was just using me to get closer to my husband.

"The end of all of this is that I left, thinking he was the a—h—e of this whole thing. It has taken me three years, talking to my ex-husband about good and bad times, and growing up, to realize I can't save the world and to use better judgment about what is a friend."

Making an identity, building an ego, feeling important through rescuing makes those rescued your means to an end other than their welfare. You need them to improve because that is how you are measuring your own worth. Some people become workaholics to serve that inner god, others find broken friends and try to fix them.

Some just turn over their lives to whoever wants a piece, because they interpret that behavior as that which will bring love and avoid all negative judgment or confrontation.

"I have been with my husband for twenty years. He has a bad habit of letting people walk all over him—not only his family members, but also people who work for us. I attempted to talk to him about this, but he never would listen to my point of view. There was always a reason why we should forgive and forget. Then, once we did, they would sh— all over us again.

"But this along with other behaviors has started to make me feel worthless."

At first, it would seem that this listener has a very weak husband. How sad. However, that is rarely the true story. This type of behavior is more self-serving than self-sacrificing. This type of behavior is generally about building a reputation through the flimsiest of means.

This is a point I've tried to drill home many times on the air: Your attempts to feel wonderful and important by having no boundaries or standards for how others outside the marriage affect you and your family is self-serving and damaging. By the way, not holding people accountable for their actions doesn't really help them. Repetitively saving their undeserving butt doesn't mature them—but it does make you feel superior. And even reflex forgiveness at its worst does not suggest reissuing a "use me" proclamation—so don't go touting forgiveness as your excuse. Please do note that along this route of self-congratulation, you willingly sacrifice the well-being and affection of those who really ought to count on you for support and protection. You are all too willing to sacrifice them for the "audience"—in your mind, the folks at enough of a distance see you as a hero. Those at home know better.

Shut Your Mouth!

I have often said on my radio program that without gossip, much of human conversation would cease and that quiet would rule the land. What some people don't get is what gossip entails. E! and A&E biographies are largely gossip. The tabloids major in gossip. Much of what passes for news is gossip. The Internet is filled with gossip (or porn). And a lot of what people talk about to each other under the umbrella of conversation is gossip.

People even gossip to themselves. A recent caller was complaining about her boyfriend. It seems that he read her journal, in which she had commentary about him and an ex-boyfriend. Evidently, he was upset by the content of what he'd read. She clearly was calling to complain about this breach of privacy and wondered if she were morally obligated to explain about the things he read. I suggested that no matter how he got this information, gossip from her friends or her journal, if she wished to continue a relationship with him she'd better clarify the upsetting points.

I frankly don't understand why people write disturbing, unflattering, scandalous things down on paper if they don't intend someone to read them. So often, in hearing about this journal-keeping, it sounds more like a place to air things that ought to be disciplined, or an opportunity to vent the ugliest, weakest, most unfortunate parts of ourselves, our thoughts and feelings. Perhaps that's the venue of spiritual or psychological counseling—where at least the venting is toward growth or depth of understanding of oneself.

I have harped endlessly on how spouses should not share their problems and complaints concerning each other with mutual friends or family. They are likely simply to side with you—so much for an unbiased sounding board. Meanwhile, you've breached the sanctity of the marriage, embarrassed your partner forever, having painted a one-sided portrait of him or her.

There are countless calls from folks who regretted telling friends and family their gripes and problems in the marriage, specifically because after the relationship normalized again, friends and family were still polarized, rejecting, critical, even hostile to the partner and the renewed relationship.

As one listener put it:

"I would like to thank you for a very practical and broad-reaching recommendation I've heard you make to callers lately. That is to refrain from discussing personal matters with uninvolved parties. We women are certainly prone to spilling our guts out to each other for little to no reason. I've always regarded it as a form of dishonesty to tell half-truths of any kind.

"I am now reduced to sharing only the most benign and anemic bits of information about my life. I admit, the more I told them the more needy I appeared. No explanation could convince them of my sanity once their sage advice had been given. I failed to take into account the destructive potential of an idle tongue."

Therein lies yet another problem in "sharing" personal information: When the advice isn't taken, then you have trouble.

On-Line Is Not Just a Chat

"When I was pregnant with our second child, my husband started several on-line friendships. He started pulling away from me, chatting at all hours of the night, sometimes about things that were none of her business. He even made long-distance phone calls. He told me one week after our second son was born, two weeks before Christmas, that he wanted a divorce. But I told him he promised me forever, he promised our children forever."

The Internet has made escaping from responsibilities and reality possible from your very own living room chair! That these cyber-affairs have become a part of our culture is evident in the new growth industry: the therapy of cyber-addiction, yet another behavior that has nothing to do with character and everything to do with outside influences and brain chemicals. I repeat, the only irresistible impulse is the one not yet resisted. This is not a disease, it is a lapse of character based upon weakness and selfishness.

At least this listener is honest enough to admit that chat-room relationships are to salve the ego, as a pretense at solving the problem:

"My husband and I were having problems that most couples have once they have been married for a time. We never seemed to have enough money, he never seemed to want to talk to me, and we did not agree on how to raise our children.

"It wasn't too long before I had my own computer and was chatting with people, spending more time with them than with my young boys. Before too long, I had met a 'wonderful' guy that hung on my every word. Of course, all my 'friends' in the chat-room encouraged me to divorce my husband and get involved with this guy in real life.

"I separated from my husband, breaking his heart, and took my kids to live in a different town. One morning, I woke up. My husband had come to pick up the kids, and I looked at his sad face. I

realized I couldn't let this man go. After all I had done to him, he still loved me. My husband and I listen and respect one another again. I can't believe how much I almost lost."

The main problem with all kinds of affairs is that they pretend that the sole source of the problems is outside you and that another "him" or "her" will solve the problems. You know better than that . . . eventually.

Yo Momma!

I used to say on the air that in the span of the quarter of a century or so that I've been on the air, I haven't gotten any father-in-law complaints. That's not true anymore. I think I've gotten five in the past three years. That still leaves thousands and thousands of complaints about mothers-in-law. They run both ways, that is, the woman's and the man's mother. There does seem to be something special about that mother-son relationship which leads to a lot of competition between daughter-in-law and mother-in-law.

Many mothers of sons have a hard time understanding that they need to turn the baton over to another woman. Instead, they may play a sickening game of tug-of-war over the loyalties of their sons. In doing so, they put their sons in the middle, as if they must choose between their mother or their wives. This can get very cruel, even evil—demanding that their sons come to visit, bring the children, but not "that woman." The sons who do that are the boys, not the men.

Many times the handwriting is on the wall, as one listener doesn't seem to see:

"I feel my fiancé chooses his family over me. He takes their side and defends them when I need him to support me. Now he is talking about when we get married and he finishes his term with the

Air Force, he wants to move onto his parents' land and rent from them. I really don't want to do this, because I feel it could destroy our relationship. He doesn't understand why I feel this way. I don't think he's gotten the point that he's on his own, and mommy and daddy aren't going to be there every day to hold his hand."

Actually, my dear, no he's not, and yes they will. You have to decide if you're going to be there to watch it.

The stories can get a whole lot worse when she does stay there to watch it:

"I knew my husband had a close relationship with his mother. His first commitment was still to his mother after we married. The day I told my husband we were expecting our first baby was the day I realized he hadn't detached himself from his mom. His response was, 'You're not going to have it, are you?' This was one of those moments in life where it starts going in slow motion, and you feel like you're having a nightmare. I was in shock and disbelief. He said he absolutely could not have this baby because his mother didn't want him to—I guess to keep him as the baby and to keep him with her and away from me or any other woman. He said that it was ultimately my decision, but if I had the baby he couldn't guarantee he'd be there next year. He gave me an ultimatum—the baby or him. And it was all so his mom wouldn't be hurt."

Well, she aborted the baby. Later, when they did have a child his mother had nothing to do with it, continuing an exclusive relationship with her son. The listener ended her painful letter:

"I wish I would have left him when he gave me the ultimatum just weeks into our marriage. Why would a husband, an intelligent, educated physician, keep as his first priority his relationship with his mother before his wife and child. I will never understand it."

I will never understand catering to it.

One male listener wrote to me admitting that he almost lost his wife and son by letting his mother intimidate him.

"Mom had always been a strong presence in our house, but I never realized the magnitude until my wife and I had our first child. Mom's domination became unbearable, but she would not lend her support or cooperate with us. When we tried to delicately confront her, she physically attacked my wife and had my older brother beat me up. After four years of her nonrepentance, and my calling Dr. Laura for advice, I gave her an ultimatum to own up and make amends, and we haven't heard from her since. Although I miss her, peace has been restored to our home."

Of course, I'm always happier when ex-communication is not the necessary option. One woman caller told me about how her father would just show up unannounced to spend the day at her home. She wanted her privacy with her husband and child, but was afraid to hurt her father's feelings—especially since she was living on land he gave them.

There's the hook: Be careful about taking such "gifts," when you understand your parents well enough to know that they feel their gift gives them appropriate entitlements, privileges, and power.

I told her to go to the door when he knocked, not let him in, and tell him: "It's a bad time now for a visit. Please give me a quick call when you're available so that we can pull this together better next time." And then, with an "I love you, Dad," give him a hug and close the door. Of course, he'll be hurt, even outraged, and I hope not vengeful. You might even have to give him back the land and actually take care of yourselves and build a future together from the bottom up. Greed is obviously a big part of this picture—those controlling parent-types count on your greedy dependency, wanting it all and now.

One listener has had it and has decided to call the meeting to order:

"I am a stay-at-home mom of two beautiful little girls. For me, the most stress comes from my in-laws. They have been coming to our home every weekend for the last two months. They stay in our home from Friday until Sunday afternoon.

"While in my home, they constantly tell me how to raise my children, and they do not follow my rules for my children. If I put them in time-out, they take them out. If I remind them to say, 'Yes, ma'am,' or 'Yes, sir,' they tell them they do not have to say that to them.

"My husband and I have discussed this, and he is nervous about saying anything to them about coming down all the time and about following the rules of the house set for the children.

"Well, I've simply told my husband that if he doesn't figure out a way to tell his parents—then the children and I will start staying at the most expensive hotel in Nebraska on the weekends while he spends quality time with his parents."

Well done. Sad that it had to be done this way. Better if each spouse would take responsibility for building a mature, adult relationship with parents and not constantly behave as though fearing being sent to his or her room without dinner!

It's Us Against Them

Many times callers struggle over the proper place for their loyalties: with their spouse or with their bio-family. "But, it's my mother/father/sister/brother . . . ," is often the lamentation which reveals a sense of "blood thicker than marital vows" confusion. Although I work very hard to have people fulfill their obligations of respect and honor to their families, I remind them that they have established a new family, over which they have primary responsibility for welfare, nurturance, well-being, and survival.

I remind listeners and callers that being supportive of their bio-families does not include sacrificing the welfare of their home, spouse, and children. For example, one caller was feeling guilty, because his parents had been pushing him to take in his wayward adult brother, out on parole again for drug arrests. My caller had several small children and a wife, who was not enthusiastic about having that big a problem to take care of or worry about or defend against (as he had bad friends and a bad temper). My caller, a decent man, didn't want to disappoint his parents, let down his "blood," nor upset his home. He didn't know what to do.

I told him that support and help came in many forms. That is, helping his brother find a place to live and helping him drive to a special appointment for a job interview was helping his brother. Calling his brother on the phone or meeting him during a lunch break to offer moral support was also helping. I told him that I believe he had no moral obligation whatsoever to put his family in jeopardy in the hopes of rehabilitating his brother. Additionally, this clearly did not put the burden where it would do the most good: on his brother.

"But what about my parents?" he asked.

"What do you mean?"

"They're going to be angry with me—disappointed in me. What do I do about that, and what do I tell them?"

"Tell them that you respect how much they care about their son and how much they want him to be and do better. Tell them you understand their desperation in wanting to protect and fix him. Tell them you have all those same feelings about your own family—and that your family comes first. They'll have to think about that one for a while, because it provides a catch-22."

It is not unusual for in-laws to put unreasonable demands and stresses on the marriage of one or more of their kin.

Why is that so? Same schoolyard clumping of mini-groups with an "us agin' them" mentality, an inability to let go, a selfish determination to control, a hostile reaction to change or difference, inherent emotional and psychological problems, and maybe even too much time on their hands.

During the week in which I worked on this very chapter, I had innumerable such calls. One was from a woman annoyed that her mother-in-law had for the past five years (married ten) yearly sibling-only reunions with her—that means no spouses (like my caller) and none of their children. At first, I responded with dismay that my caller would be upset about one night out of three hundred and sixty-five; except, it was for five nights, Thursday through Sunday. Another caller wondered whether it was okay for her husband and two adolescent children to spend six weeks vacationing with his parents without her, because she had to work (he was a public school teacher with the summer off). Yet another caller said her husband had received only two plane tickets as a gift from his out-of-state mother, enough for himself and their son. "Does that sound right or nice to you?" she asked.

"No."

"When we were dating, one of the things that was a bond between my wife and me was having to survive difficult families, in which we didn't seem to fit or have much in common. We seemed to be in sync about keeping our distance, protecting privacy and adult individuality."

This listener had difficult in-laws in stereo. Which, of course, made it a lot easier for him and his wife to band together in mutual support—or so the writer thought.

"After we married, even as the pattern of destructive/everyday evils continued on the part of my in-laws (who turned out to be really disgusting, compared to my merely frightened, confused, annoying family), my wife insisted on having much more involvement with them than I thought healthy, and she would never

stand up to their rudeness, destructive comments, and manipula-
tions. It turned out that doing it 'her' way meant doing nothing
except eating dirt, and having a wedge grow larger and larger
between us, and seeing my wife continue being emotionally/psy-
chologically crippled in general."

It is in these situations that I always prescribe serious psychotherapy. Without the growth of personal dignity and a
respect for the integrity of oneself and the new marriage and
family, such Stupid Liaisons will be destructive to the potential happiness and success of any marriage.

And sometimes, when a healthy balance cannot be
reached, withdrawal is necessary:

"It was a very painful decision for my husband not to have any-
thing to do with his family. I am grieved that my husband had to
make that decision." This listener's marriage did survive the
attempt of his family to break them up because, due to her
heritage, she was "not one of them."

"Now, Honey, You Are Not Allowed to Play . . . With Grandma/pa!"

Another point of confusion about honoring your parents as
an adult with a family to protect is the issue of serious bad
parental behaviors: drug use, shacking-up, consorting with
drug dealers and child molesters (here's the "but I love him,"
and "he's different now" excuse to ignore), blatant affairs, a
series of lovers, vulgar language, violent behaviors, and so
forth—I've heard it all. So much for the wisdom and sobriety
that's supposed to come with age!

Not only do more and more older parents engage in such
seamy behavior, they often try to entangle their children in the
fray by asking for lodging with the lover (while still married to
the other parent), demanding that they have access to the

grandchildren (who would be at some risk), offering their adult child an entry into their immoral or illegal activities, and generally asserting that they should be accepted without judgment for whatever they do simply because they are the parent.

No way. Your first loyalty is to the family you created in love and commitment.

Your Adult Children

Now that I've made it clear that your obligation is to your marriage and family, what about when your children become adults? This is especially complicated when you are in a second (third, fourth . . .) marriage with all the sense of guilt for messing up your children's lives with a broken home, and not being there to do what a father/mother is supposed to do on a daily basis. This scenario generally includes a grossly inappropriate overindulgence of bad behaviors by your adult children, an attempt to rescue them no matter what their own responsibility and need for accountability, and a general continued messing up of their lives and your marriage.

Here's a commentary on this issue by a listener:

"My husband has two grown kids who have their own partners and kids and he continually bails out his daughter with any problem she may phone him with—which is fairly constant.

"I have kept out of things until I had to mention something to him about boundaries and why he still feels he needs to give her money. I got the reply that it's none of my business and I wouldn't understand because I've never had my own kids and that I should keep right out of it.

"This excuse I've heard more than once as an excuse for bad boundaries and from parents who enable their kids throughout their adult lives; the result inevitably is that the adult child never

learns consequences for their own choices. In fact, he is making up for his own guilt for his parenting style and it infuriates me."

The guilt-ridden mishandling of children from a prior marriage is probably the major contributor to the statistic that second marriages collapse at greater rates than first. It is natural for in-laws to favor their own; and for "parents" to do the same; it is natural for there to be issues with ex-spouses because of history, extended family, and children; it is natural that there be unresolved personal, emotional problems due to the loss of the prior marriage; and it is natural that you realize navigating this isn't as easy as you thought it would be—the new love partner isn't a panacea.

It Often Does Come Down to a Choice

So many times I've heard the phrase, "I don't think I should have to choose," when a caller is complaining about someone their spouse doesn't get along with, isn't treated well by, or outright disdains. My answer: "Yes, my dear, sometimes you just have to make a choice."

"My sister and my husband do not get along at all. Although I care about my sister deeply, I only see her when my husband is not around. If there is a family function, such as a reunion or holiday, they are both adult enough to put their differences aside for the good of the family. I do not believe, as much as their personalities conflict, that either of them should be put in a situation where they have to bicker and argue.

"When it comes down to it, my sister and my husband do not make me choose a side to go on. They hate each other, but they don't expect me to hate either one. I would take my marriage in a second over my sister."

This listener letter demonstrates that there can be honor among enemies, and that she realizes that her ultimate loyalty is with her husband. That means, no, not for the sake of mommy's feelings make sure that everyone is always happy and getting along. Sometimes, that just can't work. Some personalities clash. At least they are being civil and not demanding that she go to war for either's sake.

If, for example, her sister were doing some of the horrible things I hear about, like making false reports of rape or child molestation against him, then it is clear, she must be completely eliminated from their lives.

Another listener, whose best friend was blatantly rude and mean to her fiancé, was asked by him not to invite the woman to their wedding.

"This upset me, because I considered her my friend. However, I agreed. Well, this terribly hurt her feelings, but I have to say it was the BEST thing I ever did. My husband means more to me than anything, and I am proud to say that 'I stood by my man!'"

If the criticisms and warnings of friends and family about your spouse are well-founded (physically violent, abusive of alcohol/drugs, blatant infidelities, destructive personality) you must contend with these truths—a head in the sand is a tush in the air. In general, the petty attitudes, and turf wars of your friends and families, their warped personality styles and ugly attitudes, must not be allowed to mess up your marriage.

You have to choose. You have to stand by your man/woman!

9
Stupid Mismatch

". . . Some advice my mother gave me:
'Don't date anyone you know you wouldn't want
to marry.
You never know whom you will fall in love
with.' "

—A (MALE) LISTENER

"One thing I have learned is that if you are determined to be stupid, no one can stop you!" writes a listener.

Why would anyone be determined to be stupid? First of all, the recognition of being "stupid" is largely hindsight. While in the midst of having some relationship or making a questionable relationship work, so many naïve and well-meaning to unhealthy and self-destructive motivations rule the day. Let's face it, once you make a decision, it's hard to let go of dreams, admit error, defeat, or failure, or accept that something you believed so great isn't. This is where all the armor of denial comes into play, as you use excuse after excuse to avoid recognizing the truth that needs to be faced for a healthy and happy life.

Two factors rule in not giving up a Stupid Mismatch. The

first is the fear that you are actually the problem: If you were different or better in some way he/she would be different. These self-doubts are powerful immobilizers. The second is the fact that breaking up is hard to do. All loss hurts and dumps us into an unknown. For too many of you, the ugly known is more appealing that the unknown. When I have helped people face the unknown, it is clear that most see it as a deep, black hole. I ask them to recognize that deep, black pits are exactly the foundation for planting a tree. It's all in the perspective.

Insta-Intimacy

"I have a son who was born out-of-wedlock. In fact, I only knew his father for eight weeks and got pregnant by error and then found out that his father has been arrested over twenty-five times for DUI's, driving on a suspended license, amphetamines, robbery, battery, and spousal abuse. He was even responsible for a DUI death of a girl he was dating while he was married. Surprise? He lied about everything.

"When I learned this man had been driving my new vehicle while on parole, I flipped, and broke it off at four weeks of pregnancy."

Even though she had the good sense to break off with him, it's far from over, and it probably will never be. Even from State Prison, he is filing suit to maintain rights to their son. In between his prison sentences, he harasses her at home and work. She is scared as well as physically and psychologically stressed out.

Is this an unusual situation? Actually, no. Because of the relaxed societal views about unmarried sex, too many men and women are getting insta-intimate, engaging their hearts, souls, psyches, and genitals in a situation that has not yet engaged their brains. The result is a constant flow of mismatched liaisons that lead to broken hearts, babies out-of-wedlock, sexually transmitted diseases, disappointments leading to hurt and a lack of trust in relationships in general, fearsome situations with threats of violence or worries about suicide, and embarrassment leading to more stupid decisions like marrying anyway and isolation to hide shameful situations.

It is true that one stupid decision tends to lead to another especially when you are desperate to deny reality ("This can't possibly be true") or try to transform an ugly reality into your dream ("With my love he/she will become what I should have picked/waited for in the first place").

One listener wrote to me about his experience of "not waiting":

"I broke one of your cardinal rules of dating and asked a woman to marry me after only six months of dating. I'm a forty-seven-year-old college-educated male and have been divorced over ten years. I've never shacked-up or remarried.

"My kids are grown, and I thought the time was right for remarriage. I met 'Ms. Right' six months ago. She was forty-four, intelligent, educated, affectionate, caring, of the same religion as me, and physically attractive. She said and did all the right things. We 'fell in love' within a month. Within four months we agreed to marry. She chose the engagement ring, and we picked a date. Sounds great, doesn't it?

"The day I was to give her the ring (three days before Christmas) she called and broke it off, saying she didn't want to get married or see me again. She refused all my requests for an explanation.

"It seems that I had overlooked the warning signs. I excused the facts that she had been married twice, had an abortion with her second husband whom she married six months after her first husband. She had been sexually involved with four men in the six years since her last divorce. It seems that she had broken up with all of them after six months of dating!

"I knew ALL THIS, and thought I was different and could change her life by being such a good guy. 'I'm not like the rest, Sweetie, I'm different and I'll save you emotionally!'

"Well now, after being dumped, I feel like an idiot for not seeing the signs. Dr. Laura, you were right. You NEED TIME to really get to know another person and watch for the warning signs."

Yeah, but he saw the warning signs. Unfortunately, that didn't stop him. Ill-placed hope is simply postponed disappointment.

Don't Have Sex Before You See the Whites of Their Eyes

Having sexual relations before any true relationship (read: marital commitment) is established is stupid behavior. When I talk to people about morality and G-d's Commandments, it is in the context of providing a view of rules as guardians, not oppressors. Religious proscriptions have the ultimate goal of preventing you from hurting yourself and/or others and to give you the purpose and motivation for a meaningful, joyous life.

The current ferocious cultural movement to disassemble the power and importance of religious motivation in behavior and decisions is frightening. If I weren't afraid of sounding too weird, I'd probably call it satanic. When, in 2001, young adult college students at SUNY at Albany can join a University-supported S&M Club, and their counterparts at Penn State can attend a Sex Faire complete with "pin the clitoris on the vagina" games, clearly the boundary between civility and perversion has been corrupted. In this milieu, it is understandable that young as well as mature people begin doubting their values and seeing their spiritual lives as perhaps downright silly.

Nonetheless, we must persevere. And sexual intimacy out-side the realm of a marital husband-and-wife commitment leads generally to tragedy.

"I am thirty-two and just ended my second marriage. It had lasted two years and involved five children: his, mine, and ours. I was pregnant before we got married, poor judgment on both our parts. We fought a lot about the children. He abused my boys mentally and physically. Counseling went nowhere because he was not much of a talker. I found out, though, that he had a lot of stressors in his life. His mom came out of the closet, and he had numerous affairs on his first wife. He'd already had one on me.

"We married because I was pregnant, and we thought it was the honorable thing to do. Wrong. It has cost not only money, but irreversible pain and hurt in many innocent lives."

I remember a wonderful public service advertisement from a Christian organization that had a young male adult asking his grandfather about "Safe Sex." The grandfather's answer was to hold up his left hand and point to his wedding ring. "Safe" here doesn't only mean protection against herpes, AIDS, venereal warts, and so on, it means safe from misunderstandings, emotional hurts from rejection and loss, unplanned pregnancies (miscarriages, out-of-wedlock births, abortions), and the obvious confusion that comes from imagining that sexual intercourse, or even pregnancy, is a promise of true intimacy, love, or commitment.

When people, especially women, have sexual intercourse with a number of partners, their self-esteem suffers, which usually leads to even stupider choices in a match as they feel "less valuable." I know. I've gotten too many of those calls.

Promiscuity is, in and of itself, Stupid Mismatching since it brings together bodies and hopes without rational, meaningful foundation.

Newton's First Law of Physics

An object in motion tends to stay in motion unless another force impedes its progress. Unfortunately, when dealing with human endeavors, the opposing force isn't always good sense.

"I was involved in a mismatched relationship for five years. We were complete opposites, and I knew it from day one. I kept telling myself and even my partner that we needed to cut our losses and move on, but he was always so sorry and wanted to work on our issues together. I told him that he wasn't a bad person, just not the type of person I wanted to be with, but he kept insisting.

"It became a habit.

"I kept trying to break up with him, and then he would say he was sorry. By this time, I was so bitter and angry with myself for settling and with him for mistreating me. Well, I kept hoping he would change, but of course he didn't, things just got worse.

"Till one day, when he went to a boat show on a Saturday and never came home again. So, in the end I was hurt—but it is probably for the best, because now I can find the right match for me."

Habit. Momentum. This listener also wrote that she had completely lost respect for herself and for him, she felt unloved, she realized she was being mistreated, she was miserable, they'd have angry fights, and still, it went on until he left her! Now, on top of all that frustration and disappointment, was the hurt of rejection in spite of the fact that she ostensibly didn't want him.

It is that patterning which leads me to believe that it isn't going to be easy for her to find the "right match," since she sees her painful problems only from the perspective of the victim, and not the coperpetrator of her own misery.

Until you understand more deeply your own motivations for choosing and staying in a "bad" or "mismatched" relationship, the chances of your moving on to a healthier one are small. "Wherever you go, there you are," is one of those clichés that actually makes sense. Where you are and what you do when you're there is a measure of yourself, not of the circumstances. For many of you anxious to put the blame for your problems outside yourself, that's a bitter pill.

"How Would I Know What's a Good Match?"

It is true that familial and societal influences have an important impact on personal expectations. As one listener wrote:

"On a 'to do' list, my then future husband wrote the number one item was pot, then the bills he needed to pay from that week's paycheck. Two children later I divorced him. He still smokes marijuana to this day, and I have fatherless kids.

"I talk to them often about making better choices than I did and about the importance of two solid, loving parents. I partially attribute this to the fact that I came from a broken home with a mother who worked and whose interests lay more with boyfriends than with her children.

"I had and have little to no clue as to how a good male-female relationship should be. I'm still trying to gain some footing for the bad choice I made twenty-two years ago."

At least she's willing to admit that these were her choices, that they weren't good, and she takes responsibility for the problems they've wrought and what she owes her children now. With this openness, there is more hope that she'll find a better "match."

You Only Think It's a Mismatch

One of the most difficult and uncomfortable concepts for people to assimilate is that of "water seeking its own level." I get call after call from people complaining about their relative's, or friend's, rotten partner—without whom their relative or friend would be or do better. When I try to explain that their relative or friend picked and wishes to maintain that partner, they struggle against the notion. Instead, they go on about manipulations, situations, and machinations.

Why? Because without that perspective, there is little hope for their relationship with their relative or friend. If their loved one is charting his or her own course, they realize that there is no place for them on that journey, and that they can't really save that person. It's over.

One caller epitomized this truth:

"I am thirty-four, and I've been with my thirty-seven-year-old boyfriend for sixteen months. He's never been married, I've been divorced once. We have no kids."

"What can I help you with?"

"I told him the other night that I have decided I want to go into counseling. I have some issues with some insecurities and mistrust, and it's affecting my relationships."

"How?"

"Distrust in how he feels about me. Questioning if there is somebody else. Just insecurities."

"Is he behaving in a way which would lead any reasonable person to have mistrust?"

"Not really."

"Not really means yes, but not big. So tell me what the yes is."

"The yes is he gives me some mixed messages at times that are real conflicting."

"What does that mean in English?"

"Well, sometimes he will talk in regards to our future together and be real clear that he wants a future with me, and then the following week he tells me things like, well, maybe we're not meant to be together. Maybe we are fooling ourselves."

"Okay, let me ask you something before you start paying $200 for forty-five minutes of therapy. What you have described is flip-flopping. Why do *you* need to go to therapy for your insecurities when *he* flip-flops? Normal people react with insecurity when somebody keeps flip-flopping on them. That is a normal response. Now, what does your average, reasonable, normal person do when they are in a relationship with somebody who flip-flops constantly?"

"I would suppose get out of the relationship, but I don't really want to get out of the relationship. Let me be clear. I've done flip-flopping as well."

"And now you've found someone to do it with."

As the conversation progressed, the caller showed a deeper awareness of "wherever I go, there I am." She said that she didn't want to go into another relationship and do the same thing. She also revealed that he didn't want her to go into counseling. I explained that his reaction made total sense in that he was too afraid to face his own problems and weaknesses and realized that if she got healthy, she would no longer want to be in an unhealthy relationship. Unhealthy people match up with unhealthy people. Healthy people match up with healthy people. One of the unhealthy parties will always try to undermine the other's attempt to get healthy, because they don't want to be alone.

"So," I continued, "at the age of thirty-four, you have to look at your life and ask, 'Do I want to stay unhealthy to have him in my life—never get better, never have better, and to be tortured like this forever?' "

"No, absolutely not. It's unfortunate, but it makes sense. Because, in other areas he's got a lot to offer."

"That's nice. But, when people aren't stable, what they have to offer becomes useless. It's like a beautiful mahogany table where all the legs are different lengths. What value is that? So it's nice that he has good qualities. You do, too. But with respect to bonding, you are not healthy, right?"

"Right."

"Then you are going to have to let go of the security of him."

"That is absolutely true."

"And this point is the point at which most people fail. They don't let go. They don't get healthy."

Picture two people crouched down, side by side. One decides to stand up. The other can either stand up with the partner or pull the partner back down. Those are the only two ways they can function together. Beware the person who tries to pull you back down.

In spite of all unfortunate family influences and subsequent problems and inner turmoil, you are still the only one responsible and capable of deciding your course. As one listener reminds us:

"My husband and I were married for two years. During that time is when I realized what kind of character I wanted in a man—characteristics my husband didn't possess: ambition, strong spiritual leadership, self-motivation, enthusiasm for life, and love of children.

"I strongly suggest waiting to get married UNTIL YOU KNOW WHO YOU ARE. If you don't know who you are, how can you know what you will need in a husband and a father to your children?"

Too many of you are not thinking of life beyond the present moment. So much necessary growth, self-awareness, and maturity must take place before such an important decision as a life's mate can be made. It takes being on your own, making a place in the world for yourself, finding your own identity, and growing spiritually. That takes time and patience.

Without taking that time and having that patience, you may be trying to find yourself in someone else's problems.

The Fear Factor

"I married him because I was so terribly afraid. I was so scared of raising two children (one from a prior failed marriage and the other our son) all by myself. Fear is a powerful force, because it disrupts our perceptions and our rationale. I kept hoping that he would become what I wanted him to be. I was wrong about that, too," wrote a listener.

The man in question was an alcoholic, chronic liar, and had actually left her to run off for a time with another woman when she was five months pregnant with his child. Right after the wedding, though, he was back with not only that "honey," but others, too.

Her postscript was reassuring:

"It was not until after I left him that I found out I was fully capable of raising my children all by myself all along. I hadn't needed to drag myself and my children through all the heartache after all."

Though it is reassuring that she's finally copped to her own responsibility, it is sad that her children, like those of so many other folks ill-equipped to take on responsibility for even themselves, will still have to pay the price.

Her story is not unusual. If there is one predominant theme for people expressing the reasons for their "Stupid Mismatches," it is fear:

"My husband is a wonderful man, but I married him more out of my fear of not being able to take care of myself rather than my love for him and a life we can build together. I got married for what I thought was security. I have the home, the cars, and various other toys, but I don't have my own self-respect."

Other Stories:

➤ *"I hung on to that relationship because I didn't think I was good enough for anyone else. At times I feel angry and bitter for the bad experiences that I had and the way I was treated. One day I came to the realization that I was guilty, too. I held on to that relationship until I felt strong enough to get on with my life. When I finally realized that I was good enough and that someone else would love me, I could let go. My life is completely turned around."*

➤   *"I have had a boyfriend since I was fifteen years old. One right after the other, I just couldn't be alone. I started dating an older man. Within three months, I learned that he was emotionally unstable, verbally abusive, and an alcoholic. I was terrified of him. Why did I date him? I didn't want to be alone. I didn't think I'd ever meet anyone. These were reasons that ran through my head so I settled for what was available.*

"The one good thing that came out of that relationship was that I actually stopped trying to find a man and started trying to find myself. I slowly became comfortable being alone. My Stupid Mismatch came from a fear of being alone or unwanted. I found myself."

It is disheartening to read so many pained letters from men and women who grabbed at relationships as a drowning man might grab for a straw. It is sad to hear from so many people who equate being wanted by someone, regardless of their qualities, with their own self-esteem.

As one listener wrote:

"It is true that self-esteem comes from accomplishing goals. To this day I keep adding things and goals to my life that validate who I am. I no longer need someone else to do that for me."

Good! Because, that's the only way self-esteem can be gained—through the "self." Or else it would be called other-esteem.

Love Is NOT Enough

It drives me absolutely crazy when callers, describing the disgusting, horrendous, destructive, immoral, cruel, stupid, and downright evil behavior of a husband/wife or boyfriend/girlfriend, ultimately pacify themselves with those four fateful words: "But I love him/her." Yikes! One of my listeners wrote to me to describe her four-year boyfriend as not giving her a ring, but hinting about a future, as not bonding with her children, as mean to her kids, as flirtatious with younger women and as one who double-dates with his twenty-four-year-old daughter's married friends, with his daughter as his "date." She then wrote:

"If this sounds like my problem, I really want to know. I had a very bad marriage and can be needy, despite my independence. Like my son, I am also very emotional and easily hurt. As I am not getting any younger, I am thinking that it may be time to move on. But when I think of losing him, I get very sad.

"I thought we were the loves of each others' lives. Now I'm not so sure if that's enough."

If I had her on the radio program, I'd ask her what in heaven's name he was actually *doing* that gave her the impression that she was the love of his life? And, I would want to know what in heaven's name she thought love was? Love is not about infatuation and lust. While emotional and physical passion are a part of love, infatuation and lust are not about the object, they reveal more about the subject. With infatuation and lust as the basis of your attraction to someone, when you get to know the real person, you become more disillusioned than with a love that grows slowly. The love that grows when lust and infatuation are controlled, is the love that grows of respect, awe, admiration, and trust, and is the love the lasts through all four seasons.

There is no "love at first sight," there is only sexual attraction and the romantic projections of our fantasies. There is no love where there is fear. There is no love where there is no emotional health or ability to communicate about emotional and practical issues. There is only desperate attachment. I work very hard to get folks to recognize that their desperate attachments are cementing them into destructive relationships, and to get them to stop using "love" as their rationalization for tolerating what they shouldn't, and to change what they should.

Recently, I had a talk with a Hassidic Jew about the formalities of dating in their community. He spoke with a glowing appreciation of the specialness of women, of love, of marriage, and of family. He related that Hassidim do not date until they are ready for marriage. Hassidim do not have any physical contact until after the wedding—and that includes holding hands. Hassidim spend hours upon weeks upon months, talking about all the realities of life, their feelings, joys, perspectives, plans, and goals, they meet each other's families and become close, and then they decide if it's a match.

I went to such a wedding. I have never been more moved by the meaningfulness and beauty of a wedding. These two really knew one another, they were totally supported by extended families and their community, and they believed that their union was a blessing to G-d.

Neither of them had past sexual relationships, abortions, or hurt feelings from failed marriages that so often lead to a cynicism or crassness in relationships. Since their relationship was not sexual, they were not distracted by mistaken notions that sex and love were the same thing. Their attraction to each other was strong, but determined to be made even more joyous and meaningful through marriage.

My point is that sexual passion and desperate attachments lead people to believe that they are in love, and that love can conquer all. These are two dangerously wrong beliefs.

"The first time, yes, we were young, and I was obsessed with, not in love with, him. The second time, ten years later, we realized we were in love, but there were other considerations—were we of the same religion, morals, beliefs, money thoughts, child-rearing thoughts, and a lot more? We spent about two years after he asked me to marry him figuring these things out and THEN I got a ring and we set a date and were married within six months in the most spiritual ceremony I could have imagined.

"Also, since we are of the same thoughts in so many ways, and we are both moral people, divorce is NOT an option, so we work out all of our problems. We don't fight or get nasty. We disagree and then we come to an agreement or understanding. No one wins or loses."

Clearly this listener was willing to grow into love, not assume its existence through passion, and was wise enough to realize that commonality in attitudes, goals, and morals is the Safe Marriage prophylactic that would truly make a difference in the quality of their lives and relationship.

I particularly enjoyed a letter I got from a twenty-seven-year-old divorced man who said that he and his first wife thought that *"Love would pay the bills and wash the dishes for us.*

"We had some pretty serious problems. I recognized that, but was too weak and wimpy to do anything drastic enough to do any good. A week before the wedding, we had a huge blow-up type fight about some basic differences in our philosophies of living. At one point, I suggested that we postpone the wedding. To which she replied that A) we would never get married, B) everybody has come to town already, C) we can't get the money back from the reception hall.

"We went into counseling. I knew that I either had to conform

to her notions and play dead, or be myself and live up to my potential, and that meant leaving. I was out of there.

"One of my main thoughts was from a question I read in your book Ten Stupid Things Men Do to Mess Up Their Lives, *which was, 'Do I want this woman to be the mother of my eighty-nine children?' I know, Dr. Laura, that I should have asked that question and many others just like it before I ever asked her to marry me. I now look at dating in a whole different light."*

In conclusion are the tips about the "questions to ask while you're dating" submitted by a listener who learned the hard way from her first Stupid Mismatched marriage:

➤ *"If you do want to marry (again), learn to share control.*

➤ *You have to like, respect, even love yourself (not in a prideful way) before you can share with someone else. Get over all your hurts before going into another relationship.*

➤ *Do not marry someone whose family hates you or whom your family hates. You marry the family, too—and it's hell.*

➤ *If you have to justify why you're with that person, especially when there are red flags flying everywhere, he/she is not the one! You don't love 'em. You love having someone around.*

➤ *Don't sleep with the person before you marry. You CAN wait and it's more rewarding.*

➤ *Wait until you are in your late twenties or early thirties to get married. Travel, work, do things in groups, and have fun. Then there is never the excuse, 'I never experienced life,' or the blame, 'You kept me back from the things I wanted to do.' Also, you learn more about yourself and about life if you take the time to grow up.*

➤   *Be able to support yourself and live by yourself for a while before you commit yourself for life to someone else. Then you know you're not desperate.*

➤   *If you are divorced and have children, wait to get remarried after the children are grown up. Concentrate on the children. They want and need at least one of the parents committed to them."*

Surviving the Stupid Mismatch

It is possible to get through life with someone with whom you are a Stupid Mismatch. Sometimes you might both grow and change in healthy ways that bring you closer together. Sometimes you will simply learn to accept the differences, cooperate in ways that limit conflict (like division of labor), and learn to enjoy the companionship, shared history, and good moments.

Other times, the ultimate loneliness that comes from the disconnect, which is a natural part of a Mismatch, brings challenges.

"They say that opposites attract. We sure did. We love each other, but that's about it. My husband is a devoted sports enthusiast. He coaches, trains, educates, and socializes in the world of sports. I feel out of place in his world. After occupying my first twenty-five years raising our kids, I'm finding we don't have much in common and I don't know how to meet him at his level. He isn't interested in the couples that I enjoy socializing with. Now that we're both about ready to retire, I'm wondering what the heck we'll do with each other!"

In these circumstances, where the Mismatch is not about unhealthy or destructive behaviors per se, I generally suggest that the more malleable of the two simply involve him- or herself in the activities of the other, period. That means this woman should go to the games her husband coaches, and hang out with his friends, and even learn to play some sport with him—like golf. Sometimes, after they get over the feeling of "giving in," people discover that they just haven't tried to expand their own horizons enough, and that they really do enjoy some aspects of the activities. Even more, they enjoy the closeness to their spouse. And, as often happens, the other less malleable spouse often feels more motivated to do the same.

Admit It, You Saw Those Ugly Red Flags

There have been times when a caller has tried to convince me that they didn't see the red flags. Once I pound on them, generally they retreat to, "Well, it wasn't so bad," or "They said they'd change," or "I thought I would be the 'perfect match' for him/her, and all would be well."

Callers admit to making excuses for drinking, violence, and various other ugly behaviors for many reasons. They don't want to be embarrassed by a(nother) marital failure; feel responsible for the problems ("You make me hit you/have an affair/drink"); believe that they're fat, ugly, and/or stupid and can't get anyone else or better; believe their love will change him/her and then they will earn his/her undying gratitude by loving him/her the way they wanted to be loved; their hormones have the better of them, besides which he/she is so good-looking and charming and so forth.

As one listener wrote:

"I was the idiot who came up with excuses to justify it all. I wasted my time sitting up half the night trying to think of ways to change him. I was the one who betrayed my faith. I was the one who almost turned my back on my own dreams."

You can't help being incredibly impressed by the folks who steel themselves and move on—some before marriage and children, others, sadly, only afterward. Where there is a profound Mismatch in fundamental values, attitudes, expectations, goals, morals, and spirituality, a healthy marriage and family will not grow. All differences are not compatible, in spite of the fact that some degree of opposites attract from a need to complete an incomplete self, yearning for its other side—as when an introvert is drawn to someone outgoing.

As one listener wisely wrote:

"A fish and a bird can fall in love, but where will they live?" We live in the details, not in the "what might be." We must have the courage and wisdom to face those details if we are to have a good life and provide one for our spouse and our children.

"My boyfriend of a year and a half, I love sooo much. I could marry him, but we believe in two totally different religions. I tried to ignore that fact for a while, but I finally realized that it would never work unless one of us converted to the other religion. I most definitely was not going to. This hurt so much, but it was the only way."

She was right. One of the most joyous bonding elements of a marriage, and for a family, is a mutually embraced spiritual life as a family worships together. People often underestimate the impact of an unshared religious life until they have children. Then, the Holy Wars begin.

I always tell people on my radio program, that there is the good news and the bad news about giving up someone who is a Stupid Mismatch. The good news is that you're freed up to do something healthy. The bad news is that it hurts for a while. It would seem that the bad news outweighs the good news most of the time. It is sad how many people can't sustain themselves through the painful, hurtful, difficult period of transition. Rather than set the focus on what will be possible, they set their focus on the now, the loss, the pain, and the disappointment. This leads straight to finding a way out of the pain. This leads straight to self-doubts ("If it's *me*, then I shouldn't leave him/her"), and excuses ("If it weren't for the drinking/job/sprained ankle, he/she wouldn't be doing this and that"), and finally what I call "noble-ization" as the best rationalization of them all ("I shouldn't think only of my happiness, I am hurting his/her feelings by judging/leaving him or her").

Don't go there. Surround yourself with wise loved ones, both friend and family, pray, talk to a secular counselor, see your clergyman, call my show! Or else this listener will be speaking for you:

"But ignoring those red flags got me only bruises and humiliation. It took away my personality and individuality. I had no opinions. The square peg (me) did not fit in the round hole, so I tried to change the shape to make it fit."

It is ironic that she used the round and square imagery to denote a mismatch, because another listener suggests that marriage and family life is only for "round" people, because:

"It's a circle of love. People who drink, lie, and cheat, who aren't emotionally healthy, kind, and compassionate, are the 'square pegs.' Thus, you can't make them your spouse without it being a very painful mismatch."

The moral of this section is to be "round" and find other such "round" folks to be your friends, and definitely your spouse.

Too Young, Too Foolish, Too Needy

Whenever callers tell me they're getting married, my first question is, "How old are you?" My second question is, "How old is he/she?" If those two numbers are too disparate or their sum is less than "fifty" I groan, grunt, and generally make rude noises of disapproval.

When callers tell me, after years of torture, disappointment, and anguish in really bad marriages, that they know they married too young, and wish they would have spoken to me all those years ago, I usually answer, "Yeah, but would you have listened to me when I said you were marrying too young?" "No," is the honest and typical response.

In a controlled environment where everyone knows everybody and everybody married early after parents researched, selected, and advised about a partner, where fidelity, commitment, and "till death do us part" is the norm, where expectations are modest and responsibilities taken seriously, there may hardly be a "too young" to marry.

Most of the world is not such a controlled environment. Most neighborhoods are amazingly fluid, the divorce-move-away-remarry-divorce rate is very high, shack-ups (temporary nesting) are the norm, children are born into nonexistent families, and the general expectation drilled into each person is maximum personal gratification. In this environment, there is definitely a "too young" to marry.

Why? Because there are so few shared strong values. Because there is so much anonymity. Because there is so much social stress. Because there is so little family and community for a proper, healthy education and so few role models of mature, responsible, stable relationships.

With social sexual norms at an all-time low, the easy investment of emotion and physicality misleads young people into believing they are experiencing something valuable, when they are not, and that they are experiencing something valuable with others who are valuable, when they are not.

"What did I do to mess up my relationship? I made commitments that I was too young to make. I failed to see the flaws that haunt our relationship today. I failed to heed advice that I received when I could still act on it. I failed to assess my personal strengths and weaknesses when I made decisions. Hindsight is 20/20, but I

should have asked for glasses when I was young—and not the rose-colored variety," writes a much sobered listener.

The mentality of a young person is generally largely unformed, too simplistic, coated with insecurities and ignorance, and steeped in fantasies and nonobjective thinking:

"Like most young men, when choosing a prospective wife, I only cared if she was attractive, and said she was attracted to me. Subsequently, I married at nineteen to a pretty girl with a great figure who was twenty-one, 'cause she liked me. I did not look at her past tendencies, such as she slept around and already had a kid out-of-wedlock that she gave up for adoption, or that none of her relationships lasted because she was vain and only cared about getting her needs met. Just 'cause someone is attracted to you and says they love you is NOT enough qualities to marry someone. I learned it all the hard way at my kids' expense."

Young people, seventeen to almost twenty-five, are at a stage in their lives when they are just beginning to be adults and are just starting to develop a unique, autonomous self. It is a difficult time, emotionally challenging, and somewhat frightening. It is not unusual to find both young men and women hurrying into relationships to find instant adulthood, maturity, security, and stability:

"Basically, I was too young and too immature to be patient to find the right man for me."

"I knew this man I was to marry was not a match for me. I was warned by parents, family, and friends. I carried on with the wedding out of Stupid Rebellion."

"When a person marries young, they have no way of judging their partner's attributes as compared to others. There just isn't enough experience for that. Youths take people at face value, and think only about the present. At age eighteen, that's what I did."

So many of the regretful testimonials I receive from people admit that the main problem of their Stupid Mismatch was the natural immaturity of youth.

It is natural to want to be loved, to want to have someone dear, to want to feel grown up and established, and to want to feel secure. When young people are virtually saturated with a media and social culture that glorifies attachments, no matter how superficial or fleeting, it is not surprising that they, in their innocence, want a piece of that action.

I have been sadly surprised by how many young men (and older, for that matter) have no sense of what it is to be a "man" anymore. I can't tell you how much disdain I have heaped on young men who call me, who marry before they have jobs, while they have debt, and with expectations of their wives working (dumping kids in day care) so that they can have the luxuries with which they were brought up or believe they should have "now." They tell me they'll be living in their parents' basement or supported by their in-laws.

I tell them that there was a time that defined manhood, and that it isn't now, by a man's ability and willingness to take on responsibility and prepare himself for his obligations. Now, all he's got to do is "find him a woman"!

Yes, there is a "too-young," and it generally leads to a Stupid Mismatch specifically because it is a carnival game of shooting at the first target that comes across, or the one that titillates for all the wrong reasons:

"First off, I married too young, which is the first mistake. Ask any seventeen-year-old and they will say they know it all, especially in the matters of love. But love was really lust. Things I was aware of, I chose to ignore as irrelevant. But the problems in my marriage today are a direct result of looking away from the problems in the beginning."

I am always impressed when people are open to admitting their weaknesses, because it is only in that assessment that you can begin to know where you have to work on yourself to build strength:

"Neither of us were ready emotionally—I didn't know how to

respect myself and share my perspective on what was right in a relationship; he didn't treat our friendship like it was anything important. Most important mismatch: I was a wanna-be-strong Christian, and he could've cared less. I didn't respect myself enough to end things, because I liked the 'security' of having a 'boyfriend.' "

In a prior era, where such realizations were countered with the realization that vows are commitments, people would strive to persevere and work through problems. In our disposable tissue culture, the same is not true. Serially broken hearts, marriages, and children's homes are now the more typical result.

As one listener, now much wiser, advises:

"I wou   lvise young women to date men very close to their age, refuse to have a sexual relationship until after they are married, meet friends of the men they date, get to know the family, and establish trust before investing too many emotions into a relationship. Otherwise, what you allow yourself to fall into is a false sense of security."

Wise words.

Too Old and Too Foolish

At the other end of the spectrum is the older man or woman who wants to deny the inevitability of the life cycle:

"I got involved with a younger woman, twenty-seven years younger than me. At first it was great and, of course, I was walking on cloud nine. Then, it hit me (after three years!) that I had no one to talk with who understood the things I was talking about. I was constantly supporting her ego and providing the support that she needed. I did not receive this from her, and it was many days that I would look at her, and wish I had someone who knew what I was talking about."

I couldn't summarize the main point of Stupid Mismatch better than that: "someone who knows what you're talking about." Whether it's children, religion, politics, sex, hobbies, love, family, morality, or decorating the living room, you need to make sure you're with someone who knows what you're talking about. It's not that you always have to agree. It is that you both have to understand, care, have compassion, be willing to compromise, determine to put the relationship first, admire each other's basic qualities, support each other's strong side, help with each other's weaker side, fix your own inadequacies, take responsibility for your actions, and respect your vows as sanctified by G-d.

10
Stupid Breakups

> *"I broke up with a guy once for snoring while watching TV. Now, I didn't tell him why—I just said I wanted to be friends.*
>
> *I also have had a guy with bad breath. That one I told why."*
>
> —A LISTENER

Another listener wrote to me about having asked her husband why, after twelve years and two children, he left her for another woman.

"He said he had to think about it. Two days later he called back to tell me his answer. He said, and I quote, 'I always wanted you to go to my mom's house and learn how to make jam, but you never did.' I was dumbfounded. All of this because I never learned how to can fruit? I said to him, 'Oh, okay . . . well, thanks.' I hung up the phone and sat there for a few minutes. Then it hit me. All of this was not because of the me that I was. It was because of the him that he was. It gave me a great tool in getting the closure I needed. There was no abuse in the marriage, no arguments . . . just not enough 'jam.' " We'll never know if he meant that figuratively or literally; probably a bit 'o both.

Fortunately, I don't get many such calls, e-mails or letters from folks whose reasons for breaking up sound quite that stupid, but I am deeply concerned by the growing number of unnecessary and unwarranted relationship breakups based on "modern" notions of rights and happiness.

About two-thirds of divorces currently are sought by women, and my male callers tell me that their wives left because of "growing apart," "not happy," "feeling underappreciated," "needs not being met," "differences in changing goals or lifestyle," "boredom," and the old favorite, "find myself."

It is important to note that violence, drug and alcohol abuse, neglect and abandonment, and promiscuous infidelity, which used to be the areas of complaint that women had about their husbands, are rarely the motivation for the wife to call it quits. In fact, it is usually the opposite. Some women seem willing to be more patient with these behaviors than to sustain themselves through the growth and effort needed for the maintenance and nurturance of a marriage when the only issue is moon spots or boredom.

I *dis*-credit feminism for this sad and sorry, embarrassing development in gender relations. Remember Gloria Steinem's proclamation that, "A woman without a man is like a fish without a bicycle"? What the heck was that about? Feminists have emphasized men as the "evil empire," oppressing their women with sex (one other prominent feminist called all sex "rape"), child-bearing and child-rearing (that's being remedied by abortions, day care, and surrogate mothering), and marriage itself (subservient, second-class citizenry). When women become "enlighted," they leave. To what?

One listener, a grandmother and recovered feminist wrote to me:

"Back in the seventies, I read The Feminine Mystique, *about*

the housewife's 'problem with no name.' I promptly left my husband all three beautiful daughters and went back to college looking for that elusive 'something' that would make me whole.

"Raised in the 'Birthplace of Women's Rights,' I quickly became a vocal feminist. It took me years to figure out what a sham the women's rights movement really is. The horrific results are all around us. The goal of feminists was, and is, destruction of the family. To that end, they have been very successful.

"I'm a grandmother now, and I try every day to correct the wrongs I've committed on my children."

Every so often I find myself going on a tear on my radio program about this very issue. I rant about the obvious negative impact on women, not to mention men, children, and society, by the warped notions of what feminists support. How does aborting babies from their bodies for reasons no more important than timing elevate a woman's consciousness? How does shacking-up with some guy(s), becoming sexually intimate in a noncommitted relationship, elevate a woman's spirituality? How does having babies out-of-wedlock, with the concomitant problems with poverty, child care, and isolation elevate a woman's status? Obviously, it doesn't. And, as I've asked time and again on my radio program, "How have you women allowed such a stupid philosophy to destroy your lives, and that of your children and society?"

Another listener wrote in with her complaint about the warnings she got from her liberal, feminist, college friends about what kind of a man she should avoid. She now believes that by listening to that, she jumped right into Stupid Breakups:

"When I was a senior in college I decided to break off my relationship with my boyfriend of two years. He was an intelligent, affectionate, religious man, who had a promising career as an attorney ahead of him and a deep, loving relationship

with his parents and five siblings. He expressed to me a desire to marry and assured me that when we had children, I would not have to work and would be able to raise our children at home.

"I was mortified! Appalled! He thinks women should stay home and raise their kids! 'What a jerk!' I explained to my equally liberal, feminist friends. Of course, they agreed. 'What year does he think this is! It's men like that who keep us down!,' one friend said.

"Well, I broke it off with him and made a 'better choice,' according to my friend. A twenty-nine-year-old college senior, with a drinking problem, who smoked, covered in shall-we-say body art, and a shaved head. He lived at home and, of course, had no job and no money."

According to her letter, her father went out and bought her my first book, *Ten Stupid Things Women Do to Mess Up Their Lives*, and is happy to report that her eyes are now open, and she is married to a wonderful man (with a job and no body art). One of the main issues of that book was my restating the obvious, which is that women want love, attachment, family, and children. Though choosing to have a major career instead is a reasonable, personal choice for some women, diminishing the value of motherhood and marriage by outright denial and attack or by relegating them to the edge of a woman's more important worker existence is cruel, because it denies the basic psychological and biological truth of women to bond and nurture; and that of men to provide and protect.

Be Wary!

Young women, brought up on all this feminist propaganda, are wary about marriage. Young men, brought up on all this feminist propaganda, are wary about women. Try being a young man in college these days, exposed to the feminist dominated reeducation process going on under the guise of neutral academics in courses in psychology, sociology, and even history! I have had innumerable men write to me about their growing fears in being able to find a nice girl who will get married and not soon after walk away with his kids and his home.

Men and women are being programmed to be wary and be careful about not getting used. Unfortunately, for too many folks, having to provide for his family, or having to raise children, is now being viewed as in that category of "being used."

In addition to the destructiveness of feminism has been the overall shifting of a society from the nobility of obligations and commitments to an emphasis on rights without a balanced emphasis on "responsibilities." Without a firm sense of responsibility to others and their needs and rights, we are a group of neurotic ants, each with our own selfish mission—and you can pretty well visualize that state of chaos!

This listener certainly could:

"There was a time I let the word divorce *into my vocabulary, and once you say it, it becomes a part of you and suddenly it consumes you. I was very close to divorce, and I was sure I no longer loved my husband. All I could think of was ME, and what I deserved, and everything I gave to him was attached to the condition that I get something in return. I am not sure that is the reason it wasn't returned—no one likes to receive with expectations. Every moment at home, all I did was complain of not having enough. I spent so much time wondering what was in it for me, that I didn't see just how much I already had! Lose yourself in SERVICE, and it is then that you will find yourself."*

Bow to the All-Important MEEE!

Face it, it's a fact, you cannot have in life, or from another person, all that you imagine you should, could, or would. Real life simply has more texture than that. Additionally, can you really imagine being all of what another person imagines they should, could, or would have? No, of course not. Spending one's time in coveting is to lose the moment of appreciation of what you do have—which generally includes many blessings and advantages. For example, though my husband can't dance to save his life (something I've always loved to do), he would give his life to save mine or our son's. Somehow, I think that's a pretty good trade-off. And, I'll bet, you could look at your relationship in the same way, once you threw away the notion that G-d put you here to gratify every desire or fantasy that plunked into your awareness.

It's that ugly movement toward self-fulfillment, with its protection of the self against the "destructive" needs of another, be it spouse or children, that has caused the largest number of Stupid Breakups.

"I believe in thinking about yourself before others—but only to an extent. If you are in a relationship it is your right to take care of yourself and put yourself before the relationship . . . but not selfishly."

Oh yeah? How do you figure that?

"For example," she continued, *"I am a college student and I will always put my education before my relationship, because it is the education that I will have forever, the guy might not be there forever."*

Now, why might the guy not be there forever? Death in the service of his country? Death by natural causes? Probably not what she is thinking. She's probably thinking about how many of her closest friends and relatives have been in and out, in and out, in and out, of various pseudo-commitments and she is worried.

As another listener wrote:

"I have talked to many of my friends whose parents are divorced. They tell me they feel personally flawed because the legacy of their parents' divorce scars them in some way that says they are part of a lineage of people who can't follow through, are capable of making huge mistakes, and who walk out when things get tough. They all doubt their ability to spot and maintain love, because they see that their parents thought they were in love, and it didn't 'work out' for them."

Interestingly, this letter was written by a young woman who says that she is part of an unusual and unfortunately small segment of the public in which her parents are still married—yet, by today's reckoning, should have been divorced.

"Did the fighting, yelling, un-child centered living make me a little neurotic and make it hard for me to become a well-adjusted adult? Yes! But one thing I could always hold on to was that my parents never divorced. I had to work through a lot of bad habits and personality flaws, but I never doubted that I would be able to be committed to someone, that I could carry though with a promise, or that I would ever marry until I was completely ready. I know my parents were not in love for most of their married life, and yet they still stayed in it. Did I see my mom as a wimp? No way. She is the strongest person I know, and I admire her greatly. My dad has had my respect from day one."

The argument is often made, in cases like this listener, that all she has learned is how to have a bad relationship. Wrong. She doesn't want the same marriage her parents had in terms of how they behaved toward each other, but she does want the same marriage, in terms of the ultimate commitment they had to family and to vows.

Ideally, they would have used their determination to commitment to improve their behavior, or become more compassionate about each other's shortcomings. Though that is not the ultimate point of commitment, it is the ultimate opportunity within commitment.

People Need to Work Harder at Marriage

One of the reasons I keep reminding people that "love is not enough" for a quality marriage is that emotions are labile, vulnerable, situational, unpredictable, and without an IQ. Commitment and respect for vows, promises, obligations, and tradition are much more worthy and predictable building blocks for a good relationship. You may get your "jollies" fantasizing about some movie star or neighbor, but nothing fills your heart with deeper affection (and perhaps passion) than watching the tenderness of your spouse with the children, having your spouse be compassionate and noncombative when you're in a mood, or having your spouse be solicitous when you feel (and look) like garbage.

If you really think there is anyone who can sustain a happy, fulfilled state all the time, you're wrong. You're also wrong if you think there is some one person out there with whom you certainly would sustain a perpetual happy, fulfilled state. You're also wrong if you think that the best of relationships don't go through stages, and phases, and problems, some seemingly insurmountable:

"My Stupid Breakup was from my second marriage. I was 'unhappy.' I've been married three times. My Priest finally explained the five Stages of Marriage to me. Stage 1: Falling in love. Stage 2: Discovering the foibles, faults, etc. Stage 3: Deciding what to do about this new knowledge. Stage 4: (If you reach it) Is the hard work involved in getting through the realities of Stage 2. Stage 5: Is the glorious falling in love at a whole new level of intimacy and commitment.

"A light went on! Now I know that when the going got tough, I got going. WOW! What a revelation. The stupid comes in when I consider the harm to my children and the pain I caused my ex-spouse. If we had known that relationships go through these stages, I think we would have been able to work through the problems."

I believe that millions of people would be able to work through their problems if they had that knowledge and support from their families, friends, and society at large. Unfortunately, there have been studies showing that even the so-called Marriage Education courses at high schools and colleges, according to current research, are negative and hostile to the institution. Ironically, those who are married are happier, healthier, and wealthier. Go figure.

In most cases, couples don't try hard enough to stay together. They don't talk about the problems, try to identify the issues, or work them out. And they don't take the time to remember what made them fall in love with each other. One listener added:

"I believe that most divorces are caused by materialism. In a way, our society is becoming corrupted by materialism. There is competition about having the best car, the biggest house, the nicest clothes—but no one seems to care about having the closest family, the most dinners together as a family, and ongoing friendships with family members."

I have written in many of my books, and reminded people on my radio program, that though divorce has been used as the easy way out of the challenges of marriage and family, the three A's—addiction, adultery, and abuse—justify divorce as a valid consideration. Nonetheless, that doesn't mean that there is never a way back from even these travesties and tragedies.

One listener wrote to me of her alcoholism and her loss of faith in marriage, G-d, and herself. She spent a year in AA, with a growing realization that she might lose her daughter.

"I knew that I did not have feelings of love for my husband, so it was a big struggle, and I knew the only way to get the feelings back,

was to have faith, pray, go to church, and get help. It was not easy, and there were times where I wanted to give up, because it is very hard living with someone you do not love, but I knew G-d wanted us to make it work. If I could just keep the faith in G-d, I knew he would give me my feelings back for my husband, and He did, indeed. We now have a five-month-old son, and we are very happy."

She went on to say that she is disgusted with what she put her daughter through and believes that parents should think more about their children than themselves and the world would be a better place. That means making your marriage work—and it does take work!

When there are terrible problems, like the three A's, it becomes a major challenge to consider whether or not to stay. When there is repentance (responsibility taken, true remorse, behaviors to repair and not repeat), there is hope. When there is no repentance, the hope is just postponed disappointment.

One listener wrote that he was still hopeful in spite of his wife's continued shack-up affair and her abandonment of the children, whom he raises alone,

"I think that people give up too easily on marriage when love, understanding, and forgiveness can help your partner remember what it was that caused them to commit to you in the first place. . . . Giving up on a marriage without attempting to prove your love and worth is a stupid reason for a breakup."

I wish him well, although reuniting with a woman who would abandon her children is nothing I can get too excited about.

I'm Finding Myself

I'm always amused by this expression, "I have to find myself." First, there is the notion of being somewhere other than where you are (some kind of cosmic lost-and-found), then there is the idea that you can't find yourself under the present circumstances of marriage and children, and finally there is the epiphany that you can't simply find yourself in the bed of someone new.

Truly, you find yourself in your commitments; you find yourself in the eyes of people who depend on you; you find yourself in your noble responses to life's challenges; you find yourself in your actions and decisions; you find yourself right where you are now.

This notion of "finding oneself" is an intellectually dishonest approach to frustration, a pouty reaction to obligations and routine, and a bratty manipulation of another's compassion and understanding.

"I dated a guy for two and a half years in college and found my true love in him. He was and is everything that I could ever want from a man. I knew in my heart that he would be a decent husband and father. A few weeks after I returned from a study-abroad trip through our school, I called off the relationship, because I felt I needed to find myself as an individual. That was the worst decision of my life. I will forever regret that breakup," writes a listener.

Why does finding oneself as an individual seem to imply that you must unload significant people from your life like your spouse, boy/girl friend, and/or parents? The answer is that the most immature part of yourself has reverted back to infanthood—wanting to be the center of the universe without obligations: You get to have, you don't have to give.

With that attitude, you will either end up alone, or with superficial escapades, and regrets for a Stupid Breakup.

Don't lie to yourself or anyone else. When you feel like it's time to get going, stay put and face whatever it is that worries or frightens you.

Welcome to Fantasy Land

What must you be thinking when you put a fantasy aside your reality and believe that the fantasy will have more depth, longevity, satisfaction, respect, promise, and meaning? The answer is that you don't think—you just imagine.

One of the newest and most destructive forces on marriage today is the Internet. Cyber-affairs are costing too many children and innocent spouses the warmth and comfort of an intact home. Both men and women are carrying on in chatrooms and develop "feelings" sufficient to propel them out of their homes and families to be with someone they "know will be everything that's missing in their lives." Everything, of course, other than a brain!

"My wife and I have been married for twenty-seven years. I thought we had a good relationship. We have had our problems, but we always seemed to work them out. To make a long story short, I bought my wife a computer two years ago, and it seemed to make her happy, because she always said she was bored. She had fun in the chatrooms, flirting and having a good time. I thought it was harmless. But, as time went on she spent more and more time on the computer. Well, seven months ago I found out that she is in love with a man that lives eleven hours away from her, whom she's never met. She lies in her bed and cries for him. She still talks to him every day and tells him she really loves him and is going to marry him.

"I love this lady with all my heart. I really don't know what to do. I know in my heart she still loves him—she tells him all the things she once told me."

I mean, really, how insensitive and cruel can one be to someone she once thought she couldn't live without? And why is anyone bored? The answer is, only because he or she is boring. Bored people rarely think of anything or anyone besides themselves and being entertained, thrilled, titillated, excited, distracted, or being the center of attention.

When people call and tell me that they're bored in their lives, or bored in their marriage, I jump on them to admit that they don't do anything to add to the well-being of themselves or their family—they just want to feel a certain feeling and, in that laziness, think that there is just some other guy or gal who'll just make it happen. Good luck.

The Grass Is Greener

"I left my husband of five years for a much younger man, hoping that the spice would reenter my life. WRONG!!! I thought I could find happiness in someone else. WRONG!!! I left my husband and hurt my three children very badly. Nine months later I realized that a lot of things were wrong . . . but with ME. I had just turned thirty, went back to work full-time, exhausted from the kids, and wanted out, yet realizing that what I was feeling was totally normal, and by leaving my husband the stress was still there because it was me!!!

"I strongly urge people to get help for themselves first and take some accountability for their actions and stay AWAY from temptation because now I realize I may have lost the best husband and father in the world all because of my self-centeredness."

This listener hit the main point of my argument, which is that when you imagine improving your life by simple demolition is to miss the truth. The truth is that you are largely the architect of the quality of your life. Therefore, begin first with renovation—of yourself: your attitudes, your reactions, your expectations, and your actions. Only then can you hope to have any credibility or power in your determination to make improvements in your relationship, marriage, and family.

Another important issue brought up by this listener, is the idea of avoiding temptation. Unfortunately, between the Internet and the workplace, a lot of temptation presents itself.

"I thought I had to go to work to get a life and get away from the kids. The money was nice, but it only caused me to feel I didn't need my husband anymore. I divorced my husband."

Well, nothing but bad things followed. At work she got lots of attention from men, and liked it. As she started to become more aware, she began to appreciate that her husband was faithful and considerate. She ended up marrying some guy who molested two of her three children. After two decades of therapy for her children and herself, she reports that they are doing better. Based on her experiences she had this closing message:

"Stay home with your kids. It keeps away so many problems. So much temptation. Stay married because, believe me, no matter how nice a guy he is or how much he loves your kids, it is never the same as their real dad."

The temptation issue is one that is too often, and inappropriately, scoffed at. It is not fashionable to say that people should not be alone with members of the opposite sex. It is not fashionable to say that married folks should not carry on solo "friendships" with members of the opposite sex. It is not popular to suggest that people avoid even the appearance of wrongdoing so as not to cause pain to their spouse. Yet, sensitivity to these behaviors strongly adds to the value of your relationship and your partner. All actions taken to preserve and protect your commitment—do just that!

Let Me Try One From Column A . . . and One From Column B

"Before my husband and I got married, I broke up with him several times and caused us both (moreso to him) a lot of pain. I broke up because I felt that it was important to try different people so I could develop an idea of what I wanted. Please tell your lis-

teners and readers that it is not necessary to try different people on like clothing. The more times you give your heart away, the more scars you carry and the less innocent devotion you have to give your spouse."

These words from a listener are most profound. There is a big difference between dating someone to determine whether or not he or she is a keeper, and dating around, as in sampling jellies, ostensibly to get a better view of what's out there.

Where young people are brought up in a loving and intact home, where religion is a significant part of their lives, when they have allowed themselves to mature to the degree of knowing what is meaningful in life, there is only the need to join with someone with whom you can celebrate these values together.

Unfortunately in our society these days, those factors are generally not the ones which function to guide people in their choices. Instead, they look around, try things to see how they work, and see if one style works better.

"When I was in university, my friends all told me that I couldn't stay with my high-school girlfriend permanently, because we would both lack the experience of the greater world out there— with other possibilities. I almost listened to them and would have lost the marriage and baby daughter that I now enjoy fifteen years later. You can have the life of adventure and wandering or life of depth and security. I prefer the latter."

The sad thing is that most people prefer the former. It is sad, because we have a society that doesn't train or support people to search and settle for depth and security. Instead, we urge people to experience, not settle, look for better, get something different; never be satisfied.

I have challenged many men and women on my radio program, who have cycled in and out of many stupid relationships, if they really thought their lives would be worse off with an arranged marriage. After some silliness, almost all of them said, "Yes, maybe if someone who knew me and knew what was good for me, and would match me with a good woman/man, my life would be better." Then they wonder about the excitement lost in the search, and the difficulties with learning to love someone from scratch. I then point out that the excitement would come from learning to love someone from scratch—someone with similar values, morals, ideals, goals, lifestyle, and life's plans. Talk about learning in safety!

"There Shalt Be No Gods Before Me," Say Mommy and Daddy

"We were married for eleven years with three small children. Our marriage was wrought with in-law problems from the beginning. We both saw how his mother despised me from the onset of our engagement. We loved each other deeply, and thought that our love would conquer all of life's adversities. My husband saw what was ongoing (insults, snubs, slams) yet was torn over his loyalties . . . his wife, should he defend her? . . . or his family, should he support them?"

I am flabbergasted by how many people are absolutely tyrannized by a clearly disturbed parent—to the extent that they will jeopardize, disrupt, or abandon their healthy, happy relationships. When they call me, they ask if they can dishonor their parents by not listening to their choice in a spouse, reprimand a destructive parent, or disconnect with a parent who is blatantly attempting to destroy their marriage. There are parents who are so insecure, mentally ill, or downright evil, that they will even sink to undermining their children's lives to feel alive, in control, powerful, and important.

Sometimes these parents will operate indirectly: offering

money with conditions, pleading desperation (illness or upset) for visits and support, virtually turning their adult, married children into their own parents, or by being punitive when their child even plants the lawn with grass that isn't the parent's preference.

I've heard it all. Recently, a male caller told me that his mother-in-law-to-be offered to give his fiancée a quarter of a million dollars if she would make him sign a prenup specifying that his name would be on nothing (like their own home). I told him not to sign and not to comment to his girlfriend about the money and to wait to see if she takes the money. I told him that if she took the money, she was not a candidate for marriage because he'd be marrying her mother. Several days later, he called back. She had, on her own, decided not to take her mother's money. Wonderful. Because if she had broken up with him because she catered to her mother's neurotic need to control and her hatred of men, that would have been a Stupid Breakup.

Since young people today seem to be more geared to "have it" than to "earn it," they find themselves obligated to their parents in the most unhealthy ways. If they live in their parents' homes, or on parental property, or in a house paid for by their parents, or live on income supplied by their parents, they seem to revert to their child-parent behaviors as though they had to be careful not to lose an allowance this week.

As I tell folks, "If you can't afford the wedding, and your own place to live, or the clothes on your back—you're not ready to get married. If you can't afford the car you'd like to have, or the neighborhood you'd like to live in, or the toys and jewelry you fantasize about, earn them. If you stay attached to your parents in an infantile manner, it will probably destroy your adult relationship."

Unresolved Personal Psychological and Emotional Issues

➤   *"I came from a broken home, my mom married a man who beat and molested me, and the only consistent support I got was from this guy who was very nice. I suggested that we see other people because I was bored and confused. I know I let a good man go and broke a heart that didn't deserve it just for novelty and insecurity."*

➤   *"My self-esteem used to be so low, that when I would be in a great relationship, and the guy started to really care, I would do anything to make things bad so that he would break up with me."*

➤   *"I broke up with her that night for no better reason than for not wanting her to ever break up with me. The saddest part was that she had no intention of doing that. I had dated a [girlfriend of mine] who cheated on me, and it broke my heart really bad since she was my first love. I guess I just didn't want to get dumped again, so I took the initiative and broke it off first. To this day I miss that girl. I guess you could say that in not wanting to be hurt by her, I hurt myself."*

➤   *"I grew up in a very dysfunctional home where my father molested me in front of my entire family, so I did not know what true love was—that is, until Ronnie and I came together. I was able to be myself and still have his love. When we became engaged my parents sat me down at the kitchen table and told me that Ronnie was controlling and brainwashing me. They told me that my mom was so upset about our relationship that it would make her lose the baby she was carrying, and if she did, it would be my fault. So, I broke off a relationship with a man whom I was crazy about and was perfect for me. My parents abused my trust in them, so they could keep me in the house to care for their kids.*

It was stupid to ignore my own instincts. I take responsibility for my actions by continuing to attend therapy. But, there will always be that part of me asking how I could be so stupid."

These are a few of the thousands of letters, faxes, and e-mails I've gotten from folks suffering from real and serious problems, stemming anywhere from simple immaturity, to painful reactions to the abuse and insanity of their original homes, to mental illness. When I talk to some of these folks on the air I remind them that everybody is capable of loving and worthy of being loved. How we all differ is in our ability to come out of ourselves to sacrifice for another, and our willingness to become vulnerable and open to somebody else.

Those qualities are sometimes not easy to come by, and for some people, quite damaged and frightened by their upbringing, it becomes a serious challenge. This is the area of searching for oneself that does have merit: *becoming* the kind of human being who can be of open heart with wisdom, not cynicism. For those of you for whom this is a challenge, promiscuity, substance abuse, and workaholism are not the solutions. Soul-searching, therapy, spiritual development, and risking are the solutions.

All these considerations are why I beg clergy to refuse to marry people who are unwilling to undergo at least six months of premarital counseling. This is the most wonderful opportunity for you to do something scary (face truths about yourself) and wonderful (become a more loving, open person).

Consider yourself an artist. As talented and creative as you are, without good tools, your best work will never be expressed. As a human being in a loving relationship, wishing to create a happy home, you are your tools; therefore, you are your own limitations. Please put aside your ego and face-saving notions to get the kind of education or therapeutic assistance you need to become the best tool you can be.

Stupid Breakups are caused by your not wanting to see the worst in yourself—and if you choose to stay blind, you will never have the love you want:

"One mistake was never taking responsibility for my own shortcomings. When I got in trouble I always expected someone to bail me out—including God. And most of the time that is what happened. I was a dreamer who never had the intestinal fortitude to stick it out until my dreams came true.

"I married two times, and did the same stupid things again, and then something happened. I was flying mining equipment into old Mexico and crashed a plane into a mountain. It should have killed me, but by the grace of God, it didn't. Two days later, I was sitting by myself on the side of the mountain, my life devastated, and said to myself that I know someone else who can do a better job with my life than I have. I had no idea why I was saying that or to whom I was talking, but I strangely felt that 2000 lbs. was lifted from my shoulders and peace and joy came upon me and everything was okay, even though I had gone broke in business, lost my second marriage, and just crashed a plane.

"With a relationship with God, and the teachings of the Bible, I got married for the third time. This marriage will work because I finally realized that love is a decision, not a feeling (commitment, covenant), and that feelings come later. We fuss and argue, but never let it interfere with our marriage covenant."

From all the correspondence I receive, it would seem true that the single most impressive tome for helping people get focused on a purposeful life and a satisfying relationship is Scripture. I believe that's because people who open themselves up to G-d are already in the mode of thinking beyond

themselves, more charitable of heart and action, more res-
olute in their intent to "work it out," and more savvy about
the deeper levels of satisfaction.

So, in conclusion, to avoid Stupid Breakups, now that
you've read this book, open up the Bible.

BOOKS BY DR. LAURA SCHLESSINGER

BAD CHILDHOOD—GOOD LIFE
How to Blossom and Thrive in Spite of an Unhappy Childhood

ISBN 0-06-057786-X (hardcover) • ISBN 0-06-057787-8 (paperback)
ISBN 0-06-085288-7 (CD)

In this important book, Dr. Laura Schlessinger shows men and women that they can have a Good Life no matter how bad their childhood.

THE PROPER CARE & FEEDING OF HUSBANDS

ISBN 0-06-052061-2 (hardcover) • ISBN 0-06-052062-0 (paperback)
ISBN 0-06-056614-0 (cassette) • ISBN 0-06-056675-2 (CD)

Dr. Laura urgently reminds women that to take proper care of their husbands is to ensure themselves the happiness and satisfaction they yearn for in marriage.

WOMAN POWER
Transform Your Man, Your Marriage, Your Life

ISBN 0-06-075323-4 (paperback)

A companion to Dr. Laura's bestselling *Proper Care & Feeding of Husbands, Woman Power* is filled with new information about the special power women have to transform their husbands, their marriages, and their lives.

TEN STUPID THINGS WOMEN DO TO MESS UP THEIR LIVES

ISBN 0-06-097649-7 (paperback) • ISBN 0-694-51513-2 (cassette)

Using real-life examples, Dr. Laura teaches women how to take responsibility for personal problems and discover their potential for growth and joy.

TEN STUPID THINGS MEN DO TO MESS UP THEIR LIVES

ISBN 0-06-092944-8 (paperback) • ISBN 0-694-51797-6 (cassette)

Dr. Laura tells men how to get their acts together and take control of their lives and their destinies— how to truly become men.

STUPID THINGS PARENTS DO TO MESS UP THEIR KIDS

ISBN 0-06-093379-8 (paperback)

Dr. Laura marshals compelling evidence of the widespread neglect of America's children and convincingly condemns the numerous rationalizations to excuse it.

Dr. Laura Schlessinger

TEN STUPID THINGS COUPLES DO TO MESS UP THEIR RELATIONSHIPS

ISBN 0-06-051260-1 (paperback)
ISBN 0-06-000055-4 (cassette) • ISBN 0-06-000058-9 (CD)

An invaluable guide for those struggling to find the right mate or to escape a bad relationship.

HOW COULD YOU DO THAT?!
The Abdication of Character, Courage, and Conscience

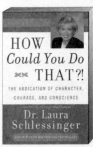

ISBN 0-06-092806-9 (paperback) • ISBN 0-694-51651-1 (cassette)

In her lively, pull-no-punches style, Dr. Laura presents a workable moral philosophy based on personal responsibility and the true happiness of the moral high ground.

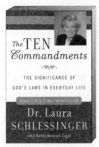

THE TEN COMMANDMENTS
The Significance of God's Laws in Everyday Life
with Rabbi Stewart Vogel

ISBN 0-06-092996-0 (paperback) • ISBN 0-694-51955-3 (cassette)

Dr. Laura shows us how adhering to the higher ideals and consistent morality found in the Commandments can create a life of greater purpose, integrity, and value.

CHILDREN'S BOOKS

WHY DO YOU LOVE ME?
ISBN 0-06-443654-3 (paperback)
A bestselling picture book about a mother's unconditional love for her son. (Ages 3–7)

BUT I WAAAANNT IT!
ISBN 0-06-443643-8 (paperback)
This picture book discusses why we want material things and what brings true happiness.

GROWING UP IS HARD
ISBN 0-06-029200-8 (hardcover)
Dr. Laura's third picture book about coping with life's disappointments and frustrations.